I0759449

The World of Jesus' Apparitions

Francisco Camilo, Ascension, *Museu Nacional d'Art de Catalunya (Barcelona, Spain).*

THE WORLD OF JESUS' APPARITIONS

WINCENTY LASZEWSKI

SOPHIA
INSTITUTE PRESS

First Published in Polish as *Świat Objawień Jezusa* © 2022 for Fronda PL, Łopuszańska 32 Street. 02-220 Warsaw.

Cover design by Emma Helstrom
Cover Art: *Ascension by Francisco Camilo* (024228-000), image derived from Museu Nacional D'Art de Catalunya / commons.wikimedia.org
Book art design, typographic design, photo layout, photo editing, and retouching: Fahrenheit 451

English translation by Anna Pietrus-Sionko

Sophia Institute Press
Box 5284, Manchester, NH 03108
1-800-888-9344
www.SophiaInstitute.com
Sophia Institute Press® is a registered trademark of Sophia Institute.

Printed in India.

Hardcover ISBN 978-1-64413-818-2
ebook ISBN 978-1-64413-819-9
Library of Congress Control Number: 2025941881

First printing

DEDICATION

"Encounters with the risen Christ characterize the Christian hope of resurrection."

Catechism of the Catholic Church, 995

To sweet, gracious, and merciful Mary, so that after this exile she may show us Jesus, the blessed fruit of her womb.

Contents

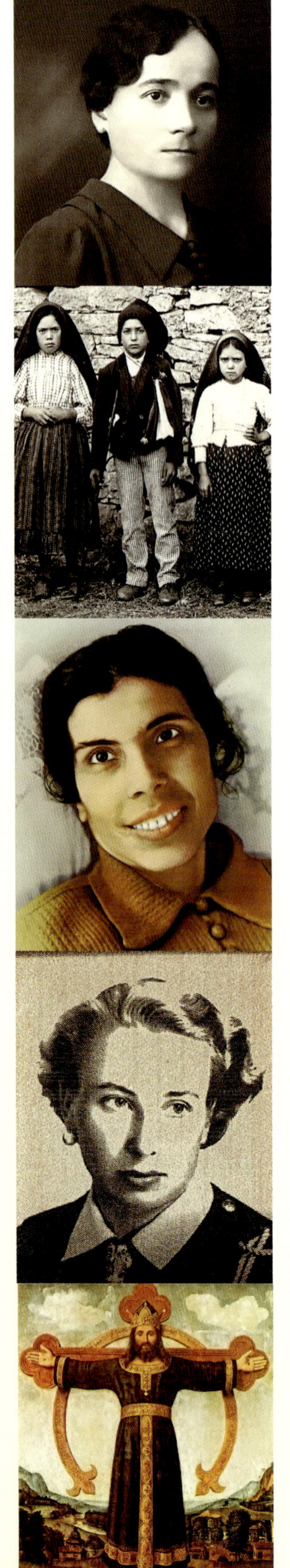

INTRODUCTION

The Catholic Church has long believed in the supernatural, and that belief persists today. The most salient example of this belief is found at the Mass, where Christ is truly present in the bread and the wine of the Eucharist. However, some also experienced the presence of Christ in an even more profound way, seeing His glorified and resurrected body while hearing His teachings.

These post-Ascension revelations may be little-known, but that doesn't stop their influence. Julian of Norwich, possibly the most popular medieval English mystic, was visited by Christ several times. Eventually, Julian wrote about Christ's apparitions to her in *Revelations of Divine Love,* the earliest book verifiably written in English by a woman. The words given to this woman by Christ would go on to have a profound effect beyond her own time and place. Although the Church has not canonized Julian of Norwich, the influence these revelations had on the Faith is immeasurable. She has been quoted by theologians, mystics, and even the *Catechism.*

Julian of Norwich also made the excellent point that these revelations only matter in what fruits they produce in us. "I am not good because of the revelation unless I love God better," she wrote, "And so it is my desire that it should be the same benefit to everyone." Christ's apparitions matter; they are signposts that speak to His mercy and power, but they only truly matter when they change our hearts and move us to follow what He teaches in these appearances.

When we compare modern apparitions of Christ with Biblical accounts, as theologian Wincenty Łaszewski does in this book, we see that the Lord never ceased His mission of mercy, and so He continues to call us to conversion and evangelism as He did in the Gospels. Jesus is the same yesterday and today and forever, as St. Paul tells us (Heb. 13:8), and that is apparent in the many apparitions of Our Lord. As with His first disciples, the modern apparitions of Christ are constantly calling us to prayer and conversion.

If you get distracted by the power and wonder of these accounts, you are certainly not alone. However, Our Lord does not mean for these revelations to be pure spectacle, and we should thus always incline our hearts to hear and live by what He teaches in His wondrous appearances. In that sense, this book is not an academic work, although you will learn a great deal, but it is a work that focuses on the message behind the appearances of Our Lord. Dr.

Łaszewski's research and observations in this book are all aimed at informing us so that we (and the world) may be converted to the Will of the Savior.

While the modern apparitions fascinate and delight us, we should remember that they are still private revelations. As such, they do not have the status of Holy Scripture, and Catholics are free to pay them no mind. Still, Jesus' modern apparitions have much to teach us, which is illuminated by comparing them to the Biblical accounts. As such, Dr. Łaszewski employs a numbering system to distinguish modern apparitions from Christ's appearances in Holy Scripture. The chapters that deal with the Lord's appearance in the Bible are numbered using the Greek alphabet. The first chapter deals with Christ at the Creation of the universe and is labeled alpha, while the final chapter, omega, discusses the Second Coming of Our Lord. As Christ is the Alpha and the Omega, the beginning and end, this is most appropriate for a book about Christ's apparitions. Meanwhile, the chapters that discuss the modern apparitions are numbered using normal Arabic numerals, starting with the visions of St. Margaret Mary Alacoque in chapter 1.

Drawing from historical and modern apparitions through this book, readers will gain significant insight into Christ's message and mission. However, it is always up to us who receive these messages to act on what He tells us. He doesn't come into this world solely to strike us with His majesty, but to make our hearts more like His. So, I join with the author in hoping that this book helps enlighten readers to Christ's ongoing mission to bring many to His merciful heart.

Michael Lichens
Editor-at-Large, Catholic Exchange

Christ's apparitions matter; they are signposts that speak to His mercy and power. But they only truly matter when they change our hearts and move us to follow what He teaches in these appearances.

El Greco, Christ Carrying the Cross, *Metropolitan Museum of Art (New York, USA).*

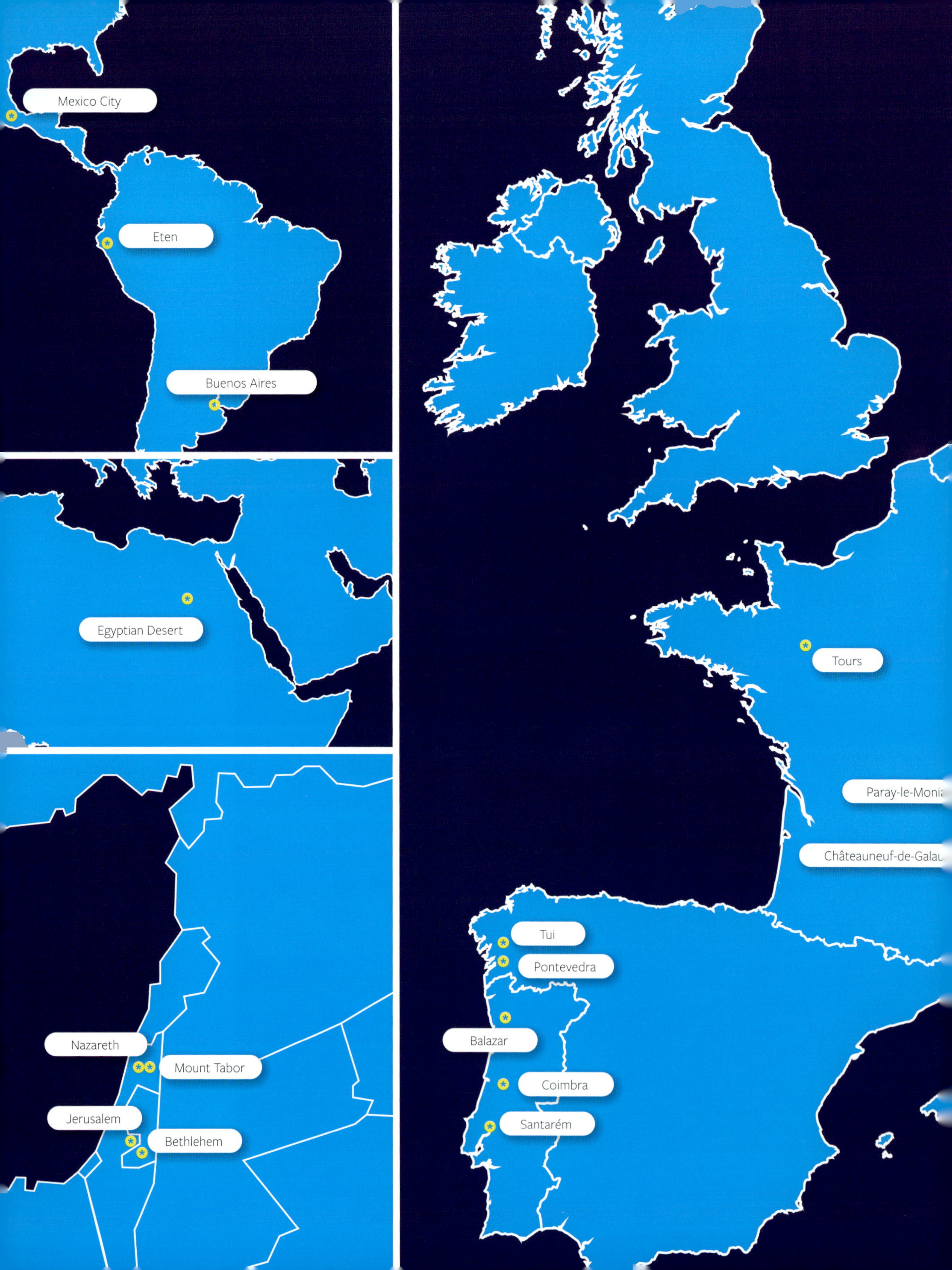

Mexico City
Eten
Buenos Aires
Egyptian Desert
Nazareth
Mount Tabor
Jerusalem
Bethlehem
Tours
Tui
Pontevedra
Balazar
Coimbra
Santarém

THE WORLD
OF JESUS' APPARITIONS
DISCUSSED IN THE BOOK
Vilnius
Szczecin
Sokółka
Płock
Kiekrz
Warsaw
Walendów
Poznań
Derdy
Parzno
Radom
Żytno
Kraków
Stara Wieś
Szczawnica
Milan
Padua
Turin
Mercatello sul Metauro
Città di Castello
Lucca
Urbania
Spotorno
Siena
Lanciano
Rome
Manoppello
San Giovanni Rotondo
Pietrelcina

➤ *Adam Styka,* Christ the King. *Parish of St. Vincent Pallotti in Warsaw. The painting depicts the Transfiguration on Mount Tabor. The Savior is accompanied by Elijah (left) and Moses (right). Christ is depicted lifting His eyes to God the Father and shielding Poland with His scepter.*

FROM THE PUBLISHER

The maps accompanying each chapter include, as needed, the birthplace of the saint traditionally associated with the name (e.g., Margaret Mary), the location where he experienced apparitions, the region

of his missionary activity — even if it was in a country other than his own — or the place of his death.

All locations are shown on maps of modern countries, with English place names.

Legend

 Apparition present in the Bible

 Apparition quoted by the Popes

 Apparition viewed favorably by the Bishop of the place

 Apparition included in the Tradition of the Catholic Church

 Apparition accepted through the sense of faith of the People of God

 Diocesan priest

 Consecrated person

 Lay person

 A visionary recognized as a saint, blessed, venerable, or servant of God

 Veneration at the place of apparitions

 Miracles and graces at the place of apparitions

 Visionary's writings

PRELUDIUM

On the previous page: The Merciful Christ *painted by Eugeniusz Kazimirowski, according to the design of St. Faustina Kowalska and with the assistance of Fr. Michał Sopoćko. According to St. Faustina's diary, Jesus appeared to her on February 22, 1931, in the cell of the convent in Płock, exactly in this form.*

➤ *A stained-glass window depicting the eucharistic miracle in Brussels in 1370, when stolen hosts intended for profanation unexpectedly began to bleed.*

PRELUDIUM

There are many apparitions of Jesus. Those described in detail number in the hundreds. Those recorded in history by a single sentence or passing reference likely number in the thousands. And beyond these lies a vast, immeasurable sea of apparitions—never noted in any chronicle, yet known to God.

The apparitions of Jesus form a kind of constant that quietly accompanies the course of human history.

But not all apparitions are genuine. History also bears witness to false apparitions—when a supposed visionary falls prey to hallucination or deception, or simply fabricates an encounter. There are also those ambiguous instances in which truth and falsehood are mingled together, like wheat and tares in the parable of Christ.

More dangerously, there are demonic apparitions, in which Satan disguises himself in the form of the Savior in order to mislead souls.

Discerning true apparitions from false ones is no simple task. Even the saints have been mistaken. But amid the multitude of supernatural encounters—visions, locutions, and revelations—there is a particular group of apparitions recorded in golden letters. These are the ones found in Divine Revelation, written under the inspiration of the Holy Spirit, and preserved in Sacred Scripture.

These biblical apparitions are infallible. They are the most important. They point with certainty to the truth of God. Strictly speaking, they would be sufficient. We could limit ourselves to these alone and lack for nothing essential.

All other apparitions are, in a sense, commentary—illuminations that reflect and deepen our understanding of what has already been revealed in the sacred books.

α
(ALPHA)
THE REVELATION OF THE INCARNATION TO THE ANGELS

On the previous page: A mosaic of the angelic choir of the Principalities, from the Baptistery of St. John, Florence.

Place of the Revelation: Heaven, at the dawn of Creation.

α

(ALPHA)

THE REVELATION OF THE INCARNATION TO THE ANGELS

THE ANGELS, THE BEGINNING OF CREATION

Before turning to the miracles woven into the fabric of the Gospel, let us first return to the opening page of Creation. There, hidden in the beginning, we find a mysterious allusion to what may be the very first revelation of Jesus—to the angels.

This revelation is not described directly in the canonical Scriptures. Yet allegorical references point to it, and we glimpse something like its mirror image in the drama of the angels' fall. In a certain sense, this may be the

The Creator holding a pair of compasses—an image echoing the verse from Proverbs 8:27: "He marked out the vault over the face of the deep."

Detail, The Creation of the World and the Expulsion from Paradise *by Giovanni di Paolo, Metropolitan Museum of Art (New York, USA).*

most decisive revelation of all, for it shaped the destiny not only of the angels, but also—indirectly—of every human soul.

According to tradition, as many as one-third of the angelic spirits said no at that moment. The book of Revelation (Revelation 12:4) is often interpreted as referring to this event when it speaks of a third of the stars swept from the heavens. But it was not God who cast them out. As St. John the Apostle writes, it was Lucifer who led their fall—who cast them down.

THE REVELATION OF THE ORDER OF THE WORLD

At this stage, we do not yet know precisely what choice the Creator placed before the angels. The *Catechism of the Catholic Church* does not say explicitly. It only offers this:

> *Scripture speaks of a sin of these angels. This 'fall' consists in the free choice of these created spirits, who radically and irrevocably rejected God and His kingdom. We find a reflection of that rebellion in the tempter's words to our first parents: 'You will be like God' (Gen 3:5). The devil 'has sinned from the beginning' (1 Jn 3:8); he is 'a liar and the father of lies' (Jn 8:44).* (CCC 392)

These may seem like sparse words. Yet a careful reading reveals much.

At the heart of this teaching lies the free but fatal choice made by Satan and those angels who followed him. They did not merely reject God; the *Catechism* adds something more. They rejected *God's Kingdom*—the divine order whose establishment was the purpose of all creation. The angels, too, were called to participate in that Kingdom. But those who sinned lost their share in it. Worse still, they took up the mission of resisting and obstructing its unfolding in the world.

What, then, is this Kingdom they rejected?

The Ancient of Days *by William Blake.*

A faint echo of the answer is already found in the *Catechism* itself—in the very passage we just quoted. The fallen angel, in tempting the first humans, utters the words: "You will be like God" (Genesis 3:5). At first glance, it seems a general temptation to pride. But hidden in that line may be the key to the great secret the angels were first shown.

It is the mystery of the *Incarnation*.

That God Himself would become man.

The serpent's words suggest not merely arrogance, but sabotage. Satan does not want God to take on human nature. He seeks to reverse the divine plan: to make man exalt himself in imitation of Satan's own rebellion, rather than receive with

humility the astonishing grace of God's condescension. *Let them be like me*, he thinks, *not like Him*. Let man strive to become God—so that God will no longer stoop to become man.

The rebellion is strategic. If Satan can tempt man to pride before the Incarnation occurs, perhaps he can forestall it altogether. Let man sin as the angels sinned. Let him fall—and be lost—before God lowers Himself to save him.

According to early Christian tradition, Satan refused homage to the mystery of the Incarnation. St. Cyprian of Carthage (†258) puts it starkly: "The sin of Lucifer was rebellion against the Incarnation."

An apocryphal first-century text, *The Life of Adam and Eve*, echoes this idea. In it, the first revelation in cosmic history is described: St. Michael the Archangel commands the angels to venerate a human being. Satan responds: "I will not pay homage to one who is lower and later than I. He should pay homage to me."

▲ *A depiction of the fourth day of Creation: God creating the sun, moon, and stars. Illustration by Julius Schnorr von Carolsfeld (1794–1872).*

▼ God Creating the World *by Jan Brueghel the Younger.*

The rejection was not only of man, but of the God who would become man.

THE WORD OF THE BIBLE

What does Sacred Scripture say about all this? Nothing directly—but much by way of allegory. This approach to reading the Bible seeks to uncover revealed truth at a level deeper than the literal. Within the historical events and figures described, we are invited to discern *types*—signs that point beyond themselves to spiritual realities more profound. Allegorical interpretation allows the faith to glimpse mysteries veiled in the fabric of history.

The rebellion of the angelic leader is presented allegorically by the prophet Isaiah in a well-known passage (Isaiah 14:12–15). From these verses, Christian tradition derived the name *Lucifer*, calling him the "Son of the Morning."

THE REVELATION OF THE INCARNATION TO THE ANGELS

We refer to him as the "Bearer of Light." But does this title suggest some special dignity? In fact, yes—and in a deeply significant way. In Scripture, light is the most mysterious of all images for God. It speaks of His presence, His purity, His radiance. It is as though light were the robe He wears when He reveals Himself to creation. "God is light," writes St. John the Evangelist (1 John 1:5). When Sister Lucia of Fatima tried to describe the Blessed Virgin, she said that Mary was formed from light, and added, simply and profoundly: "That light was God."

To bear light, then, was no small privilege. Lucifer held an extraordinary place in the order of creation. He stood closer to God than any other creature. No wonder, then, that he came to believe in his own greatness—his uniqueness. Surely no other being was so united to God. His name became a mark of permanence: he would always be *Lucifer*, always the one nearest to the divine.

I will scale the heavens;
Above the stars of God
I will set up my throne;
I will take my seat on the Mount of Assembly,
on the heights of Zaphon.
I will ascend above the tops of the clouds;
I will be like the Most High!
(Isaiah 14:13–14)

"I will be like the Most High." Here we hear a foreshadowing of the temptation whispered to humanity in Eden—the very same aspiration to divinity, the very same pride. Lucifer draws mankind into his own fall. He invites man to repeat the sin that cast him from Heaven.

He wishes for us to share in his darkness.

And darkness, as we know, is the opposite of light—the absence of God's presence, and with it, the absence of joy. As St. John writes, "In him there is no darkness at all" (1 John 1:5).

Lucas Cranach, The Creation of the World, color version, from the Bible translated by Martin Luther, 1534.

Stained glass of the seven archangels—Michael, Gabriel, Uriel, Chamuel, Raphael, Jophiel, and Zadkiel—1862, Church of St. Michael and All Angels (Brighton, United Kingdom).

But this self-assurance was already pride. And pride of this magnitude soon became blindness—the most dangerous form of pride. One more step, and he crossed the line.

Tradition links Lucifer to the words spoken in Isaiah:

A HUMILIATING PLAN

The Fathers of the Church teach that the angelic rebellion occurred *immediately* after the Creation of the world. It was then that the angels were granted the first revelation of Jesus in all of history. The

Mosaic of four archangels in the Church of St. John (Warminster, United Kingdom).

Orthodox icon depicting the Child Jesus surrounded by the seven archangels.

Creator unveiled to them the mystery at the heart of His eternal plan: the *Incarnation*—that *God would become man* (cf. John 1:14), and remain so for all eternity.

One can imagine the proud Lucifer responding with incredulity: *"Why would He not become an angel?"* If God were to assume a nature other than His own, would it not be most fitting—most glorious—to take on the form of the highest of all created beings? Lucifer might have thought: *Then I would not only be the one closest to God—I would be one with Him!*

But God willed something else. He chose not the greatest, but the least. He chose not pure spirit, but flesh and blood. He chose man—creatures of dust and limitation—as the center of His redemptive plan. Not those who stand in Heaven, but those who crawl upon the earth.

In Lucifer's eyes, this was an unthinkable insult. If God were to take on any form, it should be angelic—not human. Thus, the devil's rebellion was born of pride: a refusal to worship a God who would stoop so low as to become man.

HUMANS ARE CREATORS LIKE GOD

There is yet another reason—one that, according to tradition, filled Lucifer with rage. In the Creator's plan, humanity is elevated in a singular and astonishing way: man alone shares in one of God's greatest attributes—the power to bring forth *immortal life*. This exalted gift is intimately

The seven choirs of angels according to St. Hildegard of Bingen, manuscript from Rupertsberg.

bound to the very first command God gives to mankind: *"Be fruitful and multiply"* (Genesis 9:1). To be capable of generating a life that has a beginning but no end is to participate in a divine mystery.

No wonder, then, that Satan directed his assault precisely at this gift—the power to create life destined for eternity.

His hatred of it has never ceased. The most visible manifestations of his influence in the modern world are found in the glorification of abortion, the promotion of sterile unions, and the growing contempt for the sacredness of life itself.

SECOND PLACE FOR THE ANGELS

Lucifer rebels at the thought of acknowledging the superiority of human nature. And this is not surprising. In the order of creation, angels come after human beings. They are not the pinnacle, but only *messengers of God*, made "for us, humans"—to announce God's word and to warn us against paths that seem alluring but end in ruin. Their role is to help guide us to the shores of eternity.

Consider this: on the day of the Incarnation, when an angel encounters a human being, who kneels before whom? The Archangel Gabriel himself, one of the

Bernhard Plockhorst, Guardian Angel.

BEGINNING OF CREATION

highest of the pure spirits, kneels before Mary of Nazareth—a human.

As St. Irenaeus writes: "The Word became the steward of the Father's glory for the benefit of mankind.... The glory of God is man fully alive." It is the human being—not the angel—who stands at the center. Lucifer cannot bear this.

The tradition that the angels fell through pride is confirmed by St. Paul, who warns that a bishop "should not be a recent convert, so that he may not become conceited and thus incur the devil's punishment" (1 Timothy 3:6).

The devil was condemned for pride.

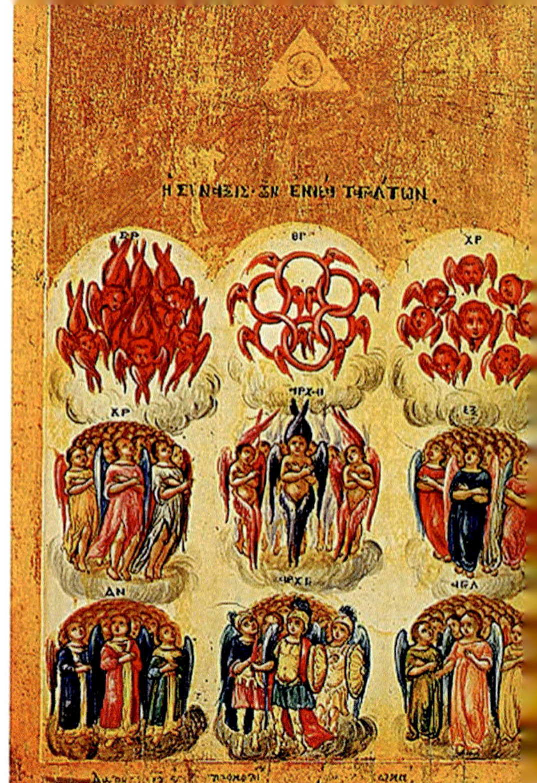

➤ *Choirs of angels immediately after Creation, illuminated by the first rays of God—according to the vision of St. Gregory the Theologian.*

CONTEMPT AND JEALOUSY

It may be that Lucifer's sin went beyond pride—that he committed an even more dreadful offense. Satan despised God for making a choice he considered beneath Him.

➤ *Eight-winged seraph. Church of St. Michael and All Angels (Shelf, United Kingdom).*

It was not merely horror at the Incarnation; it was contempt for God Himself.

Then came envy. The jealous angel did not want God to share His love and closeness with other creatures—love and closeness that had once been his. He wanted God to remain God in the splendor of majesty—or, if He must take on another form, to become an angel. But not a man. Satan refused to accept God as one who becomes human.

So when God revealed to the angels His plan to create humankind—and with it, the future Incarnation of His Son—Satan rejected what he saw as a humiliating design.

He would not bow to Jesus, God in flesh and blood. Instead, he spoke the words preserved in Christian tradition: *Non serviam*—"I will not serve."

"I WILL NOT SERVE!"

The origin of the cry *Non serviam* lies in the Hebrew *lo e'ebod*, drawn from the book of Jeremiah. The prophet declares, in words often read allegorically: "Long ago you broke

your yoke, you tore off your bonds. You said, 'I will not serve!'" (Jeremiah 2:20). In its original context, these words are spoken of the people of Israel, who reject the worship of God. But tradition applies them more broadly—to the first rebellion against God, the refusal to accept His Will.

This theme reappears in the Jewish apocryphon *The Penitence of Adam*, which describes Satan's refusal to honor man as made in the image of God. The text attributes these words to Satan:

> *I will not bow down to him who is later than I, for I am earlier. Why should I bow to him? The other angels who were with me heard this. My words pleased them, and they did not bow down to you, Adam. Then God was angry with me and ordered us to be driven from our dwelling place and cast down to earth—me and the angels who agreed with me.*

Francesco Botticini, The Assumption of the Virgin Mary, *1475–1476, National Gallery (London, United Kingdom). Depicted are three hierarchies and nine orders of angels, each with different characteristics.*

Josef Führich and Leopold Schulz, The Fall of the Angel, *fresco, portal at the organ loft, parish church in Altlerchenfeld (Vienna, Austria).*

Left: Paul Gustave Louis Christophe Doré, Paradise Lost.

Right: Fragment of the panel Paradise Lost *by Hieronymus Bosch—the casting down of angels and Lucifer.*

According to Bl. John Duns Scotus (†1308), the fall of Satan occurred immediately after the Creation of man, when God revealed to the angels His plan that the Eternal Word would become flesh. The rebellion, then, was provoked by the revelation of the Incarnation—a plan so astonishing it shook the spiritual world to its foundations. Confronted with this unexpected exaltation of humanity, the angels were subjected to a test of loyalty. Not all were faithful.

Some theologians hold that the angels' response to the mystery of the Incarnation determined their eternal destiny. And as a consequence, it has also shaped the course of human history.

John Duns Scotus, known as the Subtle Doctor.

THE VISION OF MARÍA OF JESUS DE ÁGREDA

Bl. María of Jesus de Ágreda (1602–1665), in her work *The Mystical City of God*, written on the basis of private revelations, portrays Satan's rebellion as a direct defiance of God's decision to become man.

First, the angels came to know the nature of God, one in His Being but three in Person; they were also commanded to pay Him sovereign homage and worship as Creator and highest Lord, infinite in His Being and perfections. They all obeyed this command willingly.... Next, God revealed to the angels that He wished to create human nature—that is, rational creatures of a lower order—so that they too would love and worship Him as their Creator and eternal Good, and fear Him. He also told them He would bestow many graces upon these human beings, and that the Second Person of the Most Holy Trinity would assume this nature and unite it personally to the Godhead. The angels would then be obliged to worship not only God but also this God-Man, humbly giving Him divine homage.... The holy and obedient angels all submitted to this command, yielding with the

Sebastiano Ricci, The Fall of the Rebel Angels, *Dulwich Picture Gallery (London, United Kingdom).*

María of Ágreda, Spanish Catholic nun, Conceptionist, mystic, and visionary.

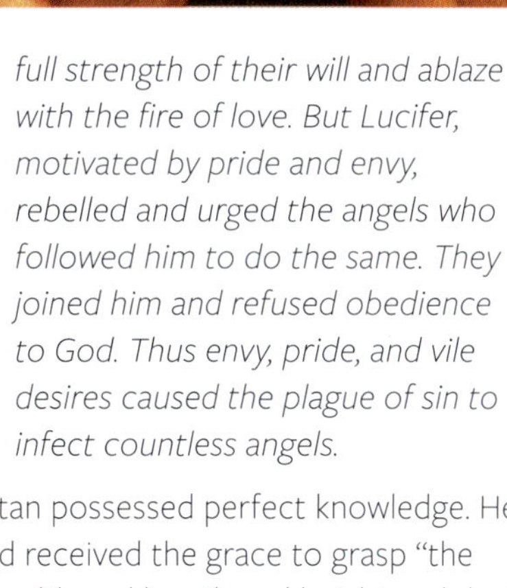

> *full strength of their will and ablaze with the fire of love. But Lucifer, motivated by pride and envy, rebelled and urged the angels who followed him to do the same. They joined him and refused obedience to God. Thus envy, pride, and vile desires caused the plague of sin to infect countless angels.*

Satan possessed perfect knowledge. He had received the grace to grasp "the breadth and length and height and depth" of God's mystery (Ephesians 3:18). He lived continually in a state of revelation, beholding God face to face. Therefore, when the divine plan for creation—and especially for the Incarnation—was revealed in that eternal and perfect light,

Guido Reni, St. Michael the Archangel Defeating Satan, *Santa Maria Immacolata a Via Veneto (Rome).*

Raphael, St. Michael Defeating Satan, *Louvre Museum (Paris, France).*

and the angel rejected it in an act of pride that hardened into contempt, he did so without ignorance. His sin, fully informed and freely chosen, became irrevocable.

ATTEMPTS BY THE PROPHETS TO DESCRIBE IT

The Fathers of the Church found allusions to Satan's fall in various Old Testament texts. One of the most striking—again interpreted allegorically—comes from the book of Ezekiel:

> *You were a seal of perfection, full of wisdom, perfect in beauty. In Eden, the garden of God, you lived; precious stones of every kind were your covering: Carnelian, topaz, and beryl, chrysolite, onyx, and jasper, sapphire, garnet, and emerald. Their mounts and settings were wrought in gold, fashioned for you the day you were created. With a cherub I placed you; I put you on the holy mountain of God, where you walked among fiery stones. Blameless were you in your ways from the day you were created, until evil was found in you. Your commerce was full of lawlessness, and you sinned. Therefore I banished you from the mountain of God; the cherub drove you out from among the*

Andrei Rublev, Icon of St. Michael the Archangel, early fifteenth century (Zvenigorod, Russia).

Pieter Bruegel, The Fall of the Rebel Angels, *Royal Museums of Fine Arts (Brussels, Belgium).*

Icon of the prophet Ezekiel. The Church Fathers saw allusions to the fall of Satan in the books of the Old Testament. One of the most interesting references—again allegorical—would come from the Book of Ezekiel.

The fall of the angels stirred the imagination of artists for centuries.

➤ *God tested Job. The fallen angel became the verifier of the biblical hero's faith and humility. William Blake,* Satan Attacking Job, *illustration for the Book of Job.*

➤ The Temptation of Christ, *a scene in the crèche of the Evangelium in the Church of Santa Maria di Dueville (Vicenza, Italy).*

➤ *Ary Scheffer,* The Temptation of Christ, *National Gallery of Victoria (Melbourne, Australia).*

> *fiery stones. Your heart had grown haughty because of your beauty; you corrupted your wisdom because of your splendor. I cast you to the ground, I made you a spectacle in the sight of kings. Because of the enormity of your guilt, and the perversity of your trade, you defiled your sanctuary. I brought fire out of you; it devoured you; I made you ashes on the ground in the eyes of all who see you. All the nations who knew you are appalled on account of you; you have become a horror, never to be again (Ezekiel 28:12–19).*

While this passage is addressed to the prince of Tyre—a human ruler—the Church Fathers, following the tradition of allegorical interpretation, saw in it a veiled reference to the first angel who fell. The figure of the cherub, whose heart was proud because of its beauty, becomes a kind of mirror in which the fall of Lucifer is reflected.

We have already seen that the prophet Isaiah also speaks of angelic pride. His words deserve to be quoted in full:

> *How you have fallen from the heavens, O Morning Star, son of the dawn! How you have been cut down to the earth, you who conquered nations! In your heart you said: "I will scale the heavens; Above the stars of God I will set up my throne; I will take my seat on the Mount of Assembly, on the heights of Zaphon. I will ascend above the tops of the clouds; I will be like the Most High!" No! Down to Sheol you will be brought to the depths of the pit!* (Isaiah 14:12–15).

WE LIVE IN THE SHADOW OF THAT REVELATION

Among those who realized how highly man was exalted by the plan of the Incarnation was Thomas Merton. On March 18, 1958, he had a remarkable mystical experience. In his *Conjectures of a Guilty Bystander*, he writes:

> *In Louisville, at the corner of Fourth and Walnut, in the center of the shopping district, I was suddenly overwhelmed with the realization that I loved all these people, that they were mine and I was theirs, that we could not be alien to one another even though we were total strangers.... I was suddenly filled with the tremendous joy of being human, a member of a race in which God Himself became incarnate. If only everybody could realize this! But it cannot be explained. There is no way of telling people that they are all walking around shining like the sun.*

Human beings shine like the sun, while Satan's light has been extinguished. No wonder, then, that the devil rages with a thirst for revenge.

That ancient revelation, granted to the angels at the dawn of Creation, casts its shadow across all of human history. From that moment onward, there has been an enemy who will not rest until he draws humanity away from God and into the darkness he himself inhabits.

The test faced by the angels reverberates through time and reaches us as well. We are tempted, like Lucifer, to cry out, "I alone matter!" It is easier, unfortunately, to say "yes" to the devil's enticement than to say "yes" to God. It feels simpler to turn away from the Creator and follow our own path—telling ourselves we will return to Him eventually. But the question remains: will we?

We do well to remember that every temptation bears the shadow of that first revelation. When Lucifer and his angels entice us, we stand, in a sense, in the shadow of the mystery first revealed at the beginning of Creation: that God would become one of us and sanctify all that is human, from conception to death. We are called to live in the light of that revelation—and unlike Lucifer, to become light ourselves.

Angels had their role in the most important moments in the history of the world. Paolo de Matteis, The Annunciation, *Saint Louis Art Museum (USA).*

β
(BETA)
AROUND THE NATIVITY OF THE LORD

On the previous page: Giorgione, Adoration of the Shepherds, *National Gallery of Art (Washington, USA).*

Place of the Revelation: Nazareth, Israel
Liturgical memorial: March 25
Bethlehem, Palestinian Authority
Liturgical memorial: December 24

(BETA)

AROUND THE NATIVITY OF THE LORD

THE BLESSED VIRGIN MARY

Once again, we find ourselves drawn close—perhaps too close. We are pausing at a moment in history which, according to many, precedes any revelation of Jesus. Theologians often identify christophanies*—that is, manifestations of Christ—with the appearances of the Risen Lord. Those events still lie years ahead: the entire earthly life of Jesus stands between.*

And yet, even now, we can already count several revelations.

At the very beginning of the Incarnation—no longer in the realm of ideas, symbolic prefigurations, or mystical allegories, but as an event rooted in time and place—God begins to disclose the mystery of His Son's descent. The eternal Logos takes on human flesh. But not flesh alone. The Incarnation is not a mere outer garment in which divinity hides. God

El Greco, Adoration of the Shepherds, *Museum of Fine Arts (Bucharest, Romania).*

Cornelis de Bruijn, View of Bethlehem from 1698.

ISRAEL

◂ *Domenico Ghirlandaio,* Adoration of the Shepherds, *Basilica of Santa Trinita (Florence, Italy).*

▾ *Taddeo Gaddi,* Annunciation to Joachim, *fresco,* Baroncelli Chapel *(Florence, Italy).*

becomes fully human: He assumes a human body, a human soul, and a human spirit. He shares our mind, our heart, our longings and fears, our suffering and hope.

His self-revelation begins with Mary. Then, still in the womb, He reveals Himself to the unborn John. He makes Himself known to Joseph, to the shepherds, to the Magi, and to Simeon and Anna in the Temple. According to certain apocryphal accounts, He also manifests His power during the flight into Egypt.

And this is only the beginning. In His public ministry, He reveals His divine identity to thousands. These, too, are revelations—though few recognized them for what they were.

NAZARETH

Everything begins near Nazareth. Here, for the second time in the history of creation, God reveals to a creature His Will to become man. It is as though this moment were a mirror image of the first page of the book of Genesis. Then, when this mystery was shown to Lucifer, it ended in catastrophe. What will happen now, when God reveals it to a human being?

Andrea Mantegna, Adoration of the Shepherds, *Metropolitan Museum of Art (New York, USA).*

On that first day, there was an angel woven of light. Now, there is a human being woven of grace: Mary of Nazareth. God, in a singular and unrepeatable act, preserved her from the stain of Original Sin—for this moment. But why such a decision? Was it a privilege? No, it was a preparation. It gave Mary the possibility of making a truly free choice.

Sin, inherited since the Fall, darkens the human intellect and inclines the will toward rebellion. Since Eden, defiance has become second nature. This helps explain why the world has seen so few saints and so much evil.

But Mary's choice had to be made in perfect freedom. To that end, God—so to speak—turned back the clock. Mary was conceived as though before the Fall. In her, unlike in the rest of us, the scales of discernment were unweighted. She stood in the original integrity of human nature.

One might object: "How is that possible? Did God reverse time?" But as the angel says at the Annunciation, "nothing will be impossible with God" (Luke 1:37). And in God's eternal plan—where time does not exist—Mary was present from the beginning. Some mystics have even claimed that in the divine mind she appeared *before the earth was made* (cf. Proverbs 8:23–24), since God, in creating the world, was already preparing for the Incarnation. He traced the course of Mary's life in such a way that it would bypass the Fall. This, for God, was no difficulty.

Accordingly, many saints—among them St. Maximilian Kolbe—have believed that the test given to the angels included the revelation of Mary as Mother of God and Queen of Heaven. Lucifer's "no," then, was not only a refusal of the Incarnation but also a rejection of the Virgin of Nazareth.

Now, at the two extremes of created freedom, we find Lucifer and Mary. And the human drama, in every generation, is a matter of siding with one or the other.

According to apocryphal sources, it was the Archangel Michael who confronted Lucifer. Now, at Nazareth, another archangel appears—Gabriel, the messenger of the Incarnation.

THE GATE OF REVELATIONS

This present revelation is a continuation of God's self-disclosure at the dawn of Creation. For what is the Annunciation, if not the unveiling of the mystery of the Son of God to the woman who is to become His mother? It is the first historical revelation of Jesus, and it will soon be followed by others.

Only days after her encounter with Gabriel and her *fiat*, Mary will witness that her Son has already begun to manifest His power. When she hurries to Ain Karim, where her elderly relative Elizabeth lives, a double miracle will occur on the threshold of that home. More important even than the greeting exchanged between the two women is the meeting of the two unborn children—which happens first.

Elizabeth and her son receive a revelation of Jesus. Elizabeth exclaims, "And how does this happen to me, that the mother of my Lord should come to me?" (Luke 1:43). How does she know that Mary is to be a mother—and of the Lord, no less? The answer is revelation. At the sound of Mary's greeting, the unborn John the Baptist begins to leap in his mother's womb. "For at the moment the sound of your greeting reached my ears, the infant in my womb leaped for joy" (Luke 1:44). John responds like the angels in Heaven, who rejoice before the face of God. How could he know who had come near, unless Jesus had revealed Himself to him, and unless the power of the Lord's presence had already touched him?

Mary, too, will now live in the continual presence of her Son—dwelling, in a sense, in the unceasing revelation of Jesus. And within the broader context of this mystery, we also see the revelation given to Joseph. In a dream, an angel—this time unnamed—says to him: "Do not be afraid ... For it is through the holy Spirit that this child has been conceived in her. She will bear a son and you are to name him Jesus,

Giotto di Bondone, Nativity of Jesus, *Scrovegni Chapel (Padua, Italy).*

Bernardo Daddi, Nativity of Jesus, *Scottish National Gallery (Edinburgh, United Kingdom).*

Flemish-Tuscan Master, Adoration of the Child, *Museo Nazionale d'Abruzzo (Italy).*

➤ *In front of the Basilica of the Nativity (Bethlehem).*

because he will save his people from their sins" (Matthew 1:20–21).

But first, everything depends on Mary's response—her answer within the framework of this unfolding revelation. It is the answer that matters most.

AN INTERIOR REVELATION

We read: "In the sixth month, the angel Gabriel was sent from God to a town of Galilee called Nazareth, to a virgin betrothed to a man named Joseph, of the house of David, and the virgin's name was Mary" (Luke 1:26–27). This is the address to which God's messenger travels from Heaven. But what unfolds is quite different from the scene most of us imagine.

According to the earliest traditions, the angel did not appear to Mary in visible form, standing before her as in so many paintings. In fact, the setting of the Annunciation may not have been Mary's house at all. Although later iconography often depicts the event indoors, at night, in a posture of prayer, there is an older tradition that places it at a well in Nazareth.

This is how the scene is depicted in the frescoes of the earliest known Christian

➤ *Geertgen tot Sint Jans,* Nativity, *National Gallery (London).*

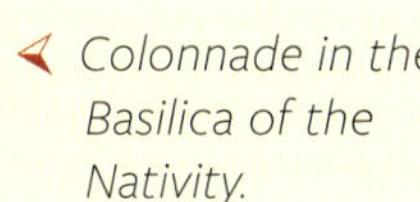

Colonnade in the Basilica of the Nativity.

church, at Dura-Europos in Syria (third century). One of the oldest written sources, the *Protoevangelium of James* (second century), describes it in similar terms:

> *And she took the pitcher and went out to draw water. And behold, she heard a voice saying to her: 'Hail, full of grace, the Lord is with you! Blessed are you among women.' And Mary looked to the right and to the left, to see whence came this voice.*

In the end, the location hardly matters. The Gospel tells us that Gabriel "came in to her," but this is not a reference to entering her house. Rather, it points to something deeper: an interior revelation. It is a direct encounter between Mary and the divine—a moment of spiritual communion at the highest level.

(It is not unlike the children of Fatima, who said they saw God within their hearts, bathed in divine light. Their vision, too, was a kind of annunciation—though still shrouded in mystery.)

Gabriel delivers his message: "Behold, you will conceive in your womb and bear a son, and you shall name him Jesus. He will be great and will be called Son of the Most High, and the Lord God will give him the throne of David his father, and he will rule over the house of Jacob forever, and of his kingdom there will be no end" (Luke 1:31–33).

And again: "The holy Spirit will come upon you, and the power of the Most High will overshadow you. Therefore the child to be born will be called holy, the Son of God" (Luke 1:35).

The content of the revelation is clear: the Virgin of Nazareth is being asked to give her consent to become the Mother of the Son of God.

And Mary—unlike Lucifer—offers a simple *yes*. "Behold, I am the handmaid of the Lord," she says; "may it be done to me according to your word" (Luke 1:38). She entrusts herself entirely to God, whose will is holy, whose wisdom is perfect, and to whom all things belong.

With that, the dialogue ends. The angel departs.

THE CREATIVE *FIAT*

Do we realize that Mary's *fiat* echoes the very words spoken by the Creator at the beginning of the world? In saying

Christmas tree in Bethlehem. During the holiday season, pilgrims from all over the world come to Bethlehem.

Orthodox altar in the Grotto of the Nativity (Bethlehem).

A star on the floor of the grotto beneath the Basilica of the Nativity marks the place where Jesus was born.

fiat—"let it be"—Mary imitates the divine command by which God formed light and darkness, sky and earth. "Let there be light" (Genesis 1:3), God declared, and there was light. *Let it be,* says Mary—and in doing so, perhaps without knowing it, she reveals what it means to be made in the image and likeness of God.

In God's plan, humanity was always meant to share in something of His creative power, a gift made visible in the lives of the saints. Mary utters a word that is not only in full harmony with God's will but also necessary for the fulfillment of His design. Only a double *fiat* is creative: the "let there be" of the Creator must be answered by the "let it be" of a creature. When a human being speaks this holiest of words, he or she begins to participate in the shaping of salvation history.

But the scene of the Annunciation could have unfolded differently. God might have heard a human *no.* That possibility was very real. On the balance of discernment lay arguments on both sides. What would tip the scale was love—a love that could be directed either toward self or toward God.

Mary did not hesitate. In her heart was a single love, and a single longing. And so she said *fiat*.

At that moment, a miracle occurred greater even than the Creation of the world from nothing: the Creator became a creature. What had seemed impossible

came to pass. As Franciszek Karpiński (†1825) writes in his *Song of the Nativity*, paradoxes are fulfilled, and impossibilities become real:

> *God is born, power grows faint,*
> *The Lord of the heavens is laid bare,*
> *The fire now stills, the radiance darkens,*
> *The Infinite has boundaries;*
> *Despised, yet wrapped in glory,*
> *Mortal, the King through all ages.*

ORDINARINESS AT THE CENTER

We pass almost imperceptibly into the scene of the Lord's Nativity—and with it, into the first public revelation of Jesus. Everything is still a "first." In a moment, the incarnate God will reveal Himself in the person of the Christ Child: first to the shepherds, then to the Magi.

Konrad von Soest, St. Joseph lighting a fire to warm the Holy Family.

Western wall of the Basilica of the Nativity.

It is a revelation unlike any other—remarkable not for its grandeur, but for its simplicity. The shepherds will enter the cave and see Mary, Joseph, and a newborn child lying in a manger. And that is all. No spectacle, no majesty—only poverty, stillness, and ordinariness.

Yet for the shepherds, this simplicity will be transformed. It is enclosed in a circle of signs: the angelic announcement, the heavenly choir, the glory of God shining around them. What they see may be ordinary, but it is illuminated by the extraordinary.

It is like a beggar seated on the steps of a church in a fairy tale. So long as no

Entrance to the Church of the Milk Grotto, where, according to tradition, Mary nursed the Christ Child while fleeing Herod's massacre.

Bilingual plaque indicating the way to the Church of the Milk Grotto. It is also visited by Muslim women desiring children.

The Door of Humility leading into the Church of the Nativity.

entourage surrounds him—no richly dressed servants, no golden carriage—he goes unnoticed, or is dismissed with contempt. But once it is revealed that the one in rags is the son of a king, everything changes.

So it is with the fields of Bethlehem. What appears to be a poor and fragile infant is, in truth, the King of kings. And those who keep watch over Him are not soldiers or nobles, but angels—more splendid than any ruler could command. If angels serve this child, then He must be the Son of God and the Savior of the world!

THE "REVELATORY ENVELOPE"

The miracle of Bethlehem did not take place in a vacuum. When Jesus was born near the town, its streets were crowded with travelers; residents were busy with daily affairs; officials assigned to the census were likely enjoying food and comfort at the inn. But the revelation was not given to them.

Mary and Joseph had been turned away. Though in urgent need, they found no welcome in the town. Bethlehem was in pursuit of profit: the census had brought a surge of business, and hospitality went to those who could pay. In that competition, the Holy Family did not matter. Pushed to the margins, they sought shelter in a cave outside the town.

And God, in revealing Himself, does not return to the city. He turns instead to those

Master of Vyšší Brod, Nativity of Jesus.

Top: John Singleton Copley, Birth of the Child, *Museum of Fine Arts (USA).*

Bottom: Interior of the Milk Grotto.

➢ *El Greco,* Adoration of the Shepherds, *Museo Nacional del Prado (Madrid, Spain).*

who—like His Son—are disregarded by the well-off, the respectable, the law-abiding. Bethlehem does not become the place of the miracle. The "envelope" of revelation unfolds on the fields beyond, where no decent person ventures at night.

Envelope? Yes, for this revelation comes wrapped in signs: in light, in the song of angels, in the dance of Heaven. Yet the Child lying in the manger participates in none of it. He is not surrounded by radiance. No music reaches the stable. No angels hover there. All of this unfolds elsewhere—in the open fields.

There, in the darkness, the angel appears. There, a light shines—"the glory of the Lord," a sign of divine favor and protection for those who seek Him. There, the angel announces the sign that will lead the shepherds to the Savior: "And this will be a sign for you: you will find an infant wrapped

➢ *Basilica of Santa Maria Maggiore in Rome, which holds the relics of the manger of Jesus.*

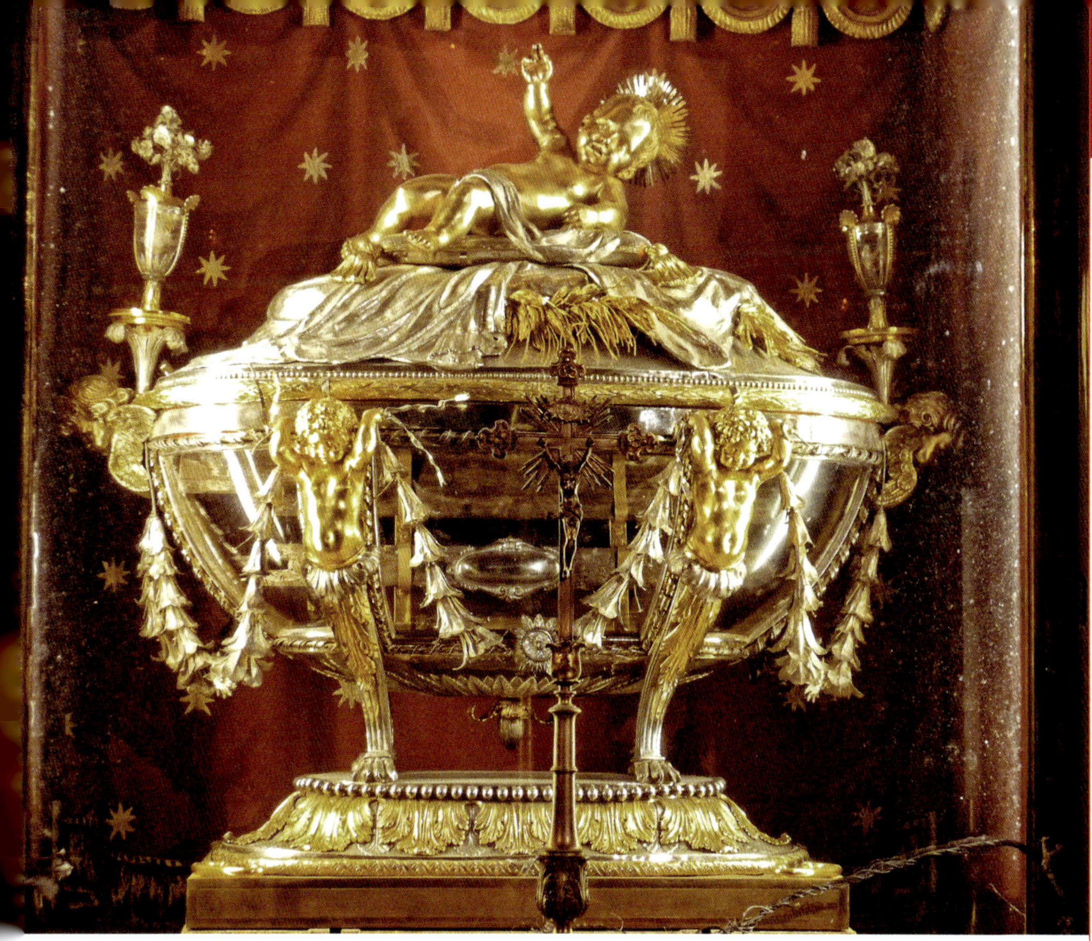

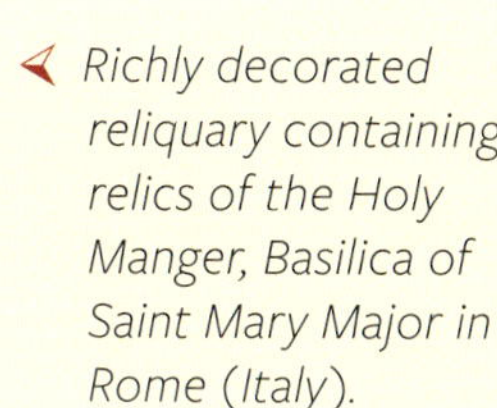

Richly decorated reliquary containing relics of the Holy Manger, Basilica of Saint Mary Major in Rome (Italy).

in swaddling cloths and lying in a manger" (Luke 2:12). And there, too, a multitude of the heavenly host appears, proclaiming glory to God and peace to those in whom He delights (cf. Luke 2:14). It is as though the ancient revelation once given to the angels—that God delights in man and desires to become one—were now echoing through the night.

The vision is brief. Soon the sky is silent again, and darkness returns. But the revelation has truly taken place. And until the shepherds go and pay homage to the Child, it remains unfinished. They now become part of it.

They go at once. They have enough signs to know they need not enter the town. They know the terrain; they know where a manger might be found. And they arrive—"So they went in haste and found Mary and Joseph, and the infant lying in the manger" (Luke 2:16).

Perhaps they do not know how to kneel. The Gospel does not tell us. It simply says that "when they saw this, they made known the message that had been told them about this child" (Luke 2:17).

And in this way, they become part of the revelation itself!

FURTHER ENCOUNTERS

We will soon hear of the aged Simeon, of whom St. Luke writes: "Now there was a man in Jerusalem whose name was Simeon. This man was righteous and devout, awaiting the consolation of Israel, and the holy Spirit was upon him.It had been revealed to him by the holy Spirit that he should not see death before he had seen the Messiah of the Lord." (Luke 2:25–26).

The fifth-century *Arabic Gospel of the Infancy* offers a striking expansion of this moment, depicting the Presentation of

Jesus in the Temple as a full revelation to the old man:

> *And Simeon the elder saw Him, and He shone like a pillar of light, carried in the arms of the Blessed Mary, the Virgin, His mother. And behold, the angels encircled Him and gave Him worship.*

This apocryphal account attempts to make sense of the reaction described in the Gospel. St. Luke tells us only that Simeon was led into the Temple by the Spirit: "He came in the Spirit into the temple" (Luke 2:27). Presumably, the same Spirit revealed to him which child—carried by a young, poor mother—was the Messiah. Perhaps Simeon did see something no one else could see. Perhaps others around him saw only a child, while to him the Christ appeared as light surrounded by angels.

At Simeon's side stands the prophetess Anna. She does not "see" God-become-man in the same immediate way, but she believes

Top: Central Romanian Master, ca. 1420, Holy Family with Angels, *Gemäldegalerie (Berlin).*

Bottom: Philipp Otto Runge, Rest During the Flight into Egypt, *Kunsthalle (Hamburg, Germany).*

Agnolo di Cosimo di Mariano, Adoration of the Shepherds.

Simeon's testimony. With him, she gives praise to the Most High.

Mary and Joseph, meanwhile, show no surprise. The mystery of the Incarnation had already been revealed to them. The signs and wonders that continue to accompany their Son do not astonish them. They have begun to live within the reality that others are only beginning to perceive.

Gerard van Honthorst, Adoration of the Shepherds, *Pomeranian State Museum (Greifswald, Germany).*

γ
(GAMMA)

THE BETHLEHEM EPIPHANY

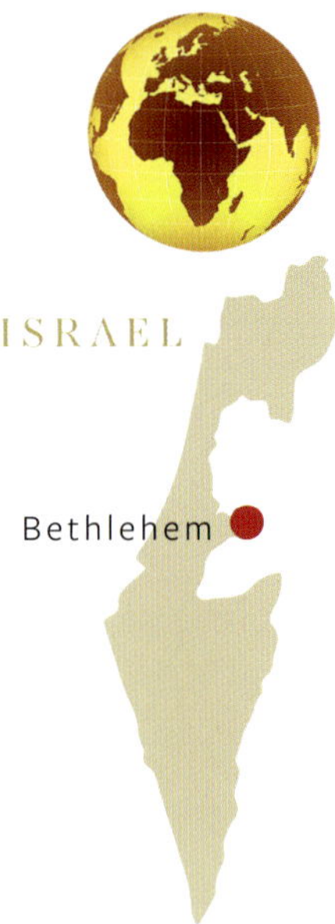

On the previous page: James Tissot, Journey of the Three Kings, *Brooklyn Museum (New York, USA).*

***Place of the Revelation:* Bethlehem, Palestinian Authority**
***Liturgical memorial:* January 6**

Master of Sant'Apollinare, The Magi Presenting Their Gifts, *mosaic (Ravenna, Italy).*

Edward Coley Burne-Jones, The Star of Bethlehem.

γ

(GAMMA)

THE BETHLEHEM EPIPHANY

SHEPHERDS FROM THE VICINITY OF BETHLEHEM, MAGI FROM THE EAST

Christian tradition is entirely certain of this: Jesus, God Incarnate, manifested His majesty and glory to humanity long before His Resurrection. One proof is among the oldest church celebrations—Epiphany, or the Manifestation of the Lord—already solemnly observed in the third century.

On a single feast day, the Church commemorated four events, each marked by a divine manifestation: the Nativity of Christ, the visit of the Magi, the baptism in the Jordan, and the miracle at the wedding in Cana of Galilee.

According to Tradition, the second of these—the visit of the Magi—is not primarily about the wise men themselves. Rather, its central focus is the mysterious star, a sign that the entire cosmos was stirred by Christ's birth and that a decisive turning point in history had occurred.

This event resembles the end of the world. In a sense, it *is* such an event, though perceptible only on the spiritual plane. The

Top left: Peter Paul Rubens, Adoration of the Magi.

Top right: Giotto di Bondone, Adoration of the Magi, *Scrovegni Chapel (Padua, Italy).*

Bottom left: Author unknown, Nativity *(Spišské Podhradie, Slovakia).*

Bottom right: Nativity from the altar of Cologne Cathedral (Germany).

➤ *El Greco,* Adoration of the Magi, *1568, Museo Soumaya (Mexico City, Mexico).*

▲ *Gospel Book from Speyer, ca. 1220. Manuscript in Badische Landesbibliothek (Karlsruhe, Germany).*

star is a divine sign of a new beginning—an instance of revelation. Strikingly, its appearance and motion parallel biblical descriptions of the apocalypse (Revelation 1:16, 20; 2:1, 28; 3:1) and the Parousia. The Star of Bethlehem, which heralds Christ's first coming, thus opens our minds to the mystery of His return. At His birth, a star—according to some apocryphal accounts—descends and radiates light upon the cave. At His second coming, the trembling of the stars signals the nearness of the Lord. Jesus Himself foretells, "The stars will fall from the sky, and the powers of the heavens will be shaken" (Matthew 24:29).

Apocryphal texts, while often popular in tone, attempt to draw out the spiritual depths of the Nativity. They suggest that Christ's first coming is, in a sense, a foreshadowing and image of His second.

If we are right to see here an analogy to the day of the Lord's return, then the star is the sign that a new time has begun—a "better age," the time of *God-with-us*. And that time has truly come.

APPARENT PROTAGONISTS

The Evangelist Matthew, who recounts the arrival of the Magi, does not call them kings but simply "magi from the East." Where did they come from? We do not know—only that, in Jesus' time, "the East" referred broadly to the lands beyond the Jordan River. On ancient maps, this could include Arabia, Babylonia, and Persia.

Apocryphal texts—which often arose to answer the unanswered questions of the faithful—provide additional details. The *Opus imperfectum in Matthaeum* places the magi by the ocean, in the far East, beyond all inhabited regions. The Armenian Gospel calls them kings of Persia, India, and Arabia; the Georgian Gospel names India, Persia, and Ethiopia; the Arabic Gospel also mentions Persia; and the *Cave of Treasures*

These gifts symbolize who Jesus is: the King who rules the world, the Priest who intercedes for grace, and the Healer who delivers us from all affliction—especially the ultimate affliction, the "malady of eternal death," the soul's damnation brought on by heeding the devil's voice.

The magi point to Christ's threefold office—but this is a later theological interpretation. In the oldest tradition, their role was to draw attention to the true protagonist of the story: the star that announced God's arrival. Perhaps only they could see it.

Just as only Stephen, in the moment of his martyrdom, saw the heavens opened, while the crowd that stoned him saw nothing unusual in the sky (Acts 7:56). Or as Bl. Maria Giannetti Taigi (†1837) saw future events unfold on a small radiant sun that hovered just above her face—visible only to her.

Rogier van der Weyden, Nativity Triptych.

Peter Paul Rubens, Adoration of the Magi *(Antwerp, Belgium).*

identifies their realms as Persia, Sheba, and Saba. Their gifts—gold, frankincense, and myrrh—might suggest Arabian origins.

But ultimately, their place of origin is not what matters—nor does the number of magi, whether two, three, six, or even twelve, as various traditions propose. The names assigned to them—three in number only because they brought three gifts—are also of little significance. These names first appear in the eighth century: Caspar (or Gaspar), Melchior, and Balthazar. They are arbitrary, nonhistorical figures, born of the human need to make the abstract concrete, to give names and identities to mysterious characters.

Tradition associates each gift with one magus: Caspar, whose name means "Guardian of the treasury," offers gold. Melchior, "God of light," presents incense. Balthazar, whose name means "O God, protect the king," brings myrrh—the rarest and most precious of the three.

Adoration of the Magi, sarcophagus plate from the Cemetery of St. Agnes in Rome, fourth century, Vatican Museum.

GOD LIT THE STAR

The astronomer and physicist Johannes Kepler (†1630) proposed that the Star of Bethlehem was the result of a conjunction between Jupiter and Saturn, which did

Adoration of the Magi, capital of a Romanesque column from Saint-Pierre, twelfth century (Chauvigny, France).

occur in 7 B.C. Others have speculated that it was Halley's Comet, also visible around that time. But the Gospel suggests something else entirely: a miraculous phenomenon. According to one Christian legend, God Himself lit the star in the sky on the day of Jesus' birth.

"There is the book of Revelation, the Bible, through which God speaks to man," say some scientists who seek to explain the star's appearance, "and there is a second book, through which He also speaks—the book of Nature." In principle, they are right. Yet in this case, theology takes precedence. For Sacred Scripture does not recount history for its own sake, but as the *history of salvation*—that is, history viewed from a supernatural perspective. And it is in that

Edward Coley Burne-Jones, The Star of Bethlehem, *Birmingham Museum and Art Gallery.*

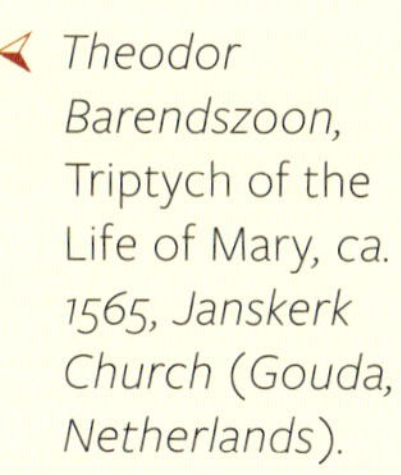

Theodor Barendszoon, Triptych of the Life of Mary, *ca. 1565, Janskerk Church (Gouda, Netherlands).*

light that the Star of Bethlehem reveals its true meaning.

What was the star? Put simply: it was a divine sign. Not a celestial body detectable by modern instruments, but a visible expression of a supernatural reality. The star was analogous to a natural star, but not identical with one. If so, then all astronomical efforts to locate it are misplaced from the outset.

What did this sign look like? A Syrian narrative describing the magi's journey to Jerusalem and their gifts to Christ recounts the mysterious light they followed: a star-like radiance, set in motion by the Most High, shining over all creation and eclipsing the sun, moon, and stars. These lesser lights became invisible in its presence. "For great indeed is the mystery of the Son of the Most High Majesty," the text proclaims. The star illuminated the magi's path first to Jerusalem, then to Bethlehem.

"We, the initiated into the mysteries, beheld the light of the star," the Eastern sages declare, "brighter than the sun, and

shown to no one else—for all others were far from its mystery and from the place where the light appeared."

Similarly, the *Protoevangelium of James* records: "We beheld an enormous star that outshone all the other stars around it, so that they were invisible. And so we knew that a king had been born to Israel, and we came to worship Him."

A REVELATION IN THE STAR

The apocrypha, expanding on the Gospel accounts, devote considerable attention to the Star of Bethlehem, seeing in it a revelation of Jesus Himself. In the work titled *On the Birth of the Savior, and on Mary, and on the Midwife*, the magi respond to Joseph's questioning:

> *Since you ask how we know, listen: we learned it from the sign of the star. It appeared to us brighter than the sun. No one can describe what it looked like. The appearance of this star means that the offspring of God will reign in the light of day.*

It did not move through the sky like the fixed stars, nor like the planets, which,

though they follow set paths in time, are changeable and wandering. The magi call these "erring bodies," unreliable for prediction. But this one did not err. It seemed the entire celestial pole, the whole expanse of the heavens, could not contain it, nor could the sun outshine its radiance, as it does with other stars. Even the sun itself appeared dimmer beside its light. It accompanied us on the journey we undertook—to Christ.

The *Arabic Gospel of the Infancy* adds: "The magi, kings of the East, saw in the sky a star like the light of the sun; it streamed from heaven to earth like a smooth band. Within the light was the image of a young maiden holding a small Child, around whom was a wreath of light."

▲ *Triptych of Crimson Ivory,* Scenes from the Life of Jesus Christ, *late tenth century (Constantinople, Turkey).*

▶ *Lorenzo Lotto,* Nativity of Jesus, *National Gallery of Art (Washington, USA).*

▶ *Sandro Botticelli,* Adoration of the Magi, *National Gallery (London, United Kingdom).*

Sandro Botticelli, Adoration of the Magi, *Uffizi Gallery (Florence, Italy). In the front row on the right is a self-portrait of the artist.*

Similarly, the *Georgian Gospel* reports: "A star appeared in India, like a full moon. Upon this moon sat a maiden of about fourteen, radiant like the sun, holding a newborn boy in her arms. The star was visible both day and night."

The *Opus imperfectum in Matthaeum* goes even further, identifying the star itself with Christ. It took the form of a small child, above whom was the sign of the cross.

In this way, the star is not merely a sign pointing to Jesus—it is a *revealing star*, a theophany. Some traditions say it manifested Jesus; others identify it with Jesus Himself.

This theme is not limited to apocryphal sources. St. Ignatius of Antioch (†108) writes, "All other stars, along with the sun

Ludovico Mazzolino, Adoration of the Magi, *Galleria Borghese (Rome, Italy).*

➤ Nativity, *anonymous master of the Church of Peribleptos (Mystras, Greece).*

and moon, became its retinue, for its light far surpassed theirs, and they were filled with fear at its novelty." St. Prudentius of Troyes (†861) adds: "It occupied the entire sky."

This was no ordinary heavenly body. It was not static, but dynamic—a living presence, a herald of God's plan. It watched over the magi, guided them, and adapted to their pace. In the worldview of the ancients—Greeks, Romans, Jews, and Christians—stars were not inert matter but living beings, endowed with reason and will. Here, the star is revealed as a divine envoy.

St. Augustine reflects: "On that day, the shepherds paid homage; today, the magi do. The shepherds were told by angels; the magi by a star. Both learned from heaven when they saw on earth the King of heaven."

A VERSION FROM THE BEGINNING OF TIME

The most extensive account of the star's appearance comes from *The Story of the Magi*. According to this apocryphal text, Adam, before his death, entrusted a testament to his son Seth. Seth updated the record and passed it down through the generations. Noah carried it into the ark, and eventually it came into the possession of the magi. This testament foretold the coming of a Savior, whose sign would be a star.

According to the account, the magi would ascend a mountain called Victorious each year to watch for this sign. Adam had written:

> *It cannot be that God would take flesh from man and descend to earth. But if this should come to pass, then a star will appear in the midst of heaven, stretching in brilliance from heaven to earth. In its center will sit a maiden on the*

Pieter Bruegel the Elder, Adoration of the Magi.

Alabaster sculpture of the Nativity, Musée de Cluny (Paris, France).

Bartolomé Esteban Murillo, Adoration of the Magi, *Toledo Museum of Art (Ohio, USA).*

brightest throne, holding the most beautiful Child. A crown of light shall rest on His head, and His hands shall hold heaven and earth—for He is the God of the world. Therefore, it is necessary to seek the place where this Child is born, the one for whom this star has appeared in the heavens. And to Him should be offered gifts: gold, incense, and myrrh.

On their way to Mount Victorious, the magi saw a pillar of light, upon which the star appeared. When they reached the summit, the sky opened like a great gateway. They beheld radiant figures bearing the star, who descended and stood above the pillar of light. The mountain was flooded with a brilliance beyond description.

From the pillar and the star, something like the hand of a small human figure reached out toward them—but they could not make Him out. Then they heard a soft and gentle voice. A small figure emerged from the light and said, "Peace be with you." It was Christ.

These depictions—each an effort to portray the mystery of the star that heralded the birth of the Son of God—seek to convey a single, luminous truth. Their message is as clear as the light of Bethlehem, which outshines all other lights.

What humanity had awaited since Adam has now been fulfilled. God has given a

Luc-Olivier Merson, Flight into Egypt, *Museum of Fine Arts (Boston, USA).*

sign: He offers the world the gift of peace, unity, and goodness. Heaven is no longer a distant afterlife but the Kingdom of God, made present and accessible through the gate of faith.

THE ENCOUNTER

When the magi reach the place marked by the star, they offer homage to Jesus. Something astonishing must have taken place—some revelation or inner illumination—for they recognize a King in the infant. Perhaps, as some apocryphal texts suggest, the light of the star revealed more than a location: a vision unfolded in the pillar of light that enveloped the cave.

The *Georgian Gospel* seeks to explain the singular nature of this moment:

> *They entered one by one to pay Him homage, bringing gifts of gold, incense, myrrh, a garment, and additional incense, all while bowing low.*
>
> *When the kings had departed, those around them asked King Balthazar, "In what form did you see Him when you entered?" He replied, "I saw Him as the Son of God, seated upon the throne of the seraphim, and the angels glorified Him."*
>
> *Caspar said, "I saw Him as the Son of God in suffering—He died and rose again—and the bodiless angels ministered to Him."*
>
> *Melchior answered, "I saw a perfect man, the Son of God. He sat upon the divine throne, judging the living and the dead, and a multitude of angels served Him."*

On their final entry into the cave, they saw a child on His mother's lap, attended by two angels. One of the angels warned them: "Do not return to Herod, that no harm befall you; let each of you go home by a different route."

▲ Gentile da Fabriano, Flight into Egypt, *predella of the Adoration of the Magi altarpiece.*

▼ Carl Spitzweg, Flight into Egypt, *Kurpfälzisches Museum (Heidelberg, Germany).*

Monumental Cathedral in Cologne. For centuries, the relics of the Three Kings have rested here.

SOMETHING BEHIND THE SCENES

It is often said that these accounts lack historical or theological credibility — that they are filled with contradictions and untrustworthy elaborations. Yet for centuries they nourished Christian devotion — and, at times, Christian sanctity. The Fathers of the Church cited them; echoes of them appear in the liturgy. Even if these events did not occur as described, the spiritual substance of the apocrypha contains no theological error. On the contrary, it can lead the faithful into deeper communion with God.

We might say these texts are *analogous*, just as the Bethlehem Star was analogous: similar to the truth, but not identical with it. How so? The apocrypha speak of the Epiphany — a real event — but they do so in a language shaped less by historical precision than by the imaginative and symbolic idioms of their time. Their imagery draws on myth and pagan expectation, not to distort revelation, but to express it in culturally accessible terms. This is not divine self-disclosure but a human attempt to portray what God has revealed.

The details do not matter — not whether the star was seen by three men, six, twelve,

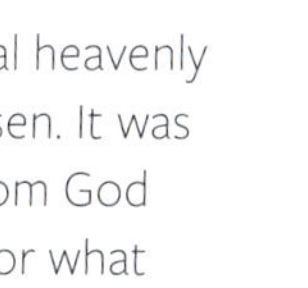

or thousands. It was not a physical heavenly body, but a sign given to the chosen. It was a *revealing* star. And those to whom God granted the vision recognized it for what it was: a sign proclaiming the birth of the God-Man.

When the star's purpose is fulfilled, it vanishes. In nearly all the apocryphal accounts, the star disappears at that very moment. Its mission is complete.

Thus ends the second "Manifestation of the Lord"—mysterious and astonishing, leaving behind more questions than answers. A revelation took place—but in what form? Paradoxically, that does not matter. What matters is the meaning: the star is the sign of a new beginning for the world.

How humanity responds to that sign is another matter entirely.

Chapel of the Three Kings in Cologne Cathedral.

Cologne Cathedral. Richly adorned reliquary in which—according to tradition—the remains of the Three Kings are kept.

δ (DELTA)

MORE THAN A MAN

On the previous page: Robert Bateman, Pool of Bethesda.

(DELTA)

MORE THAN A MAN

THE PEOPLE OF ISRAEL, YEAR 1–33

Place of the Revelation: Holy Land

God is among us—God Incarnate. "The Word became flesh and made his dwelling among us," we read in the Gospel of John (John 1:14). The divine Logos became, like every human being, a pilgrim—a transient presence in the world, one of us. The "tent" conceals the divinity of Mary's Son from human eyes. Like every man, Jesus writes the story of His earthly life day by day—unrecognized.

Yet when He emerges from His hidden life and begins His public ministry, He gradually unveils the mystery. At that moment, the book of revelations is opened. Jesus begins to manifest His power—but not yet His person. People believe in His miracles, but not in Him.

The key to understanding Christ's miracles as signs of salvation lies in the words of St. Augustine: "That He became man for the sake of humanity did more for our salvation than all that He did among mankind." This is a profound theological truth. And yet, the fact that God became man did not, in itself, change the hearts of men.

Gerbrand van den Eeckhout, Christ in the Synagogue at Nazareth, *National Gallery of Ireland.*

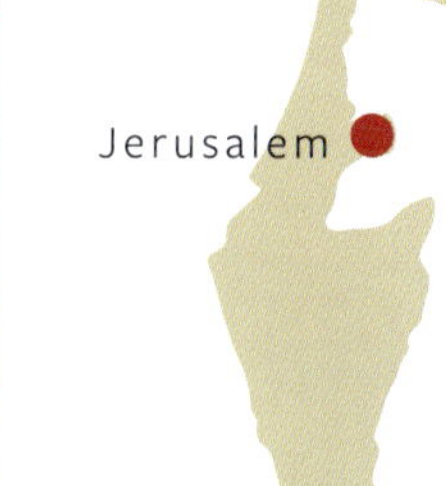

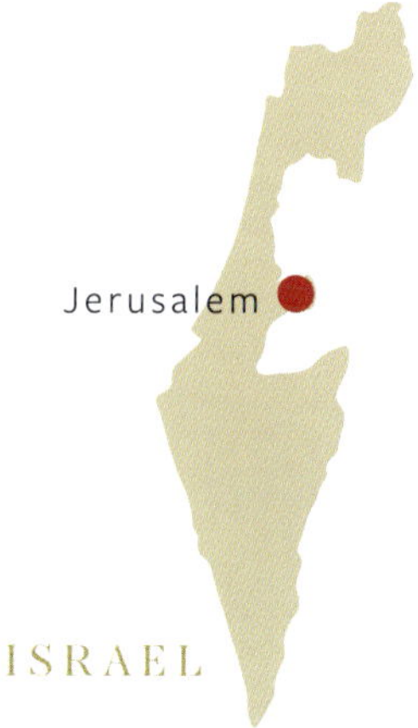

Carl Heinrich Bloch, Sermon on the Mount, *Frederiksborg Hillerød Museum (Denmark).*

NOT A DIVINE ELECT

That God "became man for the sake of humanity," and that His Incarnation "did more for our salvation than all that He did among mankind," appears to leave history untouched. The world overlooks the presence of the God-Man. It does not recognize Him. It fails to see that, by entering ordinary human life, God has sanctified every part of it—giving it light, meaning, and the power to be transformed.

An apt illustration is found in a miracle Jesus performs out of necessity. In His hometown of Nazareth, to avoid being killed, He is compelled to reveal something of His divinity. The episode, recorded by both Mark and Matthew, recounts Jesus' appearance in the local synagogue:

Michael Angelo Immenraet, Jesus and the Canaanite Woman.

José Ferraz de Almeida Júnior, Baptism of Jesus, *Pinacoteca do Estado (São Paulo, Brazil).*

1–33

➤ Duccio di Buoninsegna, Raising of Lazarus, Kimbell Art Museum, Fort Worth (Texas, USA).

▲ Nazareth depicted on a Byzantine mosaic.

➤ Jesus Discusses with the Pharisees, French school, Bowyer Bible, Bolton Museum (United Kingdom).

> *He departed from there and came to his native place, accompanied by his disciples. When the sabbath came he began to teach in the synagogue, and many who heard him were astonished. They said, "Where did this man get all this? What kind of wisdom has been given him? What mighty deeds are wrought by his hands! Is he not the carpenter, the son of Mary, and the brother of James and Joses and Judas and Simon? And are not his sisters here with us?" And they took offense at him.* (Mark 6:1–3)

At first, the people respond with wonder. But almost immediately, they retreat into the safety of the familiar. What had briefly sparked awe now provokes skepticism. They conclude, in essence, "This is only appearance. Jesus is pretending to be someone He is not."

Those who lived alongside Him for thirty years see nothing remarkable. They do not realize that God Himself has become one of them, stepping into their drab, ordinary lives—and sanctifying even

that greyness with infinite significance. Yet their ignorance is not entirely blameworthy. Jesus had hidden His divinity beneath the most unassuming humanity. For three decades, He worked, spoke, and lived like anyone else. There were no signs, no wonders, no outward marks of the divine. He was, in every respect, an ordinary man.

This concealment was not incidental but deliberate. It was part of the divine plan: men were to learn to recognize God in the face of an ordinary man. But that recognition lies at the end of the Gospel, not its beginning.

When Jesus returns to Nazareth with His disciples, the townspeople hesitate. His words provoke not faith, but fury. Luke records:

> *They rose up, drove him out of the town, and led him to the brow of the hill on which their town had been built, to hurl him down headlong. But he passed through the midst of them and went away.* (Luke 4:29–30)

▲ *Claes Cornelisz Moeyaert,* Raising of Lazarus*, 1627, National Museum (Warsaw).*

Here is one of those rare moments when Jesus reveals Himself. Just as the mob is about to cast Him down, something inexplicable occurs: the crowd is frozen—like flies caught in tar. And Jesus walks away, untouched.

When the "tar dissolves" and things return to normal, the townspeople will ask in bewilderment, "What happened?" But this does not mean they have come to believe.

Once again, we are struck by how little has changed. God knows that the greatest miracle is not to still a storm or raise the dead, but to transform a human being. It was easier to create man from the dust than to re-form him into the likeness of grace—to make him "a new man" in Christ (cf. Ephesians 4:24).

The Savior Himself affirms this in the parable of the rich man and Lazarus.

EVEN IF ONE SHOULD RISE FROM THE DEAD...

In the parable of the rich man and Lazarus, the rich man—now tormented in Hell—pleads with Abraham to send the deceased Lazarus to warn his brothers: "For I have five brothers, so that he may warn them, lest they too come to this place of torment." Abraham replies, "They have Moses and the Prophets; let them listen to them." But the man persists: "No, father Abraham; but if someone from the dead goes to them, they will repent." To this, Abraham answers, "If they will not listen to Moses and the prophets, neither will they be persuaded if someone should rise from the dead" (Luke 16:19–31).

Jesus knows that even a miraculous revelation—His own, or that of one risen from the dead—is not enough to produce faith. Revelation, in itself, changes little. To

Julius Schnorr von Carolsfeld, Wedding at Cana, *Hamburger Kunsthalle (Germany).*

most, Jesus appears as an extraordinary man, endowed with power, performing wonders, teaching with an authority that stirs the heart. He seems to echo something people have always longed for. And so they acknowledge Him as a wonder-worker, perhaps even a prophet—but not as the Son of God.

It is as though they were saying: "Yes, we admit—Jesus is more than a man. But He cannot be God. Surely, God cannot become man!"

We may recall that even Adam, in the apocryphal tradition, doubted that such a thing could happen—that God could take human form.

Only the Resurrection will serve as the decisive proof of Jesus' divinity.

THEY BELIEVED IN CANA

Jesus reveals His divine power for the first time at a wedding in Cana of Galilee, where He is present with His disciples. The story is well known: the wine runs out. Mary speaks to Him. He responds briefly, then instructs the servants to fill the stone jars with water. Once the jars are filled to the brim, He tells them to draw some out and bring it to the headwaiter.

The water is transformed into exquisite wine. The miracle occurs almost incidentally—Jesus makes no dramatic gesture. It happens as if with the snap of a finger. And yet, it requires the servants' labor: their obedience prepares the ground for what St. John calls the first revelation of Jesus' glory.

MORE THAN A MAN

The miracle takes place in vessels common to Judea—stone jars made of soft local limestone. Under the Mosaic Law, stone could not become ritually impure, unlike ceramic. Any water stored in such vessels remained clean for Jewish use. Thus, Jesus transforms into wine the very water that the Law had deemed pure—He does not abolish ritual, but fulfills and transfigures it.

How great was this miracle? Those jars held an enormous volume of water—enough to fill roughly 750 modern wine bottles. The scale is not lost on the Evangelist. Yet more important is the effect: "His disciples began to believe in him" (John 2:11). At first glance, the miracle seems to achieve its goal.

But not entirely. The faith born that day in the disciples is still incomplete. They begin to trust Him, but they do not yet understand who He is. Shortly thereafter, they will

The Wedding Church in Cana (Kafr Kanna, Israel). Historians still debate which of the towns named Cana once hosted Jesus and Mary.

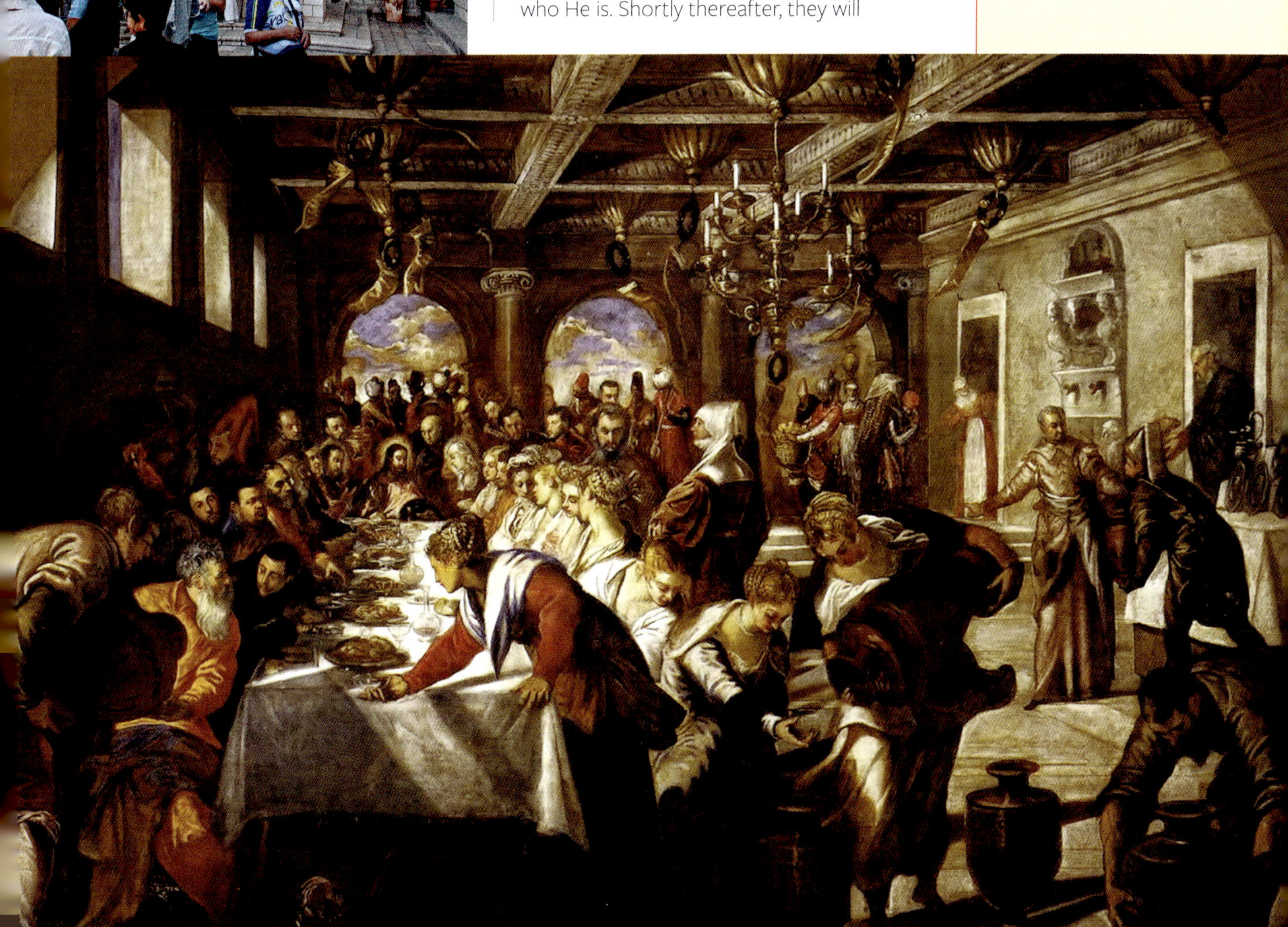

Jacopo Tintoretto, Wedding at Cana, *Basilica of Santa Maria della Salute (Venice, Italy).*

proclaim Him the greatest of the prophets, the one destined to restore the kingdom to Israel. Even when Peter confesses Jesus as "the Son of the living God," he does not yet grasp Christ's divine nature. He means a favored one of God—chosen, beloved, and empowered—not the eternal Word made flesh.

Jesus turned water into wine. But in the eyes of His disciples, He had not yet become God.

THE PARALYTIC AND GOD'S POWER

The Gospels report that even when Jesus performs acts only God can perform, people still fail to recognize His divinity. This remains true even when He calls Himself the *Son of Man*—a title explicitly associated with the Messiah—and acts with the authority that name implies. The Pharisees' response is not ignorance but disingenuousness. When Jesus later invokes that title before Pilate, they take it as an intolerable blasphemy, demanding His execution.

They know what the title signifies. They know Daniel's vision:

> *As the visions during the night continued, I saw coming with the clouds of heaven*
> *One like a son of man.*
> *When he reached the Ancient of Days*

Paolo Veronese, Raising of the Young Man from Nain, *Kunsthistorisches Museum (Vienna, Austria).*

Artus Wolffort, Healing of the Paralytic at the Pool of Bethesda, *Art Gallery of Ontario (Canada).*

and was presented before him,
He received dominion, splendor, and kingship;
all nations, peoples and tongues will serve him.
His dominion is an everlasting dominion
that shall not pass away,
his kingship, one that shall not be destroyed. (Daniel 7:13–14)

Let us return to the scene.

One day, while Jesus is teaching, Pharisees and scribes sit among the crowd—delegates from every village in Galilee, Judea, and Jerusalem. The power of the Lord is with Him to heal. Some men arrive, carrying on a bed a paralyzed man. Unable to reach Jesus through the crowd, they climb onto the roof and lower the man through the tiles into the room below. Seeing their faith, Jesus says to him, "Man, your sins are forgiven you."

Immediately, the scribes and Pharisees begin to murmur: "Who is this who speaks

Byzantine mosaic: Christ Heals the Man with the Withered Hand, *Cathedral of Monreale (Sicily, Italy).*

Left: Nicolas Colombel, Healing of the Man Born Blind.

Right: Stained Glass: Healing of the Paralytic in Capernaum, Metropolitan Museum of Art (New York, USA).

blasphemies? Who can forgive sins but God alone?"

Jesus, perceiving their thoughts, answers: "Why do you question in your hearts? Which is easier—to say, 'Your sins are forgiven you,' or to say, 'Rise and walk'? But so that you may know that the Son of Man has authority on earth to forgive sins"—He turns to the paralyzed man—"I say to you, rise, pick up your bed, and go home." And the man rises at once, takes up his bed, and departs, glorifying God.

Amazement seizes the crowd. They glorify God and are filled with awe, saying, "We have seen incredible things today" (Luke 5:26).

Jesus has plainly shown that He is God. Only God can forgive sins—and Jesus does exactly that. Yet the crowd fixes its attention on the visible miracle: the man walking. They forget—or fail to grasp—the deeper miracle: that sins have been forgiven, and that the authority to do so belongs to the One standing before them.

The Pharisees do not forget. But what ought to have been proof becomes, for them, grounds for condemnation. In Jesus, they see not the fulfillment of prophecy, but a threat to their world. And so, the clearer the sign, the more urgently they seek His death.

IN THE WRONG DIRECTION

The Gospels recount at least thirty-five remarkable miracles performed by Jesus: physical healings, exorcisms, raisings of the dead, and demonstrations of power over nature. Each was meant to confirm His divine authority and invite belief in Him.

But the people believed *differently*. To them, Jesus became the long-awaited figure who would fulfill *their* hopes. And here lies the fracture: God has one plan; humanity another.

The miracles stirred popular enthusiasm to the point that many seemed ready to follow Him even into danger. But that readiness was an illusion. When real peril arrived, even the apostles abandoned Him. One betrayed Him; another denied Him; the rest fled in fear. What changed? Why did they so quickly desert the one they had loved and followed?

The answer is found in the Gospel account of the disciples on the road to Emmaus:

> *Now that very day two of them were going to a village seven miles from Jerusalem called Emmaus, and they were conversing about all the things that had occurred. And it happened that while they were conversing and debating, Jesus himself drew near and walked with them, but their eyes were prevented from recognizing him. He asked them, "What are you discussing as you walk along?" They stopped, looking downcast. One of them, named Cleopas, said to him in reply, "Are you the only visitor to Jerusalem who does not know of the things that have taken place there in these days?" And he replied to them, "What sort of things?" They said to him, "The things that happened to Jesus the Nazarene, who was a prophet mighty in deed and word before God and all the people, how our chief priests and rulers both handed him over to a sentence of death and crucified him. But we were hoping that he would be the one to redeem Israel."* (Luke 24:13–21)

It is already after Good Friday. Jesus is dead. The movement is over. He was not crowned king, but mocked and executed in a crown of thorns. He did not lead the apostles into the kingdom they envisioned, but passed into the shadow

Left: Bernhard Rode, Healing of the Paralytic, *illustration from 1780.*

Right: Byzantine mosaic: Jesus Healing the Leper.

of death. He was not the triumphant liberator they imagined, but a man of sorrows, acquainted with grief. And they were not prepared to become like Him.

"But we had hoped," say the disciples as they leave Jerusalem behind—its danger, its disappointment. Fear now drives them, not hope. The mission they once embraced has become a liability. They are no longer "the chosen." They must retreat, return to old lives, and erase the traces of their discipleship.

They are disillusioned with Jesus because they had imposed on Him their own desires. They did not ask what He came to give; they told Him what they wanted Him to be.

They wanted Jesus to serve their dreams.

This is captured vividly in a scene from Matthew's Gospel:

> *Then the mother of the sons of Zebedee approached him with her sons and did him homage, wishing to ask him for something. He said to her, "What do you wish?" She answered him, "Command that these two sons of mine sit, one at your right and the other at your left, in your kingdom."* (Matthew 20:20–21)

▲ *Hans von Kulmbach,* Mary Salome and Zebedee with Their Sons James and John the Evangelist.

▼ *Theodoor Rombouts,* Christ Driving the Merchants from the Temple, *Museum of Fine Arts (Antwerp, Belgium).*

Jean-Baptiste Jouvenet, Christ Expelling the Money Changers from the Temple, *Musée des Beaux-Arts (Lyon, France)*.

Jesus did not fulfill the disciples' dreams. He *was* the Messiah, but not as they had conceived Him. He *did* bring salvation, but not the kind they expected. His Kingdom, His authority, and His victory were of another order entirely. Though He had spoken of this for three years, they had not understood—perhaps because they had not truly wanted to.

THEIR JESUS

Jesus says one word—*yama*—and they hear another—*gora*. As in Japanese, where *Fujiyama* means Mount Fuji, yet the suffix "yama" (mountain) might go unnoticed by non-speakers. The same word carries wholly different meanings. Jesus speaks of eternal joy; they hear temporal bliss. He speaks of the riches of grace; they imagine gold bars.

The effect of His signs and revelations is, paradoxically, the opposite of what He intends. Rather than opening hearts to the truth, they reinforce the disciples' conviction that *their* dreams are about to be fulfilled. So strong is their attachment to these hopes that they become, in a sense, *grace-proof*—impervious to revelation, deaf to the divine.

Their Jesus was meant to overthrow the Romans, restore the kingdom of Israel, and reign as a glorious, beloved monarch. Even after the Resurrection, their questions betray the same longing: "Lord, are you at this time going to restore the kingdom to Israel?" (Acts 1:6).

They still dream of becoming "somebodies" beside Him—sharing in glory, power, fame, and wealth. It is all imagined in worldly terms, according to the fleeting standards of the age. The kingdom they expect is political, not spiritual.

Heinrich Hofmann, Christ and the Rich Young Ruler, *Riverside Church (New York, USA)*.

They clung to these aspirations so tenaciously that nothing else could enter. Even the signs and wonders they witnessed were interpreted through that lens.

When Jesus failed to fulfill these expectations, He disappointed them. One betrayed Him. Another denied Him. The rest abandoned Him. The Master was left alone.

The disciples returned only after the Resurrection—and after the descent of the Comforter Spirit, the final lesson the Master gave them.

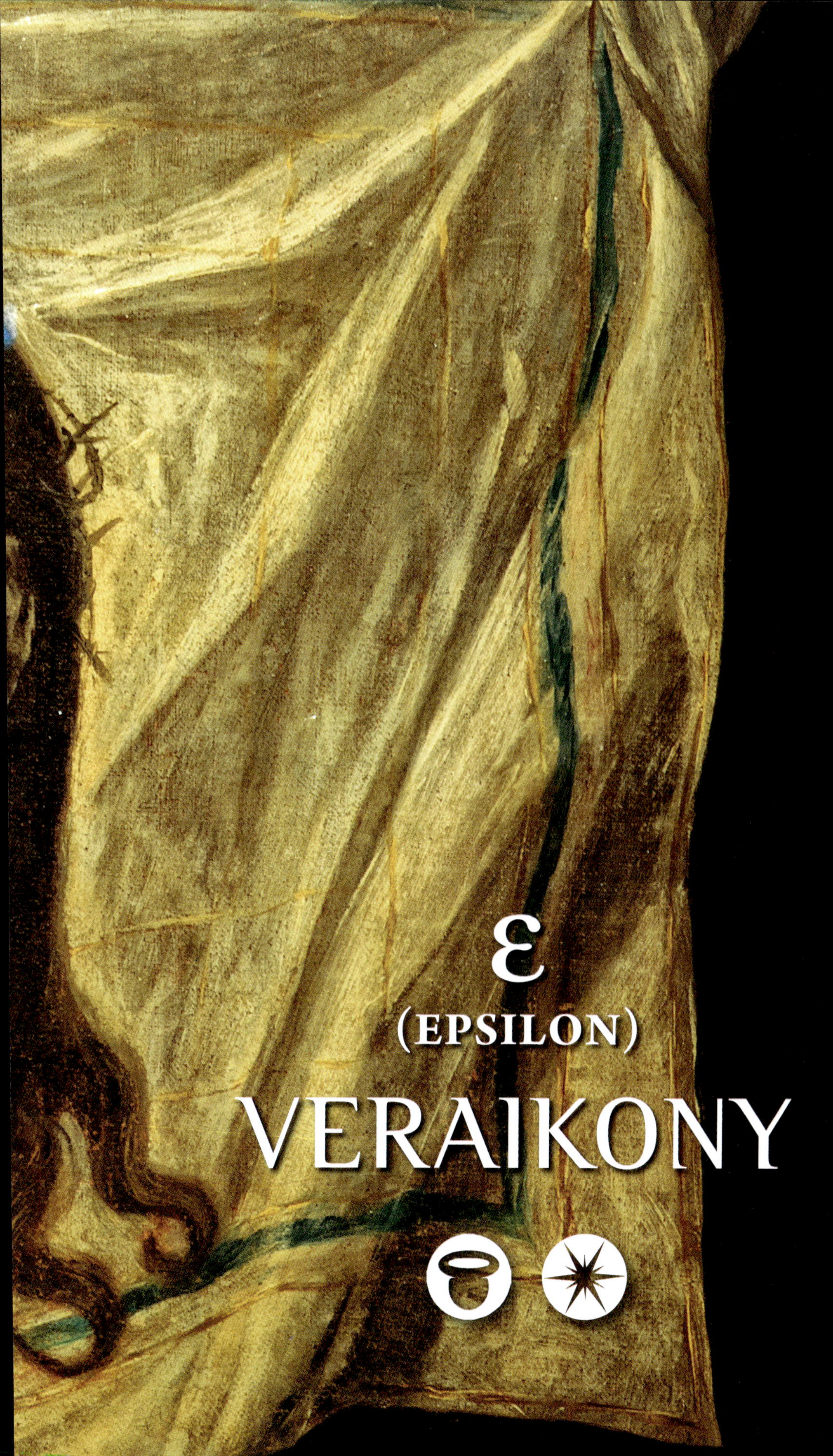

ε
(EPSILON)
VERAIKONY

On the previous page: El Greco, Veil of Veronica, *Museum of Contemporary Art Goulandris (Athens, Greece).*

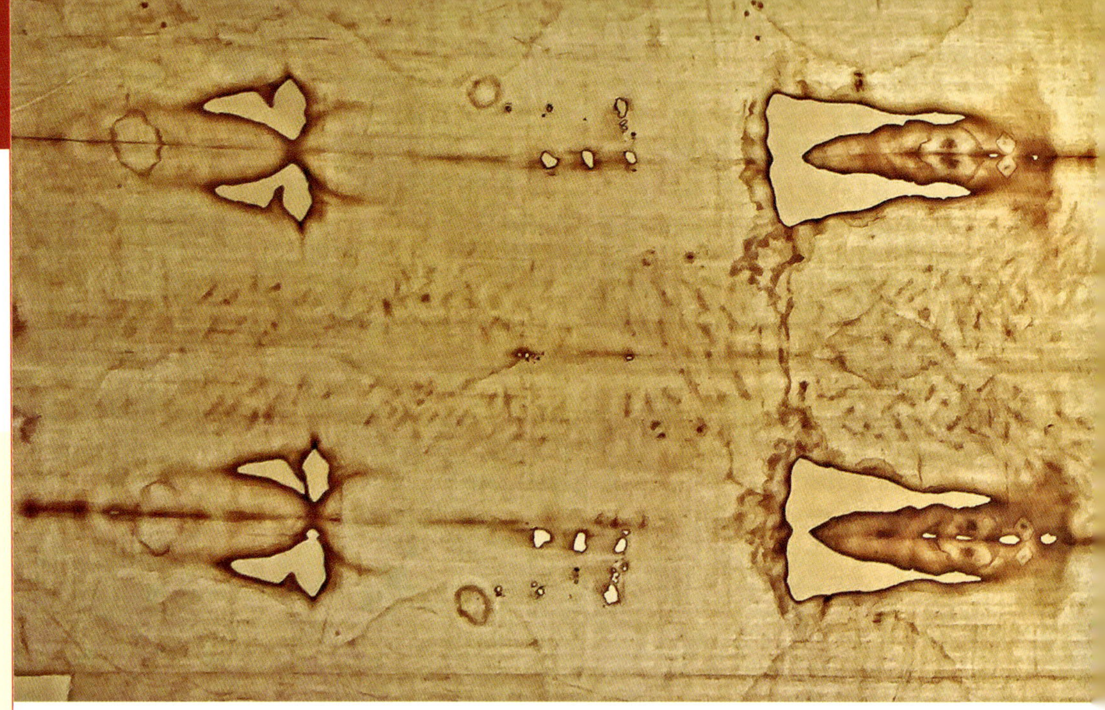

The most mysterious of the images not made by human hands: The Shroud of Turin. Scientists still cannot explain how it could have been created.

***Place of the Revelation:* Jerusalem, on the path of Jesus' journeys, Israel, Palestine**
***Liturgical memorial:* St. Veronica, February 4**

Mattia Preti, St. Veronica with the Veil, *Los Angeles County Museum of Art (USA).*

ε

(EPSILON)

VERAIKONY

THE ENVOY OF ABGAR V THE BLACK, VERONICA, BEFORE A.D. 33

In the peculiar epoch of the Renaissance, the atmosphere of the sacred that had once permeated every aspect of life in Western Europe began to recede. That is why, today, we often struggle to understand the significance once attributed to icons—especially the acheiropoieta, or "images not made by human hands." For early generations of Christians, these were not merely sacred art, but direct revelations of Jesus' divinity and power.

Today, they are often viewed as devotional objects—religious artwork whose symbolism is seldom read or felt. Their function as places of revelation has, in most cases, been lost. But there are exceptions.

Can a sacred image still be a place of revelation? Absolutely. This is attested not only in the legends of living icons and miracle-working images, but in the personal experience of those who have preserved in their hearts a natural sensitivity to the sacred.

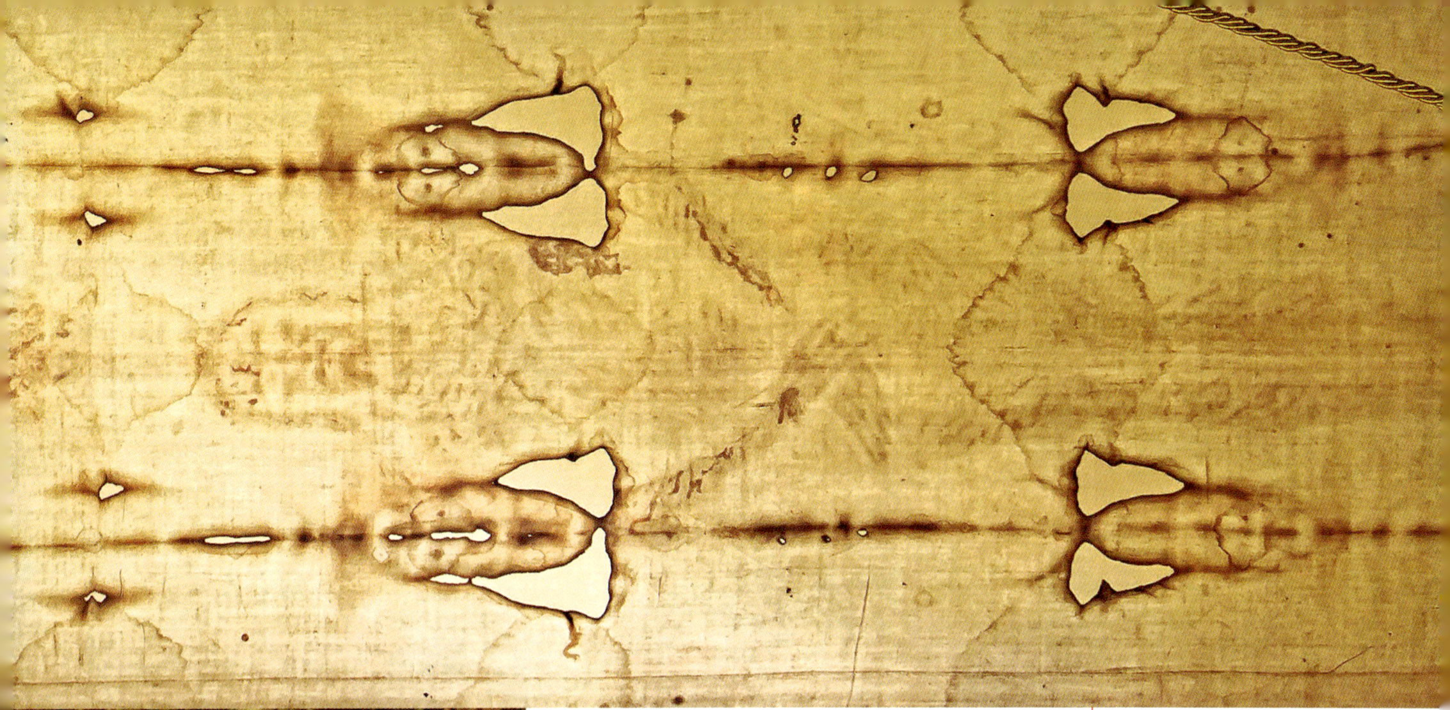

Thomas Merton offered moving testimony to this in 1965, when he received a hand-painted icon from Mount Athos. He wrote:

> *Where should I begin? I have never received from anyone in my entire life such a precious and magnificent gift. I have no words to express how deeply I was moved, standing face-to-face with this holy and wondrous presence that became my portion.... At first, I could scarcely believe.... This is the perfect act of timeless veneration. I shall never tire of gazing at this icon. There is here a spiritual presence and reality—truly Taboric light—which seems to pour forth without measure from the Heart of the Virgin and the Child, as though They were one heart. This light streams into the entire universe. It is immeasurably beautiful. And full of silence.*

For Merton, the icon of the Mother of God with the Child was a treasure beyond words. He kept it near him always. On his final journey—to Thailand in 1968, where he died tragically by accidental

King Abgar received the image from Edessa, which restored his health.

The handing over of the Holy Mandylion (image from Edessa) to the Byzantines by the inhabitants of Edessa in AD 944.

El Greco, St. Veronica Holding the Veil.

Simon Ushakov, The Savior Not Made by Hands, *1677.*

electrocution—he brought with him only five personal items. Alongside a watch, dark sunglasses, the Cistercian breviary, and a rosary, he carried that icon.

WHERE DO THEY COME FROM?

Some believe that the first icons—portraits of the Savior—were created even before the Lord's Ascension. According to this view, it was in the days following the Resurrection, as Jesus appeared to His disciples, that the earliest attempts were made to preserve the memory of His appearance through visual representation.

This opinion is found, for instance, in Eusebius of Caesarea (†339), whose testimony is particularly striking given his personal disapproval of icons. Eusebius belonged to a strand of early Christian thought that regarded images as remnants of the pagan world—unfit for Christian worship and to be condemned by the Church.

Yet even Eusebius, in his *Ecclesiastical History*, acknowledges the existence of sacred images. He refers to the famous *mandylion*, and writes: "I have seen many portraits of the Savior ... which have been preserved to our times." More intriguingly still, he recounts a visit to the home of the woman healed by Jesus of a flow of blood (cf. Matthew 9:20–22), where, according to tradition, a sculpture commemorating the miracle stood from the first century:

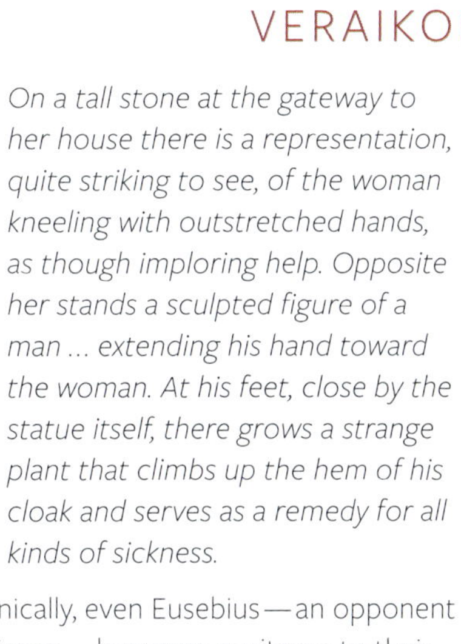

VERAIKONY

> *On a tall stone at the gateway to her house there is a representation, quite striking to see, of the woman kneeling with outstretched hands, as though imploring help. Opposite her stands a sculpted figure of a man ... extending his hand toward the woman. At his feet, close by the statue itself, there grows a strange plant that climbs up the hem of his cloak and serves as a remedy for all kinds of sickness.*

Ironically, even Eusebius—an opponent of icons—becomes a witness to their antiquity.

Contrary to the iconoclasts, many early Christians believed that Jesus Himself had given permission—even a command—to produce images. They held that He had offered His "true icon" to the Church as a

Poster for the exposition of the Shroud, approved by Pope Pius IX, 1898.

Painting by della Rovere showing the method of placing the Shroud over the Body of Christ, Galleria Sabauda (Turin, Italy).

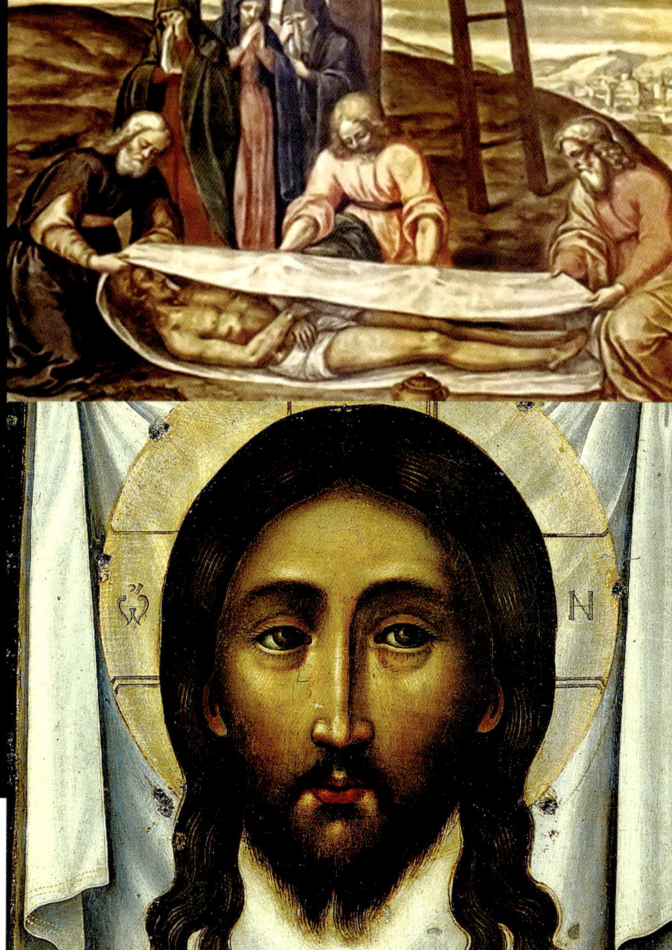

PRE 33 A.D.

Original image of the face of Christ visible on the Shroud.

The same image shown in spatial (3D) form.

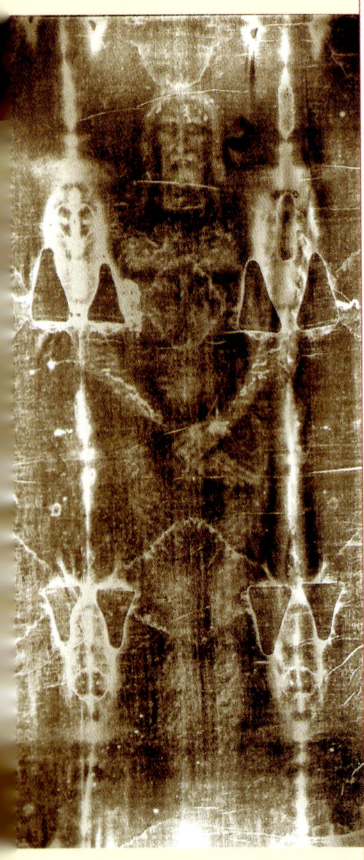

Negative image of the Shroud of Turin.

gift, perhaps even before the Ascension. Long before the first followers of Christ ever entered an icon studio, they believed the Savior had already revealed His face.

ACHEIROPOIETA AND VERAIKONY

Images said to have arisen supernaturally—without the hand of a human artist—are called *acheiropoieta*. The term comes from the Greek: *a* ("not"), *cheir* ("hand"), and *poietos* ("made"). These are the works that, according to tradition, Jesus Himself gave to His followers.

If such images truly originated through the direct action of the Savior, then their very existence is miraculous. But even if they are not, in the strict sense, *acheiropoieta*, they remain wondrous. This is one of the mysteries of faith: for many believers, to stand before such an image is to encounter the living Christ. These icons were—and for many still are—places of revelation.

"Was Jesus a painter, then?" a skeptic might ask. But the question misleads. It is better to say that the Lord *gave us His images*. Tradition refers to these as *veraikony*—from the Latin *vera icona*, meaning "true icon." The emphasis lies not on the mode of their creation, but on the authenticity of what they depict: the true face of the Savior.

The most famous *veraikon* is said to be the veil of Veronica, on which the face of Jesus was imprinted when she wiped His brow on the way to Golgotha. Yet this is not the earliest icon associated with Christ. That distinction belongs to the *mandylion*, the cloth sent to King Abgar of Edessa. Tradition also venerates the Shroud of Turin as a sacred image possibly bearing Christ's likeness.

Even if these traditions are rooted more in pious belief than verifiable history, the faith of the early Christians in their authenticity is undeniable. They believed they possessed a work of the Master—a true likeness of His face. That belief was deepened by the miracles reportedly associated with such images, which led them to the conviction that God could be encountered through an icon, that He reveals Himself through visible form.

Indeed, the entire tradition of icons is founded on this conviction: that divine light and power can dwell in sacred images.

AN EXAMPLE OF A MIRACLE

We need not rely on faith alone. Numerous pieces of early evidence

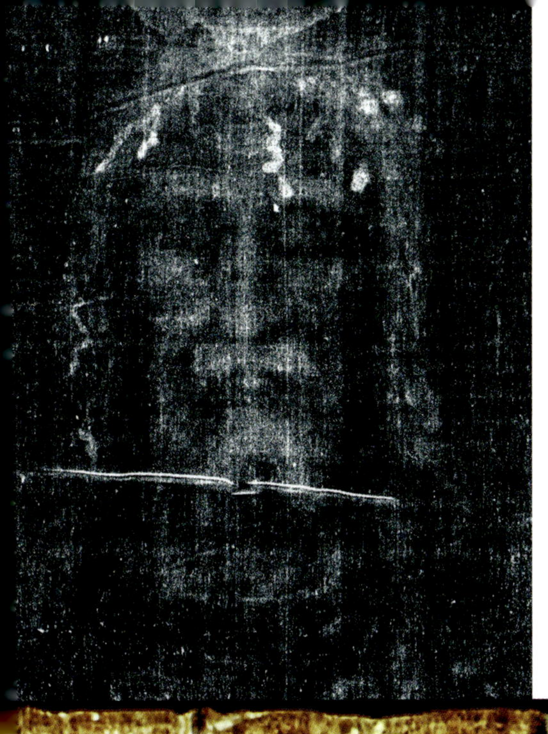

support the belief that the first images of Jesus, including Veronica's veil, the *mandylion*, and the Shroud of Turin, were not crafted by human hands but came from Heaven. The miracles associated with them, too, may be understood as manifestations of Christ Himself.

One such miracle occurred in Rome in 1849. At the time, Pope Pius IX—due to political turmoil and conflict with secular authorities—was living in exile in Gaeta, near Naples. Meanwhile, a solemn exposition of St. Veronica's veil was being held in St. Peter's Basilica.

Face of the man from the Shroud processed via computer enhancement.

The Shroud viewed in 3D.

Head of Jesus reconstructed by Prof. Jorge Almenar of Oviedo based on research on the Shroud.

PRE 33 A.D.

➤ Otto van Veen, *Christ Meets Veronica*, Royal Museums of Fine Arts (Brussels, Belgium).

➤ Robert Campin, *St. Veronica with the Veil*, Städel Museum (Frankfurt am Main, Germany). Noteworthy is the semi-transparent material of the veil. It is likely the artist saw the Veil of Manoppello.

On the third day of the exhibition—significantly, the Feast of the Epiphany—the veil suddenly changed. The face of Christ, previously faint, took on vivid color and began to radiate light. The transformation was visible to all present. So striking was the phenomenon that the basilica clergy ordered the bells of Rome to be rung, summoning the faithful to witness it. The miracle lasted for three hours and was formally recorded in the basilica's chronicles.

The Holy Face preserved in the Armenian Church of St. Bartholomew (Genoa, Italy).

Thus, in the heart of the nineteenth century, Jesus revealed Himself once more through His *veraikon*—the "true icon."

AN APOCRYPHAL, TRULY FIRST ICON

One image "not made by human hands" is the *mandylion*, and it deserves our fullest attention. Its origin is tied to the story of King Abgar V the Black of Edessa, who suffered from leprosy and sent his servant Ananias Tabularius to summon Jesus to his palace.

We read of this in the *Georgian Gospel*:

> *The envoy of the Armenian king came to Jesus, bowed before Him, and delivered the royal letter. The letter read: "If all believe in You because they have seen You, then*

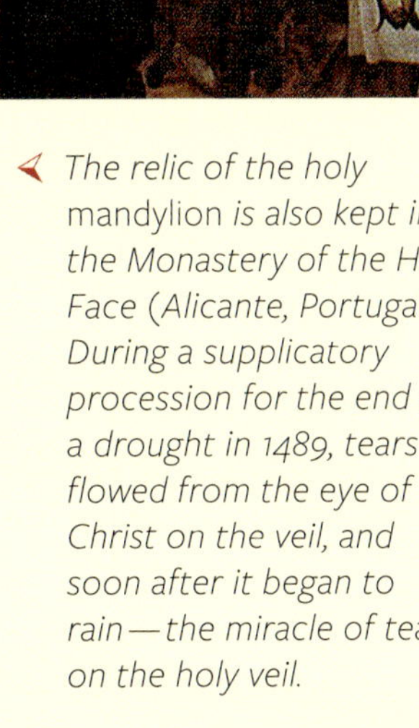

The relic of the holy mandylion *is also kept in the Monastery of the Holy Face (Alicante, Portugal). During a supplicatory procession for the end of a drought in 1489, tears flowed from the eye of Christ on the veil, and soon after it began to rain—the miracle of tears on the holy veil.*

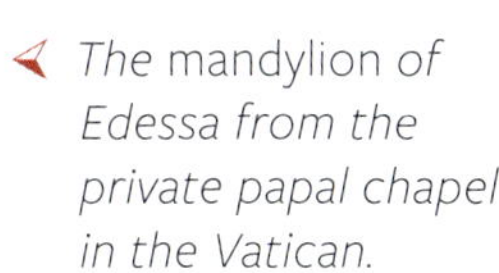

The mandylion of Edessa from the private papal chapel in the Vatican.

Basilica in Manoppello, where the veil with the mysterious image of the Savior is kept.

I, though I have not seen You, have believed that You are the Son of God who came down from heaven to save fallen humankind. I too am physically undone; if You so will, come to my land and heal me."

According to what may be the earliest version of this letter — the Syriac one preserved by the historian Eusebius — the king also wrote: "I have heard that the Jews are murmuring against You and want to harm You. I possess a very small but honorable city, sufficient for us both."

It is touching: Abgar wanted to save the Savior from the death awaiting Him at the hands of the Pharisees.

Though this royal letter was never considered authentic, its content was so theological that the Church used it in the liturgy for centuries. It even appears in eleventh-century manuscripts compiled by Irish monks.

VERAIKONY

St. Veronica with the Veil, *ca. 1420, Alte Pinakothek (Munich, Germany)*.

Responding to the ailing king's plea, Jesus replied, "I cannot go there." Then the envoy Ananias summoned a painter and ordered him to paint an image of Jesus for the king.

The painter struggled to depict the Savior. When Jesus asked why he was painting Him, the man replied: "Lord, I wish to paint Your face for our king." He added, "Our king greatly desires to see You. For he commanded us thus: 'If He does not come Himself, then paint Him and bring me His image, and I will already be healed by that alone.'" Hearing this, Jesus performed a miracle: "He took a linen cloth, pressed it to His face, and thus His countenance was imprinted on the cloth as it truly appeared."

A remarkable detail is mentioned in passing in this apocryphal Gospel: the envoys did not bring only the image to Edessa. Along with it came Christ's prayer and blessing!

Chapel of St. Veronica in St. Peter's Basilica (Vatican).

Image of the face of the Savior preserved on byssus, a material derived from Mediterranean mussels, on which it is not possible to paint effectively. So how was it created?

Despite the passage of centuries and constant exposure to daylight, the image does not fade or lose sharpness.

It bore the presence of the Savior. Little wonder that when the messenger brought the cloth to the king, and Abgar looked upon the Holy Face, a miracle took place. He beheld Jesus—and was healed.

There is another revealing thread here. Jesus promised Abgar that, after His return to the Father, He would send him one of the apostles. In the document discovered by Eusebius, we read that St. Thomas, called Addai, came to Edessa.

"Addai began to heal people in the name of Christ. When news of this reached Abgar, he suspected that this was indeed the disciple Jesus had promised to send him." And when Addai appeared before the king, "Abgar saw a great vision upon his face."

What was it? We do not know. Perhaps it was another manifestation of Jesus—this time through the person of His disciple.

Again, we see a theme that runs through many of the Lord's revelations—and one that will prove to be the most important of all.

Many hold that the image given to King Abgar was the *mandylion*. Even a late third- or early fourth-century text hostile to icons acknowledges its existence. (Though it should be noted that its authenticity is not a matter of Christian faith.) Nonetheless, it is a fact that, regardless of its historical

Master of the Legend of St. Ursula, Angels Holding the Veil of Veronica.

origin, the *mandylion* became the standard model for portraying the Savior's face. The cross-shaped halo it bears marks Him as Christ, distinct from all other saints in iconography.

Abgar—a verifiably historical figure who did convert to Christianity—is venerated as a saint in the Orthodox, Syriac, and Armenian Churches. He was even depicted on Armenian currency, holding a flag bearing the *mandylion*.

THE MANOPPELLO *VERAIKON*

We turn now to the second *veraikon*: Veronica's veil.

Only the apocrypha tell of a woman wiping the bloodied face of Jesus on His way to the Cross and of the Savior's face being imprinted on the cloth. Mentions of the incident appear, for example, in the

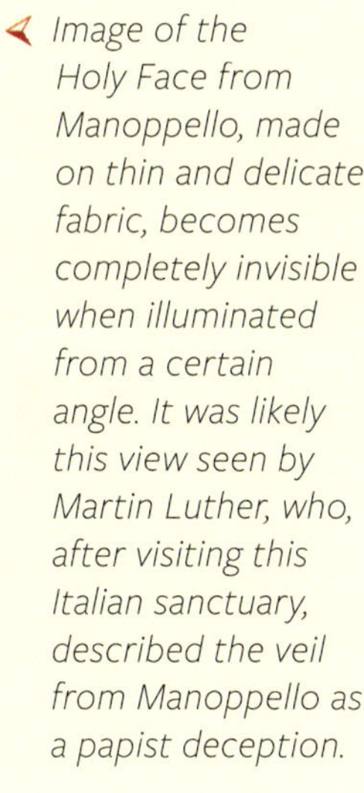

Image of the Holy Face from Manoppello, made on thin and delicate fabric, becomes completely invisible when illuminated from a certain angle. It was likely this view seen by Martin Luther, who, after visiting this Italian sanctuary, described the veil from Manoppello as a papist deception.

fourth-century *Gospel of Nicodemus* (also called the *Acts of Pilate*). The tradition connected with this event was strong, and by the fourth century the existence of St. Veronica and her veil was widely acknowledged. It is even possible that the apocrypha borrowed the story of Veronica from an older tradition, rather than having invented the belief in a *veraikon* themselves.

Interestingly, Veronica and her deed are commemorated in the Church-approved devotion of the Stations of the Cross (Station VI). Although official approval came only in the nineteenth century, it made the story an object of meditation for generations of Christians—even to the present day.

Is St. Veronica a legendary figure? Undoubtedly, her name is of legendary origin, deriving from the Latin *vera icona* ("true image"). Yet there is some evidence that she was a historical person who received a new name—"Veronica"—in connection with the greatest event of her life.

Much suggests that the "true icon," that is, the original Veronica's veil, is preserved in the Italian town of Manoppello. This cloth, known as the *Volto Santo* (the Holy Face), is a small piece of fabric measuring only 17 centimeters in width and 24 centimeters in length. It depicts the disfigured face of Christ on His way to Golgotha.

Science has not been able to determine how this image was formed or what gives the Holy Face its mysterious color, beauty, and vibrant quality. No trace of paint has been found on the fibers; the image is perfectly visible from both sides, yet there are no pigments at all. Under different lighting, the veil seems to change, to "live." In bright light, it reveals a three-dimensional face, almost holographic. Held against strong light, it becomes transparent.

Under fluorescent lighting, the *Volto Santo* looks precisely as Gertrude of Helfta—a thirteenth-century

Top: Reliquary in the cathedral in Oviedo (Spain), where the sudarium—the cloth used to wrap the face of Christ after the Crucifixion—is kept.

Bottom: The Sudarium of Oviedo shows nearly perfect consistency of the bloodstains of Jesus with those on the Shroud of Turin.

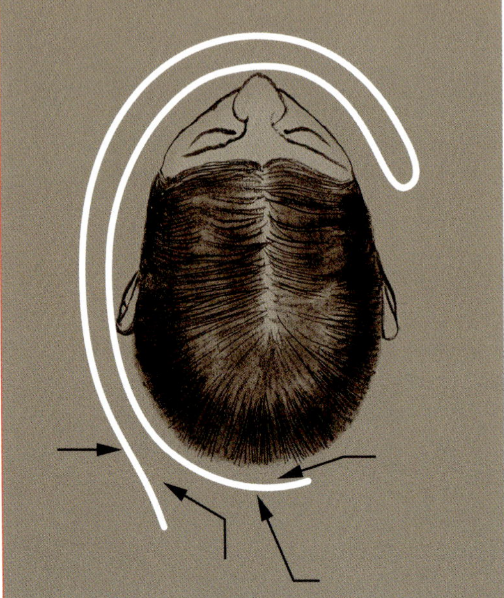

Diagram showing how the sudarium was wrapped around the head.

mystic—described Christ's face when beholding Veronica's veil in a vision.

The cloth is so delicate that it could be folded and placed in a nutshell. It is made of the rarest ancient fabric: *byssus*, or "sea silk." From a technical standpoint, it is impossible to paint anything on sea silk—let alone produce an image as perfect as that found in Manoppello. By scientific standards, the image of the Divine Face has no right to exist.

Intriguingly, when the face from Manoppello is superimposed on the face from the Shroud of Turin, they match so precisely that some speak of a graphical-mathematical proof that they depict one and the same Person.

Is this a revelation? Probably not, at least by the usual criteria. Unless someone stands before such a mysterious image in the way Thomas Merton once contemplated the icon from Mount Athos—then he too might see the divine light pouring forth upon the entire universe.

Computer overlay of the Veil of Manoppello and the Shroud of Turin shows perfect alignment.

Also demonstrating striking consistency with the Shroud of Turin are the images: Salvator Mundi *by Leonardo da Vinci and* The Vilnius Divine Mercy Christ *by Eugeniusz Kazimirowski, modeled by Fr. Michał Sopoćko.*

ζ
(ZETA)
"TABORIZATION"

On the previous page: Mount Tabor on the horizon.

Place of the Revelation: Mount Tabor, Israel
Liturgical memorial: August 6

(ZETA)

"TABORIZATION"

THE APOSTLES PETER, JAMES, JOHN, A.D. 33

This is a mystical narrative. With just a step further into the Synoptic accounts, certain mysterious patterns begin to emerge—perhaps degrees of knowing and experiencing God.

There are six days of preparation. There is Jesus' initiative to take three disciples. There is the journey to the mountaintop and prayer on the world's rooftop.

There is revelation, and the appearance of the pillars of Old Testament history, along with the theme of exodus. There is happiness and fear. There is the cloud that both reveals and conceals. There is the

Basilica of the Transfiguration of the Lord on Mount Tabor (northern Israel).

Mount Tabor is an isolated elevation (588 m) at the eastern edge of the Jezreel Valley (Lower Galilee, Israel).

voice from Heaven—and finally, homage paid. A concentrated mysticism.

Everything begins a few days earlier. Jesus is near Caesarea Philippi. It is there, when He asks who people say He is, that Peter professes faith in Christ—in His greatness. He says: "You are the Messiah, the Son of the living God" (Matthew 16:16).

CLOSE TO THE PASSION

This moment launches a new theme in Jesus' teaching. The Savior begins to foretell His Passion: "From that time on, Jesus began to show his disciples that he must go to Jerusalem and suffer greatly from the elders, the chief priests, and the scribes, and be killed and on the third day be raised" (Matthew 16:21).

But what if, in His teaching, Jesus emphasizes the resurrection, while the disciples focus only on what is but a means—the suffering? They want it neither for Jesus nor for themselves. In fact, they do not even understand what rising from the dead means.

Six days have passed since the confession of faith and the first prediction of the Passion. Across this time—as long as the Creation of the world (a deliberate analogy)—Jesus and the apostles have walked nearly ninety kilometers. At last, they arrive at the foot of a solitary mountain.

It is Mount Tabor, rising in Galilee, whose summit towers nearly six hundred meters above sea level. For many, it symbolizes beauty. Through Jeremiah, God had said: "As I live, says the King whose name is Lord of hosts, like Tabor above mountains, like Carmel above the sea, he comes" (Jeremiah 46:18). One day, the Maker of the world Himself will come "like Tabor": solitary, majestic, awe-inspiring, visible from afar.

It is a marvelous round mountain—approachable from any direction on level ground, and then ascended heavenward. Many trails lead to the top.

ISRAEL

One of the most famous paintings depicting the Transfiguration: Raphael, 1520, (Vatican Pinacoteca).

Pasquale Ottini, St. Mark Writing the Gospel Under the Dictation of St. Peter.

Left: Michelangelo, *Moses*, Basilica of St. Peter in Chains (Rome, Italy).

Right: Carl Heinrich Bloch, *Transfiguration of Jesus*, 1872

"And behold, Moses and Elijah appeared to them, conversing with him."

There the apostles will be taken out of the world. Everything lies far below them. Everything is distant.

"Jesus took Peter, James, and John his brother, and led them up a high mountain by themselves," we read in the Gospel (Matthew 17:1).

They have been chosen as witnesses. Their testimony will be needed in the time of trial. There are three of them, for the Law teaches that a testimony is valid if it rests on the word of two—or better, three—witnesses (cf. 1 Timothy 5:19).

On the summit of Tabor, a one-of-a-kind revelation of Jesus takes place. The Gospel says:

And he was transfigured before them; his face shone like the sun and his clothes became white as light. And behold, Moses and Elijah appeared to them, conversing with him. Then Peter said to Jesus in reply, "Lord, it is good that we are here. If you wish, I will make three tents here, one for you, one for Moses, and one for Elijah." While he was still speaking, behold, a bright cloud cast a shadow over them, then from the cloud came a voice that said, "This is my beloved Son, with whom I am well pleased; listen to him." When the disciples heard

this, they fell prostrate and were very much afraid. But Jesus came and touched them, saying, "Rise, and do not be afraid." And when the disciples raised their eyes, they saw no one else but Jesus alone. (Matthew 17:2–8)

LIGHT

On Mount Tabor, Jesus reveals His identity to humanity. We read that as He prayed, "he was transfigured before them, and his clothes became dazzling white, such as no fuller on earth could bleach them" (Mark 9:2–3). This revelation is a sign and foreshadowing of the resurrection. The miracle witnessed by Peter, James, and John points ahead to the Resurrection of Christ.

But as we will see in a moment—turning to the New Testament letters—the Transfiguration signifies still more. Its message is richer. It shows that the resurrection is not for Christ alone, but for all. It concerns the humanity of Jesus, and with Him, the destiny of all human nature. Created in God's image at the beginning, humanity will be transformed in the end, regaining its true condition: divine light.

Hence St. Macarius of Egypt (†390) understood Christianity as the renewal of human nature: "Just as when the Lord ascended the mountain and was 'transfigured' into His divine glory, so there are souls even now in this present time that are enlightened and glorified together

St. Macarius of Egypt and a Cherub.

"What is now visible only to the enlightened soul—perceived "within"—will one day be visible outwardly, in a transfigured body," says St. Macarius the Great.

Left: Icon of the Prophets Elijah and Enoch, seventeenth century, Historical Museum (Sanok).

Right: Icon of the Transfiguration of the Lord, 1516 (Yaroslavl, Russia).

with Him; and on the last day their bodies too will be glorified and flashing with light." What is now visible only to the enlightened soul—perceived "within"—will one day be visible outwardly, in a transfigured body.

What the apostles behold on Tabor will one day be true of all the saved. For now, Christ's eternity and glory are seen only by the "inner man." As St. Paul writes: "For God who said, "Let light shine out of darkness," has shone in our hearts to bring to light the knowledge of the glory of God on the face of [Jesus] Christ" (2 Corinthians 4:6). Christ appears as He truly is: the Son of God.

This is what awaits all humanity. The apostolic letters make it clear. St. Paul proclaims: "We also await a savior, the Lord Jesus Christ. He will change our lowly body to conform with his glorified body by the power that enables him also to bring all things into subjection to himself" (Philippians 3:20–21).

The Church's liturgy echoes this. The preface for the Feast of the Transfiguration

➤ *Gerard Hoet,* God Takes Enoch into Heaven, *Bible from 1728.*

➤ *Left: Lorenzo Lotto,* Transfiguration on Mount Tabor, *Museo Civico Villa Colloredo Mels (Recanati, Italy).*

➤ *Right: Transfiguration of Christ—part of a Byzantine-style iconostasis, mid-twelfth century, Monastery of St. Catherine on Mount Sinai (Egypt).*

reads: "On this day on Mount Tabor, Christ transformed the darkness of human nature and gave it a share in His divine brightness ... He revealed His glory before chosen witnesses, and His body, like ours, shone with a wondrous radiance."

In the transfigured Jesus, the glory of God shines forth. This is precisely what icons show. The light that appears on the face of Jesus—and on the saints—comes not from without, but from within, filled with God. Jesus (and, after Him, every saint) becomes a source of divine light, greater than any earthly radiance. That is why, for example, in icons of the Transfiguration, the sun does not illuminate Jesus; instead, it casts a shadow.

Thomas Merton, who encountered God in prayer through a holy icon, coined a term for this: "taborization"—everything becoming light, pouring out upon the world. He wrote: "What one 'sees' in prayer before an icon is not an external portrayal of the saint, but an interior presence of light, which is the glory of the transfigured Christ, an experience passed on in faith from generation to generation by those who have 'seen,' reaching back to the Apostles." Do we not hear here the voice of St. Macarius the Hermit?

APOCRYPHAL EXPLANATIONS

Chapter fourteen of the *First Book of Enoch* describes the holy man's ascent into Heaven. When Enoch enters a cosmic temple built of fire and crystal, he sees at its center the Great Glory: a figure wearing "a robe shining more brightly than the sun, whiter than any snow." This passage calls to mind the Transfiguration of Jesus, whose clothing "became dazzling white,

Johann Heinrich Tischbein the Elder, Transfiguration of Christ, *1764, Lutheran Church in Kassel/Graben (Germany).*

A.D. 33

Pietro Perugino, Transfiguration, Collegio del Cambio.

Icon of Zephaniah, seventeenth century (Northern Russia).

such as no fuller on earth could bleach them" (Mark 9:3).

The heavenly context of Enoch's vision, with its figure in dazzling white garments, suggests to us that Jesus' Transfiguration reveals what lies beneath the surface of His body—His divinity.

In the *Second Book of Enoch*, when its hero ascends to Heaven, he hears God say to the angel Michael: "Take Enoch and strip him of his earthly garments, and anoint him with the delightful oil, and clothe him in the robe of glory." Enoch explains: "Michael removed my clothes. He anointed me with the wondrous oil; the appearance of that oil is greater than the greatest light, its ointment like sweet dew, and its fragrance like myrrh; it shines like the sun. I looked at myself, and I had become like one of the glorious ones; there was no visible difference." Enoch is described as being

Interior of the Basilica of the Transfiguration on Mount Tabor.

Basilica of the Transfiguration of the Lord on Mount Tabor.

Benedict XVI: "We never perceive the pure object; rather, we see it through the filter of our senses, which must 'translate' it for us."

transformed into an angelic being by the changing of his garments.

It is the same in the *Apocalypse of Zephaniah*: just before the heavens are opened, Zephaniah is surrounded by angelic beings. "Thousands of thousands and myriads of myriads of angels gave glory to God. I myself put on an angelic garment."

We cite these apocryphal texts to show how Jewish witnesses could have understood Jesus' Transfiguration. Here, certainly, God used what we might call a "cultural filter" (to use Benedict XVI's term), placing His message in signs comprehensible to particular people.

Indeed, as Prefect of the Congregation for the Doctrine of the Faith, Benedict wrote that any vision "is necessarily linked to limits.... Even in external perception, the subjective factor plays a role: we never perceive the pure object; rather, we see it through the filter of our senses, which must 'translate' it for us.... The subject—the person seeing—views in keeping with his concrete capacities, in accord with the resources of his imagination and understanding.... The seer contributes essentially to the shaping of the image of what he sees. The single image that is revealed must be proportionate to him and respond to his abilities. Thus such

St. Matthew writing the Gospel, with an angel holding a book, Islamic miniature, ca. 1530.

visions are never mere 'photographs' of supernatural reality."

This explains much.

Peter, James, and John see "as they are able"—in the manner of the Old Testament apocrypha. But they understand that Jesus is God, and that His body has already reached the condition that one day will be theirs as well—just as it came to Enoch or Zephaniah.

TESTIMONY

The Transfiguration is described by three evangelists—Luke, Matthew, and Mark—but none of these three was on the mountain with Christ. Do we have an account from Peter, James, or John themselves?

A reference to the events on Mount Tabor appears in the Second Letter of St. Peter. The apostle confirms what he presumably shared with the others:

> *We did not follow cleverly devised myths when we made known to you the power and coming of our*

Giovanni Antonio de' Sacchis, St. Mark.

Top right: Transfiguration of Jesus, *Novgorod School, fifteenth century.*

Maarten van Heemskerck, St. Luke Painting the Virgin Mary, *Frans Hals Museum (Haarlem, Netherlands).*

Lord Jesus Christ, but we had been eyewitnesses of his majesty. For he received honor and glory from God the Father when that unique declaration came to him from the majestic glory, "This is my Son, my beloved, with whom I am well pleased." We ourselves heard this voice come from heaven while we were with him on the holy mountain. (2 Peter 1:16–18)

For Peter—through the filter of his own senses—the Transfiguration revealed "the majesty of Jesus," which lay in possessing—bodily!—the honor and glory of God Himself.

Until the day of the Resurrection, this was the greatest revelation of Jesus' divinity.

EXODUS

Why did the Transfiguration take place? The *Catechism of the Catholic Church* explains:

> *Christ's Transfiguration aims at strengthening the apostles' faith in anticipation of His Passion. The ascent onto the "high mountain" prepares for the ascent to Calvary. Christ, Head of the Church, shows what His Body contains and radiates in the sacraments: "the hope of glory."* (CCC 568)

Indeed, if we note that the revelation on Tabor was not only a vision but also included words heard by the apostles, the miracle gains new depth. Moses and Elijah speak of Jesus' departure, which is to be

Giovanni Bellini, Transfiguration on Mount Tabor, *Museo di Capodimonte (Naples, Italy).*

Exodus is a word inseparably tied to the history of God's chosen people.

accomplished in Jerusalem. To describe this "departure," the evangelist uses the word *exodus*. This is a fundamental biblical term, filled with meaning: liberation and victory.

Once again, we have a cultural filter. The apostles hear of the *exodus* of Israel from Egypt. They must translate that into what they will soon witness.

They know *exodus* is a word inseparably tied to the history of God's chosen people. It speaks of freedom from slavery, great signs and wonders, and entry into a land that, in truth, was theirs from the beginning. One might say that from God's perspective, *exodus* means returning to oneself. In that event, even Pharaoh's might proved helpless.

After the Passion and death—the events of the Passover—there will come the Resurrection: the return to the Father, to the land of eternity.

A VISION OF THE KINGDOM

It is no coincidence that, in Luke's Gospel, before they set out toward Tabor, Jesus announces: "Truly I say to you, there are some standing here who will not taste death until they see the kingdom of God" (Luke 9:27).

The Savior assures His disciples that among them are those who will not experience death before they see the Kingdom of God.

These words have often been interpreted

Ivan Aivazovsky, Crossing of the Red Sea by the Jews, *1891.*

The apostles are thus given the task of interpreting the events of Holy Week through the lens of the biblical Passover—on the night before the exodus, the Jews sacrificed an unblemished lamb, and its blood protected the children of Israel from death—and of the exodus itself.

as a prophecy that the end of the world would occur before the first generation of Christians died out. As we know, that interpretation was false: the world continues to this day.

The phrase "the kingdom of God" can refer to realities other than the final replacement of the temporal world with the eternal. Jesus assures them that the Kingdom of God is enfleshed in Him, and so it might be "seen," were Christ to reveal it—if He wished to show it to His disciples in an extraordinary, miraculous way during His earthly life.

Did such a manifestation of the Kingdom occur? Indeed it did. Luke, who records Jesus' statement about not tasting death before seeing the Kingdom, subsequently recounts the Transfiguration. Pope Benedict XVI, in his *Jesus of Nazareth*, states that we should understand Jesus' words precisely in this way, for the positioning of the promise immediately before the Transfiguration clearly links it to the revelation on Mount Tabor.

> *To some—that is, the three disciples who accompany Jesus to the mountain—it is promised that they will personally witness the kingdom of God coming "in power."*
> *On that mountain, all three see the*

Pope Benedict XVI.

Left: God the Father on the Throne, *late fifteenth century (Westphalia, Germany).*

Right: The Gospel According to St. Matthew from the Ethiopian Bible, British Library (London, United Kingdom).

glory of the kingdom of God shining forth from Jesus. On that mountain, they stand in the shadow of the holy cloud of God. On that mountain—in the conversation of the transfigured Jesus with the Law and the Prophets—they realize that the true Feast of Tabernacles has come. On that mountain, they discover that Jesus Himself is the living Torah, the complete Word of God. On that mountain, they see the "power" (dynamis) *of the kingdom that arrives in Christ.*

Thus we have the key to understanding the cryptic words spoken just before the Transfiguration. Jesus was not referring to the imminent end of the world; He was speaking of beholding in Him—the Son of God—the glory of God.

OBEDIENCE

We come at last to the second vital truth conveyed by the message of this revelation: "This is My beloved Son, listen to Him."

After the Resurrection, the apostles did indeed obey the heavenly command. We read in the Acts of the Apostles:

> *When they had brought them in and made them stand before the Sanhedrin, the high priest questioned them, "We gave you strict orders [did we not?] to stop teaching in that name. Yet you have filled Jerusalem with your teaching and want to bring this man's blood upon us." But Peter and the apostles said in reply, "We must obey God rather than men. The God of our ancestors raised Jesus, though you*

Jacques Tissot (1836–1902), Reconstruction of Jerusalem and the Temple of Herod, *Brooklyn Museum.*

had him killed by hanging him on a tree. God exalted him at his right hand as leader and savior to grant Israel repentance and forgiveness of sins. We are witnesses of these things, as is the holy Spirit that God has given to those who obey him."

When they heard this, they became infuriated and wanted to put them to death. (Acts 5:27–33)

Perhaps this obedience to Jesus is the most crucial message of Tabor. Listening to the beloved Son of the Father means that what the apostles saw in visible signs will one day become their own possession as well. There is no participation in the Transfiguration apart from obedience. There will be no *taborization* for us if God is not our first and final authority.

Two disciples, Peter and John, are sent to prepare the Passover, National Library of Wales.

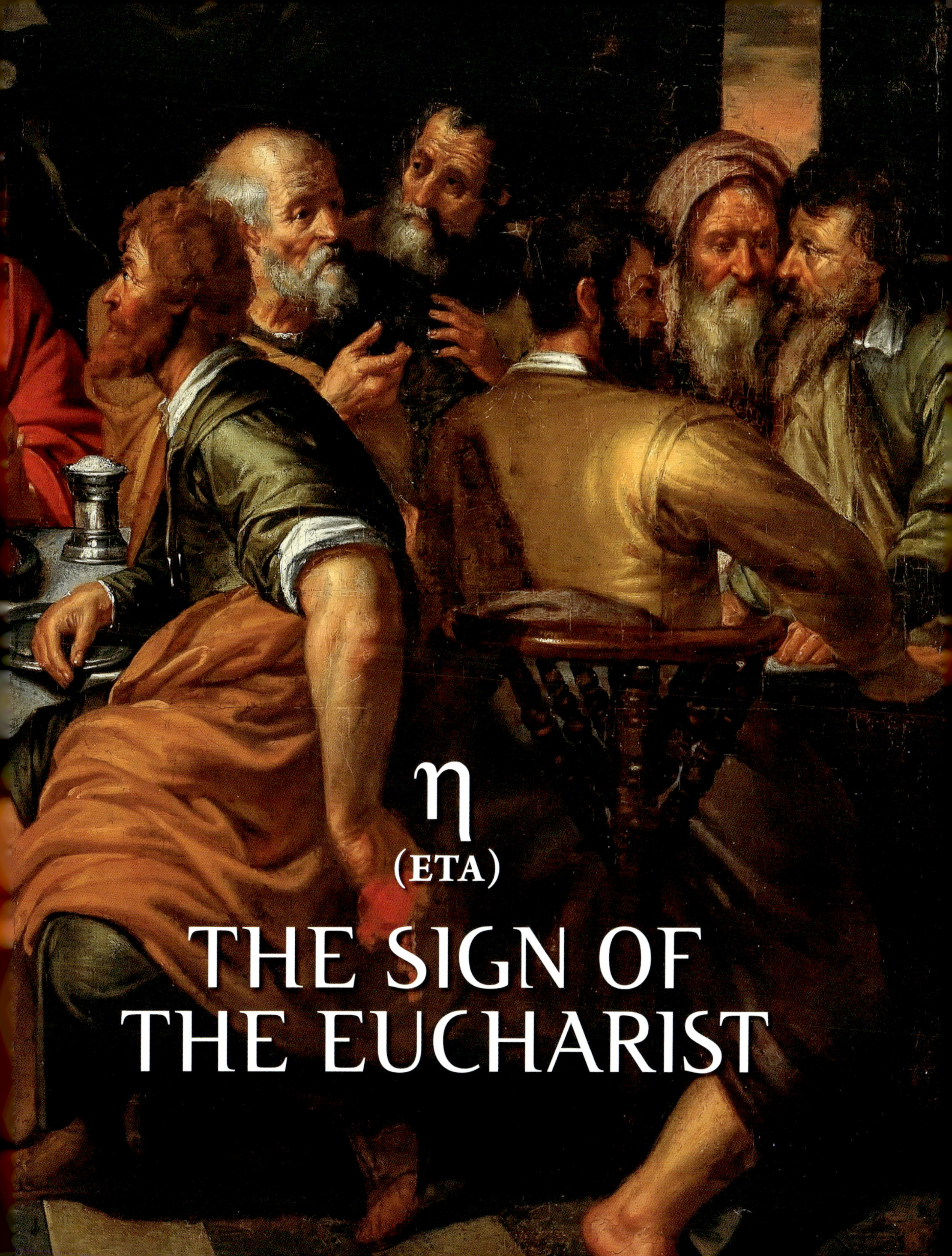
η
(ETA)
THE SIGN OF
THE EUCHARIST

Benjamin West, The Last Supper.

On the previous page: Artus Wolffort, The Last Supper *(Nijmegen, Netherlands).*

Place of the Revelation:* *Jerusalem, Israel, then hundreds of other places—the Egyptian desert, Eten, Bolsena, Santarém, and so forth

Top left: Joan de Joanes, Christ as the Eucharistic Redeemer.

Bottom left: Nicolas Poussin, Institution of the Eucharist.

Top right: Fresco of the Last Supper, sixteenth century, Monastery in Kremikovtsi (Bulgaria).

Bottom right: Giovanni Domenico Tiepolo, The Last Supper.

(ETA)

THE SIGN OF THE EUCHARIST

THE APOSTLES—A.D. 33, THE ELDER-HERMIT—5TH CENTURY, MARCO LOPEZ—1649

Eucharistic miracles form a special category of miracles. Some are even described as revelations. Christ, who is truly present in the Eucharist under the appearances of bread and wine, sometimes reveals Himself as Body and Blood, thereby unveiling His mystery. But this is not the mystery of His divinity, as in the earliest revelations of the biblical era. Rather, it is the mystery of His human agony.

Some devout believers say that a eucharistic miracle occurs tens of thousands of times each day, because every celebration of the Mass brings about the greatest of miracles—transubstantiation. It is indeed true that when the priest pronounces the words of Consecration, and the substance of the bread ceases to be bread and becomes the Body of Christ (and likewise the wine becomes His Blood), a supreme miracle takes place. But it is a hidden one,

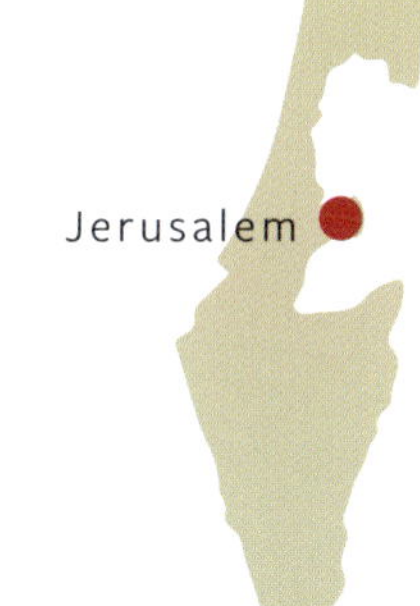

for the transformation occurs invisibly. Though this is the greatest supernatural mystery, we cannot call it a miracle in the sensory or empirical sense. It is not a "revelation" or a "sign" that can be seen or measured; it is an object of faith.

There is, however, another kind of eucharistic miracle—those that are perceptible to the senses.

THE APOSTLES DO NOT UNDERSTAND WHAT THEY ARE PARTAKING IN

Let us begin at the source. What do we believe? St. Matthew tells us that, on the day before His death, during the Last Supper:

> *While they were eating, Jesus took bread, said the blessing, broke it, and giving it to his disciples said, "Take and eat; this is my body." Then he*

Michael Bernhardt, The Last Supper, *Museu de Montserrat (Barcelona, Spain).*

Duccio di Buoninsegna, Washing of the Feet and The Last Supper, *Museo dell'Opera del Duomo (Siena, Italy).*

took a cup, gave thanks, and gave it to them, saying, "Drink from it, all of you, for this is my blood of the covenant, which will be shed on behalf of many for the forgiveness of sins." (Matthew 26:26–28)

Yet in the eyes of the apostles, this moment was neither a visible miracle nor any kind of revelation. To them, the supper simply continued—remaining, to the end, an ordinary Passover meal.

Why was the institution of the Eucharist not recognized as a miracle or a sign by Jesus' closest disciples? Perhaps they were too attached to the familiar rituals of the Passover, unable to perceive anything new. Or perhaps they misunderstood Jesus' words and actions because they were still clinging to their own expectations of His mission. After all, they believed He would be the king who would free Israel from Roman rule. Words about giving His body and shedding His blood did not fit their image of the Messiah.

Where mystics perceive Jesus transforming into bread and wine, the apostles saw nothing at all.

Only after the Resurrection did they begin to understand the meaning of His mysterious words and gestures. They came to see that Jesus had truly given Himself to them in the Eucharist—not just symbolically, but in reality. It was not merely a memorial, but a real making-present. In

time, they would teach that by the words of Christ, repeated by the priest, and by the invocation of the Holy Spirit, the bread and wine become the Body and Blood of Christ—and that this miracle will endure until the end of the world.

A DIFFICULT TRUTH OF FAITH

It does not come easily to human beings to accept this truth of faith. Throughout history, in every generation, many have struggled to believe in the mystery of Christ hidden in the Host. Even today, for many—devout though they may be—this truth is far from self-evident. A lack of belief in this "hidden miracle" has led some to leave the Church. This is not surprising, for one cannot truly be Catholic without believing that the bread and wine become the Body and Blood of Jesus.

Wilhelm List, Christ with Bread and Wine.

Giovanni Domenico Tiepolo, Institution of the Eucharist, *Statens Museum for Kunst (Copenhagen, Denmark)*.

Cathedral in Valencia. The chalice that, according to tradition, was used by Christ during the Last Supper, also known as the Holy Grail.

Equally unsurprising is that the first announcement of the Eucharist caused division among Jesus' own followers: "This is a hard saying; who can listen to it?" (see John 6:60). The *Catechism of the Catholic Church* (CCC 1336) cites these very words from John's Gospel.

The Eucharist is both the summary and the crowning expression of the entire Catholic faith. "Our way of thinking is attuned to the Eucharist, and the Eucharist in turn confirms our way of thinking," the Church teaches (CCC 1327).

Leonardo da Vinci, The Last Supper, *ca. 1492–1498, Santa Maria delle Grazie Monastery (Milan, Italy).*

THE LAST SUPPER AS SEEN IN MYSTICAL LIGHT

The visionary Bl. Anne Catherine Emmerich (†1824) describes a vision of the institution of the Eucharist that the Lord granted her:

I watched all these actions with the greatest emotion, and they reminded me very much of the Holy Mass. The longer it went on, the deeper His concentration and tenderness grew. Finally, He said: "Now I wish to give you everything I have—namely, Myself." As He spoke these words, it seemed that His body became transparent, like a radiant shadow. Continually praying in deep recollection, Jesus broke the loaves.... From the first portion, He pinched off a small piece with His fingertips and placed it into the chalice. At that very moment, I had a vision as though the Blessed Virgin were receiving the Most Holy Sacrament, even though she had not been in the room before. I saw her seated opposite Jesus at the

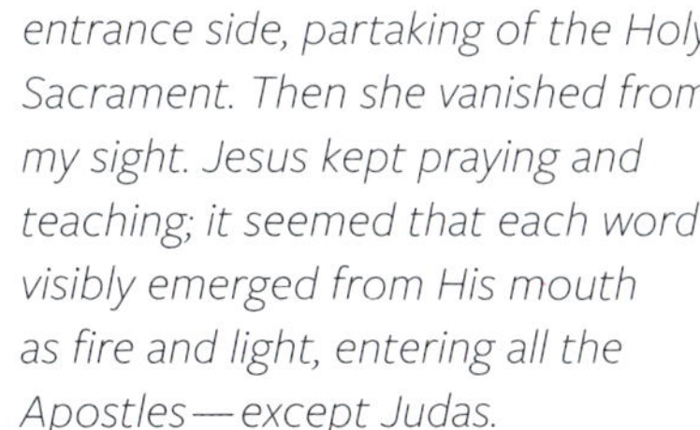

> *entrance side, partaking of the Holy Sacrament. Then she vanished from my sight. Jesus kept praying and teaching; it seemed that each word visibly emerged from His mouth as fire and light, entering all the Apostles—except Judas.*

She continues:

> *At length Jesus took [the bread] and said: "Take and eat; this is My Body, which will be given up for you." With His right hand He made a gesture over the dish, as though blessing it. At that same moment, a brightness emanated from Him;*

The Last Supper—*the first Eucharist depicted by Juan de Juanes, 1562, Museo del Prado (Madrid, Spain). The painting features the chalice from Valencia.*

Pascal Dagnan-Bouveret, The Last Supper, *Musée d'Orsay (Paris, France).*

> *His words came forth from His lips like fire, and the bread too shone brightly. Thus illumined, it entered the mouths of the Apostles, as though Jesus Himself were flowing into them. Light penetrated all of them; only Judas remained in darkness.... Then Jesus raised the chalice [toward His face] and, inclining over it, spoke the words of consecration. During this action, Jesus was transfigured and became almost entirely transparent, as though He was one with what He was about to give the Apostles.*

Wanda Malczewska (†1896) records similar words of the Savior, offering practical guidance on receiving the Sacrament of the Eucharist:

> *Judas ... received the Sacrament of My Body and Blood unworthily. This ... crime blinded him and turned him into a traitor. Here you have a manifest proof of how terrible are the consequences of receiving Holy Communion unworthily.... Judas, having received Communion sacrilegiously, murdered Me in his heart, and now, by delivering Me into the hands of the Jews, he will murder Me upon the Cross.... I desire that everyone receive Holy Communion as often as possible, but without sin, with hearts aflame with love, with souls longing to receive Me. Before receiving Communion, let them pray much and strive for interior recollection and true sorrow for sins. Let them feel within themselves a spiritual hunger and an unquenched thirst for partaking of this heavenly Food.... For just as daily food*

Top: The Upper Room in Jerusalem, where Jesus celebrated the Last Supper.

Bottom: Architectural details of the Cenacle (Upper Room).

Carl Heinrich Bloch, Judas Fleeing from the Last Supper.

Stained-glass window in St. John the Baptist Church in Yeovil. Judas is depicted with an unusual black halo (United Kingdom).

Pimen Ushakov, The Last Supper, *1685, Lavra in the Moscow region (Sergiyev Posad, Russia).*

consumed without appetite will not benefit but may even harm the body, so too the spiritual Food I give in Holy Communion, if received without real desire, out of mere habit, will not yield the fruit of salvation for the soul.... Let them set aside thoughts of earthly concerns, and speak warmly and sincerely with Me, present in their souls.... Those wishing to receive Holy Communion every day, or at least several times a week, ought to differ from their neighbors in daily life. They should be more devout, more humble, gentler, and more patient. They must work harder at reining in the flesh and subduing their passions. Rising in the morning, let them turn their thoughts to Me, hidden in the Blessed Sacrament; before setting out for church, let them avoid quarrels and strive for inner recollection. Upon returning home, let them preserve the same recollection, and handle all household tasks peacefully, without shouting. It is appalling to see people who receive Holy Communion daily live no differently than others, for they bear witness that they receive Me unworthily; and whoever receives Me unworthily shall have no part with Me in heaven, and may share Judas's fate.

THE EARLIEST EUCHARISTIC REVELATION

From the earliest centuries of Christianity, we have writings and hagiographies that recount wondrous events connected to the Eucharist. One might suppose this is, in part, why the first generations of believers left behind so few records of private revelations from Jesus—because they lived in constant contact with the revelation already present in the Eucharist.

They experienced, firsthand, what saints in later centuries would only come to describe. They had no need of further revelations.

The following is the oldest known account of a eucharistic miracle that also served as a revelation of Jesus in the form of a Child. It was recorded by the Desert Fathers of Egypt in the fifth century.

Abba Daniel tells of an elder-hermit who, despite his austere and disciplined life, could not bring himself to believe that the Bread he received in the Eucharist was truly the Body of Christ. When two other elders learned of his doubt, they encouraged him to pray for a week, asking God for the grace to understand the truth. The *First Book of the Elders* recounts:

> *When the week was over, on Sunday they came to church and sat there apart—the three of them together on one mat, with that elder in the middle. Their eyes were opened, and*

Left: Hurghada. Egyptian desert near the Red Sea.

Right: Abba Daniel on an Orthodox icon.

Icon showing the Transubstantiation. Jesus Himself is the Eucharist.

▲ Church of St. Francis in Lanciano, witness to the great eucharistic miracle of the eighth century (Italy).

▼ Consecrated Host that began to bleed on June 2, 1649, in Eten, Peru, during the feast of Corpus Christi.

when the bread was placed on the holy altar, they saw, as it were, a little child.

And when the priest stretched out his hand to break the bread, behold, an angel of God descended from heaven with a sword, sacrificed the Child, and poured His blood into the chalice. As the priest broke the bread into small pieces, so too the angel divided the Child into small parts.

Finally, when it was time to come forward and receive the holy species, that elder—and he alone—received a piece of bloody flesh. Horrified at the sight, he cried out: "I believe, Lord, that the bread is Your Body, and the wine is Your Blood!"

And immediately what he held in his hand was changed into bread, according to the rite. Gratefully he received it; and the other elders said to him: "God knows man's nature, and that he cannot eat raw flesh. That is why He changes His Body into bread and His Blood into wine, for those who receive them in faith."

THE CHILD ONCE AGAIN

A similar revelation involving the appearance of the Child—though different in essence—took place on June 2, 1649, in the Peruvian town of Eten, during the exposition of the Blessed Sacrament for the Feast of Corpus Christi. At the end of the service, Franciscan Brother Jerome de Silva Manrique was preparing to return the monstrance to the tabernacle, having just blessed the congregation. Suddenly, in the Host, the radiant face of a Child appeared, crowned with brown curls falling to His shoulders.

Reliquary from Lanciano—cyborium from the Church of St. Francis.

The miracle in Lanciano—despite the passing of time, the Body of Christ has not decayed.

All the faithful present in the church witnessed it.

The revelation occurred again on July 22 of the same year, during the town's celebration in honor of St. Mary Magdalene, their patroness. The superior of the friary, Marco Lopez, testified that during the exposition of the Blessed Sacrament, "the Divine Child Jesus again appeared in the Host, clothed in a burgundy tunic. Beneath it was a shirt that reached halfway down His chest, in accordance with the custom of South American Indians."

The fifth-century revelation is of a different nature. Unlike the Peruvian miracle, it did not merely involve the appearance of the Child in the Host, but the actual transformation of the eucharistic bread into the flesh of Christ—flesh that the doubting hermit was called to consume. In the centuries that followed, both kinds of eucharistic revelations would be recorded

Cathedral in Orvieto, which houses relics of the eucharistic miracle of Bolsena, 1263.

Papal procession with the relics of the eucharistic miracle in Orvieto, Italy.

The blood-stained cloth was sent to the pope, who was in Orvieto at the time (Umbria, Italy).

in the testimonies left by visionaries throughout the Christian world.

BODY AND BLOOD

The transformation of bread into human flesh and wine into human blood is the first kind of eucharistic manifestation. This type of miracle has reportedly occurred in Lanciano (700), Buenos Aires (1996), and more recently in Sokółka (2008) and Legnica (2013). A related form, known as a "manifestation of blood," took place in Bolsena (1263), Siena (1330), Macerata (1356), and Guadalajara (2013). Let us briefly consider the first of these.

In 1263, Fr. Peter of Prague made a pilgrimage to Rome, visiting the tombs of the Holy Apostles Peter and Paul. At the time, he was troubled by a growing heresy that denied the Real Presence of Christ in the Blessed Sacrament—and he himself had begun to struggle with doubt. Hoping to recover his faith, he stopped in the town of Bolsena and offered Mass at the tomb of St. Christina.

During the Consecration, as he elevated the Host over the chalice, he saw it begin to bleed profusely. Startled, he paused the Mass, wrapped the bleeding Host in the bloodstained corporal, and hurried toward the sacristy, intending to hide what had

Left: Reliquary with the corporal (Orvieto, Italy).

Right: Opened corporal with the Blood of the Lord cloth in the cathedral in Orvieto (Italy).

Stone with Blood remnants from the eucharistic miracle in Bolsena, 1263.

Eucharistic miracle in Sokółka.

"The sample sent for evaluation ... indicates heart muscle tissue," and more precisely, tissue taken from the pre-mortem, agonal period.

happened. But drops of blood began falling to the floor, and the faithful rushed to the altar, astonished at the sight of the corporal bearing twenty-five marks of Christ's blood.

SCIENCE'S CONCLUSIONS

Scientists have investigated numerous accounts of eucharistic miracles from around the world. In many cases, their findings point to a remarkable conclusion: the consecrated bread was transformed into human heart tissue—specifically, tissue from a person in the throes of intense suffering.

In 1971, using modern scientific methods, researchers conducted an in-depth examination of the relics from the Lanciano miracle (circa 750), in which the Host reportedly turned into human flesh. Their analysis confirmed that the material was indeed cardiac muscle of human origin.

Similarly, two pathology professors who studied the miracle in Sokółka concluded: "The sample sent for evaluation ... indicates heart muscle tissue," and more precisely, tissue taken from the *pre-mortem, agonal period*—that is, from a person undergoing the final, extreme agony before death.

Eucharistic blood, such as that found at Bolsena, has also defied natural explanation. In these cases, the blood has remained fresh, with intact proteins, enzymes, and living red and white blood cells—as if it had been freshly drawn, even after centuries have passed.

OTHER FORMS OF MANIFESTATIONS AND SIGNS

Another form of eucharistic revelation is the manifestation of light. One striking example comes from the thirteenth century, in Santarém, Portugal, where the Host reportedly shone with a mysterious radiance so intense that it penetrated the walls of its casket and filled the interior of the home with light.

History also records another kind of eucharistic manifestation: the reception of Holy Communion from supernatural beings. St. Clement and St. Catherine of Siena are said to have received the Eucharist directly from Christ Himself, while St. Bonaventure

Everyone who had the opportunity to observe the Sokółka miracle closely and under magnification was amazed to see that the Host, in a strange, irregular way, intertwines with the tissue of Jesus' heart. Without a microscope, it is impossible to clearly distinguish the boundary between them.

and St. Stanislaus Kostka received it from angels. We may also recall the eucharistic miracle at Fatima in 1916. The three shepherd children saw drops of blood fall from the Host into a chalice held by the Angel of Portugal, who then gave them Holy Communion.

AN ESCHATOLOGICAL DIMENSION

For many, the Eucharist is itself a revelation of what awaits humanity at the end of time. As the *Catechism of the Catholic Church* teaches, "The Church knows that the Lord comes even now in the Eucharist and that He is here in our midst, though His presence is veiled" (*CCC* 1404). This is why the Church celebrates the Eucharist "awaiting the blessed hope and the coming of our Savior, Jesus Christ," praying that one day we may "rejoice forever at Your glory, when You will wipe away every tear from our eyes; for seeing You, our God, as You are, we shall be like You for all the ages and praise You without end through Christ our Lord."

The *Catechism* continues: "There is no surer pledge or clearer sign of this great hope of new heavens and a new earth 'in which righteousness dwells' (2 Peter 3:13) than the Eucharist. Indeed, every time this mystery is celebrated, 'the work of our redemption is carried out,' and we 'break the one bread that provides the medicine of immortality, the antidote against death, and gives us life in Jesus Christ forever'" (*CCC* 1405).

It is no wonder, then, that for mystics and saints, the Eucharist was not only a renewal of hope for the coming of God's Kingdom—it was a real making-present of that Kingdom here and now.

The basilica in Sokółka has become a destination for pilgrims from all over the world. Numerous Orthodox Christians from Belarus have also come here.

θ (THETA)

A CHRISTOPHANY IN SHEOL

On the previous page: Joakim Skovgaard, Christ in the Realm of the Dead, *City Museum (Copenhagen, Denmark).*

***Place of the Revelation:* Sheol**
***Liturgical memorial:* Good Friday**

(THETA)

A CHRISTOPHANY IN SHEOL

THE ABODE OF THE DEAD, A.D. 33

"Descended into hell"—this is one of the key articles of faith, and yet it remains one of the most perplexing for many today. We repeat these words about Jesus descending ad infernum *whenever we recite the Apostles' Creed, professing our belief in His descent into the realm of the dead:* "I believe ... in Jesus Christ ... who ... descended into hell."

➤ *Bartolomé Bermejo,* Christ Leading the Patriarchs to Paradise, *Casa Amatller (Barcelona, Spain).*

This truth is placed between the declarations "He died and was buried" and "on the third day He rose again." Death, burial, and resurrection are clearly historical realities—central to our redemption. But what are we to make of His descent into the depths? Is that, too, a real event within the scope of Jesus' redemptive mission?

VIEWS OF DEATH IN THE ANCIENT MIDDLE EAST

In antiquity, the peoples of the Near East believed the universe had a simple, ordered structure: a three-tiered cosmos

◄ *Duccio di Buoninsegna,* Descent into the Abyss (*fragment*).

▼ *Fragment of the Hell fresco from the medieval Church of St. Nicholas (Raduyl, Bulgaria).*

consisting of the heavens, the earth, and the underworld.

The gods dwelled in the heavens; the earth was given to human beings and other mortal creatures; and the underworld was the realm of the dead. To descend into that lowest realm was to die.

WHAT IS "DEATH"?

What does it mean "to die," if—according to another dogma of our faith—man is immortal? He has a beginning, but no end. Perhaps we should understand death not as the end of existence, but as the end of earthly life, and think of it in theological rather than merely biological terms.

The *Catechism of the Catholic Church* strongly suggests this perspective: "The abode of the dead to which Christ went down after dying is called 'hell'—Sheol or Hades—because those who are there are deprived of the vision of God" (*CCC* 633).

Death, then, is the absence of the vision of God—only that, and yet that is everything.

In the ancient worldview, there were thought to be two "hells": an upper and a lower. The book of Wisdom distinguishes these two conditions—the state of the righteous and the state of the wicked (cf. Wisdom 3:1, 4, 10). The first was associated with hope and the expectation of beholding God; the second with despair and final separation from Him. The former awaited God's coming; the latter, "the land of no return," was a dark and silent void.

➤ Rapid Transit to Sheol—Where We Are All Going, According to the Reverend Dr. Morgan Dix—*by Joseph Ferdinand Keppler,* Puck Magazine, *1888.*

Human beings are, by nature, immortal. As the Preface for Christian funerals says, "life is changed, not ended." Yet in the state where one does not see God, one may truly be called "dead," for without the vision of God, life is stripped of its purpose and fulfillment. It is also stripped of the happiness that, according to the Creator's plan, belongs to the heart of human life—both now and in eternity. The Church founded by Christ was established to make that happiness possible.

But how can one reach the goal of human existence—God's glory—if "God is not there"? How can one possess eternal joy if He is absent?

In Sheol, "there is no God"—no presence, no voice, no light. It is a place of utter isolation. And so it remains... until Christ speaks there. And when He does, the dead behold Him, they see God, and they give Him glory.

A PATH TRAVELED IN FULL

Jesus was crucified and died. He was buried. At that moment—for all except His Mother—His story seemed to have ended. He had departed, gone to dwell in Sheol.

➤ *Albrecht Dürer,* Christ's Descent into the Abyss, *woodcut, ca. 1510.*

Late Byzantine *fresco,* Descent into Hell (*Anastasis*), *Church of Chora in Constantinople* (*now Istanbul*).

But that is not the truth. He did not *remain* there. If He had, Sheol would, by definition, cease to exist. For Sheol is the realm of God's absence—and where God is present, Sheol can no longer be. Therefore, Jesus' descent into the underworld marks the *end* of Sheol.

We should not speak of Him *dwelling* there, but of Him *entering* it. And the moment He enters, Sheol's time is over.

Why did He descend so far? Because Christ was fully man, even unto death. He experienced everything truly human. He gave meaning to all things and sanctified them—even the fate that awaited us after death, though not the fate Sheol had in store. "He loved his own in the world and he loved them to the end" (John 13:1).

He passed through the final gate of human loneliness, which He had already known on the Cross: "My God, my God, why have you forsaken me?" (Matthew 27:46). In His Passion and death, He descended into the abyss of human abandonment. He tasted the emptiness of Sheol, remained in solidarity with the living—and then, in the tomb, with the dead. But Christ's entrance into death meant the destruction of death's domain.

The Letter to the Hebrews teaches that Jesus fully partook of "flesh and blood," so that "through death he might destroy the one who has the power of death, that is, the devil" (Hebrews 2:14). Apocryphal writings delight in recounting the shock and dismay of Death and Satan at seeing their "territory" seized from them.

How did Jesus become the Victor over death, Hell, and Satan? The *Catechism of the Catholic Church* describes two dimensions to His descent into Hell. First, Jesus truly died—He experienced death like every human being and arrived in the place of the dead. But second, He entered as the Savior, the conqueror of death. He did not merely console the imprisoned souls—He restored them to life and gave it in fullness. The dead saw God. This, theology tells us, is salvation.

Follower of *Hieronymus Bosch,* Descent into Hell, *Metropolitan Museum of Art (New York, USA).*

THE JUST AWAITING THE VOICE OF THE SON OF MAN

In Old Testament times, the righteous in Sheol were believed to be waiting for the coming of the Son of Man. Their rightful state was one of expectation—of hope fixed on the Redeemer who was to come.

The prophet Daniel foresaw this moment: "Many of those who sleep in the dust of the earth shall awake; some to everlasting life, others to reproach and everlasting disgrace" (Daniel 12:2). It is Christ the Messiah who will awaken them.

The Gospel of John records Jesus Himself saying, "the hour is coming and is now here when the dead will hear the voice of the Son of God, and those who hear will live" (John 5:25).

St. Peter confirms this mystery: "For Christ also suffered for sins once, the righteous for the sake of the unrighteous, that he might lead you to God. Put to death

Fra Angelico, Last Judgment *(detail), Museo Nazionale di San Marco (Florence, Italy).*

in the flesh, he was brought to life in the spirit. In it he also went to preach to the spirits in prison" (1 Peter 3:18–20).

In other words, the hour of Jesus' death is inseparable from the revelation of the Messiah to the dead. They hear His voice.

GATES SWUNG OPEN

Again, let us turn to the *Catechism of the Catholic Church*: "The dead Christ, in His soul united to His divine Person, descended into the realm of the dead. He opened heaven's gates for the just who had gone before Him" (*CCC* 635, 636, 637).

This truth is vividly expressed in an ancient reading from the Liturgy of the Hours—*An Ancient Homily for Holy Saturday*—which brings to life St. Peter's words that "the gospel was preached even to the dead" (1 Peter 4:6). In this homily, Christ descends into the abyss of death, bearing life to those in darkness:

> *To you, Adam, I give this command:*
> *Awake, you who sleep! I did not create you to remain bound in the underworld.*
> *Rise from the dead, for I am the Life of the dead.*
> *Arise, you who are the work of My hands.*
> *Arise, you who are My image, made in My likeness.*
> *Rise, let us go from here!*

Apocryphal texts depict this mystery with lavish splendor. In the *Odes of Solomon*, an early Christian poetic work, we find a meditation on the Messiah's liberating descent:

> *Only the Most High, in all His perfection, knew me and believed in me.*
> *In His mercy, He exalted me and lifted my mind to the heights of truth.*
> *From there, He stretched out before me the path of His footsteps, and I opened doors hitherto locked.*
> *I burst through the iron bars;*
> *the chains that bound me were dissolved like fire, melting before me.*

Adam, Eve, and the Patriarchs follow Jesus from Hell to Heaven—fragment of a Russian icon of John the Baptist recounting Christ's descent to the righteous in Sheol, seventeenth century (Solovetsky Monastery, Russia).

Follower of *Hieronymus Bosch,* Descent into Hell, *Metropolitan Museum of Art (New York, USA).*

Nothing was closed to me anymore, for I became the gate of all things.
I went to all my prisoners to free them; I would leave none bound, nor any who would bind.
I poured out my knowledge upon them, along with mediation.
I scattered the seeds of my fruits in their hearts and transformed them.
They received my blessing and possessed life; they gathered around me, and they were redeemed.
Thus they became my members, and I—their head.

In the *Gospel of Bartholomew*, the event is cast in dramatic dialogue. Beelzebub—also called Death—tries to reassure Hades that there is no danger in Christ's descent. But Hades, aware of the truth, cries out in terror:

Pay no heed to your sweet talk! My belly is ripping, my insides burn. Surely it is none other than God Himself who has descended here! Alas, where shall I flee from His countenance, from the might of the great King?

A SCENE FROM THE GOSPEL OF NICODEMUS

Here is how the *Gospel of Nicodemus* describes these events:

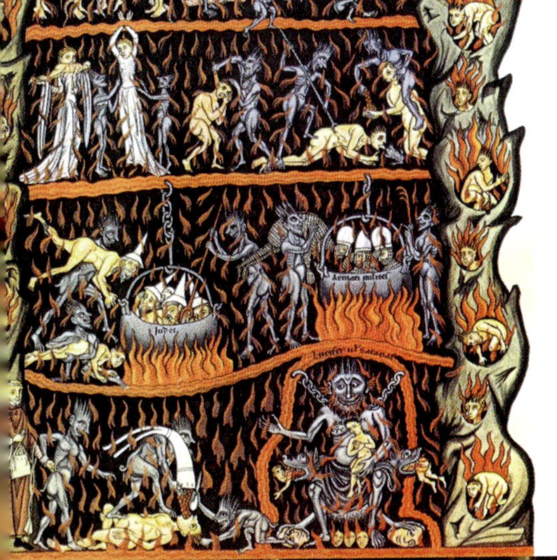

While the departed spirits were in the darkness of the underworld, a golden radiance shone forth and illuminated them all.... Great joy and gladness arose among them. Hades said to his wicked servitors: "Close, you monsters, the bronze gates, and bar the iron locks, and stand firm, lest we be taken captive—we who hold our captives in bondage!"

LAND OF THE DEAD

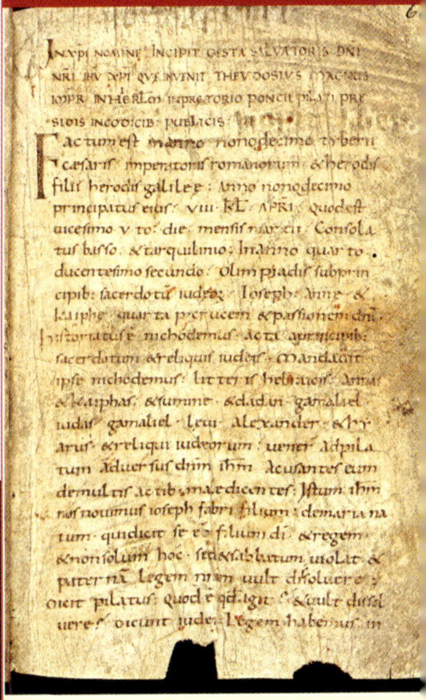

IN XPI NOMINE INCIPIT GESTA SALVATORIS DNI
NRI IHV XPI QVÆ INVENIT THEVDOSIVS MAGNVS
IMPR IN HIERLM IN PRETORIO PONCII PILATI PRE
SIDIS IN CODICIB PUBLICIS
Factum est in anno nonodecimo tyberii
cesaris imperatoris romanorum et herodis
filii herodis galileę: Anno nonodecimo
principatus eius · VIII · KL · APRI · quod est
uicesimo v to die mensis marcii · Consola
tus basso et tarquilinio: In anno quarto
ducentesimo secundo olimpiadis sub prin
cipib: sacerdotu iudeor · Ioseph · Anne et
kaiphe quarta per crucem et passionem dni
historiatus e nichodemus acta a principib:
sacerdotum et reliquis iudeis · Mandauit
ipse nichodemus litteris hebraicis · Annas
et kaiphas et summe et dadan gamaliel
iudas gamaliel · leui · Alexander et Iyr
arus et reliqui iudeorum · uenerunt ad pila
tum aduersus dnm ihm accusantes eum
de multis actibus mala dicentes: Istum ihm
nos nouimus ioseph fabri filium: de maria na
tum · qui dicit se esse filium di et regem
et non solum hoc · sed et sabbatum uiolat et
paternam legem nram uult dissoluere
dicit pilatus: Quod est quod agit et uult dissol
uere? dicunt iudei: Legem habemus in

Right: *Manuscript of the Gospel of Nicodemus, ninth or tenth century,* Einsiedeln Abbey Library.

Left: Hell—*illustration from* Hortus Deliciarum (The Garden of Delights) *by Abbess Herrad of Landsberg, ca. 1180* (Germany).

Follower of Hieronymus Bosch, Visitation of Sheol, *fifteenth century,* Philadelphia Museum of Art (USA).

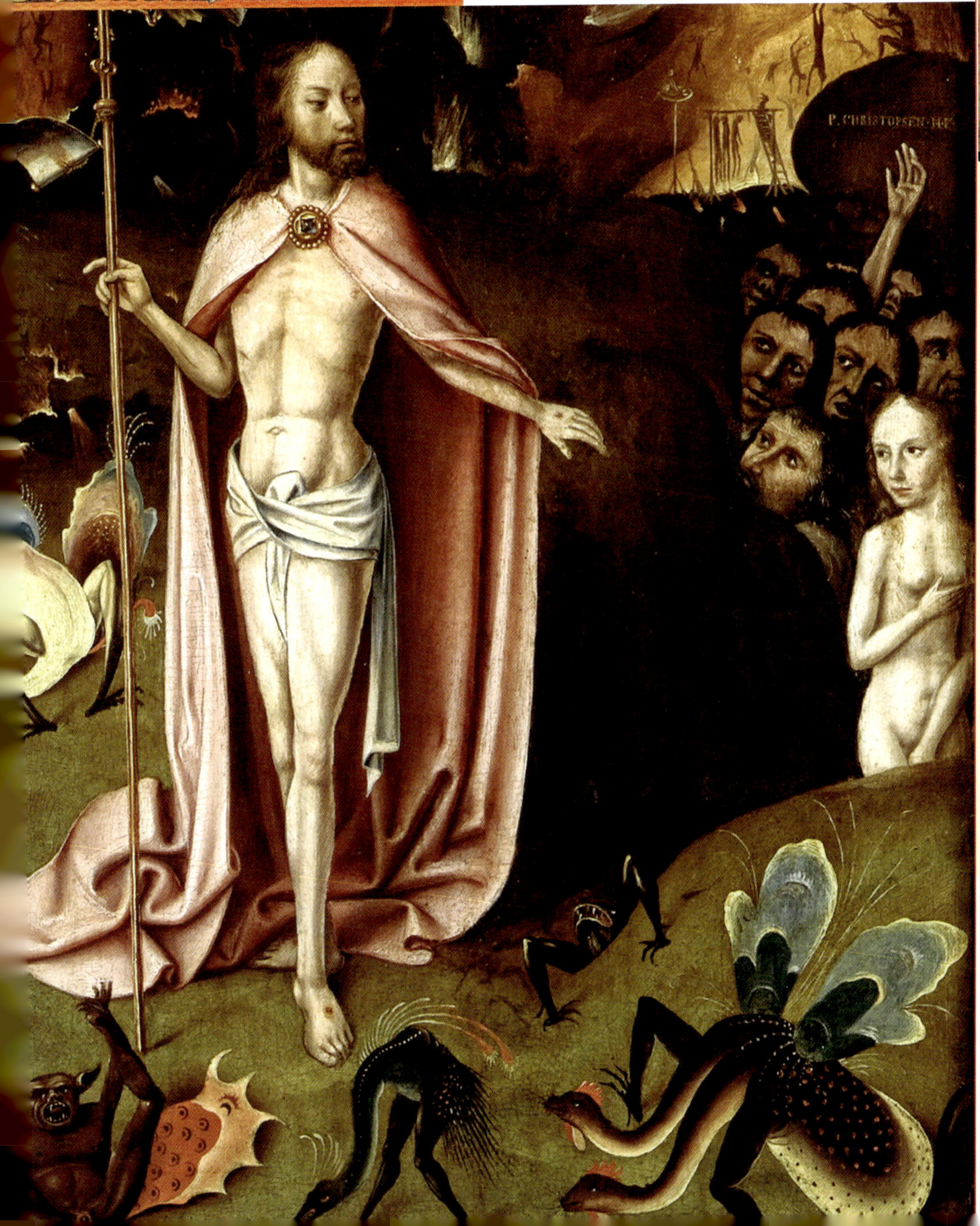

Their attempt at locking up availed nothing, for the King of Glory arrived in human form, the Lord of Majesty, scattering everlasting darkness and breaking the bonds that none could undo.

When Hades, Death, and their wicked servants, along with the cruel tormentors, beheld light in their domain, they were terrified at seeing such brilliance in the realm of darkness, and upon seeing Christ in their midst, they cried out: "We are overthrown by You! Who are You, who come from the Lord to our shame? ... Who are You who entered our domain unshaken? You show no fear of our threats, and indeed You plan to free everyone from our chains. Are You that Jesus our prince Satan spoke of—He who through His death on the cross took possession of the entire world?"

Then the King of Glory trampled Death in His majesty, seized the prince Satan, and handed him over to Hades. He drew Adam into His radiance, and they emerged from the abyss—Adam, Eve, and a host of saints; Enoch and Elijah, who had been taken up alive into heaven; the poor man bearing the Cross—Dismas, the good thief to whom Christ had promised paradise while on the Cross.

This dramatic portrayal expands on St. Peter's teaching, offering a vivid meditation on how the righteous of the Old Testament received Christ's redemption. It presents not only a descent into Sheol, but a triumph—Christ's

➤ *Andrea Mantegna,* Jesus' Descent into Limbo, *on loan to the Frick Museum in New York from the collection of Barbara Piasecka-Johnson (USA).*

➤ Left: Descent into the Abyss, *painting from the large reredos, ca. 1430–1450, old cathedral in Salamanca.*

➤ *Right: Manuscript from the Hengwrt-Peniarth Collection,* Jesus Descends into Hell and Leads Adam by the Hand. *On the scroll in the border: the motto* Entretenir Dieu le veuille *("May God sustain it").*

◄ *John Climacus,* The Ladder to Paradise, *twelfth century, Monastery of St. Catherine, Mount Sinai (Egypt).*

St. John Climacus described Christian life as a ladder with thirty rungs. Monks are tempted by demons and encouraged by angels, and at the summit Christ welcomes them (cf. the vision of St. Bridget of Sweden).

revelation to the dead as the decisive moment of salvation.

Is this merely an apocryphal vision, to be set aside with caution? Not entirely—for similar imagery and theology appear in the Church's liturgical life. In the Byzantine tradition, the *Paschal Homily* attributed to Pseudo-Chrysostom echoes the same victorious spirit:

> *When You [O Christ] met it down below, Hades was filled with bitterness, for it was abolished. Filled with anguish, for it was defeated.*
>
> *Where, O death, is your victory? Christ is risen, and you are overthrown.*

And in the *Anaphora of Saint Basil*, the Church prays:

> *Christ descended into Hades through the Cross, that He might*

bring all things to completion, and
He loosened the pangs of death.

These liturgical texts confirm that what the apocryphal visionaries expressed with poetic force, the Church herself proclaims with solemn conviction: Christ's descent into the realm of the dead was not defeat, but victory—the radiant unveiling of redemption to those who waited in hope.

THEOLOGY OF HELL

The *Catechism of the Catholic Church* clarifies that "Jesus experienced death as all humans do, and His soul joined theirs in the realm of the dead. There, however,

Pablo de Céspedes, Descent of Jesus Christ into the Abyss, *Indianapolis Museum of Art (USA).*

Fra Angelico, Christ Leads the Souls of the Just out of Hell, *fresco, ca. 1430.*

He descended as Savior, proclaiming the Good News to the imprisoned spirits" (*CCC* 632). As we have seen, 1 Peter 3:19 testifies: "[In the Spirit] he also went to preach to the spirits in prison." The gates of Sheol, it turns out, are not strong enough to resist Christ and His Church.

But what does it mean to say that Jesus "descended into hell"? Does this include the "lower hell," the place of the eternally damned? Did His light shine there, too?

This question has long perplexed theologians. For if Christ had entered the abode of the damned and fully revealed His divinity there, that place—defined by separation from God—would no longer exist. And yet, Hell does still exist.

The Church's tradition, guided especially by St. Thomas Aquinas, offers a careful distinction. According to Aquinas, one can be present in a place in two ways: either through one's power and effective action,

Jacopo Tintoretto, Descent into Hell, *Church of San Cassiano (Venice, Italy).*

or through one's full personal presence. In the Hell of the condemned, Christ was present by His divine power—His justice, majesty, and dominion—but He did not manifest Himself personally. His presence there was not saving, but judicial. It exposed the shame of the damned, revealing their rejection of grace and their definitive refusal to choose Him.

In contrast, Christ entered *personally* into that part of the realm of the dead where the righteous waited. This is what tradition calls the "upper hell"—the limbo of the just. There, He did not merely act by divine power; He revealed His very person as the Risen Lord. It was to *them* that He brought salvation.

In this way, Christ touched every depth of death's domain. He descended to the lowest places, but only those who had awaited Him in hope could receive Him. Salvation, as always, is a gift—but one that must be desired and freely accepted.

The revelation of Christ in the realm of the righteous is perhaps the most beautiful encounter between the Savior and humanity in all history. They welcomed Him with joy. They saw the Light, and they entered into it. And they remain there, in glory, forever.

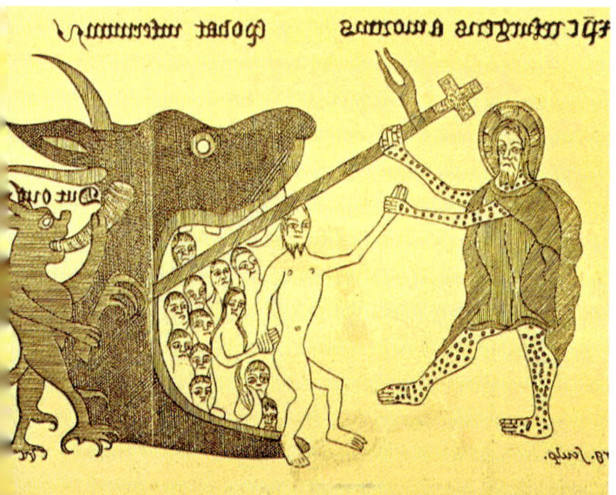

Michael Burghers, Descent into Hell, *engraving, 1647–1727.*

WILL THE PAROUSIA BE SIMILAR?

Let us once again turn to the apocrypha. The *Ethiopic Book of Enoch*, the *Book of Jubilees*, the *Assumption of Moses*, the *Fourth Book of Ezra*, and both the Greek and Syriac versions of the *Apocalypse of Baruch* describe Christ's descent into the underworld as the ultimate event—occurring on the "Day of Yahweh," the day of final judgment. On that day, not only the inhabitants of Sheol, but the entire cosmos, will undergo upheaval and transformation. The Messiah will bring Satan's dominion to an end. The dead will rise from the abyss, and God's chosen people will at last receive their long-promised freedom.

Indeed, one may discern a profound parallel between Christ's descent into Hell and His future revelation at the end of time, when He will "judge the living and the dead." To contemplate this earlier article of faith may help us better grasp the mystery of the Parousia and the meaning of the final judgment.

As the book of Revelation suggests, the revealing light of the Savior will bring either life or death. For some, it will be the fulfillment of hope; for others, the moment of final loss—a "second death," which is eternal separation from God. This will not be annihilation. The damned will not cease to exist, for they are immortal. But their unending existence, cut off from God's light and grace, will be a tormented sojourn in the loneliness of the "lower hell."

Domenico Beccafumi, Christ's Descent into Hell, *Pinacoteca Nazionale (Siena, Italy).*

Follower of Hieronymus Bosch, Christ Breaking Down the Gates of Hell, *Royal Collection, Buckingham Palace (United Kingdom).*

ι

(IOTA)

THE RESURRECTION

Only the empty Tomb remains …

Place of the Revelation: Jerusalem
Liturgical memorial: Easter Sunday—The Resurrection of the Lord

The Exit from the Abyss—*mosaic by an unknown artist in the Greek monastery of Hosios Loukas, eleventh century.*

(IOTA)

THE RESURRECTION

A REVELATION WITHOUT WITNESSES, A.D. 33

The greatest of all revelations—one that had no human witnesses. We might say it took place in the presence of angels alone, echoing the world's beginning, when God first revealed to the heavenly spirits His plan to take on human flesh. Now, He reveals the completion of that plan: God becomes man for eternity. The Resurrection of the body of Jesus takes place—a human body, glorified.

St. John begins his First Epistle with an exclamation of awe: "Life was made manifest!" Did he consider himself a witness of the Resurrection? Yes—because the Resurrection is not merely a moment in history. It is a state of existence. It is not just something that *happened*—it *endures*. In this sense, the apostles were witnesses not only to the risen Jesus but to His very rising.

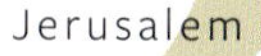

Andrea Mantegna, The Resurrection of Christ, *Musée des Beaux-Arts de Tours (France).*

Angel Sitting at the Empty Tomb—*folio 117r, Pericopes, Henry II, ca. 1002–1012 (Reichenau, Germany).*

Thus John could write:

> *What was from the beginning, what we have heard, what we have seen with our eyes, what we looked upon and touched with our hands concerns the Word of life—for the life was made visible; we have seen it and testify to it and proclaim to you the eternal life that was with the Father and was made visible to us—what we have seen and heard we proclaim now to you, so that you too may have fellowship with us; for our fellowship is with the Father and with his Son, Jesus Christ.* (1 John 1:1–3)

For John the Evangelist, the Resurrection was nothing less than the revelation of eternal life.

NOT A MERE REVIVIFICATION

The Resurrection was a true, literal, physical restoration of Jesus' life by the reunion of His body with His soul and spirit. Yet it was not a return to earthly life. It was the rising of His body from the dead into eternal life—a wholly different reality and a vital sign of God's plan.

Germain Pilon, Jesus Christ, *part of the marble sculptural group* The Resurrection, *before 1572, Louvre (Paris, France).*

Top: Anastasis—symbolic representation of Christ's Resurrection. Slab from a Roman sarcophagus of the Passion type, ca. AD 350. From excavations by Princess of Chablais in Tor Marancia, 1817–1821.

Bottom: Hans Multscher, The Resurrection of Jesus Christ, *Wurzach Altarpiece, ca. 1430, Gemäldegalerie (Berlin, Germany).*

In rising, Christ not only confirmed His identity as the Son of God but also revealed mankind's divine destiny. As St. Paul declares, "But now Christ has been raised from the dead, the firstfruits of those who have fallen asleep" (1 Corinthians 15:20). And again: "In Christ shall all be brought to life" (1 Corinthians 15:22).

St. Paul insists that "if Christ has not been raised, then empty [too] is our preaching; empty, too, your faith" (1 Corinthians 15:14). Without the Resurrection, Christians would be the most pitiable of people—for then Christ would not be the Son of God, God would have no plan to exalt humanity above the angels, and our bodies would not rise in glory. The earthly realm would be all that mattered. In such a world, one could speak only of *resuscitation*, not *resurrection*.

Making this distinction—between *revivification* or *resuscitation* and *resurrection*—is essential. The Resurrection of Jesus is entirely different even from that mysterious moment at His death when the tombs opened and some of the dead rose. St. Matthew records:

> *Tombs were opened, and the bodies of many saints who had fallen asleep were raised. And coming forth from their tombs after his resurrection, they entered the holy city and appeared to many. (Matthew 27:52–53)*

What did early Christian sources say about that event? St. Ignatius of Antioch, writing in A.D. 108, proposed that those who rose were Old Testament prophets. Apocryphal writings suggest otherwise, mentioning not only prophets but also two deceased sons of Simeon of Arimathea, who testified before a council about Jesus'

Top: Mosaic in one of the chapels of the Basilica of Our Lady of the Rosary in Lourdes (lower level): The Resurrection.

Bottom: Noël Coypel, The Resurrection of the Lord, *Musée des Beaux-Arts de Rouen (France).*

➤ *Fourteenth-century alabaster sculpture,* The Resurrection of Christ, *British Museum (London, United Kingdom).*

➤ *Annibale Carracci,* The Resurrection of Christ, *Louvre (Paris, France).*

descent into Hades to liberate its inhabitants.

The Resurrection also differs from the miracles Jesus Himself worked during His ministry—such as raising Lazarus, Jairus's daughter, or the young man at Nain. These people returned to earthly life and later died again. But Jesus "died once" and now "lives for God" (Romans 6:10). He did not return to ordinary biological life. He will never suffer bodily death again, for His is already a "glorified body" (Philippians 3:21)—a "spiritual body" (1 Corinthians 15:44).

He is the first of His kind, and all humanity awaits the resurrection of the body at the end of time. The Niceno-Constantinopolitan Creed proclaims, "I believe in the resurrection of the body and life everlasting." This is the eternal

life promised to the righteous—life in a glorified body, sharing in the radiance of God.

But if, throughout our lives, we echo Lucifer's "no," we shall rise, too—but only to judgment. We will remain in Hell, in a body that was made to be glorious but is now crushed by everlasting evil. Scripture calls this "the resurrection of damnation" (cf. John 5:29).

DID HE REALLY DIE?

Perhaps Jesus did not die at all? Some have suggested He merely survived the Crucifixion, and that His later appearances to the disciples were a deception. But no—He most certainly died. No one could survive the horrors of Golgotha. Even before reaching the hill, Jesus was close to death. After enduring a brutal scourging at the hands of Roman soldiers, He was so weakened that His executioners feared He might not survive the journey to the place of execution. That is why they

compelled Simon of Cyrene to carry His Cross.

On Golgotha, they nailed Him to the wood. Massive iron spikes were driven through His wrists, stretching His limbs across the beam and crushing the nerves—pain so excruciating it could have caused death by shock alone. Once the Cross was lifted upright, His body sagged forward. He could inhale, but exhaling required lifting Himself painfully by His feet and arms. Each breath became an act of torment. Without strength to rise, He would eventually be unable to breathe at all.

To hasten death, Roman executioners would break a man's legs. That was the fate of the two thieves crucified beside Him. Once their legs were broken, they could no longer lift themselves to breathe, and so they suffocated.

But Jesus had already died. One soldier thrust a spear into His side to confirm it—checking whether there was any reaction or sign of life. There was none.

THE RESURRECTION

And under Roman law, that meant only one thing: He was dead.

THE APOCRYPHA

Many witnessed Jesus' death, but no one was an eyewitness to the Resurrection itself. None of the Gospels describes how it happened in physical terms. No one can recount it from a natural perspective, for it is a transcendent event—beyond human comprehension, beyond the scope of our senses or earthly experience.

And yet, it is a fact. The apocrypha attempt to name it.

Before turning to those accounts, we should first note what the canonical Gospels tell us: the first to discover the empty tomb were women. At that time, the testimony of women was not accepted in court; their word was considered unreliable. Therefore, if the Resurrection accounts were a fabrication, they would not have chosen women as the first witnesses. That detail alone gives strong reason to trust the accounts: it must have happened just that way. And after all, Jesus had foretold it

Piero della Francesca, The Resurrection, *Museo Civico di Sansepolcro (Italy).*

Alonso López de Herrera, The Resurrection of Christ.

Courtyard of the Church of the Holy Sepulchre. On the right side stands the Chapel of the Franks.

clearly: He would suffer, die, and rise again (Mark 9:31).

The most extensive apocryphal account of the Resurrection is found in the *Gospel of Peter*. Before quoting it, let us consider the judgment of St. Eusebius of Caesarea (†339). In his *Ecclesiastical History*, he remarked: "We obtained this Gospel from those who used it.... We have read it and judge that for the most part it adheres to the true teaching of the Savior, though some parts differ."

What does the *Gospel of Peter* say? We read:

> *On the night when the Lord's Day was dawning, and the soldiers were keeping watch at the tomb ... a great voice sounded in heaven. And they saw the heavens open, and two men descend clothed in a great radiance.*
>
> *Approaching the tomb, the stone that closed it rolled away by itself, and it shifted aside, and the tomb opened, and the two men went in. Seeing this, the soldiers awakened*

The Basilica of the Holy Sepulchre in Jerusalem.

The Church of the Holy Sepulchre, from Views in the Ottoman Dominions, Europe, Asia, and Some Mediterranean Islands (1810), *illustrated by Luigi Mayer (1755–1803).*

the centurion and the elders ... and told them what they had witnessed.

And again they saw three men coming forth from the tomb, two supporting the other, and a cross following them. And the heads of the two reached to heaven, but the head of the one they bore along rose beyond the heavens.

Similarly, the *Gospel of Nicodemus* describes an angel in white garments, with a face like lightning, descending amid an earthquake and thunder to roll away the stone from the tomb's entrance.

In Pilate's apocryphal *Report*, we read of a multitude of majestic, radiant men, whose thunderous voice announces the Resurrection and calls the dead to rise:

A group of exalted men appeared, clothed in garments of glory, and they called out with a voice like mighty thunder:
"Jesus the Crucified has risen from the dead! Come forth, all you who are imprisoned as captives in the depths of Hades!"

The *Gospel of Nicodemus* also records the testimony of one of the guards at the tomb:

While we were guarding the tomb of Jesus, there was a violent

Right: Pilgrims at the Holy Sepulchre.

Left: Sanctuary of the Holy Sepulchre, April 10, 1839. Color lithograph by Louis Haghe after David Roberts, 1842.

Top: Orthodox Chapel of the Crucifixion in the Basilica of the Holy Sepulchre.

Bottom: Arcosolium—the tomb in which the Body of Jesus was laid.

earthquake, and we saw an angel of God who rolled away the stone and sat upon it; his face shone like lightning, and his garments were white as snow. We, for fear, became as though dead.

A MYSTERY

Origen once wrote:

> *The doctrine of the Resurrection is complicated and obscure; of all dogmas it most needs an explanation by a perfect wise man—one who might show that it befits God, and is a sublime doctrine, that what Scripture calls "the garment of souls" has within it a creative principle, so that in this garment the righteous "groan, longing not to be unclothed but to be further clothed."*

To this day, the Resurrection stirs controversy. "In no point does the Christian faith encounter more opposition than in regard to the resurrection of the body," observes St. Augustine. And yet—*Christ is risen*. He is the sign and pledge of our own resurrection.

It is not only reason that resists this truth. Within us lies a fear that affirming the Resurrection entails far-reaching consequences—ones that demand a radical change of life.

St. Ignatius of Antioch gives voice to that transformation:

> *I seek Him who died for us; I long for Him who rose for us. And my birth is close at hand.... Let me receive the pure light. Once I attain it, I shall be a complete human being.*

Dome of the Anastasis Rotunda above the edicule of the Holy Sepulchre.

Steel structure reinforcing the edicule of the Holy Sepulchre.

1
The Most Important Heart

1673

On the Previous Page: Stained-glass image of Christ appearing to St. Margaret Mary Alacoque.

➤ *Virgilio Mattoni de la Fuente, Chapel of the Sacred Heart of Jesus, Church of San Andrés (Seville, Spain).*

➤ *Unknown painter,* Vision of the Heart of Jesus of St. Margaret Mary Alacoque, *Shrine of Our Lady (Maplewood, USA).*

Place of Apparition:
Paray-le-Monial, France
Date and Place of Birth:
July 22, 1647,
Hautecour, France
Date and Place of Death:
October 17, 1690,
Paray-le-Monial, France
Visionary as a religious
(Order of the Visitation of Holy Mary)
Beatification:
September 18, 1864
Canonization:
May 13, 1920
(Benedict XV)
Liturgical memorial:
October 14
Works: Spiritual Memoir, Letters of St. Margaret Mary Alacoque

➤ *Fragment of stained glass, Vision of St. Margaret Mary Alacoque.*

1

THE MOST IMPORTANT HEART

MARGARET MARY ALACOQUE, 1673

Before us stands one of the few figures closely associated with the revelations of Jesus. And rightly so: hers are among the most public revelations in Christian history. From Margaret Mary Alacoque's encounters with the Savior, we have received the practice of the nine First Fridays, the Solemnity of the Most Sacred Heart of Jesus celebrated during the octave of Corpus Christi, the Holy Hour of Reparation, and devotion to the Heart of Jesus as an act of reparation. In the previous generation, the image of the Sacred Heart could be found in nearly every Catholic home—another fruit of her legacy.

Not a small inheritance from a cloistered nun who lived only forty-three years. Her influence on Christian piety is summed up in four revelations. Tradition calls them the "great" ones, and most of what we know about Margaret Mary's mystical experiences comes from these alone. Meanwhile, careful scholars have counted seventy-six other encounters with Jesus. But they have often missed the deeper truth: she spoke of her experiences only out of obedience. There may well have been more—many more.

Because Margaret was not only "innocent as a dove." As it is written in the Gospel:

> *"Behold, I am sending you like sheep in the midst of wolves; so be shrewd as serpents and simple as doves."* (Matthew 10:16)

She could also be as cunning as a serpent, finding subtle ways to conceal her spiritual secrets. One example will suffice: nearly everything we know about her encounters with Jesus comes from her autobiography, which she wrote

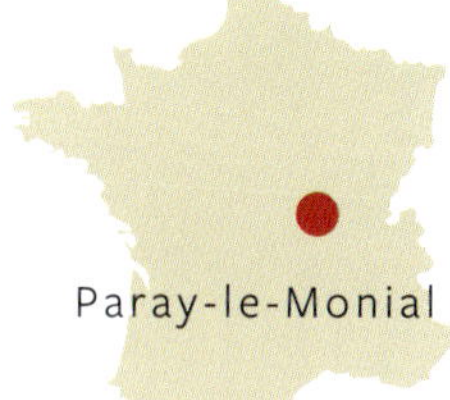

Right: *Corrado Mezzana,* Bl. Mary of the Divine Heart with St. Margaret Mary Alacoque.

only because her confessor ordered it. Knowing her well, he immediately forbade her to burn the manuscript—fully aware that this is precisely what she would have done. Obedience required her to record her spiritual life, but nothing explicitly prevented her from destroying the manuscript later. After all, his command had not covered that possibility.

In the end, she never completed the account. She stopped four years before her death, after her spiritual director read what she had written and returned it to her without explicitly asking her to continue. As she lay dying in great pain, she pleaded with the sister caring for her to retrieve the notebook from a locked cupboard in her cell and burn it. Why? Because Sister Claude de Farges could do what Margaret herself

Margaret Mary Alacoque, Parish Church of St. Gordian and St. Epimachus (Merazhofen, Germany).

St. Margaret Mary Alacoque receiving a vision of the Sacred Heart of Jesus, detail from the altar in the Church of St. Catherine (Lille, France).

could not. The confessor's prohibition bound only Margaret—not anyone else.

Fortunately, the sister did not carry out the request. Because of that refusal, Margaret Mary's notes have come down to us, and in them we find many extraordinary details about her encounters with Jesus.

THE UNYIELDING FRAMEWORK OF OBEDIENCE

What stands out most in reading her autobiography? The striking realization that Jesus enclosed Margaret Mary's entire path to salvation within the strict bounds of religious obedience. And how unyielding those bounds prove to be—even the holiest zeal must not transgress them.

Two incidents illustrate this principle, both involving direct intervention from Jesus.

The Visitation rule prescribed a nightly "discipline"—the sisters' practice of self-flagellation before bed. Each sister carried it out privately in her cell, the duration marked by the recitation of the *Ave Maris Stella*, a Marian hymn still included among the Night Prayer options in the Liturgy of the Hours. Reciting the hymn takes long enough that the discipline would typically involve at least twenty-eight strokes.

The more zealous might go beyond that—striking themselves at every word rather than at each verse. Margaret Mary was likely one of them. One evening, as she scourged herself in rhythm with the hymn, Jesus appeared to her and said briefly, "This is for me." Overjoyed, she continued even after the prayer ended, hoping to give her Savior greater joy. Then Jesus, still watching, said again: "But this is for the devil."

"That made me stop immediately," she wrote.

Another moment reveals a similar lesson. In the autumn of 1679, Margaret, overwhelmed with love, took a sharp instrument and carved the name of Jesus into her chest. She wanted a visible mark of her total belonging to Him. The wounds were deep and soon infected—but she rejoiced, for now she had something to offer the Lord.

But the rule required that any illness be reported to the superior. When Margaret revealed the wound, the mother superior not only reprimanded her and imposed a severe penance but also ordered her to see the infirmarian. Her secret would now become public. Then Jesus intervened. He healed her wound so she would not have to show it to anyone. But because she had acted without the superior's consent, Jesus told her—and here we leave the final word to Margaret herself—"He said that the carved word, which had cost me so much pain, would no longer be visible. Even the earlier marks that were on my body would vanish."

Earlier marks? This had been her second attempt to inscribe the name of Jesus on her heart.

Polish devotional image from the early twentieth century.

Left: Stained glass in St. Patrick's Church in Columbus (Ohio, USA).

Right: Corrado Giaquinto, St. Margaret Mary Alacoque contemplating the Sacred Heart of Jesus.

1673

➤ *Epitaph of Margaret Mary Alacoque in the Church of the Visitation in Paray-le-Monial.*

THE BEGINNING

Let us begin at the beginning. Margaret Mary Alacoque was born on July 22, 1647, in Lauthecourt, a small village in Burgundy. She was the fifth of seven children in the household of a prosperous notary. From her earliest years, she was marked by sanctity. At barely four years old, she made a vow of lifelong chastity to Jesus. Remarkably, she later admitted that at the time, she did not yet understand the full meaning of the vow. Even more astonishing is what Jesus revealed to her in adulthood: that the vow had been inspired by Him. He said to her, "I chose you to be my bride, and when you made your vow of chastity, we pledged mutual faithfulness. It was I who prompted you to do it before the world could occupy your heart in any way."

From that moment on, her heart belonged wholly to God.

"It was enough for someone to say that God would be offended," she wrote, "and that made me instantly stop and turn away from whatever I was about to do."

Elsewhere she recalls, "Whenever I wanted to join in my companions' games, I always felt something calling me, drawing me aside to some little corner, giving me no rest until I followed that prompting."

Holy *from always* and *for always*—so her confessors would later describe her. They attest that Margaret Mary remained free from grave sin throughout her life, preserving the purity of her baptismal grace.

TOWARD THE CONVENT

Margaret was eight years old when her father died. After his death, several of his female relatives—her paternal grandmother, Jeanne Dalaroche; her aunt, Benoit Alacoque; and her grandaunt, Benoit de Meulin—moved into the family home. Believing themselves the rightful heirs of the wealthy notary, they treated his widow and children like servants. Margaret endured countless humiliations under their rule. They sought to control every aspect of her life, even dictating when she could leave or return home. By

FRANCE

contrast, a convent must have seemed a small paradise. The situation changed only when her eldest brother came of age, reclaimed the property, and restored the family to their home.

As if that suffering were not enough, Margaret also endured a long and painful illness during her youth. For four years, she was bedridden. "I couldn't walk," she wrote. "My bones were piercing my skin." When she was miraculously healed through the intercession of the Blessed Mother, the desire for religious life began to take root in her heart.

That desire was fulfilled when she was twenty-four. In May 1671, she entered the Order of the Visitation in Paray-le-Monial, just thirty kilometers from her hometown.

Burning Heart of Jesus, stained-glass fragment.

Claude de la Colombière, spiritual director of St. Margaret Mary Alacoque, apostle of the Sacred Heart of Jesus.

Stained glass from the Cathedral in Covington (Kentucky, USA).

➤ *Armand Cambon,* Vision of Margaret Mary Alacoque, *Cathedral of Notre-Dame de l'Assomption (Montauban, France).*

Though family and friends had encouraged her to join the Ursulines—where she had studied as a child—Jesus revealed that He wished her to enter a community under the Blessed Mother's protection.

It was behind the cloister walls that Margaret began to perceive the supernatural more clearly. Her revelations emerged from the context of her religious formation, which centered above all on obedience.

From her earliest months in the convent, she began to encounter Jesus regularly. Most of these revelations were closely connected to adoration of the Blessed Sacrament and reception of Holy Communion.

ALWAYS PRESENT

In time, the visions became only an added grace, for Margaret began to sense the continual presence of Jesus beside her. "From then on," she wrote, "He was always with me in the form of the Crucified, or the *Ecce Homo* [the Scourged One], or bearing His cross." She adds, "I saw and felt Him near me, and heard His voice far better than if it were through my bodily senses."

Of one such encounter, she writes, "I am unable to express it. I can only say that He adorned me and treated me like His bride on Mount Tabor"—that is, He allowed her to share in His glory, the same glory revealed on that holy mountain during His earthly life.

REJECTED

For Margaret, convent life often resembled Purgatory. And indeed, that is what it became for her: a place of purification, preparing her for full union with God. She was misunderstood by the

➤ Sacred Heart of Jesus, *mosaic in the apse of the Basilica of the Sacred Heart (Paris, France).*

other sisters, ridiculed, and scorned. They mocked her, humiliated her, and treated her as slow or incapable—even in the simplest tasks. Margaret never tried to explain that many of her mishaps were caused by the devil: objects knocked from her hands, sudden stumbles and falls. Who would have believed her?

Her suffering was compounded by fragile health, which often confined her to the infirmary for months at a time. Even the superior doubted her fitness for religious life. No one believed her visions were genuine; some suspected demonic possession. At one point, the prioress demanded proof: Jesus must restore Margaret's health for six months to show the visions were not from the devil.

Shrine of St. Margaret Mary Alacoque and St. Claude de la Colombière, apse and front of the basilica (Paray-le-Monial, France).

1673

➤ *Veneration of the relics of St. Margaret Mary Alacoque (Valladolid, Spain).*

The Lord healed her immediately. On another occasion, He was asked to prove she could endure the austerities of convent life. Each time, Christ "obediently" gave the sign required.

The first ten years of her religious life were marked by trial and humiliation. "Religious life is a purgatory," Margaret confessed. In the closing lines of her sixty-four-page autobiography, she writes:

> *A purgatory of humiliations and shame in which my sufferings were indescribable. Yet I always felt a deep peace, as though nothing could take it from me, even though inwardly I was often shaken—either by my passions or by my Enemy. He tried every effort, yet he never prevailed.*

Elsewhere in her memoirs, she writes: "I let Him act, surrendering to Him. Life is for me such a heavy cross that my only consolation is the vision of the reign of the Heart of my glorified Savior."

Only in 1683 did her circumstances begin to improve.

A HEART AFLAME

In December 1673, Jesus again appeared to Margaret—this time in a revelation

➤ *Stained glass of the Revelation of the Sacred Heart of Jesus, Church of St. John the Baptist (New York, New York).*

Fresco depicting Margaret Mary Alacoque, Church of Our Lady of the Sacred Heart in Piazza Navona (Rome, Italy).

of extraordinary intimacy. He invited her to take the place of St. John at His side during the Last Supper and allowed her to rest her head upon His Heart. There, He revealed to her the marvels of His love, assuring her that He wished these wonders to be made known to the whole world. He told her that He had chosen her to proclaim them, and that all she had experienced up to that point had been preparation for this mission. Everything that would follow, He said, would serve the fulfillment of God's plan.

During this revelation, Jesus showed her His Heart, aflame with divine fire, and said: "My divine Heart is so inflamed with love for mankind that it can no longer contain these blazing flames within My breast. It desires to pour them out through you and enrich humanity with My treasures."

In all the revelations given to Margaret, this was the central theme: His Heart, His infinite love, the tragedy that so few turn to it, and the mystery that man, created by God, cannot be happy until he accepts his Creator's love and is set ablaze by it in return.

At that moment, Margaret writes,

> *He asked me for my heart, and I begged Him to take it. He did so and placed it within His glorified Heart, where I saw mine as but a tiny atom being consumed in that great furnace; then He took it out as a burning flame in the shape of a heart and put it back where He had taken it from.*

A TEST

Human beings are always free—even in the face of God. So one time, Jesus, wanting the right to claim her entire life, presented Margaret Mary with two paths. Let's read her notes:

> *This one Love of my soul showed Himself to me, holding in one hand the picture of the happiest life imaginable for a religious: a life of peace, filled with consolations both interior and exterior, together with perfect health, the applause and respect of others, and many other things agreeable to nature. In the other hand He held the image of a poor, wretched life, continually crucified by all manner of humiliations, scorn, and hardship, especially suffering in body and mind. He offered me these two pictures, saying: "Choose, my daughter, whichever pleases you more. I will grant you the same graces on either path."*
>
> *Falling at His feet to adore Him, I answered: "O my Lord, I desire nothing but You, and I am content with whatever choice You make for me."*
>
> *Jesus chose the better option for her—the second path. Margaret,*

trembling with dread, said yes. Her body recoiled at the thought of suffering, but her heart remained at peace.

We are not surprised. We know from accounts of the early martyrs that they, too, found peace even in the face of anguish.

Afterward, Margaret heard these words: "God can, when He wills, draw His glory even from our smallest actions," and Jesus added: "Great graces are often joined to what seems to us of little importance."

THE DAY OF DEPARTURE

Such was Margaret's life — marked by trials, illness, and seemingly humble tasks. She pulled weeds in the garden, assisted the infirmarian in the clinic, and swept the corridors. It is true that near the end of her life, the prioress appointed her assistant and novice mistress. But by then, Margaret regarded every task as equal in worth.

Suddenly, she fell ill once more. This time, the disease advanced rapidly.

Her notes do not extend to this final period. We do not know whether her superior again asked Jesus to heal her, or whether Margaret had been told by the Lord that He was already waiting for her at the threshold of eternity. Her hidden spiritual life in those final days remains unknown. We learn only from her sisters that Margaret Mary Alacoque died shortly after receiving the last sacraments.

Faithful from around the world entrust their intentions to the holy visionary. Relics of St. Margaret Mary Alacoque in the National Shrine of the Sacred Heart (Makati, Philippines).

Her final words were: "I need nothing but God and to lose myself in the Heart of Jesus." And then she passed into the eternity she had long longed for.

It was October 17, 1690.

SOMETHING RETURNS IN 1929

One might well end here with Margaret's own words: "You know enough. Walk faithfully, cheerfully, and willingly by the light God gives you." Yet the revelations of Paray-le-Monial are not fully exhausted. One more aspect calls for reflection.

It is rare for a revelation to "return" after many decades, as though Heaven were reminding us of what had already been said. But that is precisely what happened with the message given to Margaret Mary: it reappeared, from another angle, in 1929. That year, the Blessed Mother appeared to Sister Lúcia, one of the visionaries of Fátima, and requested the consecration of Russia to her Immaculate Heart. She warned of grave consequences if her request were ignored, and added pointedly: "They will regret it, like the king of France... but it will be too late."

What was she referring to?

In 1689, Margaret Mary had made various efforts to communicate a divine request to King Louis XIV, the so-called Sun King. Jesus asked that the king establish public devotion to His Sacred Heart, consecrate both himself and the nation to it, build a church in its honor to house an image of His Heart, and request that the pope approve a Mass formulary in its name.

The message did reach Louis XIV. But he received it with indifference—a culpable negligence. Neither he nor his successors fulfilled the request. Only one exception stands out: Queen Marie Leszczyńska, the wife of Louis XV, who had a chapel built at Versailles in honor of the Most Sacred Heart of Jesus.

Exactly one hundred years after the Savior's appeal, the French Revolution broke out. The monarchy fell. Louis XVI, the last king of France, was guillotined on January 21, 1793. Even his last-ditch vow—made in prison—to consecrate himself, his family, and his kingdom to the Sacred Heart if he were restored to the throne came too late. He left prison not for freedom, but for the scaffold.

One hundred years had passed. Heaven's patience was spent.

In her apparition to Sister Lúcia, the Blessed Mother recalled the message once given at Paray-le-Monial—a warning of what follows when God's appeals are disregarded. In this light, the revelations entrusted to Margaret Mary Alacoque take on a renewed and solemn significance.

Flag of Canadian Catholics used by French Catholics until the 1950s. In the center, the Burning Heart of Jesus; in the corners—royal lilies.

Personal act of consecration to the Heart of Jesus written by St. Margaret Mary Alacoque.

Patch of the Sacred Heart of the French Royal Catholic Army. Insignia of royalist insurgents during the Vendée Uprising, 1793.

2
"IT SEEMS TO ME..."

1663

Place of Apparition:
Mercatello, Città di Castello, Italy
Date and Place of Birth:
December 27, 1660, Mercatello, Italy
Date and Place of Death:
July 19, 1727, Città di Castello, Italy
Visionary as laywoman and nun (Capuchin Poor Clares)
Beatification:
June 17, 1802 (Pius VII)
Canonization:
May 26, 1839 (Gregory XVI)
Liturgical memorial: July 9
Works: Diary

2

"IT SEEMS TO ME..."

VERONICA GIULIANI, 1663

One of the greatest mystical figures in the history of the Church—compared to St. Teresa of Ávila and St. Francis of Assisi—yet still shrouded in obscurity. Could this be part of God's design, that the knowledge of her experiences remain reserved for a few chosen souls? From a human standpoint, it seems unjust. Her account of God is rich, profound, and deeply inspiring. Her spiritual experiences not only reach the highest heights of mystical theology but also echo and deepen those of earlier great mystics.

Collegiate Church of St. Peter and St. Paul in the hometown of Veronica Giuliani (Mercatello, Italy).

The revelations given to Veronica add many previously unknown details to the mystical biography of St. Catherine of Siena—that saint who received a ring from Christ, invisible to the world. Why, then, is Veronica so little known? Is it mere unpopularity? Or might we consider a more sobering possibility: that the ruler of this world has had a hand in suppressing attention to her witness?

What we do know of her life comes from a remarkable source. At the command of her confessor, Veronica began keeping a spiritual diary in April 1693—and continued for the next thirty-four years. Her final entries date from 1727. The result is monumental: an autobiography that fills an entire bookshelf, totaling more than 22,000 pages.

A GREAT AUTOBIOGRAPHY

Writing the diary was, for Veronica, a great penance. Yet she knew it was the Will of Christ. Her certainty came not only from her obedience to spiritual directors and religious superiors—obedience which, for her, always expressed the Will of God—but also from two explicit promises the Savior made to her. She wrote: "The Lord made me understand that I am to write down everything, because He wills it. These writings will benefit many souls. He wants it for the good of the whole of Christendom." And she records His words to her: "I want everything to be revealed. These are My works, My gifts, My special graces, and they will be for My glory."

It is no surprise, then, that the devil often sought to hinder her. He would hide or break her pencils and at times even attack her physically. She recounts one episode: "After Matins, when I wanted to do my act of obedience and write for fifteen minutes, suddenly I was struck in the eye and heard a voice saying: 'Cursed writings!'"

This is characteristic of how the devil acts. As with many revelations, so too with works written under divine inspiration: if he cannot prevent the visions themselves or persuade the seer to abandon the task, he resorts to subtler deceptions. He may assume the appearance of Christ or

The spiritual diary of St. Veronica consists of forty-two volumes, twenty-two thousand pages, and fills an entire bookshelf. It was written over thirty-four years.

➤ *Mercatello, the hometown of St. Veronica Giuliani, located by the Metauro River (Italy).*

➤ *Città di Castello—the city where the great saint passed away (Umbria, Italy).*

the Blessed Virgin, speaking in a language outwardly pious but inwardly false, aiming to seduce the soul into error. He casts his net subtly, and if the visionary is not vigilant, the deception can be fatal. A favored soul may begin to believe herself above others—"since others do not receive such lofty experiences"—or reject obedience to the Church—"since I speak with God directly." In such cases, the devil has already prevailed.

When even this fails—as it did with Veronica—he tries another tactic: to obscure the message. He clouds the revelation in obscurity, distracts with superficial details, or buries it beneath what the world considers "more important." He distorts, minimizes, and misleads—anything to keep attention away from what God has made known.

Is this why the revelations granted to Veronica remain largely unknown or misunderstood? If they were not meant for us, why did Our Lady intervene in the final years of Veronica's life to ensure their completion? For the last fifteen years, when Veronica was so weakened by illness that she could hardly concentrate, the Blessed Mother herself helped her continue. The mystic testifies that an image of the Sorrowful Mother in her cell came alive, and that Mary personally dictated the final chapters of the diary.

There is even a visible sign of this transition: Veronica suddenly begins to write about herself in the second person, as though another were describing her life.

CHOSEN IN CHILDHOOD

Veronica was born on December 27, 1660, in Mercatello, and baptized with the name Ursula. She was blessed with a saintly mother, Benedetta Mancini, whose influence left a profound mark on her life. A woman of deep devotion, Benedetta would read to Ursula and her four sisters the lives of the saints and martyrs. Through these stories, the young Ursula's heart was stirred with a longing to imitate them. But she chose perhaps the most demanding model: St. Rose of Lima. From an early age, she yearned to suffer for love of Jesus as Rose had, and she began to embrace severe penances.

Was her choice of Rose merely personal, or was it inspired from above? All signs point to a heavenly prompting. Even as a small child, Ursula began to experience mystical graces. When she was just three or four years old, she saw the Child Jesus in the garden as she was picking flowers. He spoke to her for the first time: "I am the true flower." From that moment, her heart burned with the desire to find and offer herself to that most beautiful of blossoms.

At the age of seven, as her mother lay dying, she consecrated each of her five children to one of the Five Holy Wounds of Christ. Ursula was dedicated to His pierced side—a mystery that would later become the very source of her most profound mystical experiences.

FIRST HOLY COMMUNION

At the age of ten, Ursula made her First Holy Communion. She later described the experience in vivid, heartfelt terms: "I believe I remember that, as I received the Sacred Host, I felt a great warmth that enflamed me. Especially my heart was on

St. Veronica Giuliani, painting from the Capuchin Poor Clares convent where the saint spent her entire life.

Façade of the Cathedral of Saints Florido and Amanzio (Città di Castello, Italy).

fire.... I was convinced that the Lord had truly come to me, and from my whole heart I said to Him: 'My God, the time has come for You to possess me completely. I belong only to You, and You alone do I desire.' I believe I remember that He replied: 'You are mine, and I am all yours.'"

From that day forward, she understood that she was called to the consecrated life. Reflecting on that moment, she exclaimed: "O God! What joy! I cannot explain what I felt. I only know that a burning desire to become a nun took hold of me, and I couldn't wait for the day I would be espoused to God."

THE CAPUCHIN POOR CLARES

At seventeen, Ursula entered the Capuchin Poor Clare convent in Città di Castello, Umbria. Bishop Sebastiani, who presided at her admission ceremony, addressed the sisters with prophetic words: "Preserve this girl like a precious treasure, for she will become a great saint." He also gave her a new name: "From now on your name shall be Sister Veronica—meaning *true* and *exceptional*—referring to you and to God alone."

She was to become a "true image" of Christ. Indeed, the name *Veronica* derives from *vera icona—true icon*. And so it came to pass: she would bear the likeness of Christ. Yet that likeness, strikingly, was also suffused with the qualities of Mary.

Not long after, she received the religious habit. On her Clothing Day, she experienced a vision in which she found herself among the saints in Heaven. "I recall," she writes, "that the Lord welcomed me warmly. He said to everyone there, 'Now she is ours.' Then He turned to me and asked, 'Tell me, what do you want?'"

Veronica recounts her response: "I remember I asked Him for three graces. First, the ability to live faithfully according

Relic of the robe of St. Veronica Giuliani.

Veronica mystically experienced the Passion of the Lord and, like her Seraphic Father St. Francis, received the stigmata. Because of the meaning of her name (True Icon) and her countless visions, photographers chose her as their patron.

Fresco on the façade of the church in Spello (Umbria, Italy).

to the state I had chosen. Second, never to depart from His holy will. Third, that He would always keep me with Him on the cross. He promised all these things, and said to me: 'I have chosen you for great things, but you must suffer much out of love for Me.'"

JESUS HANDS OVER HIS CROWN

One of the most significant days in Veronica's mystical life was April 4, 1681. She had long prayed for this grace. "I recall," she writes, "that from the beginning, when I became a nun, I always begged the Lord to let me share in some way in the suffering of His Passion."

That year, on Good Friday, her prayer was answered. "It seemed I had a vision. The Lord appeared to me, covered in wounds and crowned with thorns. I felt sorrow as He felt sorrow, and at the same time a deep

Pope Gregory XVI canonized Veronica on May 26, 1839.

contrition for my sins. I was torn between two extremes: His infinite love and my ingratitude. It seemed I said to Him: 'My Lord, enough of my ingratitude and sins. Now I want to love You. Come, O Lord, give me that crown, so that these thorns might speak in my place of how greatly I desire to love You.'"

Then, she writes, "The Lord drew closer ... took the crown from His head and spoke some words I cannot remember. He set it on mine, and it seemed to me I felt the thorns piercing into my lips, ears, entire head, eyes, temples, and brain. The pain was terrible. I collapsed to the ground as though dead. The Lord raised me up and said: 'As long as you live, you will feel these pains—more or less, depending on My will.' I collapsed again, and He raised me. I collapsed a third time..."

Following this experience, her head became so swollen that the sisters brought her to a doctor. She underwent several painful procedures, but no one could determine the cause of her condition.

THE ARRIVAL OF CATHERINE OF SIENA

Once, Veronica received a striking and unusual revelation. She saw Jesus enthroned, seated with the Blessed Virgin and St. Catherine of Siena. Could this have been the *Byzantine throne*—that wide, majestic seat spoken of in the book of Revelation (3:21), upon which Christ may enthrone whomever He chooses to share in His authority? Veronica perceived Mary and Catherine, the latter a mystic whose experiences we have already touched upon.

In the vision, Catherine wore a crown of thorns. The Lord removed it from her head and replaced it with a crown adorned with precious gems. Then, He placed Catherine's crown of thorns upon Veronica's head.

➤ *Cloister of the Church and former Convent of San Domenico (Città di Castello, Italy).*

Immediately, Veronica felt searing pain. In that moment, she understood: this was the same suffering Catherine had endured when she received the mystical grace of the thorn-crown. But she also knew what lay beyond it. One day, these thorns would be transformed into jewels.

It is a mysterious and compelling image. One cannot help but wonder: to whom might Jesus one day appear with Veronica at His side, offering *her* crown of thorns?

For now, we do not know.

A VISION OF THREE GROUPS OF PEOPLE

Veronica was granted many supernatural visions. Not only of Heaven, nor solely of intimate conversations with Jesus, Mary, and the saints. She also saw Purgatory—and even glimpses of Hell, at times presented to her by the devil himself.

➤ *Vision of St. Veronica Giuliani from her sanctuary in Mercatello (Marche, Italy).*

In one vision, Jesus showed her a vast plain crowded with souls bearing heavy crosses upon their backs. Their garments varied in color, but all had their faces bowed to the earth, unable to lift their eyes. These were people of every station, each burdened by suffering—for no one passes through life without a cross. Yet these souls could not lift their gaze to Heaven. Their pain had not drawn them closer to Christ but, instead, weighed them down and estranged them from Him.

Veronica was then shown a second group. These souls were clothed in white—most of them religious. Jesus appeared among them, radiant in glory. Yet only a few turned their faces toward Him. Struck by this, Veronica cried out: "I regret I do not have as many eyes as there are souls here, so that I might gaze at my Greatest Good with limitless love."

She then noticed a kind of veil between these souls and the Lord—a barrier that obscured their joy in His presence. God allowed her to understand its cause: they lacked purity of intention. Though consecrated, they remained absorbed in worldly preoccupations. Their hearts clung to things that were not God. Veronica ends this part of her account with sober clarity: "These souls are cold, and where there is cold, sin follows; where there is sin, God is offended—the Great Creator. Then ... justice ... punishment."

Finally, she saw a third group: souls so disfigured they appeared monstrous. She heard a terrible pronouncement: "For these there is no longer any mercy of Mine. They are, and forever shall be, deprived of Me."

Shocked, Veronica cried out, "O Lord, where is Your compassion? Who are they? Are they dead or alive?" The Lord allowed her to understand: they were not the dead, but the living. And she heard the awful reply: "They are those who have died to grace."

Devotional image from the early 20th century depicting St. Veronica Giuliani.

MYSTICAL ESPOUSALS

Shortly before Lent in 1694, Veronica received another remarkable vision. She saw Jesus enthroned, with St. Catherine of Siena at His side and surrounded by many angels. The Lord said to her: "Behold Catherine, My beloved bride. I give her to you as your companion, so that she may intercede between Me and you." Taking Catherine by the hand, He showed Veronica the radiant ring on the saint's finger, sparkling with divine light. Veronica understood then that she, too, would receive a spousal ring on Easter.

On Easter Sunday, the moment she received Holy Communion, she heard a heavenly choir singing: "Come, bride of Christ."

And so it was. On Easter Sunday, the moment she received Holy Communion, she heard a heavenly choir singing: "Come, bride of Christ." Falling into ecstasy, she beheld Jesus in all His glory, His wounds shining like precious gems. He sat upon a throne of gold and jewels, radiant beyond description. Then Catherine appeared, clothed in a splendid mantle. Veronica fixed her eyes on the Lord and wrote:

> *He was so beautiful that I cannot describe it. His hands, feet, and side—His wounds—were so dazzling that they appeared not as wounds but as exquisite gems. Only the wound in His side seemed open, with rays shining out like the sun. Inside that holy wound was the ring I was to wear.*

The visionary gazes at Jesus and notes: "He was so beautiful that I cannot describe it. His hands, feet, and side—His wounds—were so dazzling that they appeared not as wounds but as exquisite gems."

She was careful in her account, repeatedly writing, *"It seems to me..."*—as if to guard against presumption. She described how Jesus raised His right hand in blessing and said, "Come, bride of Christ." Once more, Veronica appeared as the spiritual heiress of Catherine of Siena. The Blessed Mother then took Catherine's Dominican cloak and placed it around Veronica. It was adorned with jewels that sparkled with every color of the rainbow—a symbol, Veronica understood, of the virtues.

At that moment, Jesus removed the ring from His open side and placed it into Mary's hands. Veronica saw it clearly: it was of gold, covered in enamel, and bore the name *Jesus*. Then, the Savior took it from Mary and placed it on Veronica's finger.

She was now His bride.

Whether the ring remained visible to her, as Catherine's had been to Catherine alone, we do not know. But this much is certain: from that moment onward, Veronica felt herself wholly enveloped by the love of Jesus. And that, to her, was far more precious than any outward sign.

TWO WOUNDS

The crown of thorns that tormented her until death, the ring that brought her joy—did the latter come to ease the former? No. Veronica did not seek relief from suffering; she embraced it. For her, suffering was not merely agony—it was joy, it was fullness, it was the path to union with her Bridegroom.

That union mattered more to her than anything else. Those who look for a balance

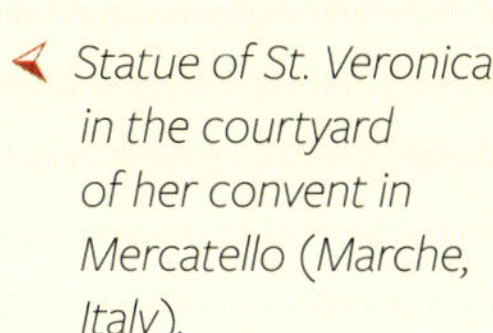

Statue of St. Veronica in the courtyard of her convent in Mercatello (Marche, Italy).

between her pain and her consolation will not find it. Her life was not shaped by alternation, but by convergence: pain *was* consolation, suffering *was* love. One sees this clearly in what occurred on Christmas Eve of 1696, when Veronica received another "unceasing suffering": a wound in her heart. In her diary, she wrote:

> *I recall that the Child Jesus held a bow and arrow in His hands, and it seemed He shot it toward my heart.*

Why would the Lord, who by now appeared to her most often as the Crucified Christ, return in the form of the Child—the *true flower* of her childhood visions? Because it was the Child Jesus who was to begin the work. He gave her a suffering mingled with sweetness, a pain that was also love. But this was only the beginning. Soon the adult Christ would inflict another, deeper wound.

Of that first wound, she wrote: "I felt immense pain. When I regained my senses, I saw that my heart had been pierced and was bleeding. I cannot express what the Lord communicated to me at that moment. I only know that I experienced intimate union with Him, and He gave me to understand that this wound was nothing

"Suddenly I beheld her as though suspended in the air, rapt in ecstasy. Before her stood an angel, filled with light, holding a golden arrow, which he thrust into Teresa's heart. She became like a fiery furnace consumed by love."

compared to the one He was about to inflict."

The wound bled for several days before closing—and it would reopen again and again.

The second wound came soon thereafter, on March 8, 1697, while she was praying before the crucifix. She writes: "When I was before Him, very close, it seemed He took His right hand from the cross and, holding the large nail in that hand, pierced my heart with it. I felt great pain, but soon came to my senses."

AND ALSO TERESA OF ÁVILA...

On one occasion, Jesus allowed Veronica to witness how He had once wounded the heart of St. Teresa of Ávila. She wrote: "Suddenly I beheld her as though suspended in the air, rapt in ecstasy. Before her stood an angel, filled with light, holding a golden arrow, which he thrust into Teresa's heart. She became like a fiery furnace consumed by love.... I believe the Lord gave me to understand that when she was thus wounded by love, she detached herself entirely from everything so thoroughly that she wanted nothing more to do with the world. She was totally removed from all and everyone, alone in God, with no other thought but Him and her soul."

Through this vision, Veronica understood—without doubt—that her own thoughts, her will, her desires must be fixed entirely on one object: God alone.

THE STIGMATA

There is no equilibrium in Veronica's life between suffering and consolation. For her, the two were not counterweights but converging realities. On Good Friday, April 5, 1697, her suffering reached a new and final intensity: she received the stigmata. She recorded the moment in her diary: "All at once, I saw five shining rays coming

Buildings of the austere convent of the Poor Clares by the Metauro.

from His wounds toward me. I watched as they turned into little flames. Four of them contained nails, and the fifth a spear, golden and aflame, which pierced my heart. The nails penetrated my hands and feet."

What she had once seen in the vision of St. Teresa—her heart pierced by the flaming arrow of divine love—Veronica now experienced in her own body. The symbolic had become literal. She was no longer merely a contemplative of the Passion; she had been drawn into it, made to bear its marks as the Bride of the Crucified.

PASSING INTO ETERNITY

Beginning in 1720, the Blessed Virgin herself began to dictate Veronica's diary. Then, seven years later—on the feast of the Annunciation, March 25, 1727—Mary instructed her to bring the spiritual autobiography to a close. When Veronica wrote the final sentence, the Blessed Mother said simply, *"Fa punto"*—"Put a period."

On June 6 of that same year, while receiving Holy Communion, Veronica suffered a stroke. For the next thirty-three days, she endured a kind of purgatory on earth, as God purified her of every last trace of sin in preparation for immediate union with Himself. Remarkably, what allowed her to die on July 9, 1727, was that—at dawn that day—her confessor finally gave her permission to depart this life. Only then was she able to go.

Her final words were: *I have found Love, Love has let Himself be seen!*

Veronica turns out to be the heir to the mission of St. Catherine. For the Mother of God covers Veronica with the mantle of the Dominican from Siena.

Veronica died on July 9, 1727. That day at dawn, she received permission from her confessor to die. Then she was finally able to depart. Her last words were: "I have found Love, Love has let Himself be seen!"

3
A MAN OF NOBLE APPEARANCE

3

A MAN OF NOBLE APPEARANCE

JOHN BOSCO, 1824

Place of Apparition: Turin, Italy
Date and Place of Birth: August 16, 1815, Becchi, Italy
Date and Place of Death: January 31, 1888, Turin, Italy
Visionary as layman and religious (Society of St. Francis de Sales)
Beatification: June 2, 1929 (Pius XI)
Canonization: April 1, 1934 (Pius XI)
Liturgical memorial: January 31
Works: Spiritual Guidelines, Dreams of Don Bosco

Here is another figure—truly extraordinary—veiled in layers of legend, yet too often overlooked where it matters most. Don Bosco is rightly regarded as a genius in the field of education, though his influence is usually confined to the formation of children and adolescents. And yet, all signs suggest that Christ intended the methods shown to this priest of Turin to serve a far broader purpose—one that concerns the Church in her entirety.

Is this not confirmed by the correspondence between St. John Paul II and the Fatima visionary, Sister Lúcia? Their letters suggest that, had the Church embraced the charism of Don Bosco, the apparitions at Fatima might never have been necessary. The peace promised by Our Lady would already have been secured, and the "errors" of which she warned might never have taken root.

"The Lord has many ways to reveal His will," Don Bosco often said. He knew this firsthand, for the revelations granted to him were extraordinary—utterly unique, even among the long history of Christian mysticism. They astonish not only in content but in their originality: more surprising than Jesus appearing as a child to lead a mystic by the hand, or as a beggar at the door, or than being transported in spirit to witness the Passion of the Lord.

Don Bosco received many such revelations. Some were personal, some typical of the mystical tradition, and

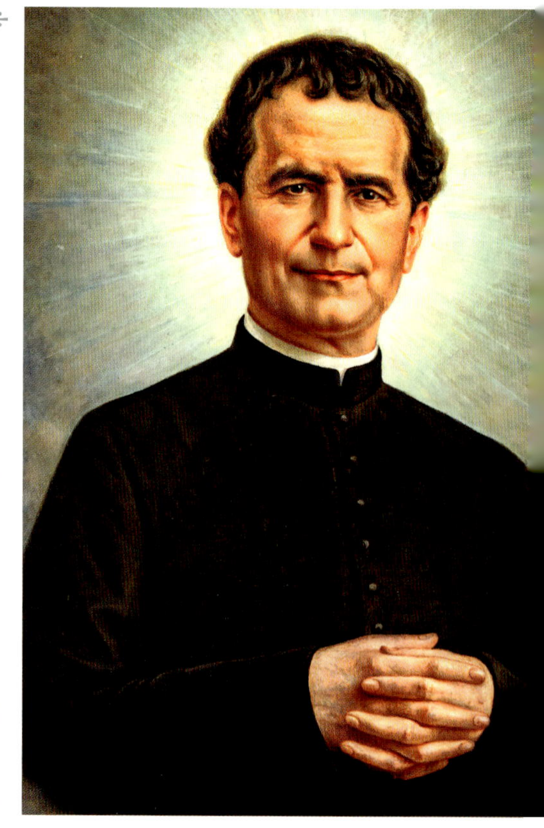

John, already as a child dedicated to Mary, carried from his family home a deep religiosity and devotion to the Blessed Mother.

ITALY

Main altar of the Basilica of Our Lady Help of Christians in Turin with an image of the Virgin Mary painted at the request of Father John.

Margaret, mother of St. John Bosco.

others wholly unusual. He would see departed friends and speak with them at length—even while traveling—where they appeared before him "as alive." His ongoing dialogue with Luigi Comollo (†1839) about the possibility of heavenly visions—mentioned at the outset of this book—remains a striking example.

But Don Bosco also received a different kind of revelation—those that resemble the parables in the Gospels. These are impossible to omit, just as one cannot recount the life of Christ without His parables. Like the Lord's teachings on the Kingdom of Heaven, Don Bosco's "dream visions" may seem at first quaint

1824

➤ *House in Becchi, near Turin, where John Bosco was born in 1815.*

▲ *Plaque commemorating John Bosco's stay in the seminary in Chieri, where the saint studied from 1835 to 1841.*

▼ *St. John Bosco was canonized by Pius XI on Easter 1934.*

or even childlike. But their meaning is anything but naive. In them we find divine messages, adapted with exquisite care to the imagination and understanding of the young.

These dreams are vivid. They are simple. And they stir the soul.

WHO IS THIS UNUSUAL VISIONARY?

John Bosco was born on August 16, 1815, in Becchi, a small village in northern Italy. He was only two years old when his father, Francis, died, leaving his mother, Margaret, to raise the family alone. From a young age, John's vocation to serve children and youth was already taking shape. Even as a small boy, he was drawn to the joy and energy of the young. Observing the popularity of traveling jugglers and street performers, he taught himself their tricks and acrobatics. Before long, he was gathering crowds in his hometown with his own magic shows—delighting his audience while weaving in prayers, hymns, and simple "sermons" echoing what he had heard in church.

It is no surprise, then, that as a priest he devoted himself entirely to the care of lost and neglected youth. His whole life—until his death in 1888—was offered for them. And through it all, Jesus guided him with countless revelations, sustaining his mission with divine light and extraordinary grace.

"INDIRECT REVELATIONS"

We might say that Jesus used John Bosco as a voice to speak directly to the neglected youth of northern Italy. His revelations were, in a sense, *indirect*—a term we will return to when we consider the visions of Fr. Leopold Mandić. For the saint of Turin did not receive visions solely for himself, but primarily for the young people entrusted to his care. These revelations were directed to them—concrete, vivid, and always with a singular aim: the salvation of each soul in his Oratory.

What was this "Oratory"? Beginning in 1844, Don Bosco began gathering at-risk boys and young men in Turin. He provided them not only with food and shelter, but with vocational training, spiritual formation, and above all, a path toward moral and religious renewal.

When he shared his visions—what he called his "dreams"—with the boys, it was never to draw attention to himself. On the contrary, he deliberately downplayed their significance, so as not to seem self-important. But he shared them because they were meant for *them*. These dreams spoke to their inner lives, warned them of danger, offered encouragement, and revealed paths of conversion.

Yet they were also revelations for him. They gave him insight into the soul of each boy, into his struggles, temptations, and spiritual condition. In that sense, each dream had two "subjects": Don Bosco, and the youth. Or perhaps it is more accurate to say that the Oratory itself—the living community of boys and their father and guide—was the collective recipient of these divine communications.

DREAMS OR HEAVENLY VISIONS?

At the end of the day, Don Bosco would share these "dreams" with his boys—usually after evening prayers, during what became known as the *goodnight talk*. In the great hall of the Oratory, with hundreds of young men gathered, you could hear a pin drop when Don Bosco began to speak. His voice, calm and fatherly, held them spellbound, especially when he recounted one of his vivid, mysterious dreams.

"Don Bosco's name and his dreams go together," wrote his earliest biographer, Fr. John Baptist Lemoyne. "If ever they were omitted, the thousands of his former students would cry out: 'But what about his dreams?'"

"I WILL GIVE YOU A TEACHER"

He had his first "dream-like vision" as a child of nine. Suddenly, the ordinary surroundings receded, replaced by another reality just as tangible to all his senses. He was back near his family home, amid a crowd of rough boys playing on a vast field. They were shouting and cursing freely. Startled by their foul language, the young Bosco tried to quiet them with shouts and fists. This got him nowhere.

Then Christ appeared. John saw a man whose face shone so brightly that he could not meet His gaze. The stranger called him by name and said: "Not with blows, but with kindness and love must you win over these friends of yours. Tell them immediately about the ugliness of sin and the value of virtue."

Don Bosco later recalled the rest of this vision:

> *Hardly knowing what I was saying, I answered,*
>
> *"Who are you that you order me to do the impossible?"*
>
> *"Precisely because it seems impossible to you, you must make it possible by obedience and by gaining knowledge."*
>
> *"Where and how shall I gain this knowledge?"*
>
> *"I will give you a Teacher," He replied, "under whose guidance you will become wise. Without her, all wisdom is foolishness."*

At that moment, Mary appeared, dressed in a robe that seemed woven of shining stars. She took him by the hand and said, "Look." He looked and saw that the rowdy boys had vanished, and in their place was a menagerie of goats, dogs, cats, bears, and other wild animals.

> *"Here is your field," said the Lady. "This is where you must work. Become humble, steadfast, and strong, and what you will see happen with these animals is what you must do for my children."*

He looked again and saw the wild beasts change into gentle lambs, frolicking around the Man and the Lady. Moved and confused, in his dream he began to sob, asking the Lady to speak more plainly. She laid her hand on his head and said, "In due time you will understand."

Exceptional care and devotion to youth made St. John Bosco the patron of young people, pupils, and students.

The bronze statue standing today in front of the basilica depicts St. John Bosco surrounded by his protégés.

Statue of Mary Help of Christians.

Relics of St. John Bosco exposed for public veneration.

The oratory founded by Father John served poor and abandoned youth as a place for meetings, games, and learning.

Thirteen years later, he did—again through a revelation.

This first vision is unusual in that Jesus appears only to inform him that He is yielding the stage to Mary. Mary would be Don Bosco's principal *Guide* (as he would call her) in these dream-visions. Jesus steps aside to let His Mother fill that role. Only at rare times in Don Bosco's visions does Christ take center stage. Typically, Mary is the leading figure.

THE VISION REPEATED

When John was twenty-two, he once more beheld the vision he had seen at age nine. Again, God placed him in another dimension: Bosco found himself looking at the valley below the Sussambrino farm, where he was on holiday. The place suddenly transformed into a large city, crowded with boys cursing and shouting. As before, he ran at them in anger, threatened them, and used his fists—until at last he ended up bruised and humiliated.

Then Christ appeared, told him to return, and introduced him to a noble Lady: "This is My Mother. Ask her." Mary looked on him with love and said: "If you wish to win over these youngsters, you must not confront them with aggression but with persuasion and kindness." And just as before, the rough boys turned into lambs, and Jesus indicated that Don Bosco was to be their shepherd.

A MEETING WITH THE SHEPHERD

In some visions, Mary remains the constant guide; in a few others, Jesus appears as a shepherd of sheep. He is Don Bosco's model, for in many dream-scenes, Don Bosco himself takes on the role of shepherd. Let us consider one of these *fairy tale-like* revelations—visions that often include childlike imagery—where Jesus the Shepherd announces that He

will show Don Bosco the flock entrusted to him. Don Bosco told his boys:

> *He led me to where there were thousands of lambs so emaciated they could barely walk. The soil was barren, dry, and sandy, without a single blade of grass or any running stream.*

When Don Bosco asked for an explanation, the Shepherd replied: "This dry, barren place is where God's word is not heard and people seek only worldly pleasures. The sheep are adults, the lambs are youth—and to them God is sending Don Bosco. This desolate land depicts the state of sin." Don Bosco continues:

> *While I stood listening and watching, suddenly I was again amazed. All those lambs changed shape. Rising onto their hind legs, they assumed human form. I went closer to see if I recognized anyone. They were all boys from the Oratory.*

TO TRANSFORM THEM BY GRACE...

But the vision didn't end. Jesus said, "Come with me, and you shall see more." Don Bosco recounts:

> *He led me to the far end of the valley, surrounded by gentle hills and enclosed by a lush hedge, into an enormous green meadow filled with*

The sanctuary built by St. John Bosco serves as the spiritual motherhouse of the Salesian work.

Façade of the Basilica of Our Lady Help of Christians, consecrated in 1868, in Turin.

1824

John Bosco, in addition to the Salesian Congregation, also founded the Institute of the Daughters of Mary Help of Christians and the Salesian Family.

The holy priest focused all his attention on lost young people. He dedicated his life to them. And Jesus helped him through hundreds of apparitions.

> *sweet-smelling grasses, wildflowers, fresh groves, and streams of crystal-clear water. There I found another multitude of young people. They were all joyful, wearing garments woven from wildflowers.*
>
> *"These shall be a great consolation for you," said my Guide.*
>
> *"And who are they?" I asked.*
>
> *"These are those who live in God's grace."*
>
> *Oh, what a sight! I can truly say I have never seen such beauty and radiance, nor could I ever have imagined such splendor. But an even greater sight lay in store.*

He continues:

> *"Come, come with me," the Shepherd told me, "and I will show you a scene that will bring you immense joy and greatly lift your spirit."*

UNTIL THEY BECOME "LIKE CHRIST"

A third vision follows, which Don Bosco again recounts to his boys:

> *He led me to yet another meadow, filled with flowers more stunning and fragrant than any I had ever seen, resembling a king's garden. There, once again, was a group of young people—though not so many. But each one was so beautiful and majestic that they surpassed those I had just left. Some of them are in the Oratory at present, some will come in the future.*
>
> *"They have preserved the lily of purity," said the Shepherd. "They are clothed in innocence alone."*
>
> *Gazing at them, I felt I was in ecstasy. Almost all wore wreaths of flowers of indescribable beauty....*

> *Their garments, so dazzlingly white, reached their feet, entwined with floral garlands matching the ones on their heads. A wondrous light emanated from those flowers, surrounding each with brilliance—and from their faces shone joy.... The loveliness of each youth multiplied itself, mirroring in the radiant, innocent faces of all the others, producing such a blaze of light that one could scarcely look at them.*

Similarly, Don Bosco as a nine-year-old could not look upon Christ. These young people, having attained holiness, had become "like Christ."

He goes on:

> *It's impossible even to imagine—let alone depict—the beauty of those young men among that ocean of glory. I approached some of*

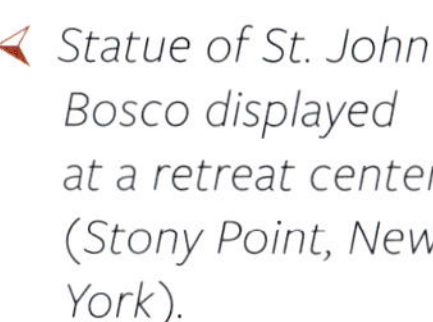
ITALY

Statue of St. John Bosco displayed at a retreat center (Stony Point, New York).

them closely. They are here, in the Oratory. And I am sure that if they could see but a tenth of their real splendor, they would be willing to face flames, be cut to pieces, to endure the harshest torments rather than lose it.

For, as the vision stressed:

Tell the boys that if they understood how precious and lovely innocence and chastity are in God's eyes, they would make every sacrifice to preserve them. Tell them not to lose heart in practicing this virtue.

Don Bosco concluded his account by saying that, enraptured by the beauty of these youths, he tried to join them—but stumbled and awoke.

A REVELATION FOR THE BOYS

"Tell the boys..." The revelation was "indirect." Jesus presented it to Don Bosco, but it was really meant for his young people. Two days after telling them of the vision, Don Bosco brought up the same "dream" again in his evening talk:

One of you asked me if he was among the innocent souls, and I replied that he was not. He also asked if his soul bore any wounds, and I answered yes.

"What do these wounds mean?" he inquired.

"Don't worry," I said, "they will heal, they'll vanish. You have no need to be ashamed of scars, any more than a soldier who fought bravely and overcame the enemy, even if he was wounded. These are glorious wounds! Yet far more glorious is the soldier who emerges from battle unscathed, for his invulnerability is the wonder of all."

Thus, with the help of these revelations, Don Bosco molded the characters of his students and placed them on the path of sainthood.

AND THERE IS THE ROSARY, TOO

We'll quote a lesser-known vision of St. John Bosco, from the Vigil of the Assumption in 1862. It took place on the meadow adjoining the courtyard where the boys were playing. Don Bosco saw a huge snake—seven or eight meters long—lying there. Mary showed it to him,

Painting from the Salesianum in Rome showing St. John Paul II and St. John Bosco as apostles of Christ.

and he, terrified, wanted to run away. But the Blessed Mother told him to stay. She needed him.

Mary took a rope in her hands and came up to Don Bosco. "Take this rope and hold it firmly," she said. "I will take the other end and, together, we will stretch it out above the serpent."

"And then?"

"Then we will drop it onto its neck."

"No! For heaven's sake!" cried Don Bosco. "Woe to us if we do that—the snake will go mad and kill us!"

"But the Guide insisted," he recalled later. "She assured me the serpent would do me no harm and reasoned with me until I complied. She lifted the rope and struck the snake's neck. It leapt and turned to bite whatever had struck it, but it entangled itself in that rope. One could say it was caught in a noose it had made for itself.

Mary shouted, 'Hold tightly! Don't let go of the rope!' She then raced off to tie the other end—holding it in her hand—to a nearby post, while I, with my portion of rope, fastened it to the window grate. Meanwhile, the snake thrashed furiously, flailing its head and powerful coils so violently that it began tearing itself apart, scattering pieces of its flesh everywhere."

Don Bosco continued:

> *Then Mary untied the rope from the post and window, rolled it up, and put it into a chest. After a moment, she opened the chest. To our amazement—mine and the boys who had run up—the rope had formed the words "Hail Mary." The*

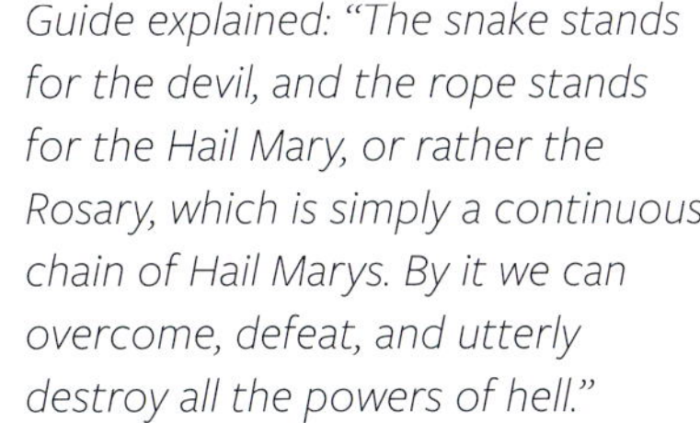

Guide explained: "The snake stands for the devil, and the rope stands for the Hail Mary, or rather the Rosary, which is simply a continuous chain of Hail Marys. By it we can overcome, defeat, and utterly destroy all the powers of hell."

That prayerful rope must be held not only by Mary, but also by human hands on earth, if it is to be a sure weapon of victory. Now we understand why Don Bosco taught the Rosary to his pupils.

HIS MOST TREASURED ONES

He died on January 31, 1888.

"I promised God that even my last breath would be for my poor boys." He remained true to that pledge. Moments before his death, his final request to his confreres concerned what had given meaning to his entire life:

> *I entrust to your care all the works God has deigned to entrust to me.... In particular, I commend to you the poor, abandoned young people who have always been the most precious treasure of my heart on earth.*

Statue of St. John Bosco in St. Peter's Basilica in the Vatican (Italy).

Relics of St. John Bosco in the cathedral in Turin (Italy).

4
LIVING WITHOUT PUBLICITY

On the previous page: Church in Parzno, where Wanda Malczewska rests.

Place of Apparition: Radom, Żytno, Parzno, Poland
Date and Place of Birth: May 15, 1822, Radom, Poland
Date and Place of Death: September 25, 1896, Parzno, Poland
Visionary as a Lay and Religious Person (Marian Friars Minor Third Order)
Beatification Process: Venerable: February 21, 2006 (Benedict XVI)
Writings: Writings of the Venerable Wanda Malczewska

Portrait of the Servant of God under the altar in Jasna Góra.

Anne Catherine Emmerich, to whom Wanda Malczewska was often compared.

4

LIVING WITHOUT PUBLICITY

WANDA MALCZEWSKA, CIRCA 1828

Some mystics believe everyone has such experiences. The supernatural world is so obvious, tangible, and personal to them that they become convinced others must experience similar mystical phenomena. They interpret the silence of others not as absence, but as a sign of universal humility and wisdom. Surely, they think, God does not wish them to speak of it—so they remain silent.

One such mystic was Wanda Malczewska, who began experiencing mystical encounters in childhood. She believed it was normal for anyone baptized and made a child of God to speak with a guardian angel or with Jesus. "In a family, you get together and talk," she reasoned—and for a child, this seemed natural. But as she grew older, she became less naïve. More than that, she noticed a change in the nature of her encounters: they became more than simple conversations. She began to have visions.

In the early 1870s, Malczewska began to witness the Passion of Christ as though it were unfolding before her eyes, as if she stood in the crowd. The seven mysterious visions she received during that time remained unknown for many years. Her contemporaries read of the apparitions of the German stigmatist Anna Catherine Emmerich, but no one asked Malczewska about Jesus' suffering—and she was glad.

POLAND

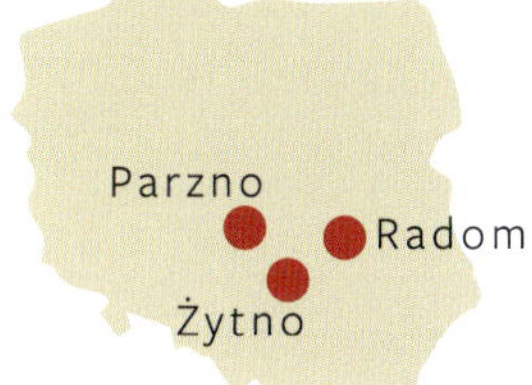

POLAND

One of two surviving photographs of Wanda Malczewska.

A SHORT PATH FROM BIG VISIONS TO SMALL TASKS

Yet some people did know that Wanda was a mystic—they had seen her supernatural experiences with their own eyes. What astonished them was how little those moments seemed to affect her daily life. Not even a trace of the extraordinary lingered in her ordinary routine. Franciszka Siemieńska, a cousin who twice witnessed Wanda's apparitions in 1874, was especially struck by this. As soon as a vision ended, Malczewska would quietly return to her everyday tasks, as though nothing unusual had happened. Not even the faintest shadow of the supernatural clung to her—if only for a moment.

However, we might say that the supernatural encounters did have some influence on Wanda. Franciszka Siemieńska was puzzled by Wanda's quietness and the serenity she radiated.

AROUND MOM'S KNEELER

Wanda Malczewska was born in Radom on May 15, 1822, and spent the first twenty-four years of her life there. Even as a child, she showed a deep spiritual sensitivity. Though its origin is hard to pinpoint, she loved to kneel at her mother's prie-dieu and meditate on the sufferings of Jesus. She listened with delight to anything concerning God and the faith. Confident in her guardian angel's care, she often asked him for help—and, remarkably, received it.

One simple example stood out. Having forgotten to bring water for the flowers

Jacek Malczewski, a famous painter and relative of the mystic.

Radom on a colorful postcard from the time.

In Parzno, near Radom, Wanda spent most of her life.

she arranged around the cross by her mother's kneeler, Wanda prayed that her guardian angel might inspire someone to help. Not long after, the family's butler, Stanislaus, appeared with a jug of water. He explained that a voice had whispered in his ear, "Wandzia needs water." Seeing no one nearby, he assumed it must have been her guardian angel—and, knowing she often prayed to him, he listened.

Wanda often shared her spiritual experiences and early visions with her mother. She once confided that, while praying at the kneeler, she heard the voice of Jesus: "My child, you will be mine forever." She understood that it was Jesus Himself speaking to her soul, and she responded joyfully: "I desire, Jesus, to belong only to You!" Then she asked Him to take her to Himself at once. But Jesus replied, "You are already thinking about heaven, innocent child. That is still too early for you."

Jesus told her that whoever wished to enter Heaven must suffer much and perform many good deeds in humility—without seeking attention, but purely out of love for Him. This, He said, was the path along which He would lead her. And indeed, it marked the course of her entire life: a life shaped by suffering and kindness, by humility and meekness.

Let us recall another encounter from her childhood. Wanda was eight years old when she received her First Holy Communion. She later described the moment in these words:

> *When the parish priest opened the Tabernacle and displayed the ciborium with the Blessed Sacrament, I saw an extraordinary brightness. It seemed to me that the whole church was on fire—that the flame engulfed us all, yet did not burn. Choirs of Holy Angels surrounded me, and the Blessed*

The baptismal certificate of the future mystic.

Mother was fixing a crown of flowers on my head.

When the parish priest placed the Sacred Host on my tongue, I experienced a sweetness beyond words and heard a voice—just as I once had beneath the cross when I was adorning it: "From now on, you are mine. You will live long in the world, but not for the world—for Me. Neither worldly pleasures nor sickness or poverty will separate you from Me. Just as I had no possessions and no place to lay My head (Matthew 8:20), so you too will have none. You will close your eyes among strangers, and there your bones will rest."

And I answered the Lord Jesus in my soul: "Lord, if I have You, I shall be happy—even if all forsake me, even if every misery befalls me. I promise

Fr. Grzegorz Augustynik, community worker and biographer of Wanda.

Title page of Fr. Augustynik's 1923 book.

MIŁOŚĆ BOGA I OJCZYZNY
OKAZANA W CZYNACH
CZYLI
ŻYWOT ŚWIĘTOBLIWEJ POLKI
PANNY
WANDY JUSTYNY NEPOMUCENY
MALCZEWSKIEJ
JEJ OBJAWIENIA I PRZEPOWIEDNIE
DOTYCZĄCE KOŚCIOŁA I POLSKI.
WYDANIE II
ZEBRAŁ I NAPISAŁ
Ks. GRZEGORZ AUGUSTYNIK
PRAŁAT DOMOWY OJCA ŚWIĘTEGO
KOMANDOR ORDERU PAPIESKIEGO
„Pro Ecclesia et Pontifice"
Kanonik h. Kaliski.
EMERYT u OJCÓW PAULINÓW na JASNEJ GÓRZE
W CZĘSTOCHOWIE.

Sandomierski Palace in Radom, the seat of the Sandomierz province commission and the Sandomierz and Radom's governors.

Left: Wanda Malczewska.

Right: Another well-known relative of Wanda, the poet Antoni Malczewski.

Less than fifty years before the Battle of Warsaw, on August 15, 1873, after Vespers, Wanda received a message from the Mother of God: "Today's feast will soon become your national holiday, for on this day you will achieve a great victory over the enemies seeking your destruction."

You, my Jesus, and I vow to You: I will remain Yours forever."

This was how an eight-year-old child responded to Christ. From that day forward, she became serious in spirit.

THE FIRST THORN AND THE VISION OF THE LATE MOTHER

And so it began. The thorns began to pierce her life, one by one. Less than a year had passed when her mother fell gravely ill. Death came soon after. Wanda never left her side, offering comfort in those final days. Her mother wept, sorrowful that she was leaving her beloved children without anyone to care for them. But Wanda gently reassured her:

> *The soul does not die. It goes to the Lord Jesus. Mama, you will always be with us. You will pray for your children in heaven, and in that way, you will not leave us as orphans.*

A remarkable event surrounded her mother's passing. Wanda missed her mother terribly. So when she heard the servants say that on All Souls' Day the souls in Purgatory come down into the church at night—and that those in a state of sanctifying grace might see a departed loved one—she resolved to seize the opportunity.

When All Souls' Day came, Wanda slipped out of the house in the evening and ran to the nearby Bernardine church. The door was still open. She entered unnoticed and hid inside. Before long, the parish clerk came to check that the church was empty and then locked the doors. Wanda was left alone. Silence settled over everything, broken only by the flickering of the sanctuary lamp. The church was nearly dark.

She later described the experience:

> *At first, fear overtook me, but I reminded myself that I had nothing*

Jerzy Kossak, Miracle on the Vistula, *1930, Museum of the Polish Army in Warsaw.*

to fear. My mother would never harm me—nor, of course, would the Lord Jesus. I went to the high altar, where the lamp was lit, knelt on the rug, and began to pray: "Jesus, let me see my mother. Let me see her once more. For this grace, I will love You even more."

In a moment, I fell asleep. I do not know how long I slept. But I was awakened by a gentle, quiet voice: "Wake up, and you will see your mother." I rubbed my eyes—and there she was. She stood before the altar, holding the prayer book I had placed in her coffin. She said to me: "Pray, and patiently endure poverty, and you will help me to leave purgatory soon."

I sprang to go to her, but she vanished like a shadow. I clung to the altar and cried out through my tears, "O Jesus, thank You for showing me my mother."

And Jesus replied, "Love Me, and you will receive even more graces."

As a result of that extraordinary experience—and from being chilled throughout the night—Wanda fainted and collapsed on the steps of the altar. That is where the parish clerk found her the next morning when he opened the church.

FREE TO SERVE THE POOR

Her mother died. Soon, Wanda's father remarried. Her relationship with her stepmother did not turn out well, and Wanda fell from her role as daughter to that of servant.

She endured her stepmother's rule in silence. Years passed, and she voiced no complaint. Eventually, a relative, Leonardowa Siemieńska, learned of her suffering. That discovery brought her time in Radom to an end. Wanda was twenty-four when her aunt brought her to Klimontów. There, she found peace. Her new family loved and respected her, and she felt at ease among them.

Left: Wanda worked as a community organizer, well ahead of her time. She arranged reading and writing lessons for children in the countryside and history lessons for adults and children. She explained historical and religious texts to those interested.

Right: Wanda's cousin Jacek Siemieński with his wife Ewa and his son.

1828

➤ *Church of the Immaculate Conception of the Blessed Virgin Mary in Żytno. When Wanda's nephew, Jacek Malczewski, vacationed here in 1872, the mystic felt inspired—she asked God to support her cousin's talent with grace and make him a great painter.*

➤ *Church in Żytno—At this altar, Wanda received many graces from God. She reconciled spouses and neighbors through her prayers.*

They began planning her future behind her back, hoping to arrange a suitable marriage. But Wanda had already made a secret vow never to marry. Soon, she found herself engaged—against her will. What could have prevented the wedding? Nothing foreseeable. Yet, quite unexpectedly, her fiancé fell gravely ill and died on the very day they were to be married. Wanda remained free.

She threw herself into service. First, she prayed for the poor and the sick, confident that God hears such prayers and offers help and direction. She prepared the critically ill for death and called for a priest when needed. She also took up the cause of education: teaching reading and writing to rural children and giving history lessons to both young and old. She encouraged all to love God and their homeland.

Before long, Wanda began to experience visions of an unusual kind—visions that concerned both God and Poland.

SERVING THROUGH PRAYER

We are not attempting to recount the full story of Wanda Malczewska's remarkable life here. It is enough to say that God led her first to Kraków, and later to Żytno. There, the parish priest, Tomasz Olkowicz, recognized her extraordinary gift for intercessory prayer. At his suggestion, Wanda began praying specifically for the reconciliation of estranged spouses and neighbors—and her prayers bore fruit. This should come as no surprise. Her petitions were not confined to formal prayer; she brought them before Jesus in the context of intimate, prolonged conversations with Him—her Lord and Bridegroom. Before long, people began to speak of her.

No one felt surprised that Wanda faced the temptation of self-satisfaction—or perhaps a little pride. The Savior reminded her:

> *When you have done all you have been commanded, say, "We are unprofitable servants; we have done what we were obliged to do."* (Luke 17:10)

This message sufficed. From then on, she never again considered herself special on her own. After all, Jesus had told her that.

GUIDED THROUGH EVERY DAY

There was another remarkable quality in this Polish mystic: Jesus began to guide her through the ordinary circumstances of daily life. He gave her counsel—teaching her how to speak to certain individuals, how to care for the children entrusted to her, and how to prepare them for their First Holy Communion. She taught them the rosary and led them before the tabernacle, nurturing in them a living faith in the Real Presence of the Lord Jesus in the Eucharist. In the summer of 1872, Wanda spent her vacation in Żytno. Her nephew, the young painter Jacek Malczewski, came to visit. Feeling moved, she prayed that God would

bless his artistic talent with grace and raise him up to become a great painter. She hoped he would be known for works that expressed both religious devotion and national history. And once again, God heard her prayer.

HIDDEN STIGMATA

As Jesus had foretold, Wanda began to experience His Passion every Good Friday, beginning in 1872. In the morning, she endured intense spiritual suffering; in the afternoon, she received hidden stigmata—wounds that were invisible to others. (They could not be made visible, for Wanda was called to remain hidden.)

She felt sharp pain near her heart, on her head where the crown of thorns had rested, and in her hands and feet, where the nails had pierced the Savior's flesh. The pain was so great that she would lose consciousness. But around five o'clock, she would revive, recover her strength, and quietly return to her daily tasks.

SEVEN VISIONS

Wanda was granted visions of the Lord's Passion. She witnessed the scenes as though she were truly present, standing among the people—from the Last Supper to the Crucifixion on Golgotha. Between these moments, Jesus spoke to her, explaining the meaning of her sufferings and entrusting her with messages.

She received seven such visions. In the first, she stood at the Last Supper; in the second, in the Garden of Gethsemane. In the third, she saw the scourging; in the fourth, Jesus' condemnation by Pilate. The fifth showed Him carrying the Cross to Calvary. In the sixth, she beheld His meeting with the Mother of Sorrows. And in the seventh, she stood at the foot of the Cross and witnessed the Crucifixion.

Why was she shown these things? Christ explained:

> *I suffer for the sins of those who spend their nights in taverns and dens of iniquity, forgetting their human dignity—that they are made in the image and likeness of God. They are only slightly lower than the angels, yet they behave like senseless beasts.*

OTHER PROPHECIES

After showing her His suffering, the Savior gave Wanda several prophecies.

While many of the Lord's messages concerned the fate of the world, some also prophesied the destiny of Poland. In one revelation, Jesus warned:

> *For the sins of debauchery, the whole world was punished with the*

▲ *The mystic received visions of Christ's Passion. She saw the scenes as if she participated in them. In the seventh apparition, she witnessed the Crucifixion.*

▼ *Jadwiga Łopatto, prioress of the Dominican nuns at the convent in Święta Anna (St. Anne) near Przyrowo.*

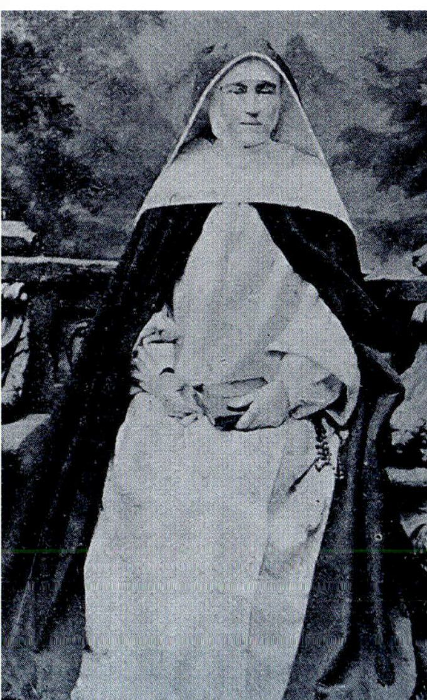

1828

Fr. Hipolit Pikalski, confessor and chaplain at St. Anne's monastery.

In 1881, Wanda became a resident at the monastery of the Dominican Sisters of St. Anne near Przyrowo. There, for eleven years, she sewed liturgical vestments and cared for the sick.

> *flood; Sodom and Gomorrah were punished with sulfurous fire. If people do not abandon these transgressions, they will be punished with bloody wars, deadly contagious diseases, and various other calamities—floods, droughts, and famine—so that, through hunger, the gluttonous and the immoral might be turned back to the path of righteousness.*
>
> *And if even this does not turn them from their ways, entire families will perish; whole nations will wither away.*

In another vision, as Wanda stood at the foot of the Cross and beheld the crucified Christ, she saw Jesus entrusting His Blessed Mother to St. John. Then she heard Him say:

> *The more a nation loves her, the more graces it will receive from Me. Even if it is condemned to destruction by its enemies, it will not perish—it will be reborn.*

MEETING WITH THE BABY JESUS

In January 1877, Wanda received a vision unlike any she had experienced before: she saw Jesus as an infant. But unlike most such apparitions, He did not appear in His Mother's arms. Instead, He sat alone upon a radiant cloud, holding a globe in His hand, with an extraordinary star shining above it. The meaning of the star remains unknown.

Wanda observed that various countries were outlined on the globe—and among them was Poland, marked with the inscription: *Mary's Kingdom*. It was a striking vision. The solitary Christ Child embraced the world, and there was a clear prophetic element: the borders of Poland—absent from the political maps of the time—appeared distinctly on the globe. Through this vision, Jesus offered a new definition of Poland: it was the Kingdom of Mary.

Yet, as with many such revelations, everything remained conditional. Jesus seemed to emphasize that Poland had a role to play. This mission might remain hidden in the divine plan, or it might enter into history and reshape the course of world events. But this latter possibility was conditional: it would come to pass only if Poland truly became Mary's Kingdom.

Some began to wonder whether this vision was connected to the earlier revelation granted to Giulio Mancinelli (1537–1618). Mancinelli had long desired to greet the Blessed Virgin with a title never before used. On the eve of the Assumption in 1608 (August 14), Mary appeared to him in extraordinary majesty and responded to his longing:

> *Why do you not call me the Queen of Poland? I have loved this kingdom very much, and I intend great things*

LE PETIT JOURNA

HEBDOMADAIRE - 37e Année
61, rue Lafayette, Paris

ILLUSTRÉ

25 Juillet 1926.
PRIX : 40 C

LE FILS DU TSAR N'EST PAS MORT

The cover of Le Petit Journal, *an issue devoted to the murder of Tsar Nicholas and his family.*

for it, for a special love for me burns in its sons.

Not even half a century passed before Mary was officially given this title in Lviv, in 1656.

At the ceremony of the Lwów Vows of King John II Casimir, even the Apostolic Nuncio cried out: "Queen of Poland—pray for us!" Yet at the time, this title remained largely symbolic. It was, in truth, a *task* for the Polish people.

Two and a half centuries later, Jesus seemed to be reminding Poland of the mission assigned to it by Heaven: that Mary was to be the Queen of Poland—and that Poland was to become *Mary's Kingdom—in practice*. It already existed in God's providential plan. Perhaps one day it would enter history as a visible reality.

Naturally, the question arises: *When* will this become part of our earthly reality? To this day, we do not know the answer.

LAST FAREWELL

After the deaths of her cousin and his mother, Wanda Malczewska moved to Parzno, where she died in 1896. She knew the exact day and hour of her passing—God had revealed it to her in an apparition. When the appointed day came, she rose early, dressed in the garments she had set aside for her funeral, requested the sacrament of the Anointing of the Sick, bade farewell to those around her, and then lay down to rest. She fell asleep with a smile—and did not awaken.

Her quiet holiness soon drew attention. A reputation for sanctity began to grow, and the Church opened her cause for beatification. Today, she is venerated as a Servant of God, just one step from being declared Blessed. This will come to pass—if Jesus wills it—and she, who was meant to live *without publicity among the people*, may yet become known to the world after death.

The destruction of the Romanov dynasty was communicated to Wanda almost half a century before the Bolshevik Revolution.

Parish church in Parzno. The semicircular presbytery houses the crypt of the Servant of God Wanda.

Prayer for the canonization of Wanda Malczewska in the crypt in Parzno.

5
GOLDEN ARROW

IHS

On the previous page: IHS monogram, Church of the Most Holy Name of Jesus (Rome, Italy).

Jesus told Mary of St. Peter about the need to spread devotion to His Holy Face.

5

GOLDEN ARROW

MARY OF ST. PETER, 1844

There are well-known cases of mystics who were pierced by a spear, sword, or arrow as part of their mystical union with Christ. These include Gertrude the Great, Teresa of Ávila, Veronica Giuliani, and Padre Pio. But in the notes left by a French mystic, we encounter a strikingly different phenomenon: a vision in which the roles of the mystic and Jesus were reversed.

Place of Apparition: Tours, France
Date and Place of Birth: October 4, 1816, Rennes, France
Date and Place of Death: July 8, 1828, Tours, France
Visionary as a Religious Person (Order of the Blessed Virgin Mary of Mount Carmel)
Beatification Process: Servant of God, no date
Works: Spiritual Diary, Letters

Now it was mankind that was given the blade to pierce the Savior—for example, in the form of a golden arrow. This startling reversal appeared in the writings of the same French mystic, who revealed something further: that mystical experiences are not necessarily the result of personal choice or early divine inspiration. Childhood piety does not, by itself, explain or determine such encounters with God.

In the early nineteenth century, we meet a striking example. A nun who cherished the Infant Jesus once expressed the simple desire "to be a donkey beside Him." Yet she was not granted visions of the Child, but rather of the tormented Face of the crucified Savior.

She was born on October 4, 1816, in Rennes, Brittany. At her Baptism, she received the name Perrine (Petronella)—a name cherished in France for its association with the Apostle Peter, whom Christ called *petra*, the rock of the Church. Yet in the final nine years of her life, she became

The lighthouse and cliffs of the Cap Fréhel peninsula (Brittany, France).

John Vespin Tabacchetti and Giovanni d'Enrico, The Road to Calvary (Detail of Christ's encounter with Veronica), Sacro Monte di Varallo (Piedmont, Italy).

known as Mary, and it is under this name that she entered history.

Though her time in the monastery was brief, it proved decisive—not only for her and her community, but for the whole of France.

However, we are not concerned here with all nine years of Maria of St. Peter's religious life—though something of her former name still echoed in the new one. What matters for our purposes are just three of those years: the brief span in which she was granted the extraordinary grace of encountering Jesus.

SLOW PROCESS

For thirty-three years, there was little to suggest that God was preparing Maria of St. Peter for supernatural encounters with Jesus. As a child, she showed no special

Château de Plessis-lèz-Tours, view of the courtyard (La Riche, France).

➤ *Juan Correa,* Triumphal Entry of Our Lord Jesus Christ into Jerusalem, *sacristy of the Metropolitan Cathedral in Mexico City (Mexico).*

signs of piety. She was willful, inattentive, and quick-tempered. She later admitted:

> *I was by nature very unkind and fractious.... My pious mother often took me to church, but I was thoughtless and inattentive there, constantly turning my head in all directions to see what was going on around me.*

Something began to change with her first Confession. Périnne made an effort to correct her difficult temperament—though at first, she relied little on God's help. But after receiving her First Holy Communion at the age of ten, a real breakthrough occurred. To the amazement of those around her, she began to change noticeably, though still depending largely on her own strength.

She later wrote:

> *I won quite a victory over my pride. Every day a poor, blind old man dressed in rags passed our door. As he approached the street corner, he needed a kind hand to guide him through. My good-hearted parents often asked me to be the one to give him the necessary help, but I was so overly proud and showed so much loathing that they eventually stopped insisting.*
>
> *One day I decided to overcome my pride. I ran out in front of the house, gently took the poor old man by the hand, and led him down the right path.*

Yet the old man did not vanish or reveal himself as Christ, as sometimes occurs in the lives of the saints. In Périnne's case, everything remained earthly—perhaps because she still relied on human effort rather than divine grace. Or perhaps the change was only meant to last for a time.

But as she prayed more deeply, her soul began to open. Her prayers were gradually accompanied by interior graces and

inspirations. One such inspiration brought with it the awareness that God was calling her to religious life.

LITTLE DONKEY OF JESUS

On November 3, 1839, Périnne entered the Carmelite Order in Tours. She was still somewhat childlike in spirit. Her desire was to be the little donkey of the Infant Jesus:

> *I offered myself to the Lord as a little donkey through the hands of Mary and Joseph.... The donkey of the Holy Infant is stubborn, avoids work, walks only on side roads—but he has decided to correct these faults. He will do everything to keep the Baby Jesus warm, he will carry Him on His journeys, and, in short, offer the Holy Family every little service he can.*

In another passage, she added:

> *I thought of my soul as a poor stable of Bethlehem, and I imagined the Holy Baby Jesus resting upon my heart. I adored Him in union with the Blessed Virgin Mary and St. Joseph. I offered to be His little pet.*

These simple, tender reflections come from the autobiography she wrote near the end of her life, at the command of her superior. She introduced it with these words:

> *Despite my great revulsion at writing about myself, I will not hesitate to obey the command. I will do what I have been instructed, with the help of the Child Jesus, into whose venerable little hand I have placed the pen, begging Him to write down the accounts of the precious graces He has granted me.*

Nun and visionary Maria Pierina de Micheli wanted to be the donkey of the infant Jesus: "I offered myself to the Lord as a little donkey through the hands of Mary and Joseph," she writes in her memoirs.

➤ St. Gatien Cathedral from Lavoisier Street (Tours, France).

A devout layman—Bl. Leo Dupont, later known as the "Saint of Tours"—began distributing a papally approved prayer in honor of the Divine Name to various religious communities.

ERA OF BLASPHEMIES

Sister Mary had lived behind the walls of the convent for four years, largely cut off from the outside world. She knew little of secular affairs and was unaware of what was taking place in the wider life of the Church. She did not even know that, on August 8, 1843, Pope Gregory XVI had established a confraternity under the patronage of St. Louis IX.

The new confraternity had a specific purpose: to offer reparation for blasphemies against the Holy Name of God. Before long, a devout layman—Bl. Leo Dupont, later known as the "Saint of Tours"—began distributing a papally approved prayer in honor of the Divine Name to various religious communities.

The text circulated widely among the city's religious orders—but it never reached the Carmel. It seems Dupont had simply overlooked the Carmelite monastery. As it turned out, this omission was providential.

▲ A sister in Carmelite habit.

PARALLEL APPARITION

Eighteen days later, as Sister Mary began her customary evening prayer, she heard the voice of the Savior. Jesus revealed that He wished to entrust her with a prayer of reparation for blasphemies against the Holy Name of God. But He added something beyond the scope of the existing papal intention: the devotion was also to make reparation for the profanation of the Lord's Day.

Upon closer examination of the messages Sister Mary received, we find that Jesus also spoke of the wounds inflicted upon His Church. He lamented:

> *Oh, you who are My friends and My faithful children, look and see if there be any sorrow like Mine. Everywhere My enemies despise and insult both My Eternal Father and My Church—the cherished Spouse of My Heart. Will no one rise up to console Me by defending the glory of My Father and the honor of My Spouse, which has been so cruelly attacked?*

France had already endured the French Revolution (1789–1799), with its devastating program of de-Christianization. In Tours, where Sister Mary lived, the memory of St. Martin—once venerated across Europe—had nearly vanished. His tomb, once a great site of pilgrimage, now lay beneath the intersection of two roads.

The busy intersection made any form of veneration at St. Martin's tomb impossible. By the mid-nineteenth century, perceptive souls saw dark clouds gathering. Freemasonry was rising in visibility and influence; communism was beginning to rally the working masses. More and more people were turning away from God.

Where once the faithful had spoken His Name in brief aspiration prayers—acts of love whispered throughout the day—it was now invoked with contempt. A kind of *satanic aspiration prayer* had emerged: the Name of God was used in cursing, to express hatred for all things sacred and for the Church herself.

The pope sought to halt this spiritual decline. And the words of Jesus, spoken to Sister Mary of St. Peter in her apparitions, were aimed at the very same purpose.

GRACE OF UNDERSTANDING

What form did Sister Mary's encounters with Christ take? The visionary consistently referred to them as *les communications*—"messages." She explained that, with one exception, she experienced no visible apparitions. The truths imparted to her were not the result of ecstatic transport, nor did they come through the natural senses.

She did not audibly hear the voice of Jesus. Nor could she precisely define the mode of communication. This very uncertainty testifies to the authenticity of her experience—she was not fabricating miracles inspired by the pious books she had read. Lacking a better term, she would simply write, "The Lord gave me to understand that…." These were not flights of imagination, nor projections of her own meditations. Rather, they were characteristic of what the Church has often called *inner visions*—real spiritual communications received not through the eyes or ears, but within the depths of the soul.

DEVOTION TO THE HOLY FACE

Between 1844 and 1847, Jesus told her to spread devotion to His Holy Face worldwide. That He advocated this devotion suggested that people who used God's name as a curse and ignored the Lord's Day did not do so

In Tours, where Sister Mary lived, the memory of St. Martin had nearly vanished. His tomb, once a great site of pilgrimage, now lay beneath the intersection of two roads.

Carmelite nun in an eighteenth-century habit.

Tours Castle (France).

The Savior assured them that if they made reparation to the Holy Face, God's justice would be replaced by mercy.

out of true conviction, but out of mindless imitation of what had become commonplace.

Contemplating the Face of Jesus was supposed to awaken people to the absurdity of their actions. The Savior assured them that if they made reparation to the Holy Face, God's justice would be replaced by mercy.

WOUND THAT BRINGS JESUS JOY

On August 26, 1843, Sister Mary recorded that Christ opened His Heart to her and revealed a profound sorrow: "This frightful sin [blasphemy] wounds His Divine Heart more grievously than all other sins. Blasphemy is a poisoned arrow, continually wounding His Divine Heart."

Mary herself observed: "Blasphemy appeared in every stratum of society with terrible vehemence..."

In response, the Savior dictated a prayer to her, which He called *the Golden Arrow*. He said: "My Name is insulted everywhere—even children blaspheme. To prevent this, I give you this Golden Arrow." Then He added, with solemn urgency: "Pay attention to this grace, because I shall ask you for an account of it." In that moment, Mary saw streams of grace flowing forth from the Sacred Heart of Jesus.

The streams of grace flowed from the very wound made by the Golden Arrow. Then Christ spoke words that startled Sister Mary more than anything else. She recorded His reassurance:

> *Those who recite this prayer will wound Me delightfully, and also heal other wounds inflicted on Me by the malice of sinners.*

As a confirmation of this promise, she again saw torrents of grace pouring forth from the Sacred Heart of Jesus, pierced—paradoxically—by love through the Golden Arrow.

Drawn now toward a deeper mystery, Mary was led to contemplate the Holy Face of Christ. She wrote:

> *Drawing me strongly to the contemplation of His adorable Face, our Divine Savior made me see, through a ray of light issuing from His august Countenance, that the Holy Face which He presented to mankind for their adoration was indeed the mirror of those unutterable Divine Perfections*

A view of the parliament building of Brittany (Rennes, France).

comprised and contained in the Most Holy Name of God.

"I saw that by thus honoring and venerating this Sacred Countenance, covered anew with outrages, we could atone for blasphemers who attack the Divinity—of which this Holy Face is the figure, the mirror, and the expression."

ALL FOR FRANCE

Mary's life revolved around three central themes: the Baby Jesus, reparation, and France. Even on her deathbed, she offered her sufferings for her beloved homeland. She felt anxious for France because Jesus had granted her a glimpse of its future. The visionary heard the same message the Blessed Mother had conveyed to St. Catherine Labouré in 1830: she heard of persecution against the Church, revolution in the streets of Paris, and the deaths of many religious. Her prayers and mortifications could not prevent it.

Left: Image of Jesus based on the Shroud of Turin.

Right: Pietro Lorenzetti, fresco in the Basilica of Assisi, 1310–1329. From Adoration of the Face of the Lord (Italy).

"I saw that by thus honoring and venerating this Sacred Countenance, covered anew with outrages, we could atone for blasphemers who attack the Divinity."

Mary's life revolved around three themes: Baby Jesus, reparation, and France.

Our Lady of Mount Carmel and the saints: Simon Stock, Angelus of Jerusalem, Mary Magdalene de' Pazzi, and Teresa of Ávila.

Stained glass with the letters IHS in St. Martin's Catholic parish church (Montmorency, France).

Jesus would let Perrine know the future: the visionary would hear the same thing the Blessed Mother had told St. Catherine Labouré in 1830. She would hear about the Church's persecution, revolution in Paris, and the death of numerous religious.

However, the events of 1870 proved to be only a brief dark episode in France's history. After all, Mary had received a "patriotic vision" from Heaven. She recorded:

> *The Lord gave me to see ... the mysterious wall protecting France from the arrows of divine justice.*

She added:

> *Jesus gave me to understand that this wall, which reached to heaven, was a spiritual exercise that I practiced every day, which was undoubtedly combined with the prayers and merits offered to God by so many holy souls for the salvation of France.*

One may guess that this spiritual exercise was her devotion to the Holy Face, with its Golden Arrow, given in the apparitions:

> *May the most holy, most sacred, most adorable, most incomprehensible, and ineffable Name of God be forever praised, blessed, adored, loved, and glorified, in heaven, on earth, and under the earth, by all the creatures of God, and by the Sacred Heart of Our Lord Jesus Christ in the most Holy Sacrament of the Altar. Amen.*

The original text listed *heaven, earth*, and "hells." Sister Mary of St. Peter felt somewhat puzzled by the words *in the hells,* but Our Lord helped her understand that His Justice was also glorified there, and that "in the hells" included Purgatory, where He was loved and glorified by the suffering souls.

"Oh, to whom shall I address Myself," the Savior said to Mary, "if not to a Carmelite, whose very vocation obliges her unceasingly to glorify My Name?"

The visionary recorded:

> *While this was taking place, I felt my soul entirely lost in God, and simultaneously I was overcome by awe as our Lord made me realize the meaning of the words spoken to Abraham—that if there could be found at least ten just souls, God would spare the guilty cities for the sake of these ten just. It also seemed to me that for the sake of those who would practice reparation for the sins committed against the majesty of God, His justice would be appeased, and He would grant mercy to the guilty.*

THERE COULD HAVE BEEN MORE APPARITIONS?

Someone might claim there could have been many more apparitions and messages if the Carmelite nun of Tours had listened more to Jesus than to her superiors. Jesus attempted repeatedly to meet her, but Mary persistently refused. She wrote:

> *At different times of the day He visited my soul, bringing a powerful impulse of His grace. I would have gladly left my work for a while—for a brief moment when I felt Him coming—so that I could listen to Him more attentively. But thinking that I should have permission to do so, I asked the Reverend Mother Superior. Since she never neglected any opportunity to train me in virtue, she told me to disregard these inner activities.... With God's grace, I listened to her wise advice.*

Altar with the image of the Holy Face of the Savior, sanctuary in Licheń, Poland.

Grégoire Guérard, St. Veronica and the Holy Women, *ca. 1530, Hôtel-Dieu de Cluny, the Wallonia-Brussels Federation Museum of Contemporary Arts (Hornu, Belgium).*

➤ *In 1876, the archbishop of Tours encouraged the faithful to practice devotion to the Holy Face of Jesus, St. Gatien Cathedral (Tours, France).*

Could there have been more apparitions? Certainly—had Sister Mary not refused these encounters, which ran contrary to the monastery rules. But there would not have been more.

There were also many occasions when the visionary not only ignored an apparition but even cut short an encounter already in progress. She wrote:

The Lord had not finished speaking when a loud bell could be heard in the parlatory, calling the sister responsible for opening the door. It was the signal for the offering. "Ah, my Jesus!"—I said—"the bell is calling me; in the name of obedience, I return to my work."

Near death, she reflected:

> *The greatest consolation now, at the hour of my death, is that I have always been obedient.*

I OFFER YOU THIS MIRACULOUS BABY

The superior, describing the final days of the visionary's life, noted, "Our dear sister foresaw the approach of her departure; in several of her letters she clearly claimed that the Lord had made known to her the time of her death."

It all began on the day of the Lord's Passion:

> *On Good Friday at three o'clock she fell to the ground to adore the dying Jesus Christ. Immediately, she felt the immense weight of Divine wrath that was about to fall on humanity. Then, renewing her act of perfect self-sacrifice to Jesus, she gave herself to Him as a burnt offering to stop the terrible blows of God's justice.*

She later added:

It seemed that Our Lord was waiting for this last generous act on her part.... Immediately [after] came a cruel illness.

Only a short time earlier, she had consecrated herself to the Child Jesus:

"My soul is completely focused on the Divine Child and His Virgin Mother," she wrote. In another letter to her superior, she said: "I was in constant contemplation of the Child Jesus in Her arms."

Now she was united with Jesus crucified. Yet the theme of the infant did not disappear. In her agony, she raised the statue of the Baby Jesus and solemnly—though quietly—pronounced these words:

> *Eternal Father, I once again offer You this Miraculous Child, Your Divine Son, as a reparation for my sins and those of all people. I offer it as an aid to our holy Mother Church, as reparation for France. Beloved Jesus, I place this work in Your hands. For Him I lived, for Him I will die!*

She died on a Saturday—the day dedicated to Mary—July 8, 1848.

"The moment the servant of God took her last breath, all our hearts were filled with the certainty that she was blessed," her superior recalled.

Her apparitions were not forgotten. The soon-famous Bl. Leo Dupont spent the next thirty years spreading the devotion Jesus had requested of Mary. In 1876, the Archbishop of Tours encouraged the faithful to embrace devotion to the Holy Face of Jesus, and in 1958, Pope Pius XII established a feast in her honor, to be celebrated throughout the Church on the eve of Ash Wednesday.

The north gable of the Archbishop's Palace in Tours. Verdicts of the bishop's court had once been proclaimed from that Renaissance balcony. After the dramatic events foretold to the visionary and after the rapid secularization of France, the palace became the Museum of Fine Arts.

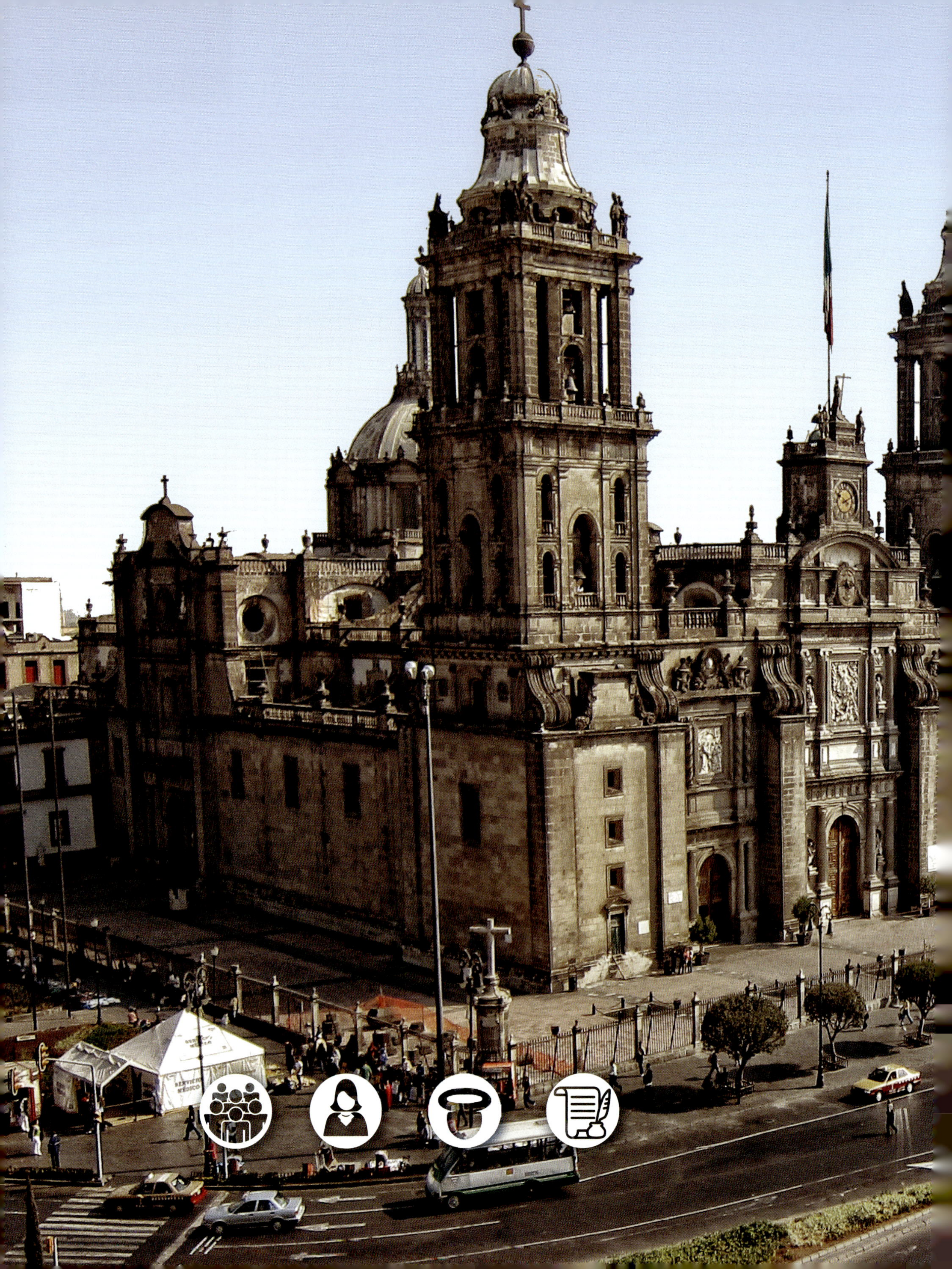

6
GIVE ME CHILDREN SO THEY LOVE YOU BETTER

1865

On the previous page: Metropolitan Cathedral in Mexico City (Mexico).

Place of Apparition: San Luis Potosi, Mexico City, Mexico
Date and Place of Birth: December 8, 1862, San Luis Potosi, Mexico
Date and Place of Death: March 3, 1937, Mexico City, Mexico
Visionary as a Secular and Religious Person (Third Order of Saint Francis)
Beatification: May 4, 2019 (Francis)
Feast: March 3
Works: Spiritual Journal

Despite social unrest during the revolution in Mexico and a difficult family situation, the mystic's heart was filled with trust and peace.

Conchita's simple life should be a role model for today's brides, wives, and mothers.

6

GIVE ME CHILDREN SO THEY LOVE YOU BETTER

MARIA CONCEPCION "CONCHITA," 1865

Her biography was unusual. It encompassed every vocation traditionally open to a woman: she was a fiancée, a wife, a mother, a widow, a grandmother, and a great-grandmother. And—thanks to a special indult from Pope Pius X—she departed this life as a nun.

She used to say that she must have had the strength of three hearts, so numerous were the duties she fulfilled each day. When she spoke of her life, she described suffering at every turn. Was that the hallmark of her spirituality—the key that opened the world of apparitions to her? No. It was love. What drew back the veil of the supernatural was love: love for her husband, for her children, but above all for Jesus. As we will see, above all in the truest and most radical sense.

She never thought of herself as exceptional. Looking at her biography, we see an ordinary woman. Her days were spent caring for her home, her husband, and her children. Outwardly, there was nothing remarkable. Even her family, when told that their mother was a great mystic and saint, replied, "We don't know if she

MEXICO

was a saint or a mystic. But she was a mom—the best mom in the world."

She was ordinary—so ordinary that she never thought of herself as specially chosen by Heaven. She insisted she had never experienced apparitions. Jesus and the Blessed Mother, she said, simply spoke to her during prayer and meditation—just as, in her view, they might speak to any of us, if only we truly knew how to pray. Perhaps she encountered Jesus and Mary because she *did* know how to pray. And perhaps anyone who truly prays and meditates is already gazing into eternity.

CHILDHOOD

Her name—long, as is common among Mexicans—was María Concepción Cabrera de Armida, though everyone called her Conchita. She was born in Mexico on December, 8, The Feast of the Immaculate Conception.

The date of her birth held deep significance for her, and she regarded it as a sign. It accompanied her throughout life, reflected in her very name: *María* after the Mother of God, and *Concepción* for the conception she was born to commemorate.

She was full of life. She loved music and poetry, played the piano, and enjoyed singing. She adored horses and was a gifted rider. She was not—as sweetened hagiographies sometimes portray the saints—a saint from birth. She herself admitted, "I did not obey my parents. I used to physically fight with my siblings, steal sweets and fruit ..." These were ordinary childhood faults, signs of a young soul just beginning to form a hierarchy of values.

Yet—and this may surprise some—these early flaws did not prevent her from experiencing supernatural encounters. We know that the baby Jesus often came to her room to play with her. But unlike in the lives of St. Rosa of Lima or St. Veronica Giuliani, the devil also appeared to her more than once, disguised as a repulsive creature, trying in vain to frighten her.

The devil—at such a young age? we asked. We knew that Jesus sometimes came to saints under ten years old, but Satan? We had not heard that before.

Could he have feared that if María opened herself to the supernatural, she would one day lead thousands to God? Was Hell already so powerless before her that the devil resorted to revealing himself—even in a childlike form—just to frighten her? After all, we knew he does

Conchita became a widow at the age of thirty-nine. Since then, she had to take care of her children's livelihood on her own.

There were not many Marian apparitions in Conchita's life. Usually, the appearing Christ told the mystic about His Holy Mother. Our Lady of Solitude of Maquinaya.

Her real name was Concepción Cabrera de Armida, although she was better known as Conchita.

not show himself to those who might still become his.

Conchita understood that to see him, even once, was to be warned—to do everything possible to avoid seeing him for eternity. Was she, even then, already beyond his reach?

SPIRITUAL SENSITIVITY

Where did this openness come from? Perhaps it was the fruit of her spirituality—a heart attuned to goodness and beauty, and a soul fascinated by the supernatural. Or perhaps it sprang from suffering. As a small child, María was so frail that a nurse had to watch over her constantly.

Or was there something more? From a young age, little Conchita gazed at the cross and began to grasp the meaning of suffering. We know that even in early childhood, she pricked her fingers with pins to share in the Lord's Passion. She was a contemplative soul, deeply devoted to prayer. For this reason, she received her First Holy Communion on her tenth birthday—much earlier than most children at the time, who typically waited until they were twelve or fourteen. Her formal schooling ended around the same time.

Nine years later, she would begin to desire holiness with radical intensity. She sought out a good confessor and imposed spiritual disciplines upon herself. Where would this path lead her?

At the age of thirty-three, in her own words, she "gave herself totally" to Jesus—imitating the Savior, who at thirty-three gave His life on the Cross. This act became the gateway to her full union with God. Soon afterward, she would experience a spiritual marriage with Christ. Then came something still more mysterious: what she called the "mystical incarnation," an event hidden even from us.

All of this took place not behind monastery walls, but amid the swift currents of her secular life.

SECULAR PATH

Conchita was turning thirteen. According to local custom, it was time for her to enter society. She began attending the theater and, though she did not enjoy them, went eagerly to the balls hosted by wealthy families.

She was repelled by the artificiality, pomp, and pretension of the balls. But she had no choice—they were her parents' will. She may have disliked dancing, but it was there

that she met the man who would become her beloved husband: Francisco de Armida.

"I was introduced to him at the ball," she later recalled. "He came to dance with me.... Then he told me very quietly that

Conchita was born in San Luis Potosi, a city located in central Mexico best known for its beautiful church dedicated to Nuestra Señora del Carmen.

he loved me. I had never imagined myself capable of having a sweetheart, so I kept quiet. Then I watched as tears rolled from his eyes. He said he was suffering because I did not want him. This softened me, and I replied, 'Is that why? Is there anything else? Well, I love you, so do not suffer for such a little thing!'"

And she did fall in love with him. But Conchita was not like other young women. Francisco likely had no idea that his beloved rose at dawn each day to begin with an unusual prayer. She placed a crown of roses on her head—not a bridal wreath, though she called it one, but something stranger, more hidden. The flowers had been woven to cover the thorns that pierced her flesh. In this way, she concealed her penance and her longing to be united with the crucified Lord.

And yet—was it not already clear that she desired to be His bride?

The rhythm of her days would follow this same pattern for many years to come.

After prayer each morning, she would go to Mass. When she returned from church, she prepared breakfast for her family and cleaned the house. Then she sewed for the poor and spent time in spiritual reading. Later, she returned to the church to visit the Blessed Sacrament, pray the Rosary, and make an examination of conscience. Afterward, she visited the sick and helped the children with their homework. And in her spare time—she wrote. (We will return to this shortly.)

Given such a pious life, one might expect her to have entered a convent. But Conchita never seriously considered that path, even though her uncle, a priest,

Holy Mary's glory in Heaven surpasses all angels and saints. It is a reflection of all the perfections God can give to His creation.

Although she wanted it very much, she never became a nun. On her initiative, the Congregation of Sisters of the Cross of the Sacred Heart of Jesus was founded in 1897.

strongly encouraged it. She believed she was unworthy of so exalted a life. To leave the world entirely and be with Jesus always seemed, to her, too high a calling. She thought of herself as too "secular."

Instead, she longed to marry, to have many children, and to serve God by loving those closest to her. Eventually, she would join the Franciscan Third Order, as many visionaries and mystics had done before her. She remained in the world—but how could she justify this, given how deeply she loved Jesus?

She found a beautiful answer. In her diary, she wrote: "Lord, I feel so incapable of loving You, so I want to get married. Give me many children to love You better than I do." And so it happened. In 1884, she married Francisco de Armida and gave birth to nine children. There might have been more—more children to love God on her behalf—had her husband not died in 1901.

I WANT IT TOO

Her time of purification had begun earlier. Already in her spiritual notes, we find difficult—at times even shocking—conversations with Jesus.

When her second child, Carlos, died at the age of six, Conchita was overcome with grief. She could not come to terms with the loss. In prayer, she heard the Lord's voice: "Whom do you wish to see—Carlito or Me?" The young mother hesitated. Then, overcoming her anguish, she whispered, "You, Lord—though I will not see my child again until eternity."

A similar moment came in September 1901, when her husband fell ill with typhoid fever. The next morning, Conchita, reciting her *roses*, surrendered everything once again to the Will of God.

She repeated the offering the next day, and the day after that. On September 15, the feast of the Seven Sorrows of the Blessed Virgin Mary, she knelt again in prayer. This time, she heard Jesus say, "Either him or Me. Choose."

For a nun behind convent walls, the choice might have been simple. But not for Conchita. Out of love for her husband, she cried out, "Lord! I choose You both!"

There was silence. Did Jesus want a different answer?

After many tears, she cried again: "I want You, Lord. I prefer You to my own soul. Whatever You want." Then, almost in desperation, she added, "Only have mercy!"

She felt as though a knife had pierced her heart. But soon the pain gave way to a deep interior peace, and she knew the Lord had poured into her the strength she

Today, Hacienda Jesus Maria houses a retreat center operating in the spirit of the Apostolate of the Cross.

would need to endure what was to come. Two days later, at the age of forty-three, Francisco surrendered his soul to God. Two more days passed, and Conchita "knew" that the Lord had released his soul from Purgatory.

Her prayer of surrender—"Jesus, if You want it, I want it too"—came to define her entire life. Through this path of loving abandonment, Jesus drew her into the world of grace and mystical union. But that did not mean the pain of loss disappeared.

Even three years after her husband's death, she wrote:

> *My heart is still struggling. My tears pour over the bread I eat—really, literally: they drip on the floor, on the crucifix. Oh my Jesus, whatever it is that You want, I want it too! I feel terribly lonely.... Mother of my soul, have mercy on me!*

MARRIAGE

Let us go back a few years. In 1894, Conchita received a grace granted to only a few of God's chosen souls: a spiritual marriage with Jesus.

When she recalled that day two years later, she wrote only, "In truth, after I had touched God and gained an imperfect understanding of His essence, I longed to fall face and heart in the dust and never get up again."

Theologians were astonished that the Lord would grant such a singular mystical grace to a woman entirely devoted to the duties of married life and motherhood. They knew of no other case like it. Spiritual marriage with Christ had always belonged to the biographies of nuns, already betrothed to Jesus through the vows of religious life. And yet, this grace was given to a wife and mother.

Conchita's experience revealed that mystical union with Christ was not incompatible with earthly marriage. The two could coexist—not in tension, but in harmony. Everything became clear through a single theological insight: marriage is a sacrament. And as such, it is a sign of Christ's love—no less, and perhaps even more visibly so, than the most solemn religious vows, which, after all, are not a sacrament.

The mystical marriage was by no means the final stage in Conchita's ascent toward union with God. Nine years later, on March 25, 1906—the Solemnity of the Annunciation of the Lord—she received a still more extraordinary grace: the mystical incarnation.

What was this grace? It was a transformation into Christ Himself.

One might wonder: on that day, praying her *roses*, did Conchita reflect on the mystery of the Incarnation and come to see that the Annunciation is not only a historical event, but a spiritual reality meant

Conchita also wished to imitate Mary in a peculiar solitude that settled in the heart of the Mother of God during the last years of her life.

Schoenstatt Shrine "Maravillas de Maria," San Luis Potosi city, Mexico.

to unfold in every soul? Did she, perhaps, receive something like what Archbishop Fulton Sheen once described?

In one of his conferences, Sheen spoke of the personal Annunciation that comes to every soul that prays deeply:

> *One day an angel sent from the throne of light comes to the Virgin kneeling in prayer and says in the silence of her heart, "Will you let me become a man?"*
>
> *This is what God says to you: Will you allow Me to become human? Will you allow Me to take on your nature? Will you allow Me to become you?*

Conchita allowed. From that moment on, her own "I" no longer mattered. For her, "to live is Christ" (Philippians 1:21). She desired not to live for herself, but that Christ might live in her: "yet I live, no longer I, but Christ lives in me" (Galatians 2:20). Her longing was for God to be all in her: "so that God may be all in all" (1 Corinthians 15:28).

Full of love for Christ and His Mother, the message written down by the visionary was an unfading inspiration for the faithful around the world.

Her will was no longer her own. Mystically transformed into Christ, she began to bear the spiritual fruits of this union in abundance.

And yet, outwardly, nothing changed. Those around her did not perceive the transformation. They did not see her sanctity, nor did they suspect the depths of her mystical life. To them, Conchita was simply a beautiful soul.

Bishop Joseph J. Madera, who witnessed her life, remarked: "Although Conchita received this extraordinary grace in 1906, she would effectively spend the rest of her life trying to fathom what had been done in her and how to respond to it." Even her second-to-last retreat, in 1935—directed by her spiritual father and friend, the Servant of God Archbishop Luís María Martínez, Archbishop of Mexico City and Primate of Mexico—was devoted to probing more deeply into this singular grace.

IHS

Once again, we have broken the chronological thread—but chronology is not essential to understanding Conchita's spiritual path. Let us go back many years. As a child, María Concepción spent long days at her family's haciendas. On occasion, she witnessed animals being branded with the owner's mark—seared into their skin with heated iron.

Years later, as her union with Jesus deepened, she began to long for something similar: to bear on her own body a visible sign that she belonged to Him. She wanted to be marked as Christ's possession. One day, she branded the letters *IHS*—short for *Iesus Christus Salvator*, Jesus Christ the Savior—onto her heart.

Sealing her devotion with blood and declaring her total belonging to Christ bore unexpected fruit. Let us listen to the mystic herself:

> *I felt as if, through the monogram, the Lord had opened some gates through which He began to pour in abundant graces. From that day onward—what a chase! How much*

➤ Among the collected memorabilia, there were numerous devotional items, photos, and everyday objects that once belonged to Conchita.

tenderness, how many graces, how many great signs of kindness toward me, a miserable mud! He did not abandon me, day or night—neither during prayer nor outside of it. "I want you to be mine. You are already mine, but I want you to be mine even more," He said to me repeatedly. "Come close to Me. I want to become engaged to you. I want to give you My name and prepare you to receive great graces."

JOY IN SUFFERING

She confessed: "There are wonderful moments during which I feel—it is very strange!—joy in suffering, and then my soul rises with a delight completely unknown to me."

The pain eased, though it did not lessen. What changed was her act of surrender to God's Will, and a newfound desire to please Him—stronger now than ever before. That day, she experienced something

The house where the visionary spent the last months of her life.

extraordinary in her soul: union in suffering. God was not a remedy for pain. He was Love—Love that endures all things. For Conchita, even suffering became joy, so long as it brought joy to her Beloved.

WRITINGS

We recalled that even as a child, Conchita loved poetry and was an avid reader. Now we must add that she also loved to write. And here was Jesus—who had taken so much from her over the course of her life—meeting her halfway to fulfill one of her deepest desires.

He said to her plainly, "Ask Me for a long life so that you can write a lot."

Conchita was destined to live a long life because she was destined to leave behind many written pages. In her, God's Will and a human longing met.

She had always dreamed of writing. She once confessed, "I have always evinced an inclination to write. From the age of sixteen, I started writing down my life, [which was] full of God."

A museum dedicated to Conchita has been established in her home. It is open to visitors.

It was a remarkable inclination, given that her formal education had gone no further than a few years of elementary school. Yet again and again she heard a heavenly prompting: "Write, write, if you want to give glory to Me."

Jesus even gave her the criteria for discerning the origin of her writing: "If what you write comes from Me, it will be for My glory. If it comes from the devil, you will be warned. If it is from yourself, you will be ridiculed—and your humility will benefit."

When her writings reached more than half a million readers, few knew who had authored them. Captivated by the content, readers remained unaware of her identity, as the works were published anonymously. Only after her death did publishers begin to attribute them to their true author—the visionary Conchita.

◀ *"God wants me to be alone," the mystic wrote.*

And it is worth noting: her works are surely read more often today than those of the great scholastic theologian.

THE END AND THE GLORY

Jesus had willed that she live a long life. Conchita returned to Him at the age of seventy-four. In the early spring of 1937, the visionary fell ill with pneumonia. She died on March 3—a date that, in the Marian calendar, marked the feast of Our Lady of the Angels.

Conchita, who had resembled the Blessed Virgin in her earthly life and had received the grace of the "mystical incarnation," now became—so we might say—*Conchita the Angel*. She entered the company of angels in Heaven, a truth the Church would later affirm in a solemn way through her beatification in 2019.

"Write, write!"—Jesus urged her throughout her life. And she obeyed. In the end, she left behind over 60,000 handwritten pages. The sheer volume of her spiritual writings rivals that of St. Thomas Aquinas.

Of course, their approaches to theology were very different, though in many ways complementary. Conchita did not produce a systematic or scholarly treatise rooted in Scripture and Tradition, as Aquinas did. Rather, she gave voice to what has been called symbolic theology: the use of material images to express realities of the spiritual and intellectual world.

Her knowledge of God came not from academic study, but from deep interior listening—from prayer, meditation, and adoration. She spoke of divine things in the language of everyday life.

▼ *The chapel where Concepción Cabrera de Armida prayed.*

7
"I WOULD LIKE TO CEASE LOVING THEM"

On the previous page: Statue in the Church of San Salvatore depicting Padre Pio helping to carry Christ's Cross (Rome, Italy).

Place of Apparitions: Pietrelcina, San Giovanni Rotondo (Italy)
Date and Place of Birth: May 25, 1887, Pietrelcina (Italy)
Date and Place of Death: September 23, 1968, San Giovanni Rotondo (Italy)
The Visionary as a Layman and Religious (Order of Friars Minor Capuchin)
Beatification: May 2, 1999 (by John Paul II)
Canonization: June 16, 2002 (by John Paul II)
Feast Day: September 23
Works: Letters

7

"I WOULD LIKE TO CEASE LOVING THEM"

FRANCESCO FORGIONE, 1875

Is there anyone who does not know St. Pio of Pietrelcina? We live in an era fascinated by him. Yet are we not often drawn more to the outward and extraordinary signs? When asked about him, people usually mention the more visible phenomena: the stigmata, healings, bilocation, levitation, prophecy, miracles, the reading of hearts, or the gift of speaking unknown languages.

Indeed, he received many charisms from God. Some have said that no one in history was granted as many. And yet, few have asked why God gave such graces to this extraordinary friar, or what the most hidden and often overlooked aspect of his life was—what lay at the heart of his vocation: his encounters with the supernatural.

He was born in 1887 in Pietrelcina, Italy, a small farming village near Naples. He came from a poor family and began working on his parents' land at the age of ten. His life was outwardly ordinary, but—even without realizing it—he was already marked out as different.

Panorama of Pietrelcina.

Pietrelcina, a small, charming town where Francesco Forgione—the future Padre Pio—was born and grew up.

ENCOUNTERS WITH HEAVEN

From a very early age, St. Pio experienced apparitions of Jesus, Mary, and his guardian angel. He regarded these encounters as entirely normal, speaking with his heavenly visitors as naturally as he spoke with those around him. For him, there was not only *this* world but *that* one as well—usually hidden from view, yet, as he believed, near, present, and accessible to all.

The daily prayers of his family, the solemn observance of Sundays, and the hymns praising God's protection all nurtured in him a deep sense of Heaven's nearness.

Padre Pio bore witness to the intersection of the natural and the

Padre Pio saying Mass.

Above the entrance to the monastery's little church, there was a window from which Padre Pio used to bless the townspeople and pilgrims.

The remarkable architecture of the church in San Giovanni Rotondo.

Padre Pio surrounded by children.

supernatural. His life showed how the two could meet—just as Jesus, one Person and our Savior, possessed two natures: divine and human. In the same way, reality itself is twofold—natural and supernatural, visible and invisible at once.

With childlike simplicity, the young Pio assumed such encounters were not unusual. He believed that anyone who had been baptized must experience similar apparitions, though such things were not spoken of in earthly terms. On the temporal plane, one conversed with those who lived within time; on the eternal plane, with those who dwell in eternity.

He was genuinely surprised to learn that such experiences were not common. In astonishment, he asked, "So—you don't see apparitions?"

AN APPARITION OF LOVE

At the age of five, he decided to consecrate himself to God. Perhaps those early conversations with Jesus and Mary, which he remembered vividly, had moved him to this decision. Around the same time, he began practicing penance and offering it to God. His mother once found him sleeping on the hard floor with a stone for a pillow and scolded him sternly. Though he gave up such outward mortifications, his inner resolve remained unchanged. Opportunities for penance were not lacking, and he embraced them daily—though only those in the invisible realm could see.

When he was ten years old, a Capuchin friar came to his village seeking alms for the order. Francesco (his baptismal name) met him and immediately recognized his own vocation. He confided to his parents that he wished to become a Franciscan. They did not object; on the contrary, they were glad to dedicate him to the Lord. Together they traveled the twenty-one kilometers to Morcone, where the monastery he dreamed of joining was located, to learn what would be required for him to become a Capuchin.

The friars welcomed the idea of accepting the future stigmatic—provided he first received the necessary education. But his parents, both illiterate, could not afford the cost. For a time, it seemed the path to religious life was closed. But was it truly? Something happened in the home of the future Padre Pio—something many biographies only briefly mention. The path remained open, but only if the family was willing to make a great sacrifice. And they were: Francesco's father went overseas to find work, hoping to earn enough to pay for his son's schooling.

The sacrifice was not only the father's. It was also a burden for the mother, who would be left without her husband, and for the children, who would grow up without their father. Life became more difficult for them all, but they accepted it willingly. It was as if they sensed that through this vocation—this path to religious life—their son and brother would become a saint, perhaps even a great one. It was a manifestation of love more wondrous than any supernatural apparition.

At the beginning of 1903, after completing the required schooling, the future visionary entered the monastery. Upon receiving the Franciscan habit, he took a new name. From that moment, he was Brother Pio—and later, after his ordination to the priesthood, Padre Pio. Why the name "Pio"? He chose it to honor St. Pius V, the patron of his native Pietrelcina.

A MYSTICAL WOUND

That is enough of his biography. Let us now turn to the apparitions that shaped his life. Which were the most significant?

A building in Orta San Giulio, in northern Italy, where an image of the Capuchin saint appeared on a wall in 1997.

The Home for the Relief of Suffering hospital in San Giovanni Rotondo.

Padre Pio devoted himself wholeheartedly to the ministry of the confessional. At times, he spent well over a dozen hours a day hearing Confessions.

Radiant angels leading pilgrims to the tomb of the Capuchin saint.

In the 1950s, a modern basilica dedicated to Our Lady of Grace was built next to the old monastery church.

A bell set in the square in front of the basilica.

Perhaps we should begin with two visions connected to his reception of the stigmata. The first resembled the vision recorded in the life of St. Teresa of Ávila, when, like the Spanish saint, Padre Pio's heart was pierced by a mystical blade.

In a letter to Father Benedetto dated August 21, 1918, he wrote:

> *I was hearing the boys' confessions on the evening of the fifth when I was suddenly gripped by intense terror at the sight of a heavenly being who appeared before my mind's eye. He held in his hand a kind of weapon, like a long, fiery steel blade. In the very moment I saw this, the figure thrust the blade into my soul with all his might. I uttered a faint cry and felt like I was going to die. I told the boy I felt ill and couldn't go on. The anguish lasted without interruption until the morning of the seventh. I cannot possibly describe how I suffered in this time of torment. My bowels felt torn and ripped by that blade, and nothing was spared. From that day on, I have been mortally wounded. Deep within my soul, I feel a wound always open and always agonizing.*

It was a mystical wound, given by Jesus. But why on that particular day? Did it have anything to do with the Confessions he was hearing? We do not know. What is certain is that the timing was no accident.

THE STIGMATA OF THE LORD'S PASSION

Less than two months later, new wounds appeared on the Capuchin's body—this time not only spiritual, but physical. They were visible and would become a source of shame and humiliation for him.

Sanctuary of St. Padre Pio in San Giovanni Rotondo. More than seven million pilgrims visit San Giovanni Rotondo each year. In terms of pilgrim numbers, Padre Pio’s sanctuary ranked second only to the Basilica of Our Lady of Guadalupe, which sees almost ten million pilgrims annually.

Padre Pio blessing a child.

It happened on September 20, 1918. The pain from the first wound had subsided after forty-five days, leaving Padre Pio with what he called a “deep peace.” But that peace would remain accompanied by suffering.

One did not exclude the other: true peace—the kind the world cannot give—was not dependent on external conditions, not even freedom from deep suffering. Recall the witness of the early martyrs. To rest in God’s hands did not mean to be spared pain. Suffering came to Padre Pio through another encounter with Jesus. He was in the choir of the church, praying before a crucifix, when the same figure who had recently pierced his soul appeared again. “In the choir, after celebrating Mass,” he wrote to Father Benedetto, “I was overcome by a sort of sweet sleep.” This “sweet sleep” likely reflected the deep peace that had settled in

The modern facade of the church dedicated to St. Padre Pio in San Giovanni Rotondo.

The Capuchin saint’s cell in San Giovanni Rotondo.

1875

➤ The body of the great mystic was placed in a crystal coffin and made accessible for public viewing.

➤ Padre Pio's sandals.

➤ Relics of Padre Pio.

his soul. In that "Edenic rest," he again met Jesus:

> *While all this was happening, I saw in front of me a mysterious Person, just like the one I had seen on August 5th, only now His hands, feet, and side were dripping blood.*

Padre Pio beheld the bleeding Christ. His wounds were still open. The sight filled him with horror. He wrote:

> *I believed I would die and would have actually died had the Lord not intervened and fortified my heart, which felt like it would burst out of my chest.*

When the spiritual agony exceeded his strength, the vision disappeared. The wounded Christ vanished—but the wounds remained. The marks he had just seen on the Savior's body now appeared on his own. "I realized my arms, legs, and side were soaked with blood," he recounted. He added:

> *Imagine the agony I felt and am practically still feeling every day. My heart bleeds constantly, especially from Thursday evening to Saturday. Dear Father, I am dying of the pain these wounds cause and of the embarrassment they cause deep in my soul. I fear I will bleed out if the Lord does not hear my heartfelt plea to rid me of this state. Will Jesus, who is so good, grant me this grace? Will He at least free me from the humiliation of these outward signs? I shall pray and not cease praying to Him to remove them. Not the wounds or the suffering—because that is impossible, for I desire to be united to Him in His pain—but these external signs that humiliate me so much and cause unbearable embarrassment.*

The stigmata would not be withdrawn from the visible world. Padre Pio bore them for another fifty years.

JESUS' COMPLAINT

They did not appear by chance. A few years earlier, following an apparition, Padre Pio had offered himself entirely to Jesus in reparation for the sins of his generation. God accepted the offering—and more:

through these outward signs on the Capuchin of San Giovanni Rotondo, He showed the world that this friar was suffering for the sins of humanity.

Moreover, the stigmata testified that Jesus continues to suffer for humanity even now. Jesus Himself revealed this to Padre Pio. In a letter to Father Agostino dated April 7, 1913, Padre Pio recalled the Savior's words:

> *Do not imagine that my suffering was limited to three hours on the cross. I will continue to suffer until the end of the world for the souls whom I love so dearly.*

A LOVE REJECTED

We hear more of this message in another of Padre Pio's encounters with Jesus, recorded in a letter to Father Agostino on March 12, 1913. There, he quoted the Savior:

> *How ungrateful people are in return for my love! I would feel less offended by them if I had loved them less.... I would like to cease loving them, but ... but alas! My heart was made for love! Cowardly and slothful people do not even try to control their temptations; on the contrary, they delight in their wickedness.... My heart is forgotten; no one cares about my love anymore; I am always in sorrow. My house has become, for many, a place of entertainment. Even my own ministers—those I have always looked upon with favor, whom I have loved as the apple of my eye—these should comfort my heart so full of bitterness; they should help me redeem souls. Yet—who would believe it?—from them I must receive ingratitude and rejection.*

Padre Pio added, "Father, it makes me ill to see Jesus weep! Have you ever felt the same?"

THE DEVIL DISGUISED AS HEAVEN

Padre Pio was a particular target of Hell's hatred. His spiritual guide, Agostino da San Marco, affirmed: "The devil appeared to him as young women, as the cross, as a young friend of the friars, as a spiritual father, as the provincial of the Capuchins, as Pope Pius X, as a guardian angel, as St. Francis of Assisi—even as the Virgin Mary." Satan used every means to tempt him.

It is no surprise that the evil one took the form of beautiful women to lure him into sin. But the prince of darkness struck at

▲ *Relics of Padre Pio.*

▼ *A modern chapel with the Capuchin's crystal coffin.*

Padre Pio celebrated every Mass with great reverence. For him, the eucharistic liturgy was true participation in Christ's Passion. He was focused, serious, immersed in prayer, and deeply moved by the miracle taking place.

an even deeper level: obedience. Padre Pio practiced this virtue with heroic devotion, which made it a target of special attack. The danger of obeying the devil was grave. How could one discern whether a command came from a legitimate superior or from a false apparition—perhaps even disguised as the pope? How could one distinguish between a true vision of the founder of his order and the devil's cunning imitation?

Saints had their ways of discerning such deceptions. You may recall how St. Martin unmasked the devil's ruses: Satan was powerless to fool him and could only lash out in rage. It is worth noting that neither Jesus nor Mary—so deeply loved by Padre Pio—prevented these attacks. The reason was simple: the devil's assaults on the holy Capuchin served God's Will. Satan caused him further suffering, and Padre Pio offered that suffering to God. Pain inflicted by the devil, when offered for sinners, held exceptional value in God's eyes. What Satan never understood was how many souls he was helping to save against his will.

WITHOUT "SWEET" RETOUCHING

Mary did not intervene when the devil attacked Padre Pio with brutality, but she gave signs of her presence and support. One such sign appeared during a violent episode. In the middle of the night, terrible noises came from Padre Pio's cell. The friars rushed in and found the room in disarray: furniture overturned and broken, anything that could be torn was torn, anything that could be smashed was smashed. Padre Pio lay alone on the floor, bruised and bleeding, his shirt shredded.

But one detail stood out: beneath his head was a pillow, perfectly arranged—soft, smooth, without a single crease. When the friars lifted him, they pointed to it and asked, simply, "And this?"

His brief reply: "That's the Madonna."

Let us add that we need not fear such attacks. The devil does not show himself to those who are not already great saints. Were he to appear to us, we might be frightened enough to convert—if not out

A statue of St. Padre Pio at a corner of the sanctuary's steps.

of love for God, then out of fear of Hell. And in that case, he would lose our soul.

He does not harass or terrify us; he hides in the shadows. As Pope Paul VI observed, Satan's greatest triumph in modern times is that people have ceased believing in his existence—and rightly so, from his perspective.

HOLY SILENCE

In the early hours of September 23, 1968, the eighty-one-year-old Padre Pio went to Confession one last time and renewed his religious vows. Holding his rosary, he repeated the names "Jesus, Mary" until the end. About two hours after midnight, he said, "I see two mothers"—his own mother and Mary—then he breathed his last.

Some members of the community at the Monastery of Our Lady of Grace in San Giovanni Rotondo later said that, in the weeks leading up to Padre Pio's death, the monastery felt transformed, as though touched by the supernatural. The invisible remained hidden from human eyes, but the air seemed charged with something beyond this world. The corridors, cells, refectory—indeed the whole monastery—were enveloped in what came to be called "spiritual silence." All sounds and conversations were subdued, as if God had turned down the volume of the temporal world so that He Himself might be heard more clearly.

NO PESTS IN PARADISE

It was not the first time the temporal world had been overshadowed by the supernatural. A similar event occurred in the spring of 1930, when the Apulia region—home to San Giovanni Rotondo—was overrun by swarms of caterpillars. They devoured everything: grass, herbs, even tree bark. Soon they descended on the land near the Capuchin monastery, stripping the almond and olive trees bare. The caterpillars tore through leaves and flowers and even gnawed into the woody husks. After two days of futile efforts to stop the destruction, the local orchard owners turned to Padre Pio for help. For many of them, almond and olive trees were their only means of survival on that rocky soil.

The friar asked his superior for permission to recite the prayer designated for such circumstances. Then he put on an alb and stole, took holy water, and went out to the ravaged groves. First, he prayed an exorcism; then he made the sign of the cross in the air and sprinkled the "nasty creatures" with holy water. By the next day, the fields and orchards were free of caterpillars. Though the trees remained stripped, something even greater occurred: those same trees yielded more fruit that year than ever before.

God had revealed His presence in nature through a miracle. But for such miracles to unfold, He needed saints like Padre Pio.

San Giovanni Rotondo, once a small Italian town, became a pilgrimage site visited by millions of pilgrims.

The stigmata of the Passion appeared early in Padre Pio's priestly life.

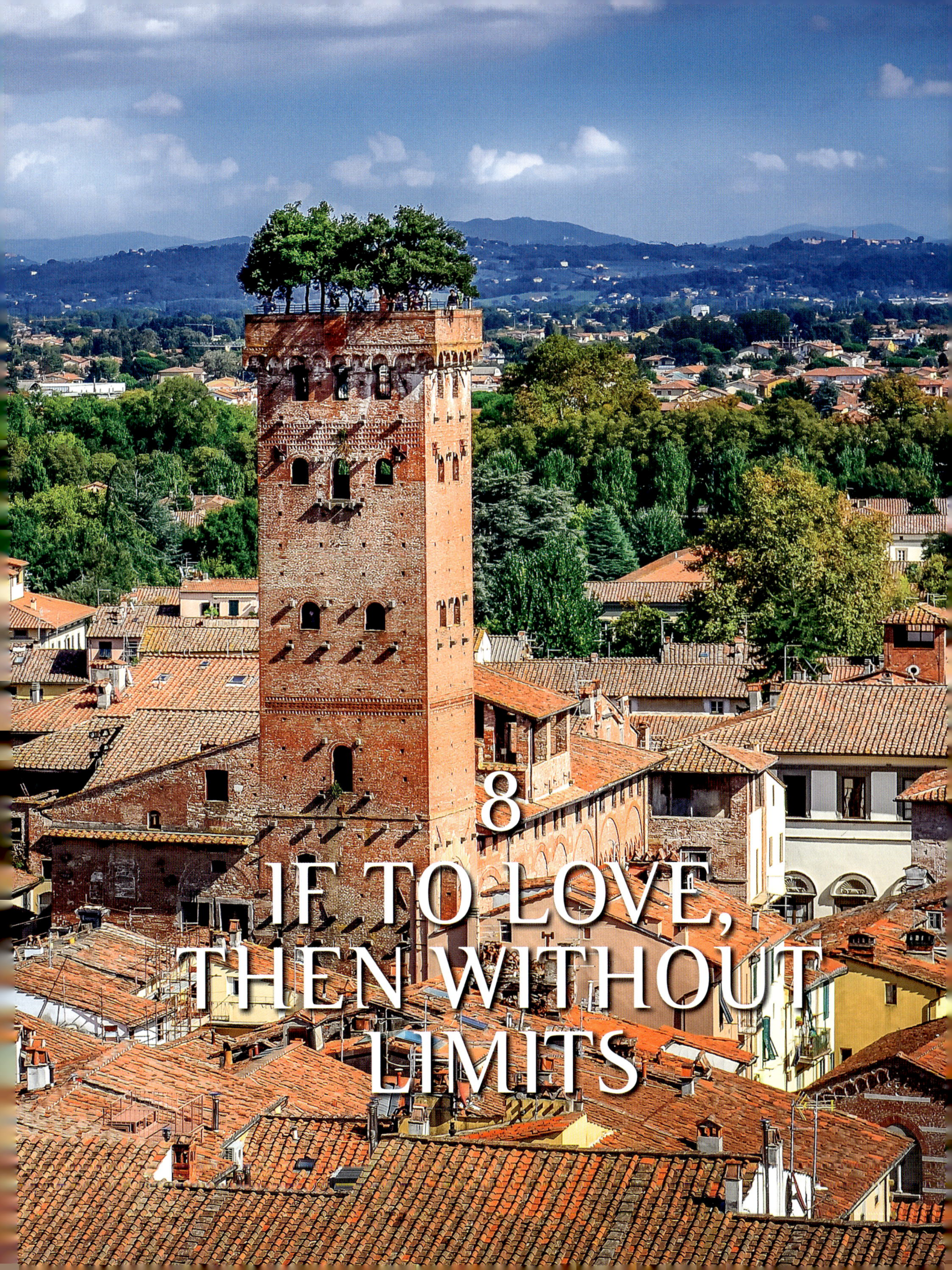

8
IF TO LOVE, THEN WITHOUT LIMITS

1887

On the previous page: Lucca, Italy.

Place of Apparition: Lucca, Italy
Date and Place of Birth: March 12, 1878, Borgonuovo, Italy
Date and Place of Death: April 11, 1903, Lucca, Italy
Beatification: May 14, 1933 (Pius XI)
Visionary as a Lay and Religious Person (Third Order of Congregation of the Passion of Jesus Christ)
Canonization: May 2, 1940 (Pius XII)
Feast: April 11
Works: Autobiography, Diary

Seven-year-old Gemma Galgani with her sister Angelina.

8

IF TO LOVE, THEN WITHOUT LIMITS

GEMMA GALGANI, 1887

Many great saints kept her image on their desks—St. Maximilian Maria Kolbe, Padre Pio, and even the more recent Don Dolindo Ruotolo. All of them read her spiritual autobiography. Was it an unusual biography? Yes—perhaps unique in all of history. The devil stole her handwritten notes, and only through exorcisms was he forced to return them. What was he so afraid of? Those writings had the power to turn souls into saints—or, more precisely, into souls willing to suffer for the salvation of others.

Was it not striking that, once again, on the map of Jesus' apparitions, we find one not centered on the beauty of Heaven or the joy of divine love—without exhortations to virtue, instructions for spiritual growth, or visions of heavenly reward? Instead, once more, Jesus appeared to ask for suffering—inviting others to share in His Passion.

Could it be that the time had come when God was calling people to become co-sufferers with Christ? That the world had grown so sinful, it needed not just reminders of God's mercy but of Christ's pain? That His suffering must be echoed in the lives of His disciples?

These questions may not all be theologically precise—but perhaps they can be reframed: did these times need witnesses to remind people of the price the Savior paid?

St. Gemma Galgani was one of those witnesses—not only to the Passion of Jesus, but a participant in it.

She might have said after St. Paul: "In my flesh I am filling up what is lacking in the afflictions of Christ on behalf of his body" (Colossians 1:24).

BURN IT IMMEDIATELY

We know about the content of Jesus' apparitions only through the spiritual writings of the visionaries themselves. By now, this seemed almost a rule. St. Gemma Galgani was another such mystic. She wrote at the request of her confessor, Father Germanus, a Passionist. In January 1900, he instructed her to record the graces she had received. Obediently, the future saint began to keep spiritual notes.

She wrote, but with a hidden hope—much like St. Margaret Mary Alacoque—that her diary would remain unknown. At the very beginning of her notes, she cautioned her confessor: "Read it and read it again as much as you want, but no one else, just you, and then burn it immediately. Do you understand?"

Father Germanus did not follow this request. The devil, however, tried to. Every surviving page of the manuscript was set on fire by him. Father Germanus later explained what had happened:

> *Gemma's manuscript, once completed, was entrusted—on my instructions—to Cecilia Giannini, in whose home the visionary was staying. Cecilia hid it in a drawer, waiting for the right moment to give it to me. A few days passed, and Gemma saw a demon entering the room through the window, where the drawer was. He laughed, then vanished into thin air. Gemma was accustomed to such phenomena and paid it little mind. Soon he returned, tormenting her again, as he often did, with foul temptations. When he failed, he gnashed his teeth and cried out, "War, war! Your book is in my hands." She wrote to tell me of this. In obedience—always her guide—she believed she was bound to report everything extraordinary to her vigilant benefactor. So she told her.*

Lucca, a small Tuscan city located near Florence and Pisa.

Left: Relics of St. Gemma.

Middle: The hallway of Gemma Galgani's house.

Right: Stark furnishings in the bedroom of the great saint.

Habit of Gemma Galgani.

> *We went and opened the drawer and found that the book was no longer there.... What could we do?... I decided to cast out the devil and thus force him to return the manuscript, if indeed he was the one who took it. With a stole and holy water, I went to the tomb of the blessed servant of God [a Passionist, Blessed Gabriel of Our Lady of Sorrows], and there—although it was almost 400 miles from Lucca—I performed an exorcism.... In the same hour, the manuscript returned to the place from which it had been taken a few days earlier. But in what condition it was! The whole thing, from top to bottom, was slightly burned, and some parts were scorched as if each page had been separately exposed to intense fire. However, they were not so damaged that the letters could not be read.*

What was the devil so afraid of? Reading her diary turned sinners into saints—and saints into great saints.

"I ASKED HIM..."

St. Maximilian Kolbe often quoted Gemma Galgani's motto: that God should be *loved without limits*. For her, to love meant to seek union. But, as she understood it, true love was not found in seeking the Glorious Jesus. As long as we remain on earth, our Bridegroom is the Suffering Jesus. Union with Him means accepting the suffering through which He invites us to share in the work of salvation.

Gemma wrote:

> *I felt a great desire to love Jesus Crucified growing in me, and at the same time a great desire to suffer and support Him in His pain. I asked Him to give me suffering—and a lot of suffering. Jesus listened to me and sent me sickness.*

Her longing for love and for suffering is most clearly expressed in a deeply mystical prayer:

> *Grant, O my God, when my lips come close to Yours to kiss You, that I may taste the gall given to You; when my arms touch Yours, that I may feel Your scourging; when my body is united to Yours in the Most Holy Eucharist; when my head comes close to Yours, that I may feel Your thorns; when my heart is close*

to Yours, that I may feel the spear that pierced You.

A JEWEL IS BORN

Gemma was born on March 12, 1878, in Borgonuovo, Tuscany. She was the fourth of eight children born to Enrico Galgani, an apothecary, and his wife, Aurelia—their first daughter. She was baptized the next day and given three names: Gemma Umberta Pia.

Her mother was troubled that no saint bore the name *Gemma*. Did this mean her daughter had no heavenly patron? But it soon became clear she had no need of one—she had Jesus. According to the meaning of her name, she was His "jewel," a title that would follow her in death. Gemma Galgani became known as the *Jewel of Christ*.

When she was two months old, the family moved to Lucca. There, her beloved mother began to suffer from tuberculosis. Gemma was deeply attached to her. Instead of playing with dolls, she preferred to sit in her lap and listen to her speak of Jesus. Years later, she would say, "It was my mother who made me want to go to heaven as a child."

"She often took me in her arms," Gemma recalled, "and many times she cried while doing so. She repeated: 'I prayed a lot for Jesus to give me a little girl. It comforted me, it's true, but it came very late. I am sick,' she told me, 'and I will have to die. I will have to leave you. And if I could take you with me, would you come?'"

She probably said yes. But at her first encounter with Jesus, the Lord would deny her that grace. Not yet. First, He would give her a foretaste of the Heaven she so deeply desired.

FIRST EXPERIENCE

She must have been a truly devout child, for she was permitted to receive her First Holy Communion at the age of eight. "There is no other choice," the priest said. "Either we allow her to receive Holy Communion, or we will see her die of grief. Yes, she is ready."

Left: Statue of Gemma in the church of Santa María del Pi in Barcelona.

Right: A portrait and memorial inscription placed on the wall of the house where the visionary died.

1887

Solemn procession through the streets of Lucca.

Aurelia and Enrico, parents of the holy visionary.

Gemma Galgani's education in a girls' school.

On the eve of receiving the Lord Jesus in the Blessed Sacrament, she wrote with deep resolve:

> *I will try to make every Confession and receive Holy Communion as if it were the last day of my life. I will often visit the Lord Jesus in the Blessed Sacrament, especially when I am distraught.*

And then—she had her first mystical experience.

What exactly happened on Friday, June 17, 1887, the feast of the Sacred Heart of Jesus, remains unknown. Even Gemma herself did not fully understand it. She wrote:

> *What took place between me and Jesus at that moment... I cannot express it.... He made me feel Him so strongly in my soul. I realized then that the pleasures of heaven are not like those of earth. I was overwhelmed by the desire to constantly abide in union with my God. I felt more and more detached from the world and more and more ready to concentrate* [*on Him*].

The next day, she confided in the priest who had heard her Confession:

> *Yesterday I experienced a day in paradise. I was constantly with Jesus, I spoke only of Jesus, I was happy with Jesus, and I even cried before Jesus.*

Gemma already felt a detachment from the world. She had tasted Heaven and knew it surpassed anything earthly. One might say, in biblical language, that she no longer desired *flesh and blood*.

What she did not yet know was that this sweetness marked only the beginning of a long bitterness. She did not yet know that God was preparing her to say *yes*—a *yes* she was not yet able to utter.

But she would. With tears.

A DIFFICULT LESSON

The first—and immediately difficult—conversation with Jesus that we know of occurred a year later, after Gemma received the Sacrament of Confirmation.

> *After the liturgical ceremony, the person who accompanied me* [*my*

confirmation sponsor] wanted to attend Mass.... I listened to the Mass as devoutly as I could, praying for my mother. At one point, I heard a voice in my heart: "Do you want to give me your mom?"

"Yes," I replied, "but only if you take me too."

"No," said the same voice. "Give me your mother of your own free will. I will take you to heaven later. I will take her to heaven, you know. Will you give her to me willingly?"

I felt compelled to say yes. After the Mass ended, I ran home. My God! I looked at my mother and cried—I couldn't help myself.

What a difficult first dialogue with Jesus. Gemma was deeply attached to her mother. She wanted to go with her. Aurelia had dreamed of the same. But the Lord had other plans—He wanted Gemma to live.

It would not be long, however. Seventeen years later, mother and daughter would be reunited in Heaven.

For now, Gemma was learning how to surrender—freely—what she did not want to let go. She was being taught to give up *flesh and blood,* to detach herself from everything that tied her to the world. She had to learn what the Apostle Paul taught: that "our struggle is not with flesh and blood but with the principalities, with the powers, with the world rulers of this present darkness, with the evil spirits in the heavens" (Ephesians 6:12).

So now, in the hierarchy of her decisions, Gemma no longer placed *flesh and blood*—her own or her family's—at the center. She placed above all the *flesh and blood of Jesus.* The affairs of His Kingdom came to mean more to her than the

Church of St. Gemma Galgani in Rome.

St. Gemma Galgani's back brace.

Church of San Michele in Foro, where Gemma received the Sacrament of Confirmation.

A modest book collection and piano in the apartment of Gemma Galgani (Lucca, Italy). Gemma's room, where she wrote her letters.

concerns of her earthly life. This was only the beginning—a difficult first lesson for an eight-year-old girl.

For now, her consent to her mother's death came more from reverence for Jesus' authority than from full submission to God's Will. And her submission was not yet joyful. Gemma already knew her mother was going to die, and that knowledge brought tears. Her beloved mother's health steadily declined. On September 17, 1895, after five years of suffering from pulmonary tuberculosis, Aurelia Galgani died.

STUBBORN AS JESUS

That first lesson had an unexpected result. Gemma learned something from Jesus—not just submission, but determination. Did He want her to follow Him? Then, like Him, she would press her case. If she had yielded her mother to His Will, perhaps He would grant her requests in return. After all, if her mother's death had been according to God's Will, so too might her pleas.

She did not always *beg* Jesus—sometimes she *bargained* with Him. In ecstasy, she once pleaded for the salvation of a particular soul. Jesus told her, with sadness, that her prayers and sacrifices would not bear fruit. The man's heart was too hardened. He had ignored too many signs, too many warnings. The Lord saw no hope. But Gemma did not give up. She turned to the intercession of the Mother of God, knowing that Jesus could not deny His Mother's request. She pleaded: "Your Mother is praying for him too. You cannot say no to her!"

She persisted:

> *I seek not Your justice, but Your grace. I know he made You weep, but do not think of his sins. Think of the blood You shed. Answer me now, Jesus. Tell me that You saved my sinner.*

Then she named the man for whom she had prayed. In the next moment, she cried out with joy: "He has been saved! You have triumphed! Jesus, always triumph like this, please!"

One of the witnesses to this ecstasy was her confessor. Upon returning home, he encountered a man in tears, who fell to his knees before him and begged to go to Confession.

It turned out that the man's name—the one who fell to his knees before the confessor—was the very name Gemma had been repeating in her conversation with Jesus just moments earlier.

Did similar moments of divine intimacy occur while she was still a student at the

Gemma's portrait often featured in the Holy Images.

Lucca at night. A street near the house where Gemma Galgani lived.

Church of St. Gemma Galgani. Relics of the mystic placed under the altar (Lucca, Italy).

convent school? Or does the following testimony simply confirm that Gemma was already in direct contact with Jesus?

One day, the superior of the sisters asked Gemma's teacher and her classmates to pray for a dying man who had stubbornly refused to receive the holy sacraments. After the prayers were finished, Gemma approached the teacher and whispered, "We have been heard." That evening, news arrived: the man had converted and been reconciled with God before his death.

TWO CROWNS

One day, something happened in Gemma's life that recalls an episode from the life of St. Maximilian Kolbe. After receiving Holy Communion, she heard the voice of Jesus: "Courage, Gemma. I am waiting for you at Calvary."

A moment later, her guardian angel appeared, holding two crowns—one of thorns, and one of white lilies.

The angel asked Gemma which crown she chose. She pointed to the crown of thorns—after all, Jesus was waiting for her

Left: A part of Gemma Galgani's tombstone (Lucca, Italy).

Right: First-class relics of St. Gemma Galgani.

One of many mementos from Gemma's apartment.

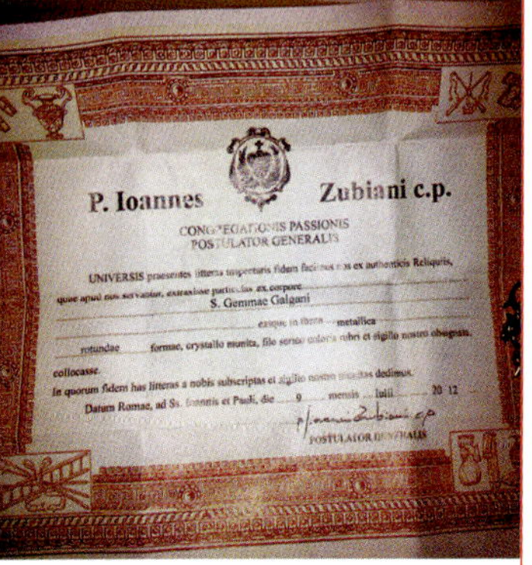

at Calvary. She did not, like St. Maximilian Kolbe, ask for both. But God would give her the other as well. Her symbol of holiness—a white lily—was no coincidence.

"HE CHOSE ME TO BE HIS CHILD"

Her Calvary was no metaphor. She began to have difficulty walking and eventually lost the use of her legs entirely. Soon after, she developed spinal tuberculosis and spent an entire year bedridden, immobilized by a plaster corset. The pain was excruciating, and the doctors were convinced she would not survive.

"I confessed," Gemma recalled, "and looked forward to the moment of going with Jesus. And—listen!—the doctors thought I didn't understand them and spoke among themselves, saying I wouldn't live until midnight. Long live Jesus!"

But she did not die. On the first Friday of the month, she received Holy Communion and began to converse with the Savior.

> *Oh, what happy moments I experienced with Jesus. He ... asked me: "Do you want to be healed?" I was moved so deeply that I could not speak, but in my heart, I answered: "Whatever You want, oh Jesus!" The grace was granted. I was healed. I got out of bed. I was happy—not so much because I had been healed, but because Jesus had chosen me to be His child. That morning, before He left me, He said: "My child, the grace you received this morning is the beginning; it will be followed by many others, even greater."*

What kind of graces would those be? For Gemma, that did not matter. The greatest joy was that Jesus had called her His child.

But we know what followed: the graces He spoke of would be suffering and stigmata. The suffering came, in part, from severe kidney inflammation, unbearable headaches, acute purulent otitis media, and two invasive surgeries—both performed without anesthesia.

Like her mother and beloved brother, Gemma also contracted tuberculosis. It would be the illness that would take her from this world. Yet throughout her suffering, she remained cheerful—and it was no mere facade. She once said: "When we are closely connected to Jesus, there is neither cross nor sorrow."

What remains, then? we might ask. Gemma's answer was simple: "We have Jesus."

LEARNING TO SUFFER

She was a master of prayer. Let us hear in her own words what she did when troubled by her inability to love Jesus as she wished: "One evening, in order to calm myself, I achieved inner concentration during prayer." It was then that she entered the world of mystical vision:

> *I found myself before the face of Jesus Crucified, who spoke to me with these words: "Look, daughter, and learn how to love!" He showed me five open wounds. "Do you see this cross, these thorns, these nails, these bruises, these scratches, these wounds, this blood? They are all the work of love—of infinite love. Do you see how much I have loved you? If you truly want to love Me, first learn to suffer, because suffering teaches you to love."*

From that moment, Gemma's one desire—the desire of one who longed to love—was to suffer.

STIGMATA UNDER THE MANTLE OF MARY

On June 8, 1899, the eve of the feast of the Sacred Heart of Jesus, Gemma received the stigmata. She wrote: "I could think of nothing but my sins and the offense they gave to God. My memory recalled all my past sins and showed me all the torments Jesus had suffered to save me."

Once again, the path to encounter Jesus was prayer—deep, interior prayer. She continued:

> *Following this interior recollection, I was quickly rapt out of my senses and found myself before my heavenly Mother [the Blessed Virgin Mary]. At her right stood my guardian angel, who told me to make an act of contrition. When I had finished, my blessed Mother said to me: "Daughter—in the name of Jesus, your sins are forgiven."*

This raises a rich theological question: could the Blessed Virgin, united with Jesus in Heaven, forgive sins? Of course not. Mary was not acting as priest or judge; she was simply declaring what God had already done. God had forgiven Gemma's sins.

And yes—even Gemma considered herself a sinner. Ask the greatest saints, and they will tell you how great their sins were.

Why did Mary appear in this moment? Gemma used to say, "If God took my mother, He left me His Mother." She often turned to the Blessed Virgin, entrusting to her the desires of her heart. Her favorite aspiratory prayer was: "Holy Virgin, make me a saint."

So it was no surprise that the Blessed Mother called her "daughter."

What followed was Gemma's remarkable account of receiving the stigmata. It began with a conversation—with Mary.

Mary was her guide and teacher in that moment.

The mystic wrote down her visions under divine inspiration.

"Jesus, my Son, loves you very much, and He wishes to give you a grace. Do you know how to make yourself worthy of it?" In my misery, I did not know what to answer. She continued: "I will be your Mother. Will you be a true daughter?"

This seemed to be the condition for receiving the grace—and for encountering Jesus.

She then spread her mantle and covered me with it. At that moment, Jesus appeared, with all His wounds open. But blood no longer flowed from them—flames of fire issued forth instead. In an instant, these flames came to touch my hands, my feet, and my heart. I felt as if I would die. I fell to the floor, but my Mother supported me, keeping me covered in her mantle. I had to remain several hours in that position, but I also felt good.

This echoes a theme familiar from the testimonies of the martyrs: suffering and joy can exist together. Gemma, wrapped in Mary's mantle, discovered that wounds do not only hurt—they have meaning. And that meaning brought peace, even happiness. In the midst of agony, *she felt good.*

She continued:

Finally, she kissed me on the forehead, and all vanished. I found myself kneeling on the floor. But I still felt intense pain in my hands, feet, and heart. I got up to go to bed and noticed that blood was flowing from the places where I felt pain. I covered them as best I could, and with the help of my angel, I managed to go to bed. These sufferings and pains, though they afflicted me, filled me with perfect peace. The next morning, I was able to go to Communion only with great difficulty, and I wore a pair of gloves to hide my hands. I could hardly stand, and I thought I might die at any moment. The sufferings lasted until 3:00 p.m. on Friday afternoon, the solemnity of the Sacred Heart of Jesus.

Left: Posthumous photo of Gemma surrounded by her family.

Right: Las mañanitas a Santa Gema, a procession with the statue of St. Gemma Galgani in the streets of Managua (Nicaragua).

Bishop Giovanni Volpi, Gemma's confessor and spiritual father, initially had sincere doubts about the origin of these wounds.

One day, despite Gemma's protests, Bishop Volpi sent her for a medical examination. The doctors dismissed the stigmata as symptoms of an unknown illness—or as the physical manifestation of religious delusion in an overly pious young woman.

The wounds of the Lord's Passion did not disappear until three years before her death. At one point, her confessor forbade her to receive the stigmata. Gemma, obedient as always, prayed for them to be taken away. They vanished—though faint white marks remained until the day she died.

DYING FOR THE LAST TIME

"I have to be crucified with Jesus. He told me that His children must be crucified," she said on her deathbed. She would remain on the cross until the very end. A witness to her final hours wrote:

> *She took the crucifix in her hands, and holding it at eye level, she said: "You see, Jesus, I really can do no more. If it is Your will, take me." Then, turning to the image of the Blessed Mother on the wall, she said: "My Mother, I commend my soul to you. Tell Jesus to be merciful to me."*

Though she was suffering terribly, she was, according to those present, "as beautiful as an angel—calm, serene, smiling as always."

She died quietly, in the presence of a local parish priest. He later said:

> *I have been present at many deathbeds, but never have I seen anyone die like Gemma—without any sign that death was near, not even a final breath. She died with a smile still on her lips. I could not convince myself that she was dead.*

Gemma passed away at the age of twenty-five. Like her beloved mother, she died of tuberculosis.

The manuscript of Gemma Galgani's spiritual diary, which a demon tried to burn despite its being hidden in a fireproof armored cash box.

9 MISSION IN THE EAST

9

MISSION IN THE EAST

LEOPOLD MANDIĆ, 1887

Place of Apparition: Padua, Italy
Date and Place of Birth: May 12, 1866, Herceg Novi, Montenegro
Date and Place of Death: July 30, 1942, Padua, Italy
Visionary as a Religious Person (Order of Friars Minor Capuchin)
Beatification: May 2, 1976 (Paul VI)
Canonization: October 16, 1983 (John Paul II)
Feast: May 12

Two confessors lived in the same era, both Capuchins, both residing in monasteries within the same country. One friar was as sharp as a scalpel cutting through an abscess; the other, as gentle as balm poured over a wound. The gentler of the two performed heavy penances on behalf of his penitents and once lamented that he was not as merciful as a true disciple of Jesus ought to be. While the first could turn people away from the confessional, deny absolution, or even raise his voice at a penitent, the second seemed capable of only one thing: showing mercy.

One was Padre Pio. The other was Leopold Mandić. Both shared the same charism—the grace to read hearts—and the same vocation: to lead souls to conversion. But their methods could not have been more different.

It was as if Jesus—on whose behalf both men granted absolution—were different in each of them. Yet it was the same Savior who denounced the Pharisees without a trace of pity, who drove out the merchants from the Temple with a whip of cords,

and who, at the same time, forgave the tax collector Matthew without condition. It was He who forgot the sins of Mary Magdalene, and who promised Paradise to the thief suffering beside Him on the cross. Two ways of Jesus. At times, the first path—the stern and uncompromising—was walked by the well-known Francesco Forgione of San Giovanni Rotondo. The second, the path of quiet mercy, was never left by Leopold Mandić of Padua. Though different in method, the stigmatist from Pietrelcina held his Paduan confrere in the highest esteem. He even asked pilgrims from northern Italy: "Why do you come to me? After all, you have a holy confessor in your own region."

A CALL TO THE EAST

Leopold Mandić was born on May 12, 1866—a date that, in the Marian calendar, honors Our Lady of Miracles. Perhaps this was no coincidence. His life would become a quiet witness to the truth that whatever is Marian must be Christian, and must shape the life of every disciple of Jesus.

For Mandić was, in a certain sense, *miraculous*. His life was filled with the presence and signs of God—not spectacular or showy, but the kind that unfold silently in the depths of the soul. He was not an outward miracle worker. Like the Blessed Mother, he was hidden from the world.

At Baptism, he was named Bogdan Ivan. But in 1884, when he took the Capuchin habit, these names were hidden beneath a new one: *Leopold,* which means "brave people." And indeed, he would carry a lifelong dream—to return to the East, to serve his "brave people."

And so he became Leopold—bravely embracing his mission. But where did that dream come from?

He was the twelfth child of Karolina Zarević and Piotr Mandić. Their impoverished home was in Herceg Novi, in

The Old Town in Herceg Novi, the hometown of St. Leopold Mandic, and the church dedicated to him (Montenegro).

ITALY

Statue of Leopold Mandić in Medjugorje, Bosnia and Herzegovina.

what is now Montenegro. At the time, the town had been under Habsburg rule since 1797 and bore the Italian name *Castelnuovo*. But was there much Italian culture in daily life? Unlikely.

This Dalmatian town was deeply divided—home to both Catholic Croatians and Orthodox Serbs, who lived in a state of mutual suspicion and tension. Even the Christian faith had become a tool of conflict. To the local Catholics, the Orthodox were heretics; to the Orthodox, the Catholics were traitors to Christ.

That fractured landscape left a deep impression on the heart of the future saint. The sign of division in his own hometown became, for him, a kind of calling. From a young age, Mandić sensed that God was inviting him to work for unity between East and West.

DIRECTION: THE MONASTERY

He must have perceived some inner voice early on—though not one he recognized as an apparition. After discerning his vocation, he left his hometown at age sixteen and walked 800 kilometers west to knock on the door of the Capuchin seminary in Udine.

He chose the Capuchin order precisely to prepare for the mission he believed God had entrusted to him.

Was his certainty the fruit of a private revelation—unknown to the world? Or was it the result of a quiet but unmistakable spiritual conviction? For Mandić, such interior clarity was equivalent to the voice of the Lord.

He later recalled that he first heard the voice of God on June 18, 1887. On that occasion, the Lord spoke to him about the return of the separated Eastern Church to unity with the Catholic Church. Interestingly,

this date came *after* his decision to join the Capuchins. Yet we know that his religious vocation had already been born out of a deep desire to serve as a missionary in the East. This means that the call he received in 1887 was not the origin of his vocation—but rather its confirmation. God Himself affirmed the mission.

LEOPOLD IS BORN

Young Mandić set out so that one day he might return—to his "brave people"—as a missionary. He was convinced it would be soon.

In the meantime, he prepared with diligence. He studied languages and eventually became fluent in Croatian, Serbian, Slovenian, Italian, Latin, and Greek. He immersed himself in the history and theology of the undivided Church, especially the period before the schism of 1054. All of this, he believed, would serve the great work of restoring Christian unity.

When he was ordained to the priesthood on September 20, 1890, he was convinced that his dream was about to be fulfilled. He immediately petitioned his superiors to send him as a missionary to the East. Their answer was no.

The monastic authorities judged Mandić unfit for such a mission. He was small in stature—just 135 centimeters (approximately four feet four inches)—frail in health, and suffered from a noticeable speech impediment. Despite these limitations, Leopold remained confident that he was pursuing the Will of God. He appealed again and again, asking that the will of his superiors be brought into harmony with the Will of Heaven. But permission never came. Obediently, he accepted their decision. In 1906, he was assigned to the friary of Santa Croce in Padua. He would remain there for the rest of his life.

Because of his speech impediment and limited ability as a preacher, Leopold's

Leopold Mandić, National Shrine of St. Michael and the Archangels (Manila, Philippines).

Mosaic with St. Leopold Mandić, the facade of a church in Rijeka, Croatia.

➤ *A crowd around the coffin of the holy friar in Zagreb Cathedral, Croatia.*

superiors assigned him to the confessional. This quiet ministry became his new vocation—and, as he would come to understand, the very instrument through which he would fulfill his original missionary calling.

Leopold discovered a deeper dimension to his mission:

> *The whole meaning of my life should be God's plan, so that I, too, in my own way, should do something so that one day, in accordance with God's Wisdom—who decides everything with power and gentleness—those separated from the East will return to Catholic unity. I must always be ready to work. We were born to work hard, and we will rest in paradise. I was called for the salvation of my people—that is, the Slavic people—and at the same time, I was called for the salvation of souls, especially by administering the sacrament of reconciliation.*

In these words, Mandić revealed two vocations: the dream of bringing unity to the Eastern Church, and the daily work of Confession. He came to understand that the latter was the path by which the former would be fulfilled.

APPARITION GIVEN TO A PENITENT

Father Leopold's heart remained in the East. For this reason, he refused to accept Italian citizenship—even during the First World War. Because of this, he was forced to move from monastery to monastery throughout southern Italy. After all, he remained a citizen of the Habsburg Empire, which was at war with Italy. At one point, he even spent a year in prison for refusing to renounce his nationality.

He always insisted: he was from the East, and he would return to the East.

He still believed, with unwavering certainty, that his vocation was the reconciliation of the divided Church. Was he mistaken? From a worldly point of view, it might seem so. But Leopold saw things differently. He knew he had to look from a broader perspective. After all, the call he had received from God and the tasks given him by his superiors must somehow share a common purpose.

What was that purpose? Jesus Himself provided the answer. "I had the opportunity to meet a good soul and give her Communion," Leopold later recalled. "After she completed her thanksgiving, she told me: 'Father, the Lord Jesus ordered me to tell you that your East is every soul you assist here in Confession.'"

This woman had received the grace of what we might call an *indirect apparition*—Jesus revealed Himself to her and gave her a message to deliver.

From that moment, Mandić understood: his mission to the East was to be fulfilled in the confessional.

The body of the holy friar on display in a crystal coffin during a ceremony.

In his notes, Leopold wrote: "Each soul who needs my ministry will become an East for me." He understood that he had been *called for the salvation of souls, especially by administering the sacrament of reconciliation*—and that this very task would become the means of fulfilling his original vocation. Every Confession he heard, every moment spent with those who came to him, became an instrument for uniting the divided Church.

It was a tool far different from the one he had imagined. It did not allow him to witness the fruits of his labor firsthand. But that did not matter. What mattered most to Mandić was that he had found peace in the harmony between God's Will and the will of his superiors. The two were not in conflict. They were, in truth, one: the Will of God spoke of the result, and the will of his superiors revealed the means.

"LOUNGE OF HOSPITALITY"

Leopold began his ministry as a confessor not in a church confessional, but in a small monastic cell. He called it the "lounge of hospitality." The room measured just six square meters (about 65 square feet), with a tiny window that looked out onto a cramped and airless courtyard. It was here that he received penitents. Each Confession was, for him, a hidden labor on behalf of the East.

He would spend over a dozen hours a day hearing Confessions—every day, for nearly forty years.

All sorts of people knocked on his door, and no two Confessions were alike. In one extraordinary case, the roles were unexpectedly reversed. Giovanni Chivato, who had avoided Confession for many years, entered the *lounge of hospitality*—and was so overwhelmed by the holiness of the friar that he instinctively sat in the confessor's place.

Leopold knelt to hear Chivato's Confession. His confreres later said, "He treated everyone as if the salvation of all humanity depended on their conversion." After long, exhausting hours in the confessional, he always went straight to the chapel. "I give the penitents light

▼ St. Leopold Mandić depicted on a stained-glass window, Church of Our Lady of Lourdes (Rijeka, Croatia).

The confessor's beatification took place thirty-four years after his death, on May 2, 1976. He was beatified by Pope Paul VI, and seven years later John Paul II proclaimed Leopold Mandić a saint for the whole Church.

penances, so I have to do the rest of the penance for them myself," he explained. "Don't worry—please put everything on my shoulders, and I will take care of it." He imposed penances on himself: long prayers, night vigils, fasting, and scourging—until he bled.

SACRIFICE

Leopold was not always appreciated by his fellow confessors. Some accused him of being too lenient—too eager, in their view, to absolve. They said that was why the line outside his door was always so long. To such criticisms, he offered the same reply:

> *Me—gentle? Mind you, I didn't die for their sins like Jesus. Is it possible to be more gentle than He was to a penitent thief? If the Lord wants to accuse me of being too lenient toward sinners, I'll tell Him that it was He who gave me the example. And I haven't even died for the salvation of souls as He did!*

JESUS REVEALS THE FATE OF PADUA

Perhaps he experienced visions in his youth. Perhaps he encountered Jesus more than once during his priesthood. We cannot say for certain. But we do know of two visions—one on June 18, 1887, and another, half a century later, on March 23, 1932.

How do we know about the second? Because afterward, Leopold was filled with sorrow. His confreres, who knew him as always cheerful, asked what troubled him. He answered: "The Lord opened my eyes, and I saw Italy in a sea of fire and blood." When they asked whether Padua would also be bombed, he replied:

> *Yes, and very much so. This church and friary will suffer. But not this little cell—for in it, God has shown so much mercy to the souls of men that it will remain untouched, as a visible sign of His goodness.*

His prophecy was fulfilled on May 14, 1944, during a bombing raid. Five bombs struck the monastery. But the *lounge of hospitality*—his tiny cell—was left intact.

DEATH

The years passed, and Mandić, increasingly frail, knew his end was near. Yet he worked as always. For him, nothing was more important than the Eucharist and the confessional.

On the last active day of his life, Leopold heard the Confessions of nearly fifty penitents.

On the morning of July 30, 1942, he fainted while preparing to celebrate Mass. He was carried to bed, where he received

the Sacrament of the Anointing of the Sick and began to pray. He died just after finishing the *Salve Regina*—the Hail, Holy Queen.

He gave his final breath with his hands raised, as if reaching for a long-awaited embrace. During the canonization process, Father Benjamin, his superior at the time, testified:

> *I, who accompanied him in his last moments, am convinced that the Mother of God accompanied him in his passage to eternity. He died repeating the* Salve Regina. *When he said the words,* O clement, O loving, O sweet Virgin Mary, *he rose, and, joyfully stretching out his arms upward—as if to touch something marvelous—he passed away.*

Did Mary, in that moment, show him Jesus, the blessed fruit of her womb, as the antiphon requests? It would have been the final and most beautiful apparition of his life.

DEFINITION OF HOLINESS

During Leopold's canonization on October 16, 1983, Pope John Paul II said:

> *His life passed without any great events: several times, in accordance with the custom of the Capuchins, he was transferred from monastery to monastery, but nothing more. His last assignment was to a friary in Padua, where he remained until his death. And yet it was into this poor, outwardly inconspicuous life that the Holy Spirit descended and ignited a new greatness—a heroic fidelity to Christ, to Franciscan ideals, to priestly service to his brothers. St. Leopold did not leave behind theological or literary works. He did not captivate others with his knowledge or found any great social institutions. To those who knew him, he was simply a poor religious friar—unassuming and frail. His greatness lies elsewhere: in self-sacrifice. In the daily offering of himself, year after year, for fifty-two years of priestly life—spent in silence, in hiddenness, in the poverty of a tiny confessional. Brother Leopold was always there: ready and smiling, prudent and modest, a discreet confidant and faithful father of souls, a respectful teacher, an understanding and patient spiritual counselor. If one were to define him with a single word, as his penitents and confreres did during his lifetime, it would be confessor. He only knew how to confess. And precisely in that lies his greatness.*

Solemn Mass at Carevom Polju in memory of St. Leopold Bogdan Mandić (Jajce, Bosnia and Herzegovina).

The statue of St. Leopold Bogdan Mandić in the Croatian National Shrine of St. Mary of Marija Bistrica.

VULTUM · TUUM · SUPER NOS

What was puzzling was that in this particular moment, Jesus first addressed her by the name she had received at Baptism: "Follow Me, Maria." Later, we read that He called Leonia His "little sister." The mystical marriage she received was not a private favor alone—it was meant to commission her as an apostle of a new path to salvation. Jesus explained:

> *I need the souls of people, for I desire to fill heaven with them. I have an excess of happiness; I want to share it, to make [souls] happy, to satiate, to enrich. Oh, to whom will I give this goodness without end that flows from My heart? It [is] born in My heart for people, My brothers, My children. There is enough for everyone, as long as they are willing to receive.*

He added: "Leonia, the path of spiritual infancy is available to all."

We already knew Mary of St. Peter, who lived in closeness to the Infant Jesus, and of course St. Thérèse of Lisieux. But Leonia was the Bride of the Infant Jesus. Was such a thing even possible? From a merely human standpoint, it seemed a contradiction. But mysticism operates according to a different logic.

SHORTEST PATH

Leonia was not destined for a long life—nor did she desire one. She already longed to leave this world and be united with God forever. In the few years remaining to her, Jesus taught her how to live out the mystery of "spiritual infancy." He wanted her to remain always aware of her own littleness, her total dependence on divine aid. "Become a little one," He said, "so that the Immaculate Mother may take you in Her arms, as She used to take the Infant Jesus."

Leonia knew that "spiritual infancy was the shortest path to heaven," and that it was even more beautiful than martyrdom,

Stara Wieś was lucky to have titans of the spirit. In the novitiate of the Jesuit college, Bl. John Beyzym and Bl. Albert Chmielowski began their spiritual journeys.

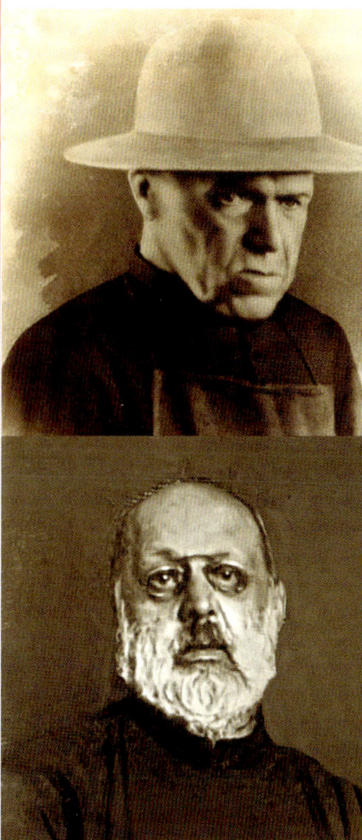

Top: The grave of the members of the Bar Confederation on the border of Stara Wieś and Brzozów.

Bottom: Family home of the mystic (Stara Wieś).

Bottom: Maria Nastał (right) with her sister, Stefania, during her elementary school years.

1903

➤ *A contemporary tomb of a mystic in the Stara Wieś.*

From Leonia's letter to Rev. Kazimierz Schmelzer: "Perhaps it's wrong that I do not fear eternity and judgment that much. After all, the saints also trembled before it, and I rather tremble with joy that I will sink in God irrevocably" (Szczawnica, November 29, 1937).

which ensured salvation. But spiritual infancy did not mean simply resting in the warmth of divine love. Though Leonia experienced spiritual ecstasies and, as she wrote, "on many nights she rested by the Heart of Jesus," she also endured suffering. She passed through spiritual dryness, which further purified her. She was also granted rare and intimate graces. Among them was the "gift of tears"—at times, she would begin weeping during prayer and be unable to stop.

TWO MORE VOWS

Following her mystical espousal, Leonia made additional vows. That moment had not been the conclusion of her journey, but the beginning of a deeper surrender. These two final vows may be seen as a practical imitation of Jesus the Infant, intended to fortify her innocence and turn her attention ever more completely toward God. In early 1936, she vowed "always to do what was more perfect." Then, in 1938, came her final vow: to "do everything out of love." Whether she acted, suffered, rejoiced, or grieved, she resolved always to remain in close union with God—more mindful of Him than of those around her, or the things that occupied her daily life.

This last vow should not surprise anyone familiar with her writings. She once recorded in her diary: "I believed Love; moreover, it seemed to me that it was no longer a faith, but a certainty, for the presence of the Lord Jesus in my soul was so noticeable and vivid that it was enough for me to close my eyes a little bit to external things, and I was with the Beloved of my soul entirely." Surely she was already among the highest ranks of saints still walking this earth—though only God knew it. She had heard: "As much as you give yourself to Me, I will give Myself to you. [If] you give yourself completely to Me, I will give Myself completely to you." And Sister Nastał gave herself completely—utterly—to Him every single day.

"I'M HAPPY"

From the moment she entered the convent, Leonia ceased thinking of herself entirely. That meant she also stopped caring for herself. The life of the Little Servant Sisters was hard: poor housing, insufficient food, and relentless labor. And to this already austere life, Leonia added frequent fasts, acts of self-scourging, and nights spent sleeping on bare wooden boards, without a mattress.

In September 1935, at the Lord's own command, she began to record her spiritual experiences. Thus began the extraordinary writings that preserve the story of her inner life.

She wrote more than four hundred pages. Some are a joy to read—such as those where she expresses her preference for the religious rule over even apparitions from Heaven, echoing the humility seen in the lives of other holy mystics. When she was awakened during the night of May 20, 1934, by the voice of Jesus saying, "I have loved you with an everlasting love," she whispered softly, "God—I love You too, but if it is You, please let me fall asleep, because I am not allowed to talk to You at this time; I am supposed to sleep until the scheduled hour." "And I fell asleep," she added.

In 1937, she developed the first symptoms of tuberculosis. In her, the illness awakened joy and the hope that reunion with Jesus was near. She received the disease as a hidden *mark of love*, offering all her impending sufferings to God. She sensed that she stood at the very threshold of eternity. With each passing moment, as the grains of her life slipped through the hourglass, God drew her more deeply into the circle of mystical union. On that final stretch, He prepared Leonia for sainthood.

"THE LITTLE FISH IS IN THE SEA"

She died on January 10, 1940, in Stara Wieś, near her family home. In her final months, she returned to the first convent she had known—the House of the Little Servant Sisters—which had become her home. She was just thirty-seven years old.

The final entry in her diary reveals the depth of her union with God, a union that already shared in the happiness of the blessed: "There are moments when the soul experiences the happiness of the blesseds in heaven and the Glory that pours the might and pleasures of heaven into the soul."

"The little fish is in the sea," wrote Leonia Nastał, "when it is below the surface of the sea, when it is a few meters deep, but it is not in the depths of the sea where it is calm, quiet, where it is safe; it is in the sea, but not in its depths. In union with God, the soul reaches the depths but does not yet know all His mysteries. This happens only when the soul passes into eternity, [and] sees Him as He is."

For her, death was a dive into eternity.

The mystic's parents, Franciszek Nastał (born 1879) and Katarzyna (née Jop), were smallholding peasants of modest means.

Venerable Servant of God Sr. Leonia Nastał with her parents and her sister's family.

12
THE KING

1907

On the previous page: Statue of Christ the King in Świebodzin, Poland.

Place of Apparition:
Kraków
Date and Place of Birth:
September 9, 1901, Jachówka, Poland
Date and Place of Death:
September 13, 1944, Kraków, Poland
Visionary as a Lay and Religious Person (Secular Franciscan Order)
Beatification Process:
November 5, 1996, Venerable Servant of God (Cardinal F. Macharski)
Works: Confessions of Inner Experiences

A stained glass window in the transept of St. John's Anglican Church (Ashfield, New South Wales).

Earthly Vanity and Divine Salvation *by Hans Memling (detail), ca. 1485 (Musée des Beaux-Arts, Strasbourg, France).*

12

THE KING

ROZALIA CELAK, 1907

Many questions arise when we turn to the figure of Rozalia Celak. Who was she, that great men of the Church—such as Cardinal Adam Sapieha and Father Pius Przezdziecki, Prior of the Jasna Góra Monastery—left such astonishing testimony about her? What role did God assign to her in the spiritual history of the Polish nation, since He prevented her from leaving the country to enter the congregation she longed to join? Why did He say simply, "I want you here," and leave her in Kraków? Was her mission a complement to the visions granted to St. Faustina? The two visionaries lived at the same time, nearly side by side, encountering the same Jesus—yet they knew nothing of one another.

She was born on September 19, 1901, in a village a few kilometers from Maków Podhalański, the first of eight children born to Tomasz and Joanna Celak. Her family was peasant, devout, deeply rooted in the faith. Before she was born, her mother consecrated her to Our Lady of the Rosary and to the Sacred Heart of Jesus. It is striking how thoroughly these two devotions would come to define her entire life.

FIRST MEETING

Like many mystics before her, she began to experience the tangible care of the Savior while still a child. At the age of seven, when she gave herself entirely to Jesus, she heard Him assure her that He would always remain at her side. But this was not her first supernatural encounter. Christ had already appeared to her a year earlier, following a harsh punishment she received after being falsely accused

of striking a classmate. As she recalled: "While I was crying, a thought suddenly came to me—to not exonerate myself again, not even with one more word, but calmly offer everything to the Lord Jesus to please Him, and at the same time I asked Jesus that I could love Him and become better every day."

Then something supernatural happened—some kind of interior encounter took place. Rozalia later wrote: "Then was my first inner encounter of the Lord Jesus with my very miserable soul; it will remain in my soul forever indelible." The accusation had been false, the suffering undeserved. Yet it brought about a meeting with Jesus and set Rozalia on the path to union with God. That path would become a path of Christ-like suffering—also undeserved—just as her childhood punishment had been.

THE KING

Rozalia came to understand that sanctity required her to "love the Lord Jesus to the point of madness, to the point of complete self-forgetfulness: to burn herself as a sacrifice on the altar of love." The defining mark of the life of the "Rose of St. Lazarus," as she was sometimes called, became suffering and sacrificial offering. This was not imposed—it was chosen, consciously and voluntarily, and even, we might say, joyfully. She wanted to answer Jesus' call with her whole life: "There is a great need for sacrifice... I ask for expiation."

Immediately, the Savior told her: "My child! You will suffer greatly.... I want to prepare you for suffering, [because] otherwise, if you were unprepared, you would collapse under this suffering. I, Jesus, I am with you, and I tell you this." At another time, He added: "My child, I give great suffering only to privileged souls. For it is with them that I share this part of Me.... Fear nothing. Fight valiantly by My Heart, from which you will draw strength for your entire life. You will receive the grace to love suffering as I, Jesus, have loved."

She did receive that grace. She loved suffering—not for its own sake, but because she saw in it a way to become

POLAND

Suffering and sacrifice became the hallmarks of Rosa of St. Lazarus's life, as the Handmaid of God was sometimes called.

Rozalia—standing first on the left in the bottom row—on the day she took the nursing exam, August 4, 1937, in front of the Narutowicz Hospital (Kraków).

more like Jesus and more perfectly united to Him.

At the same time, Rozalia was increasingly convinced that suffering, united with the Savior's Passion, did more than sanctify her personally—it *took over* her faculties in a mysterious way. It helped erase sin, converted sinners, and opened Heaven for others. This was why she actively sought suffering. She understood that God's Will was for "everyone to be saved" (1 Timothy 2:4). She would not preach sermons, write theological works, or perform miracles. Her influence would reach others invisibly—through suffering hidden from the eyes of the world. "With what arguments should I convince the world?" St. John Paul II asked in 1993. The following year he added, "The pope must suffer, so that all families and the whole world can see that there is a gospel—I could say—that is superior: the gospel of suffering, with which we must prepare for the future." Rozalia understood this.

Rozalia Celakówna in the winter of 1938 on the Dietl Planty in Kraków.

SUFFERING IS GRACE

Suffering, for her, was a grace greater than the gift of working miracles. Its fruit was what she called "invisible miracles." This word—*invisible*—was crucial, for it set apart the "people of suffering" from miracle workers, whose signs were astonishing and public. The grace of performing miracles was a calling to point explicitly and visibly to God and eternity. "Invisible" miracles, by contrast, were not signs at all. Only God saw them. Their effects were known only to those souls who, unknown to themselves, had been kept from the gates of Hell or brought to the gates of Heaven through someone else's suffering. The one who bore such suffering never knew what had been accomplished, nor did they seek to know.

Rozalia made this clear. She assured us that she lived not for "supernatural rewards," and once said to the Savior: "I don't want to do anything out of self-interest." And she added: "Even if You cast me into hell after my death, then I will rejoice in the fact that I served You not for reward, but out of love, and also [rejoice] in the fact that I did not serve the world [but You]." Perhaps it was precisely because she was not motivated by reward that she found so much happiness. For her, suffering was not an obstacle to joy—it was a necessary instrument of it. As she wrote in her diary: "Sometimes it seemed to me that my heart could not bear such happiness, that it had to stop beating. I don't know why, but I felt so happy suffering, that suffering ceased to be suffering."

DARK NIGHT

Let us return to Rozalia's early years. She must have advanced spiritually at a pace known only to the greatest saints. At just eighteen years old, she entered the "night of the spirit"—a period when God withdraws all consolations, leaving the soul in utter spiritual darkness, as though He did not exist. Rozalia endured this inner

Funeral of Rozalia Celakówna—Sisters of Charity in the funeral procession.

night for seven long years. It was not until 1926, through the intervention of the Blessed Mother, that the darkness lifted.

Mary left a lasting imprint on her life and remained a strong presence in it. At age fifteen, Rozalia had received a special grace: the smile of Our Lady and the promise that Mary would teach her how to love Jesus and lead her to Him. She had already begun to live the principle known in Catholic theology: *Per Mariam ad Jesum*—"through Mary to Jesus." Our Lady, herself, prepared Rozalia for her mission. That same year, she miraculously healed Rozalia of a terminal illness. Two years later, at the feet of the Blessed Virgin, Rozalia made a vow of chastity. Then, at twenty-four, she received the grace of perfect liberation from temptations against that virtue. She was, by then, already following in Mary's footsteps, living a life of total consecration. And remarkably, all of this unfolded during her spiritual night.

In 1924, she decided to leave her family home and move to Kraków. She longed to enter religious life but could not discern

Jesus in the Church of the Sacred Heart of Jesus in Berlin (Germany).

Sculpture of Christ the King at the entrance to the Cenacle (Jasna Góra).

Mosaic tympanum above the entrance to the cathedral in Florence.

The interior of Rozalia's house in Jachówka.

A stained-glass window bearing the words Tu Rex Gloriae Christe, by William Earley, 1933, St. Joseph's Church (Toomevara, Ireland).

which congregation to join. She found temporary work in a hospital as unlicensed nursing staff. In the dermatology ward, she came face to face with the physical and moral misery of the world, caring for patients suffering from venereal diseases. Providence seemed to have led her to this place, to which she would remain connected for the rest of her life. It was here that she came to understand how deeply the world was immersed in sin.

Eventually, she sought admission to the Poor Clares. But she lacked the physical strength for their rigorous life. After less than four months, she was forced to return to her work at St. Lazarus Hospital. It was then that her spiritual night ended and her encounters with Jesus began. The Lord was preparing her not for a cloistered vocation, but for a unique mission in the world.

VISIONS

She began to receive great and terrifying visions. The most famous of these Rozalia described in vivid detail:

> *I found myself in the spirit in Stradom, Kraków, near St. Agnes Street. I saw a terrible commotion among the people of the city, who were fleeing in panic in all directions. Among them were people of every class, with suitcases, briefcases, and bundles, fleeing their workplaces and responsibilities. I watched these crowds with astonishment, and also with anxiety.*
>
> *Beside me stood a serious-looking gentleman. He faced the fleeing people. His face was sorrowful, yet full of solemn dignity—there was something divine about him. After a moment, he lifted his eyes to the sky. At that instant, his face became majestic, solemn, and serene, yet still marked by profound sorrow. I looked at him with awe and*

> *reverence. There was something about him that stirred the heart, and I became convinced that he was not from this world.*
>
> *Then I too looked up and saw the sky filling with terrible, black, heavy clouds. They spread across the heavens from the west. I was overcome with fear. The unknown man turned to me and said:*
>
> *Child, look carefully at what will happen. What you see now will soon become a reality. There will be a terrible time for Poland. The thunderstorm signifies God's punishment that will fall on the Polish nation for turning away from the Lord God through sinful living. The Polish nation is committing grave sins and crimes—the worst of which are sins against chastity, murder, and hatred. Yet there is a way for Poland to be saved: if it acknowledges Me as its King and Lord by enthroning Me, not only in*

individual hearts or communities, but in the whole nation, with the government at its head. This acknowledgment must be confirmed by the renunciation of sin and a complete return to God.... Only in Me is rescue for Poland.

I thought it was St. Joseph, so I said to him: "St. Joseph, please tell me what all this means because I do not understand these things myself." This unknown, important person looked at me with kindness, but it was not St. Joseph. Who it was, I don't know. I asked Him, "when will it happen?" He told me that it would happen soon, but I did not dare to ask him about the year, month, and day of this disaster. Suddenly, something strange happened: the houses from Dietl Street to Market Square disappeared. I saw a huge square where people of all estates gathered. Most of the people I saw were village people with baskets, intelligentsia, workers, Jews, etc., who were carrying stones to the construction site. So I continued to ask this unknown man: "Tell me, St. Joseph, what are they going to build? What are these stones, bricks, sand, wood, and other items they are carrying here for?" Then the countenance of this stranger became strangely radiant and majestic and He told me: "Look, child, and soon you will know what will be built here." Christ will reign from here. In a moment, I saw a statue of the Sacred Heart of Jesus in the square. It was of such enormous size that nothing—no house nor any church could compare to it. The Lord Jesus was so high up on this monument that not only all of Poland but also the whole world could see Him. What this monument looked like, how people all over the world saw the Lord Jesus, this I could not comprehend nor describe because the things of God, things of spirit, could not be expressed in human language. All eyes were turned to the Lord Jesus, who stood over the whole world in beautiful radiance. At this monument, people of all estates made offerings, also in the form of lovely flowers in white and red. [To describe] what a decoration it was, [one could] only compare it to [things of] heaven, not earth. This stranger gave me to understand that at the feet of Christ, such a sacrifice had to be made: prayers and various offerings flowing from pure hearts, and martyrdom, to wash away the crimes of the whole world, not just Poland itself, but Poland in the first place. Suddenly, the sky cleared up beautifully, and all the black clouds disappeared from the horizon. The

▼ The entrance to the St. Lazarus Hospital on Kopernika Street in Kraków.

▲ Coat of arms of Galicia and Lodomeria on the seal of St. Lazarus Hospital in Kraków, early years of the twentieth century.

The Superior General of the Order of Saint Paul the First Hermit, Fr. Pius Przezdziecki O.S.P.P.E., influenced by the suggestion of his confrere, Fr. Kazimierz Zygmunt Dobrzycki—Rozalia's confessor—corresponded with Cardinal Hlond (pictured on the right) regarding enthronement, and in May 1938, at the Eucharistic Congress in Budapest, delivered a missive to him on the matter.

The grave of Rozalia Celak at the Rakowicki Cemetery in Kraków.

sun, moon, and stars appeared in the sky, and it was not ordinary daylight, but one that I could not describe. The stranger spoke to me: "See, child! The Kingdom of Christ is coming to Poland through the Enthronement." After a while, surrounded by clergy and faithful, His Eminence, the Primate of Poland Cardinal Hlond walked to this monument. In a few moments, His Eminence solemnly recited the act of offering all of Poland to the Sacred Heart of Jesus.

MULTIDIMENSIONAL AND BLURRED VISION

It was an image not from this world, and so its meaning could not be taken literally. Many questions remained unanswered. For instance: what was supposed to happen in Poland that would be so momentous that a statue of the Sacred Heart of Christ, located in Kraków, could be seen by the whole world? Or: who was the guide in the vision—this unusual *mister*? Was it Christ Himself, since a similar figure had appeared in the visions of St. John Bosco? Would Cardinal August Hlond, in fact, be the one to perform the act of enthronement? Or perhaps the vision pointed not to a literal future event, but to an ideal—the enthronement *should* have taken place then and there.

That is very plausible. After all, Jesus told Rozalia that such an act would have prevented the outbreak of the Second World War. But maybe it was not Cardinal Hlond in particular, but the spirituality he represented—especially Marian—that mattered most. Or perhaps the vision referred simply to the need for a spiritual leader of the Church in Poland, not any one individual.

On one hand, the message seemed to be that Christ desired the act of consecration to occur before September 1939. On the other, the vision appeared to anticipate a future enthronement—one prepared by intense national suffering. This could refer solely to the war years, or perhaps to something even more extensive. The vision was multidimensional and appeared to contain elements that might seem mutually exclusive.

Yet, when viewed on their proper levels, all these elements harmonized and revealed themselves as parts of a greater whole.

The plans of Divine Providence are never immediately clear. The answers to these questions will likely be understood only once the vision entrusted to Rozalia becomes part of the visible history of the Church and the nation.

But let us return to Rozalia's notes.

She concluded the description of the vision in these words: "Once again I heard a voice: 'What you are watching now will happen soon, but there has to be a lot of suffering first!' I no longer saw the strange man. In a mysterious way, he moved away from me and went somewhere. The vision disappeared, bringing into my soul a deep peace and certainty that truly the Lord Jesus would reign in Poland through the Enthronement."

The mysterious vision foretold the coming of the Kingdom of God in Poland. While we did not know when it would be fulfilled, we did know *how*. All of it "would happen through the Inthronization," and its fruit would be the "Reign of Christ" in Poland. Beyond that, we knew little. But we recall the words of Jesus, which Rozalia recorded in a letter to her confessor, Fr. Dobrzycki:

> *Why do you worry and think in human terms? (as I pondered the words "now or never"), is God's time [the same as] human time, am I not preparing the hearts of people for this sublime moment, which the Enthronement is supposed to be? Do you think that my words are not to be fulfilled? Have you not seen all that was to come and is now coming true? Be at peace, child, for that*

The main altar of the Church of the Sacred Heart of Jesus in Kraków.

▲ The main altar of the Church of the Sacred Heart of Jesus in Kraków.

▼ Sculpture above the entrance to this church.

which troubles you does not come from the Spirit of God. The Spirit of God is a spirit of peace, not of confusion.

GOD'S PLANS

Rozalia Celak's vocation did not require enclosure behind monastery walls. It could be fulfilled just as well—and perhaps even more perfectly—in the world. This is why Jesus desired her to remain in secular life. Immersed in the daily lives of laypeople, Rozalia found endless opportunities to carry out the mission entrusted to her. The Savior said:

> *I have plans for your soul, but in order for them to be realized in you, you must be ... trampled, spurned, and crucified, and you must love a hidden life in imitation of My life in Nazareth, and avoid such deeds that would elevate you in the eyes of people, for such deeds, I tell you once again, have no value in my eyes.*

And so Rozalia chose, freely and consciously, a life that was obscure, unknown, quiet, and lonely. The Lord had shown her that the most beautiful reality is *smallness*—a spiritual posture that He said was the very foundation of Nazareth.

In one apparition, the Blessed Virgin said to her:

> *My child, if you want to please me, love this hidden life very much... —this way is most sublime because it is so simple.*

Rozalia echoed this in a letter to her confessor:

> *The Lord Jesus asked me: "And what kind of life did I, Jesus, lead in Nazareth?" So I answered that I knew only that the Lord Jesus led a hidden life, unknown to anyone except the Blessed Virgin Mary and St. Joseph until the thirtieth year of His earthly life, because the Holy Gospel tells us nothing more than these words: "He went down with them and came to Nazareth, and was obedient to them" (Luke 2:51).*

Then the Lord Jesus said to her with great love: "Yes, my child, I was hidden for so many years, and only three years remained for apostolic activity because I wanted to give you an example of how precious hiding oneself is in My Divine eyes. This is an invaluable grace that I give to you so that, in this way, you may become like Me. So, my child, out of love for Me, love to be forgotten. O Child! Love Me like Mary. Live in such a way as to draw no attention to yourself. That kind of life will protect you from pride."

END OF LIFE — HEAVEN

We speak of Rozalia Celak's earthly life, but should we not also speak of what characterizes her life in Heaven? Jesus assured her: "My dear child, for your mercy and forbearance towards your neighbors, you will go straight to be united with Me. I will place you close to My Heart among Its worshippers in heaven."

Rozalia continued her service to the sick until the end. In 1944, on the Nativity of the Blessed Virgin Mary—September 8—she attended Holy Mass for the final time. Upon returning home, she felt suddenly weak and ill. Two days later, a doctor diagnosed her with Plaut-Vincent's angina. Her strength declined quickly. The next day, she was admitted to "her hospital," St. Lazarus Hospital. The following day, she received the Sacrament of the Anointing of the Sick; the day after that, she died.

That is all the biography records. And yet her role was immense. She was an instrument of God.

The Lord told her:

> *My child, you must live by faith and trust [Me], trust that despite the greatest difficulties, this work will be carried out so that you may know that I am acting on My own—you are only tools in My hands. The more you forget yourselves and the deeper you descend into the chasm of self-annihilation, the more freely I will be able to work in your souls.*

This message is at once demanding and profound. It teaches us what man must do, and what God desires to do. The Lord wants people to trust Him, to forget themselves, and to open themselves entirely to His Will. In this sense, man must "disappear"—not in destruction, but in surrender—so that God may take his place. By giving ourselves to God in love, we give Him space in the world.

Rozalia, under the guidance of Jesus, learned to imitate Our Lady. She became a place where God could act.

Jesus Christ the King of the Universe statue in Świebodzin, Poland, designed by Miroslaw Patecki and erected in 2010. The sculpture in Świebodzin referred in form to the Christ the Redeemer statue in Rio de Janeiro. In terms of height, it is currently the second-tallest statue of Jesus Christ in the world.

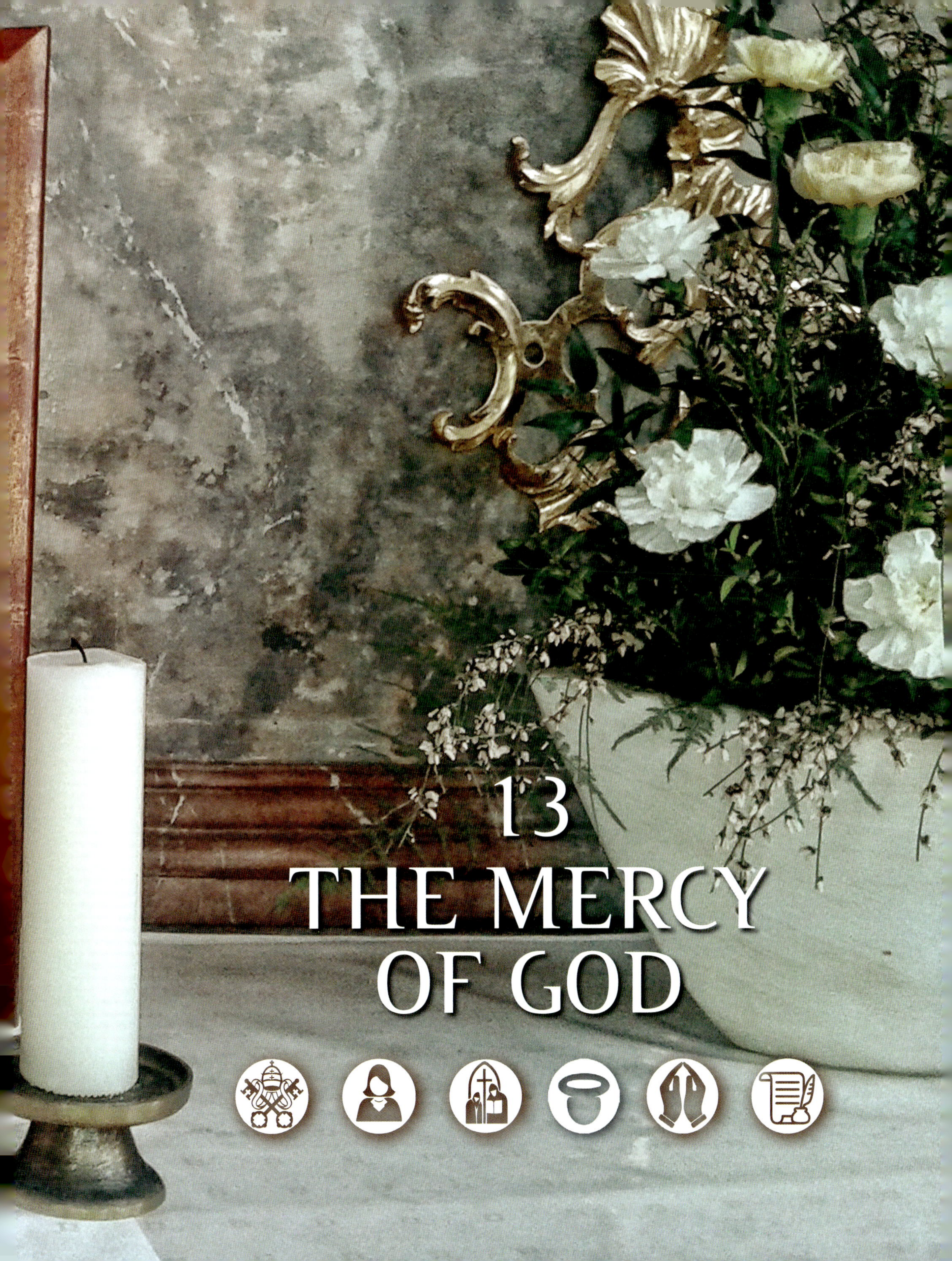

13
THE MERCY OF GOD

1924

Place of Apparition: Głogowiec, Płock, Vilnius, Warsaw, Kiekrz, Walendów, Derdy, Kraków, Poland
Date and Place of Birth: August 25, 1905, Głogowiec, Poland
Date and Place of Death: October 5, 1938, Kraków, Poland
Visionary as a Lay and Religious Person (The Congregation of the Sisters of Our Lady of Mercy)
Beatification: April 18, 1993, (John Paul II)
Canonization: April 30, 2000 (John Paul II)
Feast: October 5
Works: Diary, Letters

13

THE MERCY OF GOD

FAUSTINA KOWALSKA, 1924

One cannot help but pay a little more attention to this visionary. Yet the question arises: is there anything more to say about her that has not already been said? After all, thousands of books have been written about her; her Diary *sells in the millions; her image adorns countless shrines; and she is quoted more frequently than politicians or popes. This is hardly surprising, since she is so closely associated with what is perhaps the most widespread devotion of our time—Divine Mercy. The words "Divine Mercy" and "St. Faustina" have become inseparable.*

And yet many still do not understand what Divine Mercy truly is, and just as many form a distorted image of this extraordinary saint. Hell, it seems, does not take kindly to her. She has been called "the secretary and apostle of the message of Divine Mercy." She herself once wrote, "I have now learned that Satan hates mercy more than anything else."

St. Faustina during a visit to her hometown of Głogowiec.

Faustina was, in many ways, like a child—simple, trusting, and sincere. The devil took advantage of this innocence and, unusually for the lives of the saints, managed to deceive her. He succeeded, for a time, in destroying her writings. At the request of her confessor, Faustina had begun to record her visions and spiritual experiences. But in 1934, Satan appeared to her twice in the guise of an angel of light (see 2 Corinthians 11:14), and urged her to destroy them. He persuaded her: "You write foolish things and only expose yourself and others to great annoyances. What do you gain from this Mercy? Why waste your time writing delusions? Burn it all, and you will be calmer and happier."

He chose his moment well: at that time, Faustina had no one to advise her. Convinced she was hearing a voice from Heaven, she obeyed the command

POLAND

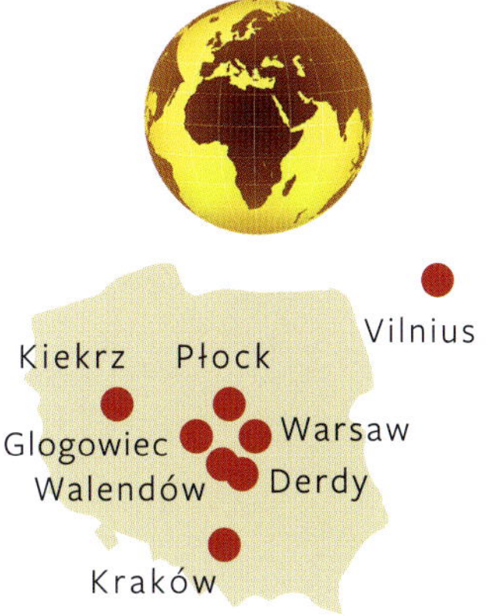

POLAND

given during the apparition, believing it to be God's Will. When her confessor returned, she told him what had happened. Fr. Sopoćko instructed her to rewrite everything, which accounts for the unusual lack of chronology in her *Diary*.

MOST OF HER LIFE WAS "IN THE WORLD"

Since 1926, Helena Kowalska had been known as Sister Maria Faustina—a name

◄ ▼ *A small museum now operates in the house that once belonged to St. Faustina's parents. It showcases items from the period when the Kowalska family lived in Głogowiec.*

At the beginning of the chapter: the chapel with the miraculous image of the Merciful Jesus and the tomb of St. Faustina (Lagiewniki).

by which she would enter history. Yet she lived in religious life for only thirteen years. The rest of her life unfolded "in the world." It was there, as with all of us, that her life began.

She was born on August 25, 1905, in the village of Głogowiec, situated between Łódź and Płock. She did not leave central Poland until she entered religious life. Her early years were spent in Głogowiec, Aleksandrów Łódzki, Łódź, and Warsaw. She was an ordinary girl from an ordinary, poor family. Like many daughters of impoverished homes, she left to work as a servant in the households of the better off. Faustina was one of them.

Was there anything remarkable about her childhood? Yes. The signs of a divine calling appeared early. When she was seven years old (it is often the case with visionaries that they first hear the voice of Jesus in childhood), during Vespers with the Exposition of the Blessed Sacrament, Helena heard a mysterious voice in her soul, calling her to a more perfect life. "Then, for the first time, God's love infected me and filled my little heart, and the Lord gave me an understanding of the things of God," she wrote in her *Diary*. "I came across no one who would have explained these things to me," she added. What this "more perfect life" would come to mean would only be revealed twelve years later.

Then once again she heard the voice of Jesus. This time what He wanted from her became obvious.

TORMENTED JESUS

She was nineteen years old—not in church, and not in prayer—but

(własnoręczny podpis osoby wyszczególnionej w dowodzie)

Stosownie do art. 19 rozp. Prezydenta R. P. z dnia 16 marca 1928 r. o ewidencji i kontroli ruchu ludności (Dz. U. R. P. Nr. 32, poz. 309) zaświadczam, że wymieniony(a) w niniejszym dowodzie

p. ....

jest obywatelem(ką) polskim(ą), co zostało stwierdzone

na podstawie ....

....

Urząd ....

Pieczęć powiatowej władzy administracji ogólnej

Nr. ....

Dnia ....

....
Podpis

▲ Fr. Michał Sopoćko, confessor and spiritual director of Sister Faustina during her stay in Vilnius.

➤ The saint's portrait in color from the time before she entered the convent, painted from a photograph.

➤ A small, modest plaque in Juliusz Słowacki Park in Łódź in remembrance of the day that changed Helena's life. The day she met Christ.

surrounded by music and dancing, when she suddenly saw the tormented Jesus. Many years later, she described the moment this way:

> *Once I was at a dance [probably in Łódź] with one of my sisters.... As I began to dance, I suddenly saw Jesus at my side, Jesus racked with pain, stripped of His clothing, all covered with wounds, who spoke these words to me: 'How long shall I put up with you and how long will you keep putting Me off?' At that moment the charming music stopped, [and] the company I was with vanished from my sight; there remained Jesus and I.*

Temporal reality dissolved before the presence of the supernatural. It was as though two worlds—one infinitely higher—occupied the same place and time. Everything disappeared: the music, the commotion, the crowd. Helena was alone with Jesus. She, dressed in a pink gown with lace; He, covered in wounds and blood. The contrast could not have been more stark. And she understood.

What did Jesus ask of her? Did He speak further? He did not need to. The movement He stirred in her heart was enough. She later wrote:

> *I took a seat by my dear sister, pretending to have a headache in order to cover up what took place in my soul. After a while I slipped out unnoticed, leaving my sister and all my companions behind and made my way to the Cathedral of St. Stanislaus Kostka.*

Her journey began there. In a matter of moments, her path would be made clear. She soon went to Warsaw, where, once again, she would be guided in a church. Faustina recalled:

> *Paying no attention to what was happening around me, I fell prostrate before the Blessed Sacrament and begged the Lord to be good enough to give me to understand what I should do next. Then I heard these words: "Go at once to Warsaw; you will enter a convent there."*

She did not hesitate. She wrote:

> *I rose from prayer, came home, and took care of things that needed to be settled. As best I could, I confided*

St. Faustina at the convent in Biała. Faustina (first on the left) stayed there in 1930–1932.

> *to my sister what took place within my soul. I told her to say goodbye to our parents, and thus, in my one dress, with no other belongings, I arrived in Warsaw.*

That day, she received two apparitions—one a vision, the other a locution. The latter carried specific instructions, but following them required great courage, or perhaps even madness. Helena set out for a large city she had never seen, wearing only the clothes on her back, with nothing but the assurance of Jesus: that in the capital, she would enter a convent. The message was brief but unmistakable.

Yet an entire year would pass before she entered religious life. Jesus had told her only that she was to join a convent in Warsaw—nothing more. The task of finding the right place fell to her alone. Through perfect cooperation with God's Will, and with the guidance of both the Lord and Our Lady, she completed this task with quiet brilliance.

She went from convent to convent, but wherever she knocked, she was turned away. At last, she came to the Sisters of Our Lady of Mercy. "When Mother Superior ... came out to meet me," she wrote, "she told me, after a short conversation, to go to the Lord of the house and ask whether He would accept me. I understood at once that I was to ask this of the Lord Jesus. With great joy, I went to the chapel and asked Jesus: 'Lord of this house, do You accept me? This is how one of these sisters told me to put the question to You.' Immediately I heard this voice: 'I do accept; you are in My Heart.'"

When she returned from the chapel, Mother Superior asked, "Well, has the Lord accepted you?" Faustina replied, "Yes." "If the Lord has accepted," she said, "then I also will accept."

"You are in My Heart"—she would hear those words again and again. Jesus Himself would mark the rhythm of her spiritual life with them.

ASKED TO BE A REPARATORY SOUL BY JESUS

Our future saint—who now bore the name Faustina—spent thirteen years among the Sisters of Our Lady of Mercy. During that time, she worked in the kitchen, the garden, the bakery, and at the convent gate. She was transferred from house to house, often tasked with the humblest of duties.

Her religious life was no path of sweetness. She suffered spiritual dryness, temptations, and deep anguish. She also endured intense physical pain from pulmonary tuberculosis, as well as exhausting labor that often surpassed her strength. She offered it all as a gift to Christ.

On Holy Thursday, 1934, Jesus asked her to offer herself as a soul of reparation—for sinners, and especially for those who had lost faith in God's mercy. She became one of those chosen souls who, in Jesus' words, "uphold the existence of mankind." He said of them: "When the number of the chosen ones is complete, the world will cease to exist."

The chapel at the Ostra Brama in Vilnius with the icon of Our Lady of Mercy.

Left: *Abiding in prayer before the miraculous image of Our Lady of Częstochowa, Faustina felt Mary's care and a special closeness to the Mother of God in her heart.*

Right: *Nuns praying in the convent chapel in Biała, which was consecrated in 1929 in the old convent building.*

What is striking here is that, in most cases, the desire to become a reparatory soul arises in the visionary's own heart. In Faustina's case, it was the Savior who asked.

NINETY-FIVE PERCENT OF HER LIFE

Many people had a mistaken image of Faustina. But this is true of most saints, and she was no exception. Most people knew only a small part of her life—perhaps five percent—and were content to leave it at that. The accounts of Jesus' apparitions and Faustina's remarkable experiences were enough to satisfy their curiosity.

But what about the other ninety-five percent? That part of her life was marked by the most ordinary and exhausting tasks—daily burdens often beyond her physical strength. These were the labors that contributed to her early death. Nearly every duty she was assigned proved too difficult for her frail body.

In the kitchen, the most taxing task was straining potatoes—she often dropped half of them on the floor. In the bakery and the bread store, the work was so strenuous that her superior sent her to a nearby village to rest and regain her strength. When she felt somewhat better, she returned to Płock and resumed the very tasks that had previously overwhelmed her.

Even work in the garden proved too much for her, and her superior eventually reassigned her to lighter responsibilities at the convent gate. Were these simple duties truly so difficult for her? One need only read two lines from her *Diary* to understand.

In the first, she wrote, "When one's health is poor, there is much one has to bear. For when one is ill, but not in bed, one is not considered to be ill."

And in another:

> *I was suffering very much, and it seemed to me I would not be*

> *able to make my adoration, but I gathered up all my willpower and, although I collapsed in my cell, I paid no attention to what ailed me, for I had the Passion of Jesus before my eyes.*

These were not exaggerations. We know that her superiors eventually excused her from the community's spiritual exercises due to her complete physical exhaustion.

Instead of participating in the full round of spiritual exercises, Faustina was instructed to recite short aspiratory prayers. Her confessor, recognizing her physical weakness, did not permit her to undertake the severe mortifications often found in the lives of other saints. She herself wrote, "I was given the permissions I asked for: to wear the bracelet for half an hour every day during Holy Mass, and in times of difficulty, to wear the belt for two hours." She was allowed to wear the narrow, spiked chain on her hand and the wire belt, but only occasionally—her body could not have endured more. Her sanctity was shaped not by dramatic penances but through hidden, daily sacrifices: "O you small, everyday sacrifices, you are to me like wildflowers which I strew over the feet of my beloved Jesus. I sometimes compare these trifles to the heroic virtues, and that is because their enduring nature demands

A building where the Polish mystic lived during her stay at the Antokol monastery.

At the behest of her confessor, Sister Faustina kept a diary for four years, where she wrote down her mystical experiences.

Monastery of the Congregation of the Sisters of Our Lady of Mercy and the Shrine of Divine Mercy in Kraków-Łagiewniki.

Fr. Joseph Andrasz SJ, the confessor of St. Faustina during her stay in Kraków.

heroism." She was misunderstood, ridiculed, and even accused of deceit. In moments of despair, she cried out, "O Jesus, I can't do it anymore." Those around her often failed to see the truth. Some believed she was pretending. When her symptoms worsened, help was not always given. Her room went unheated for weeks, and her needs were overlooked. And yet, she accepted it all. Reflecting on the day she received the religious habit, she wrote, "The day I took the [religious] habit, God let me understand how much I was to suffer. I clearly saw to what I was committing myself."

TEMPTATION

One day, she saw Jesus in great majesty. He said to her, "My daughter, if you wish, I will this instant create a new world, more beautiful than this one, and you will live there for the rest of your life." This was a test. Faustina answered, "I don't want any worlds. I want You, Jesus.... I am very much surprised at Your offer, my Jesus; what are those worlds to me? ... Everything that is not You is nothing to me."

During her stay in Kiekrz, she once walked down to the lake. There, on the surface of the water, she saw Jesus, who said to her, "All this I created for you, My spouse; and know that all this beauty is nothing compared to what I have prepared for you in eternity." Her soul was flooded with such consolation that she remained there until evening, though it seemed to her like only a brief moment.

WITH THE INFANT JESUS

St. Faustina was a visionary—and not just any visionary, but the one to whom the Merciful Jesus appeared. Yet it is often forgotten that she also received numerous apparitions of the Infant Jesus. It may be that He appeared to her in this form more often than any other. These apparitions followed a familiar pattern. Faustina often saw Our Lady holding the Child in her arms. But these were not merely Marian apparitions, for Jesus was

not silent. He, too, spoke with the nun from Głogowiec.

During one such vision, Faustina saw her confessor kneeling at Mary's feet, speaking with her. She could not record what was said between them, because, as she wrote, "I was busy talking with the Infant Jesus, who came down from His Mother's arms and approached me." This simple note from her *Diary* reveals much.

An apparition of Mary often became an apparition of Jesus. The Infant Jesus frequently appeared to Faustina on His own as well. "In the evening," she once noted, "a little child came and woke me up. The child seemed about a year old." Jesus instructed her to look up at the sky and asked, "Do you see this moon and these stars?... These stars are the souls of faithful Christians, and the moon is the souls of the religious.... Such is the difference in heaven between the soul of a religious and the soul of a faithful Christian." Why did Jesus speak to her in the form of a child rather than an adult? Because His form was itself a sign—one He explained: "True greatness is in loving God and in humility." These were the virtues of a child.

The main church of the Sanctuary of Divine Mercy in Kraków-Łagiewniki can accommodate 5,000 people (approx. 1,800 seats). *Above the building rises an observation tower, measuring seventy-seven meters.*

1924

Coffin with the relics of St. Faustina in Kraków-Łagiewniki.

Monastery with the Shrine of Mercy in Kraków-Łagiewniki.

The Infant Jesus often appeared to Faustina during Holy Mass. "When I see the Infant Jesus during Holy Mass," she wrote, "it is not always the same: sometimes He is very joyous, and sometimes He is not even looking at the chapel. At present, He is often very joyful when our confessor [Fr. Sopoćko] offers Holy Mass." She described another such moment: "One day, after Holy Communion, I suddenly saw the Infant Jesus standing by my kneeler and holding on to it with His two little hands."

At times, the Infant Jesus appeared in the consecrated Host. She recalled: "During the shepherdess' service I saw the Infant Jesus in the Host" and "during Midnight Mass, I again saw the little Infant Jesus, extremely beautiful, joyfully stretching out His little arms to me."

Faustina recorded two especially striking visions. In the first, Jesus appeared in place of the priest, but in the form of a child. "Once when my confessor [Fr. Sopoćko] was saying Mass, I saw, as usual, the Child Jesus on the altar, from the time of the Offertory. However, a moment before the Elevation, the priest vanished from my sight, and Jesus alone remained. When the moment of the Elevation approached, Jesus took the Host and the chalice in His little hands and raised them together, looking up to heaven, and a moment later I again saw my confessor. I asked the Child Jesus where the priest had been during the time I had not seen him. Jesus answered, 'In My Heart.'"

Faustina also received a rare and extraordinary grace—one known from the lives of saints such as Anthony of Padua and Stanislaus Kostka: she took the Infant Jesus into her arms. "I saw Our Lady with the Infant Jesus.... The most holy Mother said to me, 'Take My Dearest Treasure,' and She handed me the Infant Jesus. When I took the Infant Jesus in my arms, the Mother of God and St. Joseph disappeared. I was left

alone with the Infant Jesus. I said to Him, 'I know that You are my Lord and Creator even though You are so tiny.'"

In another entry, she wrote:

> *I often see the Child Jesus during Holy Mass. He is extremely beautiful. He appears to be about one year old. Once, when I saw the same Child during Mass in our chapel, I was seized with a violent desire and an irresistible longing to approach the altar and take the Child Jesus. At that moment, the Child Jesus was standing by me on the side of my kneeler, and He leaned with His two little hands against my shoulder, gracious and joyful, His look deep and penetrating.*

Elsewhere in the *Diary*, she describes an event that took place during a Mass celebrated by her confessor, Fr. Andrasz, just before the moment of Elevation: "During a Mass celebrated by Fr. Andrasz, a moment before the Elevation, God's presence pervaded my soul, which was drawn to the altar. Then I saw the Mother of God with the Infant Jesus. The Infant Jesus was holding onto the hand of Our Lady. A moment later, the Infant Jesus ran with joy to the center of the altar, and the Mother of God said to me, 'See with what assurance I entrust Jesus into his hands. In the same way, you are to entrust your soul and be like a child to him.'" The Blessed Mother was speaking about Faustina's confessor—but also offering a lesson in childlike trust.

BROKEN IN THE HOST

The most astonishing of Faustina's visions were those of Jesus in the broken Host. In one such vision, she saw the Infant Jesus standing beside her at her kneeler, resting both hands on her shoulder. But when the priest broke the consecrated Host, "Jesus was once again on the altar and was broken and consumed by the priest. After Holy Communion, I saw Jesus in the same way in my heart and felt Him physically in my heart throughout the day."

A second description is even more moving. During a Mass celebrated by Fr. Andrasz, Faustina again saw the Mother of God, with the Infant Jesus holding Her hand. Jesus ran joyfully to the center of the altar. Then, she wrote, "He [Fr. Andrasz] broke up this beautiful Child, and living blood flowed forth. Father bent forward and received the true and living Jesus into himself. Had he eaten Him? I do not know how this took place. Jesus, Jesus, I cannot keep up with You, for in an instant, You become incomprehensible to me."

MERCY FOR THE WHOLE WORLD

Faustina's most important mission was to be "the secretary of Jesus." On February 22, 1931, she went to her cell to rest and suddenly saw the Savior. She wrote: "In the evening, when I was in my cell, I saw the Lord Jesus clothed in a white garment. One hand [was] raised in the gesture of blessing, the other was touching the garment at the breast. From beneath the garment, slightly drawn aside at the breast, there were emanating two large rays, one red, the other pale. In silence I kept my gaze fixed on the Lord; my soul was struck with awe, but also with great joy."

One of the most famous images of St. Faustina Kowalska.

The sanctuary and the commons around it witnessed the enthronement of Christ as King and Lord.

After a moment, Jesus spoke: "Paint an image according to the pattern you see, with the signature: *Jesus, I trust in You.* I desire that this image be venerated, first in your chapel, and [then] throughout the world." He added, "I promise that the soul that will venerate this image will not perish. I also promise victory over [its] enemies already here on earth, especially at the hour of death. I Myself will defend it as My own glory."

Jesus revealed that the enemies from which He promised to defend souls were Satan and the world. He also said: "Let the sinner not be afraid to approach Me. The flames of mercy are burning Me—clamoring to be spent; I want to pour them out upon these souls." At that moment, Faustina heard Him express a sorrow similar to what He once revealed to St. Margaret Mary Alacoque: "Distrust on the part of souls is tearing at My insides. The distrust of a chosen soul causes Me even greater pain; despite My inexhaustible love for them they do not trust Me. Even My death is not enough for them."

Jesus revealed the devotion to Divine Mercy to Faustina a second time, after a retreat in preparation for her perpetual vows. This vision, though similar to the one in Płock, took a slightly different form. "After the renewal of vows and Holy Communion," she wrote, "I suddenly saw the Lord Jesus, who said to me with great kindness, 'My daughter, look at My merciful Heart.' As I fixed my gaze on the Most Sacred Heart, the same rays of light, as are represented in the image as blood and water, came forth from it, and I understood how great was the Lord's mercy." Then He said again, "My daughter, speak to priests about this inconceivable mercy of Mine. The flames of mercy are burning Me—clamoring to be spent; I want to keep pouring them out upon souls; souls just don't want to believe in My goodness."

At the instruction of her confessor, Faustina asked Jesus to explain the meaning of the rays in the image. A few days later, she heard Him say interiorly: "The two rays denote Blood and Water. The pale ray stands for the Water which makes souls righteous. The red ray stands for the Blood which is the life of souls. These two rays issued forth from the very depths of My tender mercy when My agonized Heart was opened by a lance on the Cross.... Mankind will not have peace until it turns with trust to My mercy.... Proclaim that mercy is the greatest attribute of God. All the works of My hands are crowned with mercy."

In June 1934, the first image was completed and delivered to Fr. Sopoćko. Faustina was disappointed—it did not match the beauty of the vision she had seen. But in the chapel, she heard Jesus say: "Not in the beauty of the color, nor of the brush lies the greatness of this image, but in My grace."

INTERCEPTED DEVOTION?

Satan did everything in his power to hinder the fulfillment of God's plan. He

The main nave of the Divine Mercy Sanctuary, the main altar with a tabernacle in the shape of a globe (Łagiewniki, Poland).

sought to draw souls away from the true path of salvation by attacking those chosen to deliver Heaven's messages. At times, he attempted to intercept the apparitions themselves—as in the case of the Marian apparitions in Gietrzwałd—or to discredit them, as he tried with the apparitions at Lourdes. And when all else failed, he tried to distort or exploit the apparitions after they had ended, twisting their message to serve his own purposes.

One example of this distortion was the way Satan exploited both the Fatima apparitions and the revelations given to Sister Faustina. In the case of Fatima, he used the devotion itself as a means of attacking the Church. He sowed suspicion by convincing many that the Vatican was hiding the true contents of the messages. He persuaded others that the consecration of the world to the Immaculate Heart of Mary had not met the proper conditions. Some even came to believe that Sister Lucia had been killed and *replaced* in the late 1940s. Others claimed she had written things she never wrote, or that what she did write had been dictated by the bishops.

Was it the same with the messages Jesus gave to Sister Faustina? No—the method was different. Here, Satan did not fabricate conspiracies about hidden documents or impersonated visionaries. Instead, he attacked the Church by turning attention to the treatment Faustina received within her own order, accusing her superiors of negligence and even suggesting they caused her death. But his main target was the message itself. And rather than opposing it directly, he twisted its meaning to suit his purposes.

Satan found a way to exploit the emphasis on mercy. "If I were Satan," wrote Ralph Martin in *The Final Confrontation*, "I would be most interested in assuring people that virtually everyone will make it to heaven, and it is almost impossible to be lost, so great is God's mercy, and so difficult is it to really commit a truly mortal sin. I would want to assure people that as long as they are not a serial killer, they have nothing to worry about."

"This truly wicked lie," the theologian continued, "has unfortunately been widely accepted by many of our fellow Catholics.

Pope Francis paying homage to St. Faustina's relics during his apostolic visit to Poland, on July 30, 2016. Chapel of Mercy, Shrine in Łagiewniki.

➤ *The window of the cell where Sister Faustina died, at the convent in Łagiewniki.*

If I were to express how very many of our fellow Catholics look at the world today, I would describe it like this: 'Broad and wide is the gate that leads to heaven and virtually everyone is going that way. Narrow and difficult is the door that leads to hell and hardly anyone is entering it.'"

Jesus said the opposite of what many presume today: "Enter through the narrow gate; for the gate is wide and the road broad that leads to destruction, and those who enter through it are many." (Matthew 7:13–14). Faustina echoed this in one of her most vivid visions. She described seeing two roads. "One day," she wrote, "I saw two roads. One was broad, covered with sand and flowers, full of joy, music, and all sorts of pleasures. People walked along it, dancing and enjoying themselves. They reached the end without realizing it. And at the end of the road, there was a horrible precipice; that is, the abyss of Hell. The souls fell blindly into it; as they walked, so they fell. And their number was so great that it was impossible to count them. And I saw the other road, or rather, a path, for it was narrow and strewn with thorns and rocks; and the people who walked along it had tears in their eyes, and all kinds of suffering befell them. Some fell down upon the rocks, but stood up immediately and went on. At the end of the road there was a magnificent garden filled with all sorts of happiness, and all these souls entered there. At the very first instant they forgot all their sufferings."

The broad road and the narrow path—Faustina's vision confirmed the solemn truth spoken by Christ Himself. To change His words, to soften or invert them, has devastating consequences. If people come to believe that there is a wide road to salvation, they will cease to resist temptation. They will no longer strive for holiness. They will not renounce sin, but instead will renounce the power of God which the Gospel proclaims. But a careful reading of the *Diary* makes this truth unavoidable: mercy comes at a great cost—on God's side, and on ours. On God's side, the price was the Cross. On the side of man, it is the same Cross.

POOR JESUS

Let us recall another apparition of Jesus—unique, and profoundly significant. During the time when Sister Faustina was assigned to work at the convent gate, Poland was enduring a severe economic crisis. She served all who came with love and compassion. One day, a poor young man knocked at the door and asked for something to eat. Sister Faustina found some soup in the kitchen, warmed it, added bread, and brought it to him. After he had eaten and returned the bowl, she recognized Him: it was Jesus.

"I AM BUSY COMMUNING WITH MY HEAVENLY FATHER"

Faustina died on October 5, 1938, in the convent at Kraków-Łagiewniki. She was only thirty-three years old—the same age as Jesus at His death. Shortly before her passing, her confessor left behind a remarkable testimony. In mid-September, he had spoken with her one last time. After leaving her room, he realized he had forgotten to give her the small booklets of the Divine Mercy prayers—prayers that had been given to her by Jesus Himself.

He returned to her cell, opened the door quietly, and saw Sister Faustina hovering above her bed, immersed in

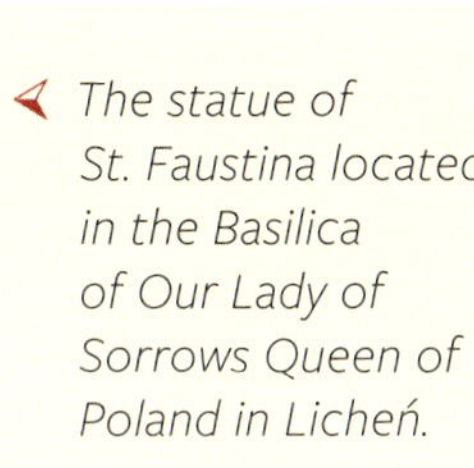

The statue of St. Faustina located in the Basilica of Our Lady of Sorrows Queen of Poland in Licheń.

prayer. "Her gaze," he later wrote, "was fixed on some invisible object, her pupils slightly dilated, and she did not take notice of my entrance. I did not want to disturb her and intended to retreat." But soon she regained awareness, noticed his presence, and apologized for not hearing him knock or enter. He handed her the prayer booklets and said goodbye. She replied simply, "See you in heaven."

When he visited her for the final time in Łagiewniki, on September 26, she no longer wished to speak — or perhaps, rather, she was no longer able. She said only, "I am busy communing with my Heavenly Father."

October 5, 1938, was the last day of Sister Faustina's earthly life. She had known it was coming for at least ten days. At 10:45 p.m., with her eyes fixed on the image of Christ, she peacefully gave up her spirit to God.

14
REPAIRING THE WORLD

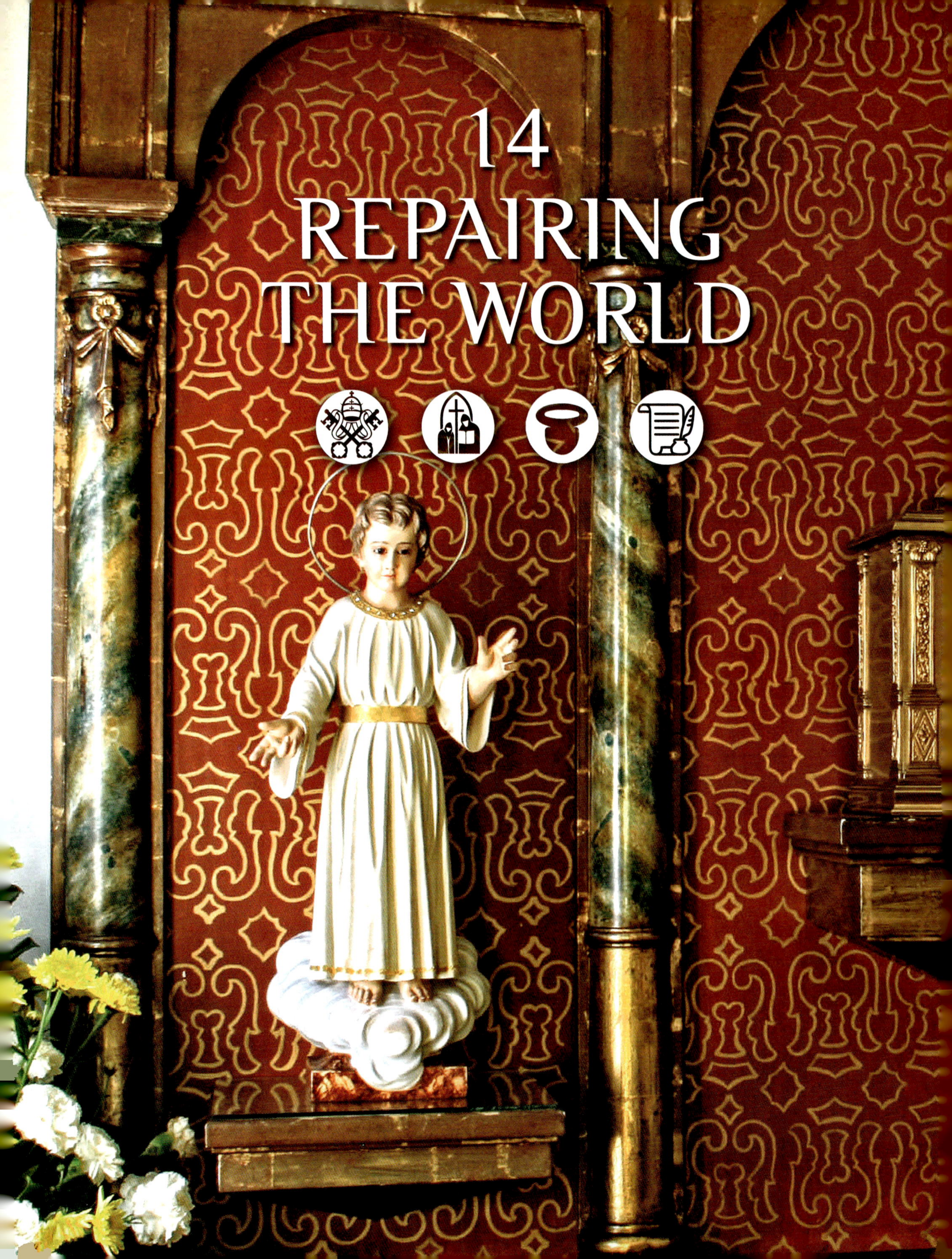

Place of Apparition: Pontevedra, Tui, Spain; Coimbra, Portugal
Date and Place of Birth: March 28, 1907, Aljustrel, Portugal
Date and Place of Death: February 13, 2005, Coimbra, Portugal
Visionary as a Lay and Religious Person (first Congregation of St. Dorothy, then Order of the Blessed Virgin Mary of Mount Carmel).
Beatification Process: Servant of God, February 13, 2008 (Pope Benedict XVI)
Works: Diary, Memoirs, Calls/Appeals from the Message of Fatima, Fatima in Lucia's Own Words

An image of the Blessed Virgin Mary from Lucia's family home.

14

REPAIRING THE WORLD

LÚCIA DE JESUS ROSA DOS SANTOS, 1925

Lúcia is the best-known of the Fatima visionaries. Unlike the other witnesses to the apparitions — Francisco and Jacinta — she lived a long life, reaching the age of ninety-eight. Until the very end, she remained active and deeply immersed in the supernatural. This long span of life was granted to her so that, through the visions and instructions she received, she might help the Church endure a time of great crisis. Yet it seemed that the height of this crisis was only just beginning. So we waited for the Vatican to reveal the full extent of the messages entrusted to her by Jesus and Mary, since we had been granted access to only a small portion of them.

Many believed that Lúcia was solely a Marian visionary. But this was not the whole truth. She also experienced numerous apparitions of Jesus — so many, in fact, that they could be measured with "a good measure, packed together, shaken down, and overflowing" (Luke 6:38). These supernatural encounters were a great treasure, meant for us all, and ought to be more widely known. Out of necessity, we limit ourselves here to just the three most important. It must also be said that the apparitions of Jesus granted to Lúcia were virtually unknown, and when

PORTUGAL

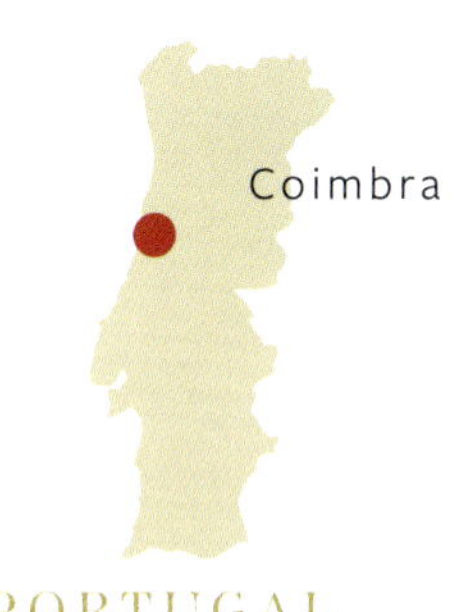

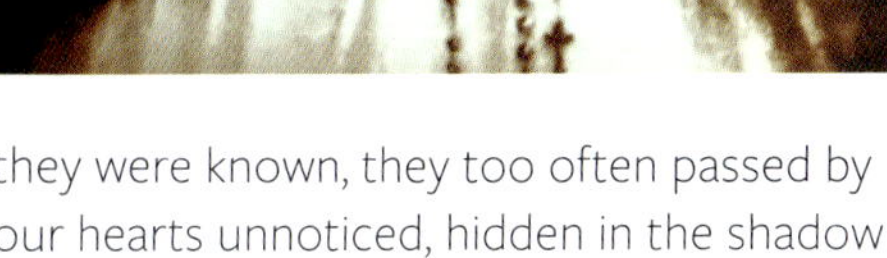

they were known, they too often passed by our hearts unnoticed, hidden in the shadow of Mary.

When we looked more closely at the content of these apparitions, it became clear that Jesus stood in the foreground, while His Mother appeared in a supporting role.

FATIMA ANNOUNCEMENT

Mary's apparitions at Fatima already pointed to the possibility that Lúcia would one day encounter Jesus directly. During the second apparition, in June 1917, the Blessed Mother foretold that the eldest of the visionaries would "stay here for some time." Strikingly, she explained that the Savior had need of Lúcia: "Jesus wishes to use you in order to make me known and loved."

Did this mean that the apparitions of Jesus served a Marian purpose? In a sense, yes—for this call to make Mary "known and loved"

Left: There was something unusual about little Lucia, something that convinced Fr. Cruz, who came to Aljustrel, that the girl was spiritually very mature.

Right: A statue of Our Lady, which smiled at Lucia, at the parish church in Fatima.

Lucia's parents took care of their daughter's religious upbringing.

1925

Before the meeting with Mary took place, an angel appeared to the children three times, preparing their hearts to receive the message of the Blessed Mother.

The Blessed Mother, by appearing to Lucia, Jacinta, and Francisco, reminded us of the dignity of children and their potential for spiritual growth.

On the last day of the Fatima apparitions, the young visionaries were surrounded by one hundred thousand people.

would indeed be the central task entrusted to Lúcia. But it was not the ultimate goal. The deeper purpose of the future apparitions would be the Church itself, because Jesus desired His Church to become like Mary. If the Church were to be conformed to her, it would bring about nothing less than a total revolution in the world.

SERVANT IN A CONVENT

We promised to examine three apparitions of Jesus, and so we begin with the first: the apparition in Pontevedra, which took place in 1925. It was unusual in character and, as it turns out, carried a hidden and additional message. Remarkably, we know of this apparition thanks to another apparition. Two years after the events in Pontevedra, Lúcia knelt before the tabernacle and asked Jesus whether the contents of that earlier vision "belonged to the Mystery." The Lord appeared to her and answered that she was free to reveal all that had taken place at that time.

Throughout her life, Lúcia experienced many similar encounters with Jesus, present in the Blessed Sacrament. At times, she found the courage to ask the Savior for help or for signs—and He responded. Yet His answers often came through unexpected coincidences, which Lúcia, with spiritual discernment, was able to recognize for what they were.

Let us return now to Pontevedra. The apparition—often mistakenly referred to as a Marian apparition—occurred on December 10, 1925. It took place in the convent at Pontevedra, yet both the beginning and the end of the encounter unfolded elsewhere. They happened "in the world," beyond the walls of the monastery.

According to the designs of Divine Providence, the apparition in Pontevedra was framed by two encounters with a young boy—who, as it was later revealed, was Jesus Himself. The first of these took place in the fall of 1925, sometime after October 26, the day Lúcia arrived in Pontevedra. No one there knew who she truly was. Since June 1921, she had gone by the name Maria das Dores. Under this name, she completed her studies in Oporto, and it was as Maria das Dores that she entered

The countless crowds of people gathered in the Cova da Iria Valley watched the extraordinary dance of the sun.

▲ ▼ ▶ *The Basilica of Our Lady of the Rosary took twenty-five years to build and was consecrated in 1953.*

the Sisters of St. Dorothy in Pontevedra. Her heartfelt dream was to teach children about Jesus.

It should be noted, however, that despite earlier assurances from the provincial superior, Lúcia was assigned to what was called the second choir. This group was made up of uneducated sisters who were even forbidden to study or write! The Fatima visionary, then, was placed in service to the first choir—the educated sisters—who were responsible for catechesis, the very work Lúcia longed to do. Her assigned duties included tending the garden and cleaning the house, kitchen, and dining room. At that time, she was still a postulant and wore secular clothing.

She swept and mopped the floors. Each day, she also stepped outside the convent gate to take out the garbage, depositing it in the container just beyond the wall.

TALKING TO A STREET KID

On one such outing, Lúcia encountered a little boy. Longing to be a teacher, she could not pass up the opportunity to speak with him. She later wrote:

> *I met a child and asked him if he knew the Hail Mary. He told me that he did. However, he did not know how to begin, so I recited this prayer with him three times. After I finished, I asked him to repeat it. At the end of the three Hail Mary's, I asked him to say it alone. As he remained silent and did not appear capable of saying it alone, I asked him if he knew the church of St. Mary. He answered yes. I then told him to go there every day and to pray thus: "Oh my Heavenly Mother, give me Your Child Jesus!" I taught him that prayer and departed.*

There seemed to be nothing extraordinary about the moment. Lúcia had gone outside the convent gate to discard the trash and had met one of the poor little ones—likely a street child, neglected both spiritually and materially. The zealous postulant spoke with him, told him about God, taught him to pray, and encouraged him to visit the church. One might be tempted to say, "And that was all."

SATURDAY APPARITION

Weeks passed within the quiet rhythm of the Dorothean convent. The brief encounter with the child faded into the background of daily tasks. Then came December 10, 1925. It was a Saturday—the day traditionally dedicated to the Blessed Mother. That day, Lúcia felt especially close to her. With a few spare moments alone in her small room, she gave herself over to meditation and prayer.

She spoke with Mary. And then, suddenly, the world of thoughts gave way to the world of vision. The Blessed Virgin appeared to Lúcia.

It is something of a sorrow that the account of this apparition was recorded in such a restrained, third-person manner. Lúcia had originally written a more personal version but later destroyed it, choosing instead to recall the events with some distance. This is how she described it:

> *On December 10, 1925, the Most Holy Virgin appeared to her [Lúcia], and by her side, elevated on a luminous cloud, was the Child Jesus. The Most Holy Virgin rested her hand on her shoulder, and as she did so, she showed her a heart encircled by thorns, which she was holding in her other hand.*

Lúcia was already familiar with this tender gesture. Four years earlier, on June 15, 1921, she had encountered the Blessed

PORTUGAL

Lucia (already as Maria das Dores) at the religious house in Porto.

Sr. Lucia in Valinhos in 1946 while identifying the site of the fourth Marian apparition.

Mother for the last time at Fatima. In her diary, she wrote of that meeting:

> *I felt your friendly and maternal hand touching me on the shoulder; I looked up and saw you; it was you, the Blessed Mother, giving me a hand and showing me the way.*

That same gesture would be repeated throughout Lúcia's life—most notably during an apparition in Tui in 1944, when she received the vision that enabled her to write down the Third Secret of Fatima. But now, she simply noted: *"Our Lady, as if to give me courage, placed her hand on my shoulder."*

REPAIRING THE WORLD

That gesture was enough. But this time, unlike the encounter four years earlier, it was not "the sweet timbre of your Mary's voice" that restored peace and light to her soul. On this day, it was Jesus who spoke first.

The Child said: "Have compassion on the Heart of your most holy Mother, covered with thorns with which ungrateful men pierce it at every moment, and there is no one to make an act of reparation to remove them."

The fact that Jesus spoke first is deeply significant. He was at the center of the vision, standing upon a "luminous cloud"—a traditional sign of divine presence. His mother would add only the necessary details to the request given by her Son.

Jesus spoke to Lúcia: *"Have compassion..."* He called for an act of reparation. In the original language, he used the word *reparação*—meaning to repair, to mend what had been damaged. This was the same word Mary had used earlier at Fatima. Through this word, Jesus called attention to truths once obvious but now too often forgotten:

1. *The world was broken.*
2. *Its corruption was the result of sin.*
3. *Only God could repair what had been broken.*

The construction of the Church of the Holy Trinity was completed in Fatima in 2007. It is now the fourth-largest Catholic shrine in the world.

4. *Our civilization had taken the wrong path—it had become a "civilization of the new," where nothing was repaired, only replaced. Yet the world, as created by God, was good. It was not a new world that was needed, but the restoration of the original—its order, beauty, and goodness.*
5. *God desired human cooperation. "God has human hands." He willed to save the world and restore its beauty through the cooperation of human beings. Thus came the request to help repair the world.*

MARY TELLS LÚCIA ABOUT THE DETAILS

But the apparition did not end there. *"What do you want me to do, Lord?"* Lúcia asked silently in her heart. The response, however, came not from him, but from Mary. She explained that this work of reparation was to be carried out through the devotion of the First Saturdays. Why this particular devotion was chosen, and what it meant in God's plan, is not the focus of our present reflection.

Then the Blessed Virgin said:

> *Look, my daughter, at my Heart, surrounded with thorns with which ungrateful men pierce me at every moment by their blasphemies and ingratitude.*
>
> *You at least try to console me, and announce in my name that I promise to assist at the hour of death, with all the graces necessary for salvation, all those who, on the first Saturday of five consecutive months, shall confess, receive Holy Communion, recite five decades of the Rosary, and keep me company for fifteen minutes while meditating on the fifteen mysteries of the Rosary, with the intention of making reparation to me.*

Puzzlingly, Lúcia wrote in her diary: "Having received this grace, how could I brush off even the smallest sacrifice that God asks of me?" At first glance, the remark seems almost unrelated—but perhaps not. For Lúcia, nothing God asked was small, and no request of Heaven could be ignored.

THE SECOND TIME

Following the apparition, Sister Lúcia did what she could to spread this new request of our Lady. But what could she do? She was just beginning her religious life, in

In response to Our Lady's appeal, many people once again reached for the rosary, returning to this form of devotion particularly beloved by Mary.

➤ *The first recipient of the Third Secret of Fatima written down by Lucia was the bishop of Leiria, José Alves Correia da Silva. This photo is usually described as him with a sealed envelope of Sister Lucia's text.*

an obscure convent of the Sisters of St. Dorothy. Days passed. Weeks passed. Two months passed.

Then, on February 15, 1926, Lúcia again went outside the convent to empty a garbage can. There she saw the same little boy to whom she had once taught a prayer to the Mother of God. She later wrote:

> *He seemed to be the same one as before, and I asked him: "Did you ask our Heavenly Mother for the Child Jesus?" The child turned to me and said: "And you, have you revealed to the world what the Heavenly Mother asked you?" And, having said that, he turned into a resplendent child.*

What a transformation! The timid boy became bold, full of authority. And how did he know about the request, about the devotion? Before Lúcia's eyes, the boy was transfigured—radiant and unmistakable. She now recognized him as Jesus.

He looked the same as when he appeared to her two months earlier at Mary's side.

THE KEY

This was an apparition that unfolded on at least two planes. A few months before the revelation concerning the First Saturday devotion, Lúcia experienced what might be called a "hidden apparition"—an encounter that, at the time, did not appear to be supernatural. Only in February 1926, when the same boy revealed his true identity, did its significance become clear. The child who had gently anticipated the December 10 apparition was Jesus Himself.

The Fatima visionary came to understand that she was surrounded by heavenly figures veiled in human form. Why was this particular request of Jesus—regarding the First Saturday devotion—framed by two such encounters? Was it to emphasize the urgency of spreading this new form of reparation? Or was God giving us a different key entirely?

Perhaps the meaning lies in this: the world can only be repaired when we begin to see Jesus in every poor child—and in every suffering person. Our treatment of the least among us is, in truth, our treatment

➤ *Sister. Lucia surrounded by postulants during her novitiate at the convent in Tui.*

of God. If the world would see Jesus, our Savior, in the poor, the earth would become a little paradise. Perhaps the First Saturday devotion was given not only as a means of reparation, but also as a way of learning to see with the eyes of Heaven. The apparition at Pontevedra is a mystery—a puzzle given to us by God to be solved.

HOLY HOUR

Let us now turn to the second of Lúcia's early apparitions, which took place in another convent of the Dorothean Sisters—this time in Tui, Spain, on June 13, 1929. We have a fairly detailed account of what occurred that night. Lúcia wrote: "I requested permission from the superior and my confessor to celebrate a holy hour every night from Thursday to Friday, from eleven o'clock until midnight."

This devotion was not unusual. Many saints—canonized and uncanonized—had kept this hour in imitation of Christ's agony in the Garden of Gethsemane. Jesus Himself had requested it of St. Margaret Mary Alacoque. Lúcia's notes reveal that she was not alone in this practice. Other sisters, too, spent that hour in adoration, seeking to console the Savior in the time He was most forsaken.

But this particular night was different. "Finding myself alone one night..." she wrote. This apparition could have no witnesses.

By this time, Lúcia was already struggling under the weight of her reputation. She had been recognized as the Fatima visionary. If the sisters had seen her receive another apparition, it might have caused scandal—or idolatry. Some of the younger nuns already looked at her as if she were a saint, offering her the reverence due only to God. There were others, too—jealous, suspicious, and unkind.

And so, Jesus chose a moment when Lúcia was alone in the chapel. She later wrote:

> *I knelt down near the Communion rail, in the middle of the chapel, to recite the prayers of the Angel, lying prostrate.... Feeling tired, I got up and continued to recite them with my arms in the form of a cross. The only light was that of the* [*sanctuary*] *lamp.*

It is worth adding that in this section of the chapel, there was an open passage between the chancel and the nave, and Lúcia had no physical support—no communion rail—on which to rest her outstretched arms.

FOUR THINGS

At this moment, four themes stand out—elements that may well have prepared the way for the vision to occur.

First, Lúcia did not kneel in her usual place, where she kept her books and prayer aids. She had not turned on the light and would not have been able to read them anyway. Instead, she knelt near the tabernacle, close to Jesus—not only spiritually, but physically. Her whole being was drawn toward Him.

1925

➤ *The Immaculate Heart of Mary constantly wounded by the thorns of blasphemies and ingratitude. It is the main content of the apparitions in Pontevedra.*

Second, there was obedience. Lúcia only began keeping this weekly holy hour after receiving permission from both her confessor and her superior.

Third, faithfulness. She prayed the words taught by the Angel of Peace to the Fatima children—a prayer she would continue to say for the rest of her life.

And fourth, perseverance. Though exhausted, she pushed through her fatigue, rising to her feet and raising her arms in the shape of a cross. It was a gesture of worship, of total offering. Without her perseverance, obedience, and fidelity to prayer, there would have been no vision at Tui—and the world would have remained without what would later be called the "prescription for peace."

VISION FORMED BY THE LIGHT

Lúcia received a vision—one of those extraordinary encounters that, as the sisters in her Carmel at Coimbra would later describe, involved her "seeing in God, as in a mirror, a film showing the life of humanity." For her, this was not rare. It had become the ordinary way in which Heaven communicated the divine mysteries.

Now, however, Lúcia was not watching the life of the world. In the mystical mirror, she saw the image of God Himself. "Suddenly," she wrote, "the whole chapel lit up with a supernatural light."

She recognized this light. She had seen it many times at Fatima. Jesus had been surrounded by it in Pontevedra. But this time was different. The entire chapel was marked by the presence of God. It was as though the whole room had become His dwelling place.

Of course, the chapel in a monastery belongs to no one but the Lord. But now, it was filled with light, as if to prepare for the magnitude of the vision that was about to be granted. What Lúcia was about to witness would stand among the most important apparitions in the history of the Church.

She did her best to describe what she saw:

> *On the altar appeared a cross of light which reached the ceiling. In a clearer light, on the upper part of*

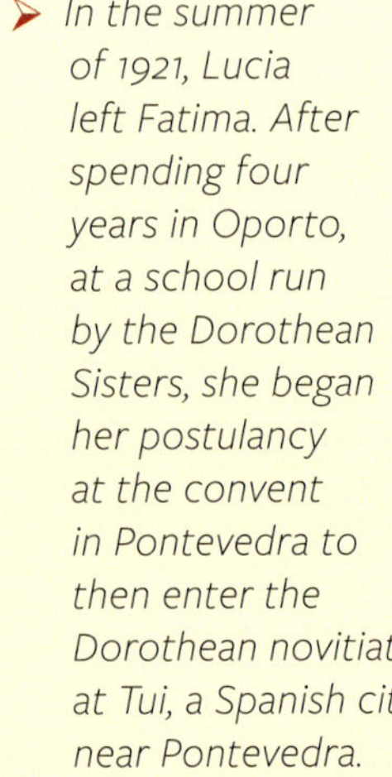

➤ *In the summer of 1921, Lucia left Fatima. After spending four years in Oporto, at a school run by the Dorothean Sisters, she began her postulancy at the convent in Pontevedra to then enter the Dorothean novitiate at Tui, a Spanish city near Pontevedra.*

the cross, could be seen the face of a man with his body to the waist, on his chest a dove, equally luminous; and nailed to the cross, the body of another man. A little below the waist, suspended in the air, could be seen a chalice and a large host, onto which some drops of blood were falling, which flowed from the face of the Crucified One and from the wound in his breast. Running down over the Host, these drops fell into the Chalice.

Everything was light. Just as it had been at Fatima.

Let us recall here Lúcia's conversation with the Dominican sculptor Fr. Thomas McGlynn, who designed the statue that stands in the niche of the Rosary Tower at the Fatima Basilica. When he asked if there had been a difference between the cloak and the tunic Mary wore during the apparitions, Lúcia answered simply: *"The cloak was a wave of light."*

Fr. McGlynn asked further questions, and Lúcia responded with quiet precision:

And the tunic was not made from light?

It was.

Then how does one distinguish between the mantle and the tunic?

There were two waves of light, one on top of the other.... It was like a ray of sunlight all around the mantle, like a thin thread.

Were the face and hands and feet of our Lady the color of light or the color of flesh?

Flesh-colored light; light which took on the color of flesh."

Lúcia also explained: "She was all light. The light had different tones—yellow and white, and other colors. It was through the variety of tones and intensities that one saw what was a hand and what was a mantle, what was a face and what was a tunic."

MYSTERY OF THE TRINITY

Such was the case again here, in the vision at Tui. The entire apparition was composed of light—light that was not merely a symbol of God, but *is* God. It was a vision that communicated, through

The room that once served as Sister Lucia's room now houses a chapel.

The appeal coming from Spain, the request to spread devotion to the Immaculate Heart of Mary in the world, is still relevant today. It is also our task.

light, something beyond the capacity of human words or the limitations of image. It attempted to depict, however incompletely, the mystery that cannot be grasped: the inner life of the Trinity.

And yet, through this flood of supernatural light, Jesus revealed to Lúcia a glimpse of the unutterable reality.

To make this mystery known, Jesus employed a cultural filter. He revealed the Holy Trinity in a form familiar to Lúcia—an image often seen in churches and devotional art: the Father above, the Son reigning from the cross, and the Holy Spirit as a dove. Yet one crucial detail stood out: the Father was not described as an old man. From Lúcia's account, one might even conclude that the Father and the Son appeared to be the same age, or at least bore a striking resemblance to one another.

What she saw was not simply an abstract doctrine, but the living Trinity in the act of redemption. God the Father, God the Son, and God the Holy Spirit are Love—not love turned inward, but a love that overflows. It is a love meant to give life to creatures made in God's image, and the wellspring of this life is the Eucharist: the acceptance of salvation offered on the Cross.

A fragment of the facade of the Church of the Pilgrim Virgin with two towers on top.

◄ *The Sanctuary of the Apparitions in Pontevedra, Spain.*

But there was more. Part of the vision of the Trinity included a human being—one of us—who stood within this mystery: the Blessed Mother.

MARY AS A PART OF THE MYSTERY OF THE HOLY TRINITY

Sister Lúcia wrote:

> *Under the right arm of the cross was our Lady with her Immaculate Heart in her hand.... (She appeared as our Lady of Fatima, with her Immaculate Heart in her left hand, without sword or roses, but with a crown of thorns and flames). Under the left arm [of the cross], in large letters, like crystalline water which flowed over the altar, forming these words: "Grace and Mercy." I understood that the mystery of the Most Holy Trinity was shown to me, and I received lights about this mystery which I am not permitted to reveal.*

Lúcia was granted an apparition that included a secret concerning the greatest mystery of the Christian faith: the Holy Trinity. This secret would remain sealed within her.

REPAIRING THE WORLD

In that vision, the "voice" of the Trinity was Our Lady. It was she who instructed Lúcia about the need for the consecration of Russia to her Immaculate Heart and for acts of reparation. The vision seemed to reveal that the Trinity, while infinitely transcendent, *opens itself* to humanity—perhaps not merely through Mary, but in such a way that we are invited to dwell within the circle of divine life itself.

The apparition revealed a profound truth: the intimate bond between Our Lady, the Holy Trinity, and the outpouring of grace and mercy upon the world. It was a theme of enormous depth, yet we must now set it aside, turning the pages of history forward by fifteen years.

THIRD FATIMA MYSTERY

It was Monday, January 3, 1944. On this day, under obedience to her superiors, Lúcia wrote down the contents of the Third Secret of Fatima and sealed the envelope. But before doing so, as she did every day, she went to the chapel at four in the afternoon—her regular hour of prayer before the Blessed Sacrament. She chose this hour because the chapel was always empty, offering solitude for her adoration.

That afternoon, while she knelt alone in prayer before the tabernacle, a new supernatural vision began—just as it had in Pontevedra. Once again, it began with a touch.

▼ *Until the end of her days, Sr. Lucia diligently answered letters and questions addressed to her from all over the world.*

1925

➤ The visionary, entering the Congregation of the Sisters of St. Dorothy, took the name Maria Lucia of Sorrows.

▲ A plaque commemorating Sr. Lucia's stay at the novitiate of the Congregation of the Sisters of St. Dorothy in Tui.

Lúcia recorded in her notes:

> *I felt the friendly, gentle, and motherly touch of a hand that touched my shoulder. I looked up and saw my beloved Mother from heaven. "Do not be afraid, God wanted to prove your obedience, faith, and humility. Be at peace and write what they order you, but do not give your opinion of its meaning."*

After this brief but intimate apparition, Lúcia wrote the secret. She noted: "I wrote [it down] without difficulty, on January 3, 1944. I was kneeling, and the bed served as my table."

Mary's touch and her words of consolation were necessary. Without them, Lúcia may not have had the peace or strength to complete the task. Yet through that act of humble obedience, the path was opened for the eventual consecration of the entire world to the Immaculate Heart of Mary.

On August 17, 1959, Fr. Pierre Paul Philippe, OP, Commissary of the Holy Office, brought the envelope containing Lúcia's letter to Pope John XXIII. He did so with the permission of Cardinal Alfredo Ottaviani. According to the official record, "After some hesitation," the Holy Father said: "We shall wait. I shall pray. I shall let you know what I decide." But Pope John XXIII ultimately chose not to open the Third Secret. The envelope was returned, unopened, to the Holy Office.

Years passed.

Then came May 13, 1981. Pope John Paul II was holding his weekly General Audience in St. Peter's Square. Without warning, the sound of gunshots rang out. One eyewitness later told the *National Catholic Register*, "That was all it was: popping sounds. I thought they were fireworks." But they were not. Four bullets struck the Holy Father—passing through his abdomen and arm, narrowly missing his heart.

As he later said, "The gunman fired the gun, but Mary guided the bullet." Through what he called her miraculous intervention, the Pope survived. Not long afterward, he requested the envelope containing the Third Part of the Secret.

Following the attempt on his life, Pope John Paul II felt a powerful urgency to consecrate the world to the Immaculate Heart of Mary. He composed a prayer—an *Act of Entrustment*—and began seeking to fulfill our Lady's request. But it would take more than one attempt before Sister Lúcia confirmed that the consecration had been carried out in accordance with Heaven's Will.

As the Congregation for the Doctrine of the Faith later stated in *The Message of Fatima*:

> *On March 25, 1984, in Saint Peter's Square, while recalling the fiat uttered by Mary at the Annunciation, the Holy Father, in spiritual union with the Bishops of the world, who had been 'convoked' beforehand, entrusted all men and women and all peoples to the Immaculate Heart of Mary.*

Lúcia personally confirmed that this solemn and universal act was exactly what our Lady had asked for: "Yes, it has been done just as our Lady asked, on March 25, 1984."

From that moment forward, further discussion or petition regarding the consecration was without foundation.

Thanks to John Paul II's decision, the contents of Lúcia's letter were finally revealed to the world on June 26, 2000. As Archbishop Tarcisio Bertone, SDB, then Secretary of the Congregation for the Doctrine of the Faith, wrote: the decision to disclose the Third Secret "brings to an end a period of history marked by tragic human lust for power and evil, yet pervaded by the merciful love of God and the watchful care of the Mother of Jesus and of the Church."

IN HER TESTAMENT

Lúcia died on February 13, 2005. She took with her the mystery of the Holy Trinity, which she had been shown but was never permitted to reveal. And yet, to those who read her writings carefully, some light still shines from that great silence.

What she did leave behind, however, was abundant. The apparitions she received over the course of her life, she gave fully to the Church. And with them, she offered her many written reflections—thousands of pages, carefully preserved, which she entitled *My Path*. She began keeping them in 1921.

"The Church is the interpreter of apparitions," Lúcia often said. "I am only a visionary."

If the Church one day judges that the world should know more of her testimony, it will possess a vast treasury: records of countless supernatural interventions in the twentieth century. For now, only a small portion of her notes has been released, with the Church's blessing.

Perhaps this is as it should be. For Lúcia always insisted that what matters most is not what remains hidden—but what has already been revealed. What we must do, above all, is fulfill the requests of Jesus and Mary that we already know.

In 1948, with special permission from Pope Pius XII, Lucia left the Sisters of St. Dorothy and entered the Order of the Blessed Virgin Mary of Mount Carmel.

Sr. Lucia was faithful to the Message of Fatima from the apparitions until her last encounter with the Blessed Mother, who ran to meet her halfway at the moment of her death.

15
“YOUR LOVE BURNED ME”

On the previous page: Painting of Marthe Robin.

Châteauneuf-de-Galaure (France) was located in the hills and covered by forest.

Place of Apparition: Châteauneuf-de-Galaure, France
Date and Place of Birth: March 13, 1902, Châteauneuf-de-Galaure, France
Date and Place of Death: February 6, 1981, Châteauneuf-de-Galaure, France
Visionary as a Lay and Religious Person (Secular Franciscan Order)
Beatification Process: Servant of God: April 1996 (Pope John Paul II), Venerable Servant of God: November 8, 2014 (Pope Francis)
Works: The Way of the Cross, Meditations

15

"YOUR LOVE BURNED ME"

MARTHE ROBIN, 1926

The person standing before us had known profound physical and moral suffering. Marthe Robin endured torments beyond what we can comprehend—suffering that defied the scale of ordinary human pain. Yet, to our astonishment, she came to accept it. In time, she gave it meaning.

She was not in any way enamored with suffering. On the contrary, in the midst of it, she longed for death as a release. "I feel broken physically and morally," she said. "I would be much better off under the ground than on it." These words date from the period before she entrusted herself to God.

But once she gave her life to Jesus, everything changed. Her suffering did not cease—but her spirit transformed. Those who visited her expected to find a woman whose face was contorted in pain. Instead, they were met with joy. In the small room where she lay paralyzed, her laughter could often be heard.

She was born on March 13, 1902, the sixth child of a humble village family. Her mother was devout, while her father wanted to keep pace with modern ideas. He considered himself a freethinker and seldom entered the church.

Why mention this detail? Because one day, when Marthe was four or perhaps five years old, Joseph Robin nailed a plain wooden cross above the front door to please his believing wife.

He showed it to the future visionary and said, "Look, there is no one on it." Was he trying to persuade the child that Christianity was a thing of the past—that even Christ had vanished from the cross? We do not know his intentions, nor do

they truly matter. What matters is Marthe's response.

"Then we will be there!" she replied without hesitation.

In that moment, she spoke a prophecy about herself.

"YOUR LOVE BURNED ME"

FIRST "MEETING"

Her father wished to be seen as an atheist. Her mother's piety was traditional and far removed from anything mystical. Yet their sixth child harbored within herself a mysterious openness to the supernatural—something neither parent could comprehend.

Perhaps her response to the empty cross sprang from an early mystical intuition. She certainly possessed a spiritual sensitivity. At age ten, when she received her First Communion—granted to her two years earlier than was usual—she experienced a kind of encounter with Jesus through the sacrament.

For now, there were many "some kind of" moments in her story. Marthe herself often used such expressions, unable to name her spiritual experiences precisely.

FRANCE

FRANCE

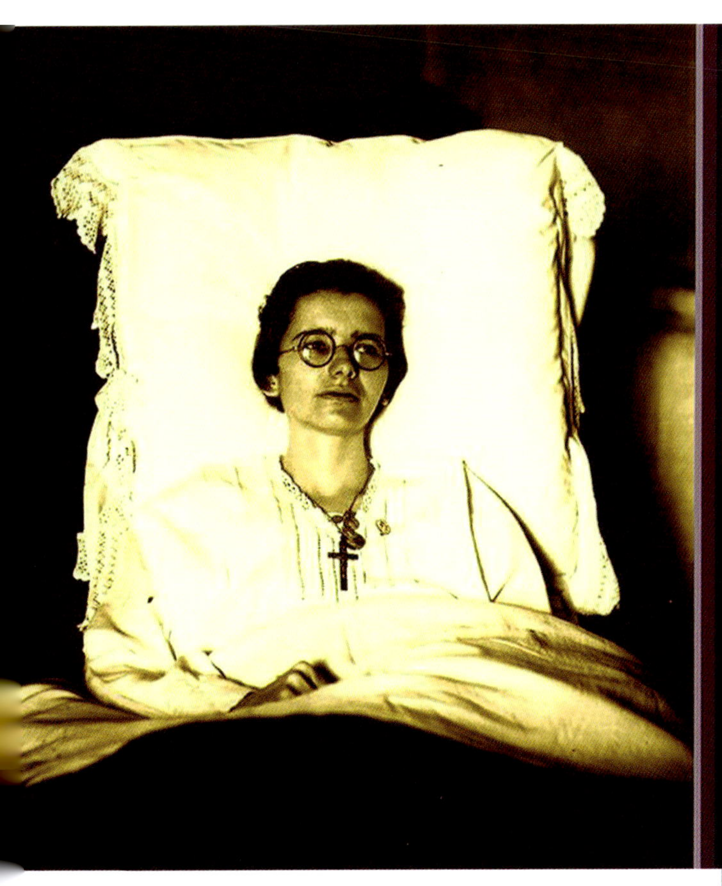

Marthe Robin was sixteen years old when she experienced her first serious health problems: unbearable headaches, paralysis of the legs and then also of the arms, and frequent stretches of complete unconsciousness.

When speaking about receiving Jesus in Holy Communion for the first time, she tried to explain: "I believe that my private communion was the moment when Our Lord took possession of my soul. I believe he had already taken hold of me at that time. My private communion was something very sweet."

Marthe felt that it was not she who received Jesus, but rather Jesus who received her. He took possession of her. This is easier to understand when one remembers that Marthe's heart was pure and wholly open to God. So when she welcomed Jesus, the Lord could fill her heart entirely with Himself and make her soul completely His—just as in the days of Eden.

It is worth noting that there was no active effort on Marthe's part. Jesus acted; Marthe only opened her heart.

St. Bonitus Church, 2008 (Châteauneuf-de-Galaure, France).

IT'S STARTING...

At the age of sixteen, she experienced her first serious health problems. She had been ill before, but her earlier ailments were common to many. Now something unusual began: unbearable headaches, paralysis first of her legs and then of her arms, and frequent episodes of complete unconsciousness. These episodes were strange in nature. It was known that she experienced some kind of apparition during these states, which we will discuss in more detail later.

During unconsciousness, Marthe seemed to exist "outside of time." For instance, in early 1921, a parish priest came to visit her. In the middle of their conversation, she lost consciousness. She awoke a month later—surprised to learn the priest had already come and gone. When he returned, Marthe resumed their conversation exactly where it had left off.

LIGHT THAT WAS IN THE PHYSICAL WORLD

That same year, on May 20, Marthe Robin received her first apparition. She was not alone. Her sister Alice—eight years her senior—slept in the same room to care for the sick girl. In the middle of the night, Alice was awakened by a radiant light that filled the entire room. The next morning, unsure if it had been a dream, she asked Marthe about it.

"Yes, there was a beautiful light," Marthe replied, "but I also saw the Blessed Virgin."

This was not merely an interior vision. Elements of the apparition—its "splinterings"—also manifested in the physical world. The light associated with it was perceptible to the senses. It was not seen by the visionary alone; her sister saw it too.

Was it not the same with the apparition of the Infant Jesus to St. Anthony?

Such "splinterings" were not always light. During the Fatima apparition in August, witnesses noted that "the air was different." There was a light with no temporal source, an altered atmosphere whose properties could not be explained, or a fragrance accompanying many apparitions—unknown to the senses beforehand.

One might ask whether such physical phenomena could be investigated using scientific tools. Perhaps, as with the study of the image of Our Lady of Guadalupe, science could uncover further signs of the supernatural—evidence of the "Creator of things visible and invisible."

This extraordinary apparition marked the beginning of the hundreds Marthe Robin would receive throughout her long life.

MEETING DURING SPIRITUAL READING

She read extensively until she lost her eyesight. Above all, she turned again and again to the Gospels. But she also drew

FRANCE

On October 15, 1925, the feast of St. Teresa of Ávila, Marthe Robin drew up her act of surrendering herself to Jesus: "Lord, my God, You have asked everything of Your little servant, so take and accept everything. Today I give myself to You completely, O beloved of my soul! It is You alone that I desire, and for Your love, I renounce everything."

strength from *The Imitation of Christ* by Thomas à Kempis. She found joy in *Story of a Soul: The Autobiography of St. Thérèse of Lisieux* and a biography of Bl. Giulia (Maria Celeste) Crostarosa (†1755). Over time, she became familiar with the lives of many saints. These readings became another kind of "place of apparition."

One day, as she set aside the book in her hands, she heard the voice of Jesus: "For you, it will be suffering." When she opened the book again, her eyes immediately fell on the words: "You must give everything to God."

"I CAN STILL HEAR HER SCREAMS"

Perhaps it is not quite right to say that God intended suffering for her. Rather, God gave meaning to the suffering that entered Marthe Robin's life—and more than that, He used it, with her consent, to accomplish His mission: the salvation of souls. Marthe was to participate in this mission.

She was not given pain as a command, something she could later boast of having endured. Jesus knew that her illness—not He—would plunge her into a sea of agony beyond human understanding.

One surviving testimony speaks to this. Marthe Robin's niece vividly remembered her aunt's suffering from their childhood.

Recalling the early stages of Marthe's illness, her niece shared: "She was screaming. I can still hear her screams.... We didn't dare approach her bed—she was crying so much, poor thing.... She told

The fireplace in Marthe's house and her bedroom with a short bed, where the visionary rested all her life.

"Jesus asked me to offer my chest and heart. Their piercing was accomplished in an even more intense way. Jesus also offered me a crown of thorns. He placed it on my head, pressing it firmly." The stigmata of the crown were perfectly visible on the visionary's head.

me: 'If you had dipped me in boiling water, I would not have suffered more.'"

It was most likely encephalitis. The paralysis that slowly overtook her body did not dull her sensitivity to pain; rather, it intensified it. It is hard to fathom how she endured such suffering—how she bore it for more than sixty years without ever losing consciousness from the pain.

SPIRITUAL BREAKTHROUGH

Suffering was not part of our nature in the beginning. It did not belong to the world as God created it. That is why, even to the end of time, mankind will never grow accustomed to pain—though the world is filled with it.

It is no wonder that Marthe struggled with suffering for many years and resisted accepting it. She dreamed of entering the Carmelite order. But for that, she needed to be healthy. And so she resisted her "Way of the Cross."

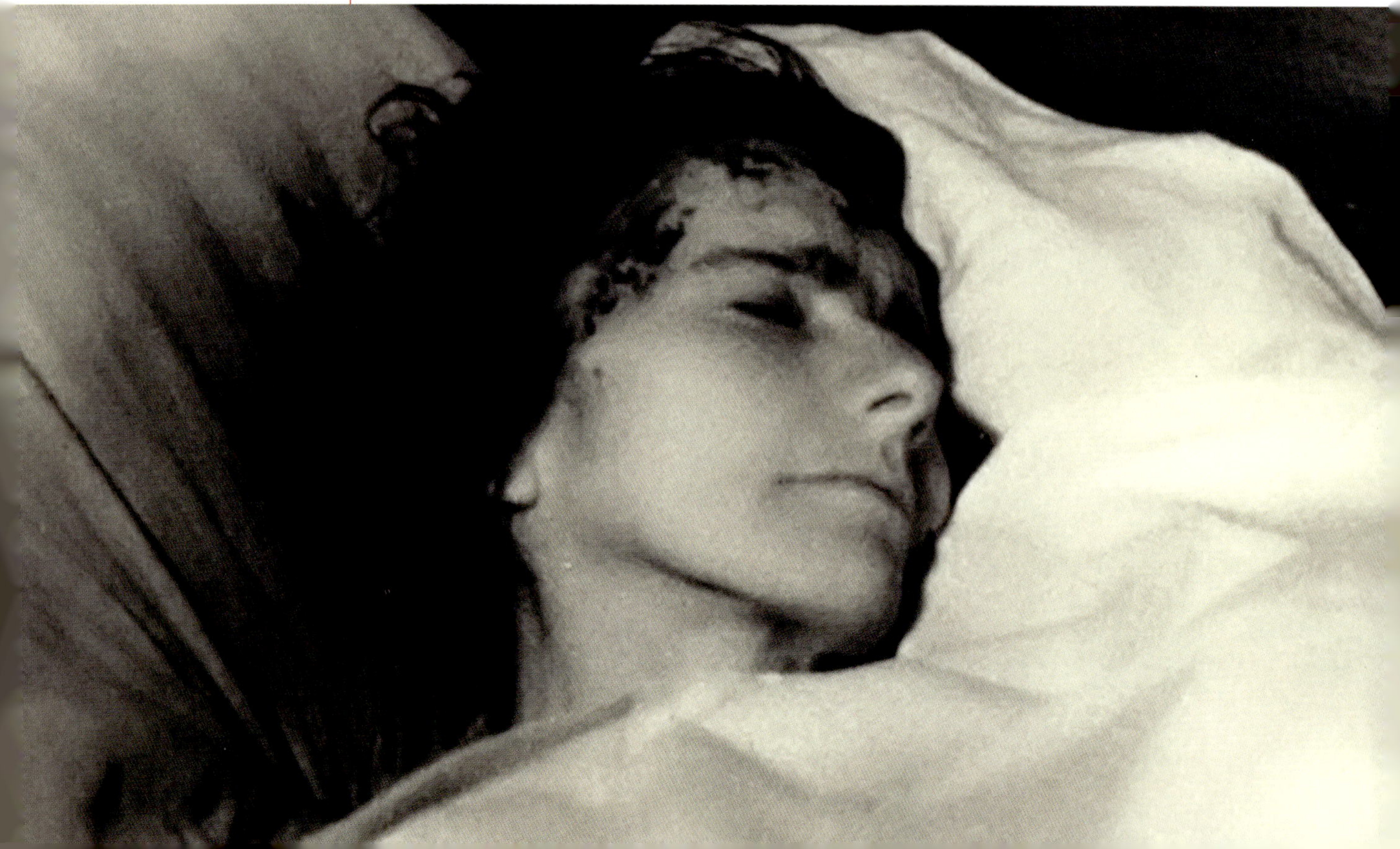

Until the autumn of 1925, she had not yet recognized her true vocation.

She had not yet understood that her vocation was not to the enclosure of a convent, but to her family home—and to the bed from which she could no longer rise. But by mid-October of that year, she came to see that the place of her sanctification would be suffering itself. That was when she made her decision.

On October 15, 1925, the feast of St. Teresa of Ávila, Marthe Robin composed her act of total self-offering to Jesus:

> *Lord, my God, You have asked everything of Your little servant, so take and accept everything. Today, I give myself to You completely, O beloved of my soul! It is You alone that I desire, and for Your love, I renounce everything.*

It was a heroic act—but, as she would later come to understand, her devotion was not yet complete. There remained in her heart a trace of "worldliness": a longing for the suffering to come to an end. At the conclusion of her offering, she wrote: "My beloved, help me, take me to You. Only in You do I wish to live, and only in You do I wish to die. Help me!"

She seemed to be heard—for her condition steadily worsened, and it appeared that death was drawing near.

On October 3, 1926, the feast of another Carmelite beloved by her—St. Thérèse of Lisieux—Marthe Robin fell into a mystical sleep that lasted three weeks. When she awoke, she told her parents that during that time she had experienced both great suffering and, paradoxically, the sweetness of God's love. "I think I will not die," she added. And she was right. More than fifty years of life still lay before her.

How did she know that the time of death had not yet come? Could it be that, in her mystical sleep, she was granted a vision of what awaited her? Whatever the case, she no longer feared pain. She had learned that when she united herself to Jesus in suffering, her pain became inseparable from joy.

This did not mean that the "sweetness of God's love" dulled the sharpness of her agony. Rather, suffering and happiness became mingled—like wine and water. They became one.

Marthe Robin's confessor, Fr. Georges Finet. Together, they established Les Foyers de Charité.

1926

➢ *Pilgrims from all over the world traveled to Marthe Robin's room in Châteauneuf-de-Galaure to pray at the visionary's bedside for the intentions entrusted to them by the sick and suffering.*

STIGMATA

On December 3, 1928, during a parish mission, two Capuchin fathers came to visit the sick—and among them, they visited Marthe Robin.

On that occasion, the visionary received the Sacrament of Reconciliation and Holy Communion. Something happened that day—something decisive. Marthe stopped struggling with herself and fully embraced the words of the act she had signed three years earlier.

"Then everything changed!" she later recounted. "After years of anxiety, sin, after many hard physical and spiritual experiences, I dared to choose Christ Jesus."

She made this choice knowing full well that to choose the Savior meant also to choose suffering. Over the next two years, she grew ever deeper into this unexpected vocation. By 1930, it seemed she was already fully united with Jesus—for that year, she received the stigmata of His Passion.

At the end of September, Jesus asked her, "Do you want to be like Me?" She replied that she did.

At the beginning of October, she had another apparition. Jesus appeared to her hanging on the Cross—but she also saw something else, something she could not describe in earthly terms. She later spoke of it as a "fiery arrow," like a "blade of light," coming forth from His Heart.

What followed? Marthe recalled:

> *Jesus first asked me to offer my hands. It seemed to me that an arrowhead came out of His Heart and split into two rays, so that each pierced one of my hands. At the same time, my hands were pierced as if from the inside. Then Jesus encouraged me to offer my legs, which I immediately did. I saw an arrowhead that again split into two parts and pierced my legs. All this took place very quickly. Then Jesus asked me to offer my chest and heart. Their piercing was accomplished in an even more intense way. Jesus also offered me a crown of thorns. He placed it on my head, pressing it firmly.*

Not long after, Marthe dictated a letter in which she reflected on what had taken place: "This year, an intimate union of my soul with God took place. My whole being has undergone a transformation as mysterious as it is profound." She added, "Despite my disability, my happiness is profound and lasting because it is Divine." And further, she exclaimed: "What a labor! What growth God has wrought in me!"

In the end, she expressed the foundation of it all: "But what leapings of the heart, what death-struggles of the will it takes to die to self!" Without this death to self, there would have been no union with Christ. There would have been no stigmata.

Marthe Robin's family grave at the cemetery in Châteauneuf-de-Galaure, France.

STAY IN PURGATORY COULD BE SHORTENED!

When Robin's mother was hospitalized in grave condition, she was brought home so that she could die near Marthe.

"At my request," wrote Fr. Finet, "the nurse brought Mrs. Robin and leaned her over Marthe, who was unconscious at the time, as she was reliving the Passion. I made Marthe's head touch her mother's lips. She kissed her and said, 'Little one!'"

This was Mrs. Robin's final expression of maternal love. She died soon after—in peace and without fear.

"Mother is entering heaven! Her purgatory is over!" Marthe said.

She confided to her confessor the content of an apparition: "The Lord has asked me to take upon myself my mother's purgatorial sufferings. So I must experience more suffering from now on—for nine months—and for the last three months I will also endure the anguish of damnation."

By accepting this suffering and offering it for her mother, Marthe delivered her from Purgatory.

LES FOYERS DE CHARITÉ (BONFIRES OF LOVE)

In 1933, Marthe received a series of visions in which Jesus revealed what He desired of her. Once again, let us hear from her:

> *Jesus spoke to me of the wonderful work He wished to accomplish here—for the glory of the Father, for the growth of His Kingdom throughout the Church, and for the renewal of the whole world, through the religious instruction that would be given here. For this work, I was to place myself under the direction of the priest whom He had chosen in His Heart from all eternity. One day, He would send this priest faithful and devoted collaborators—men and women to absolve, instruct, and nourish souls, and to lead them into His love.*

Jesus desired this to be *something new*—a work in which all its members would be holy, shining with the example of supernatural life, and acting always in love: "This bonfire, burning even in the remotest corners of the earth, will be a

A lobby in the main building at the Foyer de Charité center in Ottrott (Grand Est, France).

Ottrott Castle, which belongs to the center.

refuge in the midst of human misery for countless sinners."

The Lord Himself spoke of the *Foyers de Charité*—the *Bonfires of Love*. He assured Marthe that through these communities, souls "will seek love and merciful love; they will understand it, feel it, and practice it."

"If this condition is met, I will pour streams of light and grace on this work and each of its members. I will perform astounding miracles there." The Lord explained that Marthe was one of the sparks of the "new Pentecost of love" and a herald of a new era of uniting hearts and nations in God's love. Once more, the theme of God's Kingdom on earth emerged. "I have chosen you to rekindle the fading love in the world," Jesus added. These words of Christ to Marthe Robin summed up her mission: to reveal God's unconditional love for all.

ONLY THE EUCHARIST

Marthe Robin suffered from full-body paralysis that so affected her esophageal muscles she could not even swallow a drop of water. The visionary ate and drank nothing due to this physical impossibility, brought on by the total immobilization of her body. For fifty years, she consumed no earthly food. The Eucharist alone sustained her. She received it only once a week—on Tuesday, and, in the final years of her life, on Wednesday evening. On the day she received Jesus in Holy Communion, she spent the morning in prayer, repeating her act of complete self-offering from October 15, 1925. That day also always included the Sacrament of Penance and Reconciliation. Each time after receiving the Eucharist, she gave a silent cry of joy and fell into ecstasy. Her face would radiate unearthly beauty and happiness.

How was this possible? The answer is found in the prayers she wrote to Jesus. "I am so happy, O my Beloved. I feel my heart beating in Your heart, I feel You in my heart, You living and almighty. The Lord in me—what a mystery! I feel like I am in paradise. One day, I will die feeling You, O my Jesus, as You beat in my heart. O my Jesus, make it be said one day that Your love has burned me, not as a result of my efforts, but by Your grace." And again she prayed: "O my God, if You already give me such peace and make me so happy on this earth, what will be in heaven?" Her thanksgiving lasted the whole day. The following morning, the ecstasy would end, and Marthe would return to her normal state.

Les Foyers de Charité—the center in Baye (France).

"When I receive Holy Communion," she explained, "it's as if a living person enters me. Each time, new life is poured into me. Jesus is in my whole body as if I have risen from the dead. Holy Communion is more than a union: it is a transformation into one." And she added, "I want to cry out to those who ask me if I eat that I eat more than they do, because I am fed by the Eucharist with the body and blood of Jesus."

"O my God, if You already give me such peace and make me so happy on this earth, what will be in heaven?" Her question was rhetorical.

Marthe died on Friday, February 6, 1981. She knew that death would take away her suffering, but not her life—nor her mission. She had assured others: "In heaven.... I will continue my beautiful mission: working so the Love will be loved, sowing the seeds of supernatural vocations..., [and] opening God's treasuries to all souls. From the heights ... I will hear them better, I will do even more." Now that she had departed this world, her dream could be fulfilled, for she was no longer limited by the frailty of the body. She could at last devote herself entirely to the task the Lord had entrusted to her.

Her great longing was being realized: "I would like to be everywhere and tell the world again and again how good God is, how much He loves people, and how He turns out to be tender and compassionate." In the communion of saints, nothing constrained her anymore.

Foyer de Charité (Courset, France).

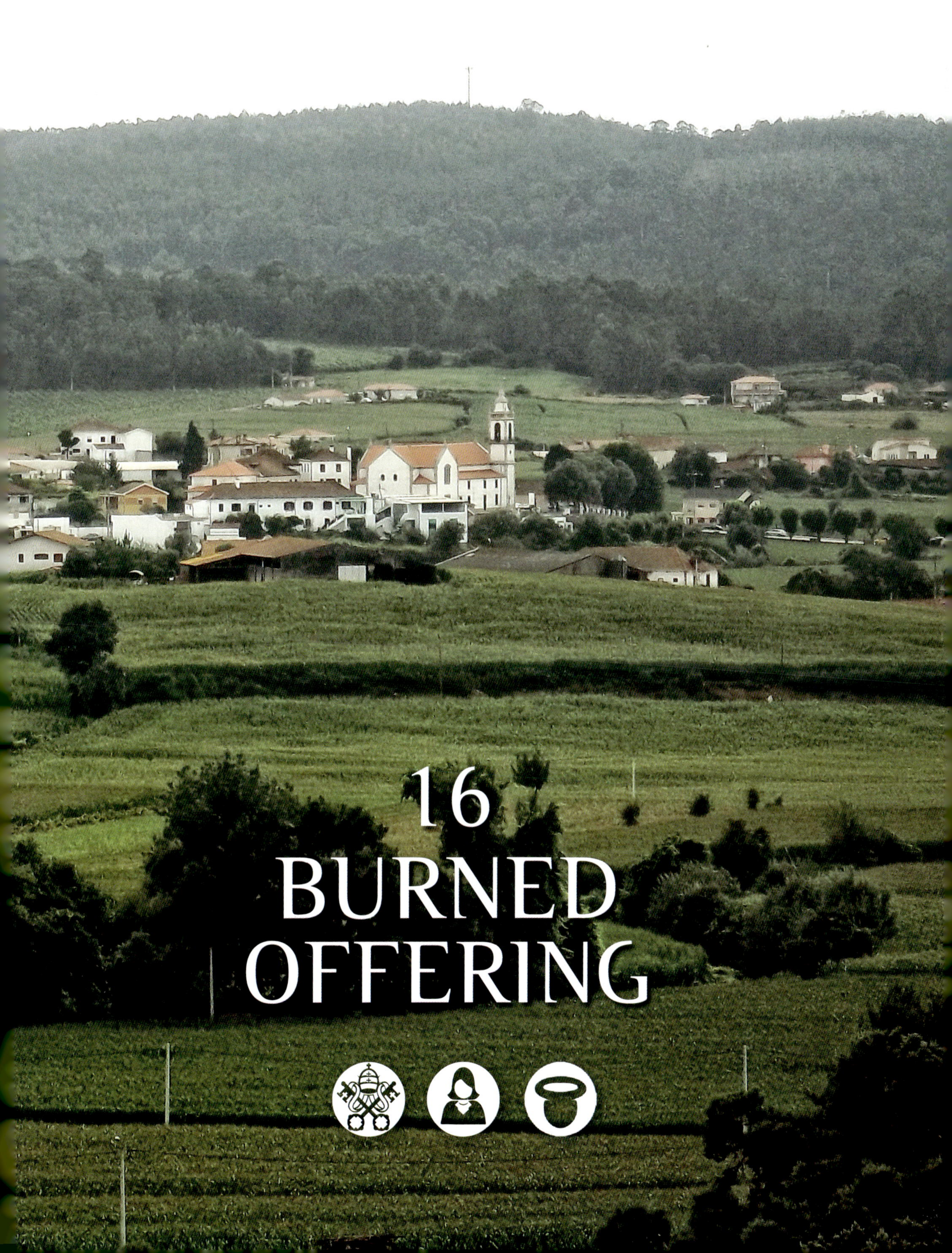

16 BURNED OFFERING

On the previous page: View of Balazar (Portugal), the home village of the mystic.

Place of Apparition:
Balazar, Portugal
Date and Place of Birth:
March 30, 1904,
Balazar, Portugal
Date and Place of Death:
October 13, 1955,
Balazar, Portugal
Visionary as a Lay and Religious Person (Association of Salesian Cooperators (ASC))
Beatification:
April 25, 2004
(John Paul II)
Feast: October 13

Senhora Ana and Deolinda—the mother and sister of Alexandrina. Below: her baptismal certificate.

16

BURNED OFFERING

ALEXANDRINA DA COSTA, 1933

Another difficult biography. Again, this is a figure no one would naturally wish to relate to. Beatified so that we might imitate her? Such a suggestion may arouse our instinctive resistance. Once again, we hear about suffering, which must be accepted out of love for God and love for others. This is a different perspective, one we do not easily understand: only suffering can save the world. It is needed, and holy people are able to accept it with a joy incomprehensible to us.

St. John Paul II wrote: "My thoughts turn to the deep mystery, and an inexhaustible subject of meditation, that the salvation of many depends on the prayers and suffering endured with patience, which the members of the Mystical Body of Jesus Christ offer for this intention." This is the shortest definition of Alexandrina da Costa's holiness. Her life had already been planned, and in God's designs, she was to become a clear sign given to the world. Mankind saw that, although the work of Redemption was completed by Christ and His suffering, Christ-like suffering, permeated by the spirit of His sacrifice, remains "the irreplaceable mediator and author of the good things which are indispensable for the world's salvation. Suffering, more than anything else, clears the way for the grace which transforms human souls."

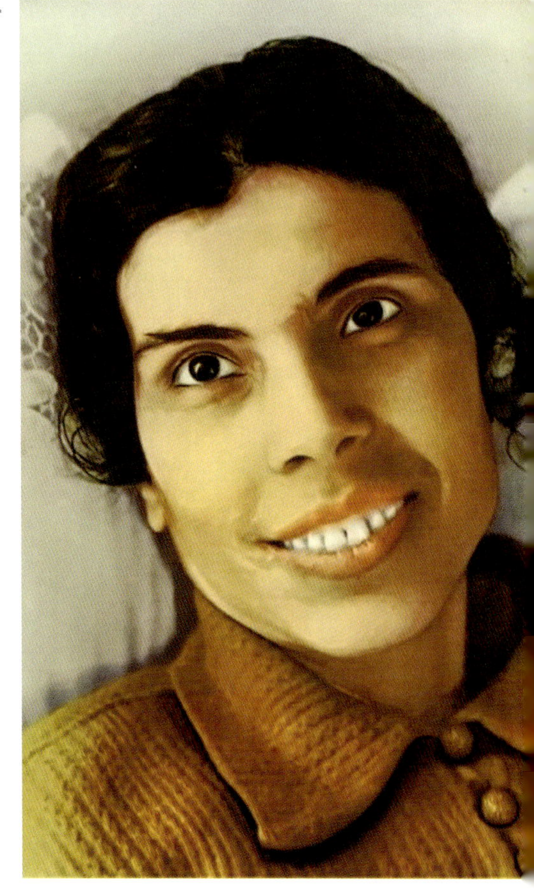

CROSS FROM THE SOIL

We are in the Portuguese village of Balazar, not far from Fatima, which everyone knows today. However, the

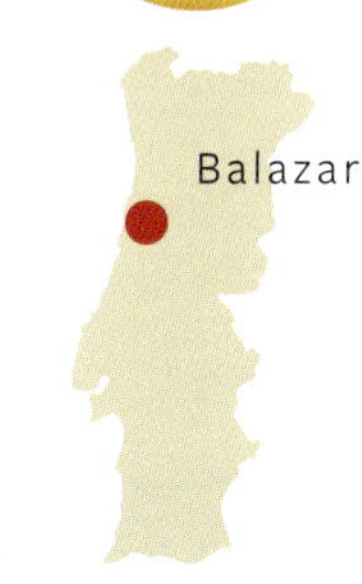

year is 1832, and so far, no one has heard anything about Fatima. On Corpus Christi (we will discover why God chose this particular day when we learn more about Alexandrina's life), villagers notice a cross formed from a thin layer of black soil across from the church.

They notified the parish priest, but he was convinced it was a prank by local youth—most likely the children of the blacksmith, he thought—and he ordered the sign of the cross to be removed. This, however, proved impossible. The cross could not be covered, destroyed by scattering black soil, or washed away with water. Each time, it reappeared the next day.

The pious residents began to see it as a sign for their village. They whispered among themselves that one day a great saint, who would suffer much, would come out of Balazar. In time, they built a shrine over the cross.

What was the meaning of the sign? The mystery remained unsolved until 1947—and again in 1955. On December fifth, 1947, a villager, Alexandrina da Costa, heard the words of Jesus:

> *You are my victim; to you I have entrusted the highest mission. And as proof of this, listen carefully and understand well. Almost a century ago, I sent to this parish the cross as a signal of your crucifixion. I did not send a cross of roses, because the cross did not grow roses, only thorns; nor was it of gold, because your virtues and your heroism would be the precious stones adorning it. The cross was of earth, because it grew from the earth. The cross was prepared; it lacked the victim, but already in the divine mind, the victim had been chosen: it was you.*

Why was this so? we ask. Jesus goes on to say:

Alexandrina's bed, in which she experienced many ecstasies and the Passion of the Lord.

Relics of the visionary.

The cross made of earth is currently protected by a steel barrier.

Evil has increased; the wave of sin has reached its high point. The victim must be immolated. You came, the world's sacrificial lamb.

And now you will leave the earth for Heaven, but the cross will remain until the end of the world, and it will always be mine. It was human perversity that prepared mine, and it was the same human perversity that prepared yours.

Jesus ended His apparition with words seemingly unrelated to the suffering He had just spoken of. He exclaimed:

Oh, how admirable are the designs of the Lord! How great and admirable they are! How many enchantments they hold!

How can one speak of suffering and delight in the same breath? Again, we touch a mystery we cannot fully comprehend. Only mystics and saints do.

A SACRIFICE THAT HAS ALWAYS EXISTED IN THE EYES OF GOD

Perhaps we will understand more by listening to what Christ said eight years later, on January 21, 1955:

More than a century ago, I showed a cross to this beloved land—a cross awaiting a victim. Everything is proof of love! Oh, Balazar, if you do not respond to me... Cross of earth for the victim who was taken from nothing, the victim chosen by God and who always existed in the eyes of God!

Redemption was part of God's eternal plan. The Creator of the world ordained the Incarnation of His Son and His Passion, culminating in the triumph of His Resurrection. Through the eyes of His Providence, He allows us, through apparitions, to glimpse not only the Passover of Jesus but also the participation of His Church in Jesus' Passion and victory.

The suffering person who "fills up what is lacking in the afflictions of Christ" (Colossians 1:24) participates in the spiritual dimension of the work of redemption, serving, like Christ, the salvation of his brothers and sisters.

Fortunately, there are such souls, like the ten righteous. Ten righteous—an insignificant number—would have been enough to save Sodom (see Genesis 18:32). Their vocations, like all vocations, are eternally planned. Theirs is the most beautiful vocation, for through their lives they most fully reflect the life of Jesus. Their vocation is the most beautiful—and, humanly speaking, the happiest.

Jesuit Fr. Mariano Pinho, the first spiritual director of the Servant of God.

The stove in Alexandrina's house and a view of her home village.

Just look at the photographs showing Alexandrina's face, lit up with a radiant smile.

Where does this joy come from? Jesus explained this in the second part of His discourse from January twenty-first. Its ending strikes a note that at first sounds like dissonance. Yet it echoes a theme that makes the words the visionary hears in ecstasy perhaps a little clearer to us. For the Savior speaks of God's gifts—of graces. We know that these—more than anything else in the universe—are the true source of happiness, although the world does not know such happiness.

Christ says to Alexandrina:

> *The victim of the world, but so enriched with celestial graces, who has given all for Heaven and who, for love of souls, accepts all! Trust, believe, my daughter! I am here. Repeat your "I believe." Trust!*

A FEW WORDS FROM THE BIOGRAPHY

Alexandrina Maria da Costa was born in 1904 in the now familiar rural village of Balazar. From the beginning, her life was marked by poverty and hard work. It should not surprise us that her piety was intertwined with dreams of happiness. The fullness of life, in her view, was affluence—something her family home lacked.

She often gazed at the statues of Our Lady of the Rosary and St. Joseph in the church, fascinated by their magnificent robes. She dreamed of one day becoming like them—not so much to be a saint, but to be rich.

This was the path she chose as a child, and perhaps she would have achieved her dream if not for a certain event. She was fourteen years old at the time, one year after the apparitions of Fatima. It was then that she, along with her sister and another

▲ *Dr. Azevedo, Alexandrina's doctor, with his patient and her family. Alexandrina is lying sideways in the frame.*

Top: In June 1944, Fr. Humberto Pasquale visits Alexandrina for the first time. He will become her second spiritual director.

girl, was attacked by three men who forced their way into the house.

Alexandrina cried out, "Jesus, help me!" and, lashing out at one of the men with her rosary, she fled. Unable to protect her chastity, she leapt from an upstairs window. Gritting her teeth and wiping the blood from her face, she seized a stout piece of wood and staggered back into the house to defend her companions. A few well-aimed blows were enough; the men fled, and the other girls were saved.

After the fall, irreversible damage occurred to her spine. The pain worsened, and Alexandrina's body was progressively overtaken by paralysis. April 14, 1924, was the first day she could no longer rise from her bed. Was even this written into Providence's plan, down to the dates? In the Marian calendar, the feast of Our Lady's apparition to St. Ludwina falls on that day.

ST. LUDWINA

The apparition took place in 1433. Ludwina had been suffering terrible torment from progressive paralysis since she was fifteen years old, after an unfortunate fall. At first, she struggled to come to terms with the suffering that filled her life. Only a conversation with a priest made her realize what a great treasure illness and pain could be. From that moment, Ludwina united herself with the Crucified Jesus and offered her sufferings for the conversion of sinners.

As a reward, God granted her numerous spiritual consolations and visions. Many were fascinated by St. Ludwina's witness, and one of her contemporaries recorded her life in detail. We know him by name: Thomas à Kempis, the author of *The Imitation of Christ*.

JESUS ASKS FOR LOVE

It is striking how similar the lives of Alexandrina and Ludwina are. Our twentieth-century mystic believed she could be healed. She did not cease asking Heaven for help. She pleaded with great faith, confident she would be heard. But Heaven had other plans. It remained silent.

As more months passed, Alexandrina gradually came to terms with the thought that she would never be healthy again. It was not yet acceptance, but resignation. The breakthrough came one day during prayer, when, contemplating the Blessed Sacrament, she was suddenly struck by the thought that the Lord Jesus in the tabernacle was also a prisoner—just like her. She began to understand. Again and again, she visited the tabernacle in spirit.

She experienced her first ecstasy in 1933. Christ asked her to love, to suffer, and to make amends for sinners. Let us note the order of His requests: first, there is love, for without love there can be no other. In that year, Alexandrina became—out of love—a reparatory soul suffering for the sinful world.

Five years later, Jesus asked her to spread the Message of Fatima by offering her sufferings to God.

What else happened in this fascinating biography? From October 1938 until March 1942, every Friday, Alexandrina suffered the wounds inflicted on Jesus during His Passion. From 1942 onward, as Jesus had foretold, her only nourishment was Holy Communion. She died on October 13, 1955. Pope John Paul II beatified her in 1995.

FIRST LIGHTS FROM THE SKY

The first visions took place in 1933. Alexandrina was then thirty-one years old and had been suffering for fifteen years. She heard Christ's compassionate voice:

> *Give me your hands, because I want to nail them with mine. Give me your feet, because I want to nail them to my feet. Give me your head, because I want to crown it with thorns as they did to me. Give me your heart, because I want to pierce it with a lance as they pierced mine. Consecrate your body to me; offer yourself wholly to me.... Help me in the redemption of mankind.*

She would hear these words again a year later. She said "yes" to Jesus' invitation to participate in His Passion.

Four years later, on October 2, 1938, she received another message. The Savior announced that she would have to pass through His Passion from Gethsemane to Calvary, but that she would not reach the *Consummatum est* ("It is finished"). Her agony would last almost twenty years.

JESUS' OFFER

"Forget the world and offer yourself to me. Throw yourself into my arms; I will choose paths for you," Jesus said to Alexandrina. "I have chosen you for me. Respond to my love. I desire to be your Bridegroom, your Beloved, your Everything. I have also chosen you for the happiness of many souls."

On feast days, thousands of people came to Balazar to see Alexandrina.

In July 1941, Alexandrina goes for the fourth time to Porto for exams. She stays in Trofa, in the home of the Sampaio family.

consolação em sofrer por amor de
Jesus. Que grande dita! Ser Jesus o m
Cireneu! Avante sempre. Caminho com
meu esposo com o amado da minha a
Tudo venço com Ele. Subo sem dificul
não deve estar longe o Calvário. Custa
muito muito querer amar. Sei e não s
o que mais hei-de fazer. Se mais algu
coisa tivesse para oferecer a Jesus me
dava. Não lhe posso dizer mais nada
Beija-a e abraça-a saudosamente a
zinha querida.

Alexandrina left behind many writings, mostly dictated, as she could not write them herself. But this note was written in her own hand.

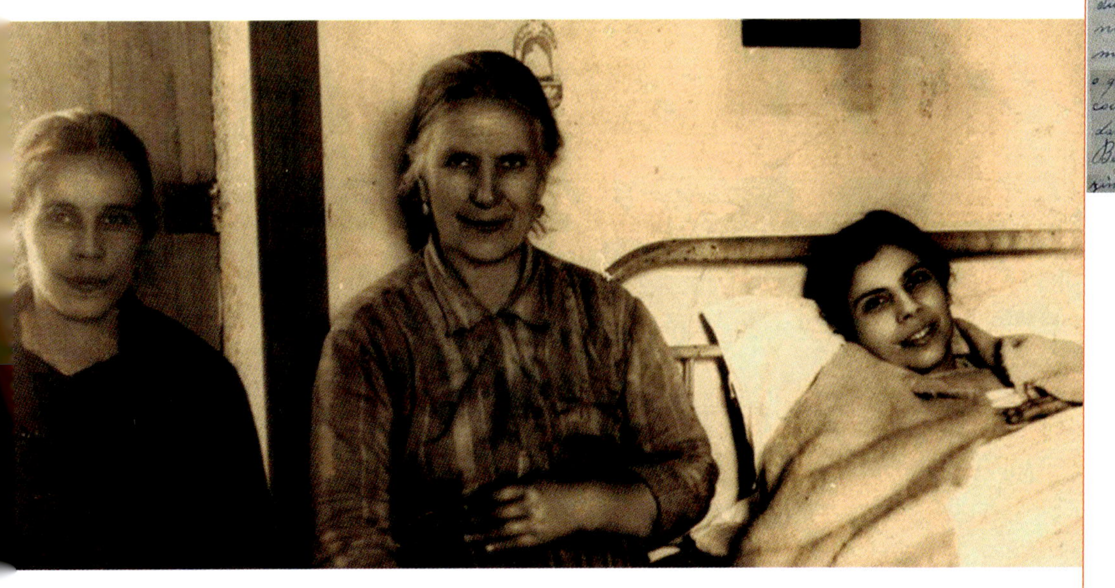

Deolinda and Ana—the mystic's sister and mother.

1933

Despite immense suffering, in 1924 Alexandrina sets out for Braga for the First National Eucharistic Congress.

"I agreed to what the Lord was proposing to me," Alexandrina confesses, "but I thought that the sacrifices He was asking me to make were only those resulting from my illness, even the greatest of them. Extraordinary phenomena never crossed my mind."

Meanwhile, Jesus entered her life: "He spoke to me day and night.... He confided in me." In this intimate closeness, Christ did not cease asking her to save sinners by offering her sufferings to Him: "Do not deny me sufferings and sacrifices for sinners! God's justice weighs down on them. You can save them."

He especially instructed her to pray for priests: "Pray for the priests: they are the workers in my vineyard; the harvest depends on them."

LAST THIRTEEN YEARS

During Holy Week of 1942, she heard the words:

> *You will not take food again on earth. Your food will be my Flesh; your blood will be my Divine Blood; your life will be my Life. You receive it from me when I unite my Heart to your heart.*

For thirteen consecutive years, Alexandrina accepted no other drink and no other food than the eucharistic Jesus. Yet her body's weight did not change, and the clarity of her mind remained unbroken. Jesus explained:

> *You are living by the Eucharist alone because I want to prove to the world the power of the Eucharist and the power of my life in souls.*

Suspicions arose that she was faking it, and on May 27, 1943, she was taken to the hospital. Locked in a separate room under constant surveillance by guards, doctors, and nurses, she remained in isolation for forty days.

At the end, the doctors issued a formal statement:

> *We testify that the bedridden woman, from June tenth to July twentieth, 1943, remained at the hospital under the day and night surveillance of impartial persons desirous of discovering the truth of her fast. Her abstinence from solids and liquids was absolute during all that time. We testify also that she retained her weight, and her temperature, breathing, blood pressure, pulse, and blood were normal, while her mental faculties remained constant and lucid, and she had not, during these forty days, any natural necessities.*

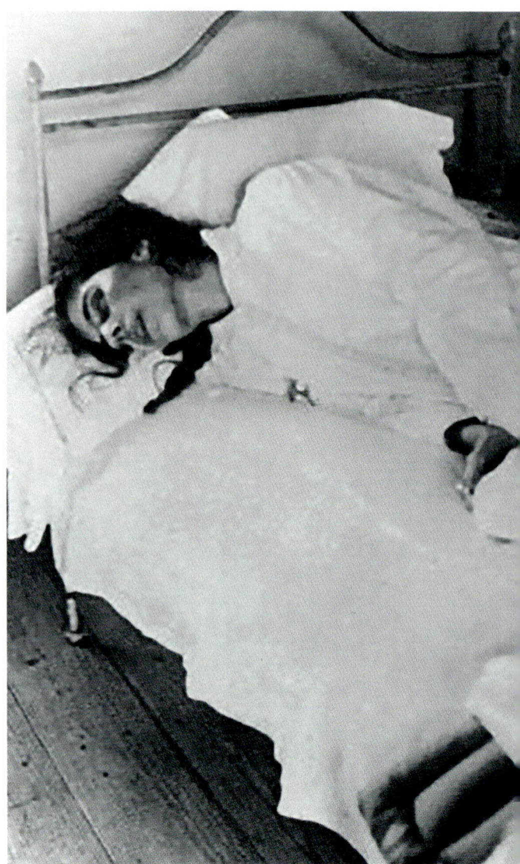

Fr. Terças from the Congregation of the Holy Spirit Missionaries published a story about Alexandrina's experience of the Passion of the Lord, which triggered a wave of unhealthy sensation.

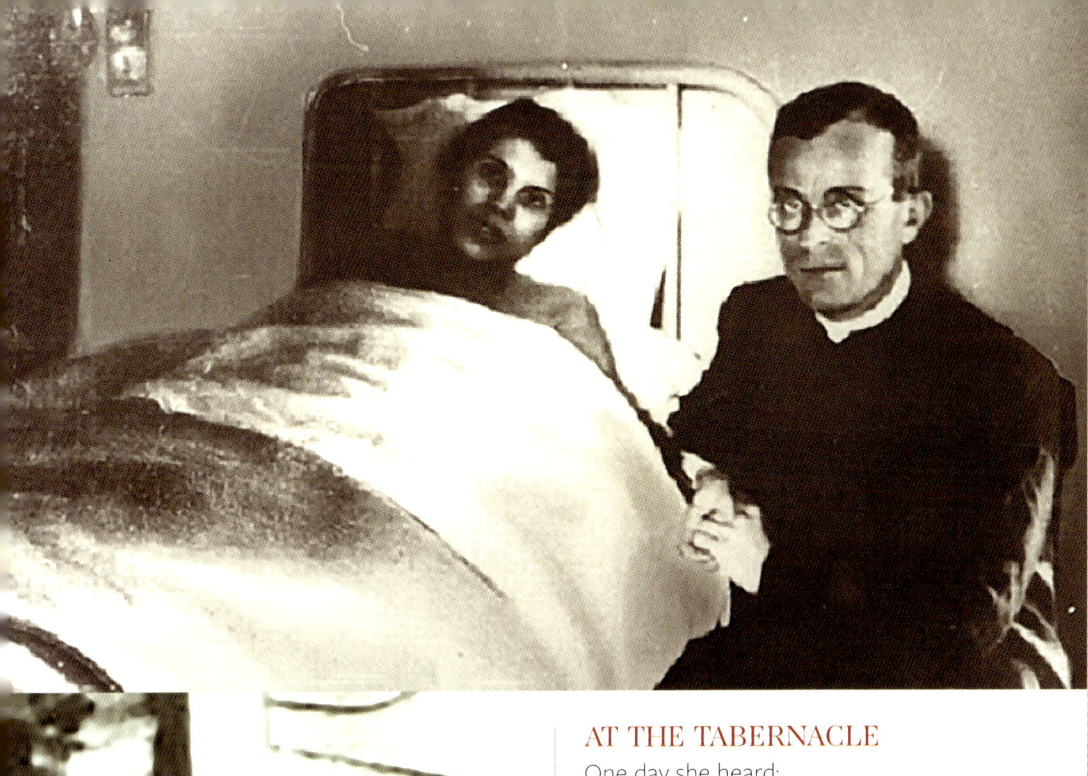

PORTUGAL

Alexandrina's confessor, Fr. Humberto Pasquale, at the bedside of his ward.

In 1938, the mystic experiences the Passion of the Lord, which is documented in photographs.

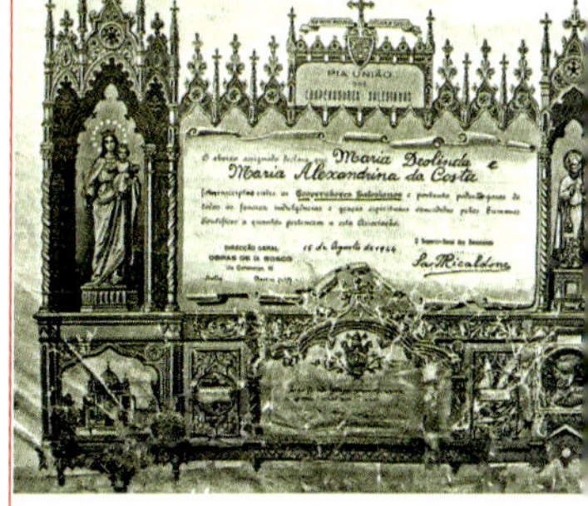

In August 1944, Alexandrina is enrolled among the Salesian Cooperators.

AT THE TABERNACLE

One day she heard:

> *Keep me company in the Blessed Sacrament. I remain in the tabernacle night and day, waiting to give my love and grace to all who would visit me. But so few come. I am so abandoned, so lonely, so offended.... Many men do not believe in my existence; they do not believe that I live in the tabernacle. They curse me. Others believe but do not love me or visit me; they live as if I were not there. I have chosen you to keep me company in these little refuges. Many of them are so wretched—but what riches inside!*

Alexandrina wrote her response with her own blood. On the reverse side of a holy picture, she inscribed:

> *With my blood, I vow to love You very much, my Jesus, and may such be my love that I die embracing the cross. I love You, and I am dying for love of You, O my beloved Jesus, and in Your tabernacles I desire to dwell.*

1933

➤ *On October 13, 1955, the one proclaimed "light and beacon of the world" sets out on her final journey, to sing with angels and saints the glory of the Most Holy Trinity.*

➤ *Her grave is visited by pilgrims from all over the world (Balazar, Portugal).*

She prayed:

> *Jesus, offer me with You as a sacrifice to the Eternal Father for the same intentions for which You offer Yourself. I wish to spend all the moments of my life, without ceasing, day or night, joyful or sad, alone or in company—always—comforting You, adoring You, loving You, glorifying You, and giving You glory. May there not be a single tabernacle anywhere in the world, not a single place where You dwell sacramentally, where now—and from now on forever—there would not be heard: Jesus, I love You! Jesus, I am all Yours! I am Your sacrifice, the sacrifice of the Eucharist, the olive lamp of Your prisons of love.*

Henceforth, the hours of her illness passed on her spiritual pilgrimage to the tabernacles, remaining at the feet of Jesus. He assured her:

> *Like Mary Magdalene, you have chosen the better part. You have chosen to love me in the tabernacles, where you can contemplate me not with the eyes of the body, but with those of the soul. I am truly present there as in Heaven—Body, Blood, Soul, and Divinity. You have chosen that which is most sublime.*

SATAN TEMPTS

The demon assaulted her with impure thoughts, temptations, and images. One night, Alexandrina no longer had the strength to fend them off and endured immense torment. She offered her powerlessness to Jesus.

Jesus responded, and the fruit of the devil's temptation became completely contrary to what the devil intended. In the midst of the sea of temptations, Alexandrina experienced her mystical marriage with Jesus!

"The devil contributes to our merits," St. Maximilian Maria Kolbe would say in one of his conferences.

It should not come as a surprise, for her heart could cry out:

> *Give me sufferings, even the most severe, as long as through them I can prove to You that I love You. I ask You for pain and love—these are the bonds that bind me to You. A thought repeatedly arises in my mind: Thy will be done always and everywhere!*

EVERYTHING IS LIGHT

On January 7, 1955, she finally heard the longed-for words:

> *This is your year! Entrust yourself to me, trust me! I never take back what I promise. My promises—the promises of the Supreme Lord—will come true. Trust! Confidence! Heaven belongs to you; there you will continue your mission.*

Indeed, she would die that very year.

As the moment of death approached, the Lord spoke to her after she received Holy Communion:

> *Daughter, now is the opportune moment to ask for the Last Rites.*
>
> *You are going to Heaven—you are going to Heaven!*

In the last moments of her life, with a heart filled with joy, she repeated:

> *I desire Heaven. I do not regret the earth. There is no more darkness in my soul. Everything in it is sunshine, life… everything in it is God.*

Just before her passing—she died on October 13, 1955, the anniversary of the last apparition at Fatima—Alexandrina exclaimed:

What light! The darkness is no longer here! It has gone! All is light! Do not sin. The pleasures of this life are worth nothing. Receive Communion, and pray the Rosary every day. This sums up everything. See you in Heaven!

The church where Alexandrina's body was laid to rest.

17
SIXTEEN-HOUR CONFESSION

The Ducal Palace in Urbania (Marche, Italy).

On the previous page: Ducal Palace (Urbino, Italy).

17

SIXTEEN-HOUR CONFESSION

MARIA TERESA CARLONI, 1952

Place of Apparition: Spotorno, Urbania
Date and Place of Birth: October 9, 1919, Urbania, Italy
Date and Place of Death: January 17, 1983, Urbania, Italy
Visionary as a Layperson
Beatification Process: Servant of God
Works: Diary from a Journey to the Holy Land, Stations of the Cross, Letters

She is well known in Poland, Hungary, and other countries of the former Eastern Bloc. In the West, however, she remains largely unnoticed. Even the residents of her hometown knew little about her. It is a pity, for Carloni was a mystic of extraordinary spiritual depth, whose life offers answers to our questions about eternity. Sadly, only a few knew her closely.

"Only a few"? This list includes such names as Pius XII, John XXIII, Paul VI, John Paul II, and Cardinals Wyszyński, Mindszenty, Slipyj, Beran, and Tomášek.

How can she be described in one sentence? Maria Teresa Carloni dedicated her entire life to the persecuted Church suffering behind the Iron Curtain.

Her spiritual experience began several years after the great wave of apparitions that took place just after the end of World War II. Her life experience only confirmed how important the message of those

interventions from Heaven was: God was calling for prayers for priests.

One day, the late Pope Pius XII appeared to Maria Teresa. He was wearing a red cassock, and when the visionary asked him, "Why do you not wear white?" he answered: "Because you love the martyrs, not the clergy. You are "anti-clerical," but I understand you. It is not your fault. You are just a victim."

He added:

> *At the end of my life, I was also "anti-clerical." Being "anti-clerical" today means being against those priests who are not priests—not against God, and not against the clergy who defend Him.*

"But where are those priests?" Maria Teresa asked.

"There are very few of them, even though there are many priests in the world," he replied. "Good night."

Showing the greatness of the priesthood became the second dimension of her life.

PROGRESS

She was born on October 9, 1919, in Urbania, a town in central Italy, into a wealthy aristocratic family. Her happy childhood ended quickly. When she was four years old, first her mother, then her father, died. She and her brother then went to live with their grandmother, a strict and demanding woman who intended to prepare them for secular careers. She paid little attention to what the children felt or needed.

It would not be right to say that she played a nurturing role in their childhood and youth. Yet when she died, it was her death that caused the breakthrough in Maria Teresa's life that led her into the world of apparitions.

At that time, no one noticed Maria's delicate sensitivity. She had no good fortune with confessors or educators. No one crossed her path who could offer true help. When she spoke of her struggles during Confession, she was often met with indifference or resentment. It is not surprising, then, that she developed resentment toward the Church. "It is not your fault," Pius XII would one day tell her.

Maria Teresa's resentment toward the clergy grew, especially as she began to see that many priests and religious did not strive for goodness, holiness, or fruitfulness. Eventually, she abandoned the Church.

Before she did so, she made one last attempt. Once again, she sought support in the confessional. Unfortunately, the seventeen-year-old girl was again mistreated by the priest. She interrupted

Spotorno

Urbania

ITALY

Maria Teresa Carloni spends World War II in Rome—studying and caring for wounded soldiers as a nurse. Though non-practicing herself, she prays for the conversion of the wounded and for eternal life for the dying.

When Maria Teresa Carloni was approaching the age of four, her parents died one after the other. Then, together with her brother, she came under the care of their grandmother. A strict and demanding woman, she planned to prepare her grandchildren for secular careers. She did not consider what the children felt or what their needs were.

Panorama of Urbania.

her Confession and walked away from the confessional.

Yet something still drew her toward God, for as she left the church, she turned around in the doorway and called out to the crucifix: "We will meet again!"

It was her farewell—for now.

NON-PRACTITIONER

Soon the war broke out. Maria Teresa Carloni spent these years studying in Rome and working as a nurse, caring for wounded soldiers. Though she was no longer a practicing Catholic, she still prayed for the conversion of the wounded and for eternal life for the dying.

"What could I do?" she wrote. "[I spent] sleepless nights on the cold floor by the sick, who were going to die anyway ... so that at least they could experience peace!"

"For months I almost forgot to sleep," she added. "I spent my nights in an empty chapel, lying prostrate before the Blessed Sacrament. What did I ask for? Nothing for myself, since I did not count myself among the living. I asked for those who had not yet been excluded from the Church."

THE YEAR OF REVIVAL

The war ended, and she returned to her hometown of Urbania. Around 1951, her grandmother fell ill. Maria Teresa once again felt as though she were back in a military hospital during the war. When she saw that her grandmother was near death, she did everything she could to ensure the woman would have time to reconcile with God.

This time she could do more than pray and fast for that intention. She approached the local parish priest, Fr. Cristoforo Campana. The priest accepted the challenge and prepared the elderly Mrs. Carloni for her death.

After her passing, Maria Teresa was left entirely alone and fell into depression.

"Crushed by all this, exhausted, possessed by the fear that I would die having done nothing of any value, by a desperate act of will I made one more attempt at Confession, vowing that it would be the last time," she confessed.

She must have cared deeply about making a good Confession, for she added a note: "I prepared myself all week, with intense prayer and strict mortifications."

What a relief and joy she found! "My parish priest," she wrote happily, "did not push me away at all, contrary to what I expected. He was not at all surprised, and did not condemn me."

The Confession, divided into three parts over sixteen hours, finally allowed her to lift a huge burden from her shoulders and restored her peace of mind. Even after dividing it into three meetings, each session lasted more than five hours.

Portal of the Church of the Dead in Urbania (Marche, Italy).

Carmelite Oratory in Maria Teresa's hometown.

The Ducal Palace in Urbania. Part of the building houses the Galleria Nazionale delle Marche—one of the most important collections of Italian Renaissance art.

An all-cleansing Confession. Every sin touched by healing grace.

Maria Teresa could now begin a new life—and in this new life, Fr. Campana became her spiritual director.

A VOICE APPEARS

Soon her first mystical experiences began. While she was staying in Spotorno, five hundred kilometers from Urbania, she began writing letters to her spiritual director. She described how she heard a person speaking to her from within, and when He stopped speaking, she responded. At first, these dialogues lasted only a few minutes, but soon they extended to as long as an hour and a half. As they grew longer, she would hastily leave whatever she was doing and hide so that others would not notice anything unusual.

Upon her return to Urbania, Fr. Campana witnessed one of these conversations between Maria Teresa and Jesus. "When she was talking to me," he recounted, "I noticed that she closed her eyes, withdrew, and began speaking to 'someone' invisible. This lasted from fifteen minutes to half an hour. Finally, everything returned to normal. She was embarrassed when she realized I was still there, and said, 'It's not my fault. Are you still here?'"

Meetings with Jesus occurred on Tuesdays and Fridays.

One day, the Voice began to address the priest through Maria Teresa:

> *I want to repeat My Passion in this creation, said the Savior. You, being her spiritual director, can accept or reject this, since you are the authority who represents Me. But know that this is My Will.*

When the priest asked who was addressing him, he received the answer:

> *I am Jesus. This soul offered herself to Me, and I accepted her sacrifice.*

The Lord added that on Good Friday, Maria Teresa would receive the hidden stigmata. Jesus explained:

> *The wounds will not appear externally, because everything must remain hidden, as you said. But later, whenever you want, you can make them visible.*

Everything was entrusted to the hands of the priest. Jesus left all decisions to him, for Fr. Campana held the power to "bind and loose" in God's name (see Matthew 16:19).

On December 20, 1952, Maria Teresa receives the grace of spiritual espousal with Jesus.

WEEKLY AGONY

When Maria Teresa regained consciousness, Fr. Campana asked her: "If Jesus wanted to unite Himself with you even more intimately, to unite you with His sufferings, what would you say?" "If He wants it, I want it too," the visionary replied. "He wants it," said the priest. She accepted Jesus' Will.

On Good Friday, April 11, 1952, Fr. Campana found her on her bed, in agony. When he asked if she was in great pain, she, with teeth clenched and barely able to open her mouth, whispered, "Yes, very much."

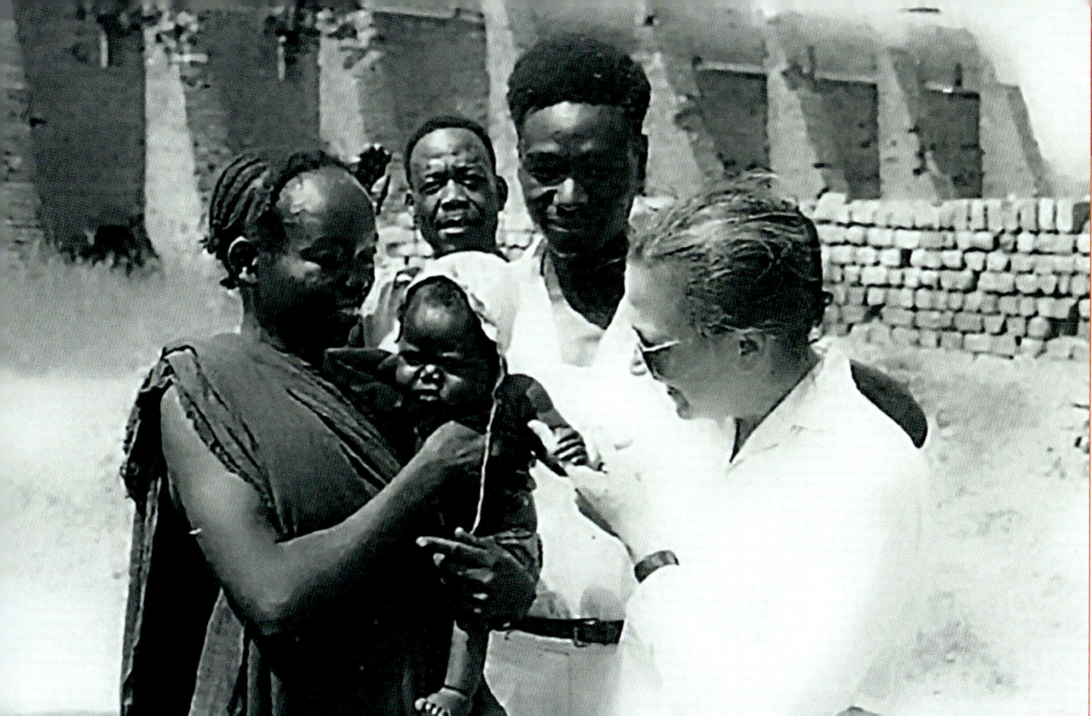

ITALY

Maria Teresa Carloni leaves as a doctor for missions in Sudan, 1960.

At three o'clock, Fr. Campana witnessed the peak of her agony and believed his spiritual daughter had died. However, after a few minutes, she opened her eyes, smiled, and said, "It happened."

She remained unable to leave her bed until midnight.

VISIBLE RING

On December 20, 1952, Maria Teresa received the grace of spiritual marriage with Jesus. The Voice asked Fr. Campana to take her to the church. When they entered, the visionary knelt before the altar, and almost immediately a dialogue between her and Jesus began.

Fr. Campana heard the Voice say to Maria Teresa:

> *Jesus agrees to be your Bridegroom, but He wants His bride to be like Him: persecuted, trampled, slandered, and always suffering in body and spirit.*

Then Jesus addressed the priest:

> *Go to the altar, lift the tablecloth, take the gold ring, and give it to my bride as a tangible sign of my marriage with her.*

The priest found the ring in the place Christ had indicated and placed it on Maria Teresa's finger, saying:

> *"This is not from me. Someone is giving it to you as a sign of His union with you."*

REPARATORY SOUL FOR RUSSIA

Her mission was about to begin. Fr. Campana recalled:

> *On January 4, 1953, Ivana Pushkin, great-granddaughter of the great Russian poet, died in Russia. She secretly professed the Catholic faith and organized an underground Church. She sacrificed her life for the salvation of Russia, omitting in her prayers and sacrifices the soul of Stalin, whose magnitude of crimes horrified her.*
>
> *One Friday afternoon, during Maria Teresa's three-hour agony, I was informed (by Jesus) of this woman's death. I was instructed to ask Maria Teresa if she was willing to become a reparatory soul in place of the deceased woman, accepting all the consequences of sacrificing*

herself for Russia and the countries dominated by it.

Maria Teresa responded as usual: "If the Lord wants it and gives me the necessary strength, I accept."

With this decision, her spiritual and physical suffering increased, and demonic attacks began as well.

A JOURNEY INTO A BYGONE ERA

Two months passed. Let us attend to Maria Teresa's confessor:

> *At the beginning of March, news was made public that Stalin had been stricken with paralysis and was near death. The following Friday, before the three-hour suffering began, the same Voice said to me: "Now I am going to ask you for something, if you allow it and if this creation agrees. Before Stalin dies, despite his crimes, I want to give him the chance of salvation, as I give to all redeemed souls. If you agree, I ask you to offer these three hours for Stalin's soul. But do not let the suffering of this creation frighten you."*
>
> *I asked Maria Teresa if she would be willing to make this sacrifice, and she agreed.*
>
> *The three-hour suffering took place, as usual, in the same secluded room. It was in the afternoon. I was present the whole time. I will never forget those three hours. I have never again seen such suffering—also in the physical sense. I cried in horror and felt like screaming: "Enough! Enough!"*

"Now I am going to ask you for something, if you allow it and if this creation agrees. Before Stalin dies, despite his crimes, I want to give him the chance of salvation, as I give to all redeemed souls. If you agree, I ask you to offer these three hours for Stalin's soul. But do not let the suffering of this creation frighten you."

There appears to be an error here. The first Friday of March 1953 fell on the sixth, and Stalin died the day before.

If the confessor's notes are accurate—and they likely are, since Maria Teresa relived the Passion of the Lord and received messages from Jesus on Fridays—then the historical account differs from the spiritual account.

Does this mean that with God there is no past tense, and that one can journey

through time, changing the fate of people and the world? This would explain the sense of plenary indulgence. Moreover, it reflects how the power of Redemption obtained by Jesus on the Cross—through His Passion and death, which occurred on a specific historical date—works both upon the past and the future.

GRACE REJECTED?

"Did Stalin make use of this last grace?" Fr. Campana asked. Until the final moments of life, the Lord offers every person the chance to repent and turn to His mercy.

"God's mercy," writes St. Faustina in her *Diary*, "Outwardly, it seems as if everything were lost, but it is not so. The soul, illumined by a ray of God's powerful final grace, turns to God in the last moment with such a power of love that, in an instant, it receives from God forgiveness of sin and punishment, while outwardly it shows no sign either of repentance or of contrition."

St. Faustina adds, however: "But—horror! There are also souls who voluntarily and consciously reject and scorn this grace!"

An account of Stalin's last moments was recorded by his daughter, Svetlana, in her diaries. When she reached her father's bedside, she realized that his condition was grave. Stalin was unconscious, his eyes closed. Svetlana sat by his side, wanting to remain with him until the end.

At one point, she noticed that the dying man opened his eyes and looked at her. She saw such extreme fear in his eyes that she herself froze in place. A few moments later, Stalin was dead.

Did he make use of his last chance? Did he open his heart when God's love flooded him?

Fr. Campana did not know the answer. However, Bl. Elena Aiello, another Italian mystic, while witnessing a vision of Hell, saw Stalin's soul there.

TRAVELING "IN THE SECOND BODY"

Monday, December 6, 1954, was the first day Jesus granted Maria Teresa the gift of bilocation. She needed this grace to assist the persecuted Church. God reached for an extraordinary means and placed it in the hands of a truly extraordinary woman.

Bilocation became a way of saving Christians behind the Iron Curtain. Though Maria Teresa remained physically in her apartment in Urbania, she would, at the same time, travel—let us call it moving "in the second body"—to other places, sometimes thousands of kilometers away from her hometown.

Maria Teresa appeared in various places of confinement where priests, bishops, and the faithful were imprisoned. She brought them help, spiritual encouragement, and sometimes even assisted in their escape or saved their lives.

Maria Teresa is friends with Bl. Stefan Wyszyński, whom she called "Brother Stefan" and whom she visited twice in Warsaw (aside from bilocation). It was the Polish cardinal who obtained for her permission to have a private chapel with the Blessed Sacrament in her apartment. A painting of Our Lady of Częstochowa hung there.

Bilocation journeys were a tremendous effort for Maria Teresa, and she returned from them mentally and physically exhausted. Among other things, these contributed to the progressive loss of health by the mystic.

Maria Teresa Carloni helped priests behind the Iron Curtain.

Left: Primate of Croatia Cardinal Alojzije Stepinac and Ustaše leader Ante Pavelić, 1941.

Right: Portrait of Stepinac on the wall of the cathedral in Zagreb (Croatia).

How did she enter these heavily guarded places? Jesus made Carloni visible only to those He permitted to see her. Although her body remained in physical form during bilocation, she passed through locked gates and barbed wire, appearing in the depths of Soviet mines or in the heart of a gulag.

Interestingly, although Jesus granted her the grace of bilocation, it was she who had to make all the decisions: how to act and how best to help those to whom she was sent. It must be said that she lacked neither cleverness nor courage.

Once, when Fr. Campana questioned her about the details of these journeys "in the second body," he asked an interesting question at the end: "When you are like this—in some place in the form of bilocation—what do you look like? Young? Old?"

She answered: "I am neither a child nor an old woman, neither big nor small, but I feel that I am in the fullness of life."

Perhaps this is a glimpse of what our bodies will be like after the resurrection.

These journeys took a tremendous toll on her. When she returned from them, she was mentally and physically exhausted. They contributed, among other things, to her progressive decline in health.

On the evening of February 2, 1976, Maria Teresa called her spiritual father, Fr. Campana, and said: "I am being insistently summoned to Russia! I'm going there!"

At a mine on the border between Lithuania and Belarus, a wall had collapsed, trapping twenty-seven prisoners from a nearby gulag who had been working there. Among them were Lithuanians and Russians, Catholics and Orthodox alike, including two Lithuanian priests, one Orthodox priest, and one subdeacon.

Nothing was done to save them, for as religious people—*religioznyi*—they had already been sentenced to death, and the collapse had been induced to carry out the sentence.

The guards, separated from the convicts by the fallen wall, suddenly saw an unknown woman approaching them.

Sensing something uncanny, they hurled heavy metal-cutting shears at her. But when she caught the tool, they fled in panic, convinced they were dealing with "dark forces."

Maria Teresa, led by divine power, made a breach in the wall with those shears. The prisoners escaped through it. First, they fled from the mine, and later from the camp itself, as their liberator, using the captured tool, cut through the barbed wire surrounding the camp at the points they had agreed upon.

Afterward, she "returned" to her first body, but was inwardly urged to go back: she still had to help the escapees find a safe hiding place.

The Russian concentration camp authorities did not initiate a search for the fugitives, for the guards at the mine—wishing to conceal the fact that they had fled because of the "dark forces"—reported to their superiors that all the prisoners had died in the collapse. Later, noticing a passage cut through the barbed wire and finding the shears nearby, they kept the discovery secret and quietly repaired the damage.

Maria Teresa now had to guide the fugitives to safety.

The Lithuanians decided to head toward the Lithuanian border at night, trusting that they would find refuge in their own country. The others were led on foot or transported in wagons by local sympathizers to places where they could hide for longer periods.

At the border post with Lithuania, Maria Teresa found a military officer who was secretly a Catholic priest. Together, they made a plan: he would ensure that his colleagues would be sleeping and would allow sixteen fugitives to pass through the barrier.

Only this priest in uniform knew that Maria Teresa was there by the grace of bilocation. The others believed she was simply a heroic Russian woman rescuing the prisoners.

Over the next few days, they all found safety with families or in other secure places. Maria Teresa was informed of each one's safe arrival by interior voices after she had already returned to Urbania.

Josyf Ivanovych Slipyj, Metropolitan Archbishop of Lviv. He spent eighteen years in the gulags. Thanks to the intervention of Pope John XXIII and President Kennedy, he was released in 1963.

Cardinal Josef Beran, Archbishop of Prague, prisoner of German concentration camps. He spent the years 1949–1963 behind bars by order of the communist authorities.

József Mindszenty, Primate of Hungary from 1945–1974, prisoner of the communists, freed during the 1956 uprising. He spent the next fifteen years hiding in the U.S. embassy.

Priests whom Maria Teresa helped:

- Top: Anton Vovk, Archbishop of Ljubljana.
- Bottom: Edward Mason, Bishop of Sudan; Comboni Missionary; Archbishop of Zagreb.
- Left: Franjo Šeper, Archbishop of Belgrade.
- Middle: Gabriel Bukatko.
- Right: Kyryl Stefan Kurteff, Bishop of Sofia.

EUCHARISTIC DISCERNMENT

Maria Teresa possessed the mystical ability to read souls and detect consecrated objects. She could distinguish between a consecrated Host and an unconsecrated wafer.

One day, Pius XII, with whom she frequently corresponded, asked her to observe the morning Masses being celebrated in the Vatican Basilica. Of the twenty-four Masses celebrated between 7:00 a.m. and 8:30 a.m., in one case, the celebrant was so distracted that no valid consecration occurred.

On the day she reported this information to the Pope, she was invited to walk with him in the Vatican Gardens. During the walk, Pius XII took out a tiny ciborium containing four Hosts and showed them to Maria Teresa. He asked, "Which of these four Hosts are consecrated?" Without hesitation, the visionary threw two of them to the ground.

At that moment, the pope said, "Let us ask the Lord to give us a sign that those remaining are consecrated." Immediately, blood stains appeared on the Hosts he was holding.

SHEPHERD IN THE HOLY LAND

In January 1967, Maria Teresa made a pilgrimage to the Holy Land with a friend. In her diary, she recalled that Jesus appeared to her three times as "the Shepherd."

The first encounter took place in the Garden of Gethsemane:

> *We were left alone in the garden ... and almost at the same second, we asked each other: "Where do you think is the place where Jesus prayed? We must be very close." From behind came an answer spoken in perfect Italian: "Indeed, you are at the place." ... We were three people, but we looked like three statues. It seemed even nature had been petrified.... I asked: "You speak Italian. Who are you?!" "I am the Shepherd." ... "You are looking for a place: here it is, about a stone's throw [from here]."*

The second time, Jesus appeared to her on Mount Tabor. He spoke of His Transfiguration and explained that it was mistakenly called a "miracle." It was

not a miracle, He said, but rather the "stopping" of a miracle—because in the Transfiguration, He revealed His true divine essence. The true "miracle" was His humanity.

She saw Jesus for the third time on the Mount of Beatitudes. She recorded His words:

> *The God of Justice will judge souls. They will not be asked about the details of their lives; they will not be asked how many hours they worked or prayed, but they will have to answer about the good they did to their neighbors. Have you been humble? Have you been meek? Did you suffer with dignity? Did you hunger and thirst for righteousness? Did you have mercy? Were you pure of heart? Were you a peacemaker? Were you persecuted because of love for me? Truly I say to you, souls will be judged from this alone, that is, from mercy.*

TOWARD THE END

In the final years of her life, the supernatural phenomena began to fade. Mystical sufferings and spiritual gifts no longer appeared. It was as if Jesus had moved the ailing Maria Teresa into retirement.

She herself recognized that her mission had been fulfilled: there was a "thaw" in the world, persecution was subsiding, and John Paul II—a pope who knew the problems of communism better than anyone else—was now sitting in the Vatican. She was allowed to depart.

Maria Teresa died on January 17, 1983, and was buried in the cemetery of her hometown of Urbania. In accordance with her wishes, her tombstone bears the words from St. Paul's letter, *Mihi vivere Christus est, et mori lucrum* (Philippians 1:21): "For to me life is Christ, and death is gain."

It may puzzle some that all documentation concerning her life and activities was transferred to the Jasna Góra Marian Shrine in Częstochowa. Why?

Let us recall her friendship with Bl. Stefan Wyszyński, whom she affectionately called "Brother Stefan," and whom—thanks to her gift of bilocation—she visited twice in Warsaw and many times in Rome. It was this Polish cardinal who obtained permission for her to have a private chapel with the Blessed Sacrament in her apartment. In that chapel, there was an image of Our Lady of Jasna Góra—the beloved Madonna of the Millennium, the Primate's great devotion. It was through her intercession that Maria Teresa prayed for the persecuted Church.

Maria Teresa Carloni died on January 17, 1983, and was buried in the cemetery in her hometown of Urbania. According to her wish, the words from the letter of St. Paul were placed on her tombstone: Mihi vivere Christus est, et mori lucrum *(Phil. 1:21) (For to me life is Christ, and death is gain).*

18
ANTI-CHURCH

On the previous page: Timothy Paul Schmalz, I Was in Prison and You Visited Me, *part of the Matthew 25 Collection.*

18

ANTI-CHURCH

ALICJA LENCZEWSKA, 1985

Her curriculum vitae is so plain that it is virtually non-existent. If we search for something unusual, we find only that she lost her father at the age of two and never married. There is also a brief episode in her life when she was a member of the Communist Party, but in her case—and in those days—it was likely necessary in order to complete her dream of finishing school and becoming a teacher.

Place of Apparition:
Gostyń, Szczecin, Poland
Date and Place of Birth:
December 5, 1934,
Warsaw, Poland
Date and Place of Death:
January 5, 2012,
Szczecin, Poland
Visionary as a Layperson
Works: Spiritual Diary.

She has a great deal of time on her hands, so she travels extensively and devotes herself to the study of art history. At some point, she returns to the Church. There is nothing extraordinary about this, either. The only detail that might catch one's attention is that she returned to the faith through reading a book about the Catholic Charismatic Renewal, after which she joined a local charismatic community. Yet even this is not uncommon.

Something different comes much later, when she is already fifty-one years old. That is when she enters the world of the supernatural—but we will only learn of it after her death. Jesus takes His time. Everything begins after more than half a century of her life has passed and only a quarter-century remains until its end. God does not need much of our time. Or perhaps He delays so long because He desires the apparitions to be as close

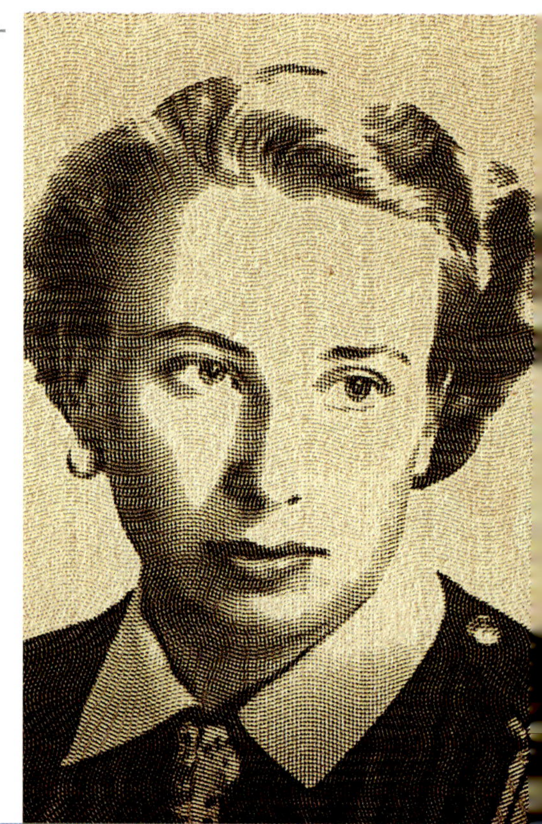

Alicja Lenczewska was born in the territory of present-day Ukraine. In 1940, she moved with her mother and older brother Sławomir to the Rzeszów region. Then the family moved to Inowrocław, and finally in 1946 settled in Szczecin.

Church of St. Margaret in Gostyń, 1985.

The first mystical encounters of Alicja Lenczewska with Jesus took place during a retreat in Gostyń in 1985.

to our times as possible. Or perhaps it is something else: perhaps He wishes to see whether the Church will listen to the multitude of His messages that He is leaving in the world today.

Maybe Jesus is waiting because He wants to see which path humanity will choose. Once He knows, He comes to a Polish charismatic woman from Szczecin. Why Poland? Why her? Her story will provide the answers.

DRAWN MAP

It is worth noting that what Heaven communicated to her remained completely unknown until the day of her death. It is as if our guess is correct: the clues Jesus passed on to Alicja were meant for later times, for our today. Reading her notes, one could say that Christ answers the questions we face now. He speaks of the impending crisis of the Church and its destiny, with purification at its center. He portrays a world possessed by evil and warns of the emergence of the anti-church. This is not mere information. The Savior draws a clear map and places signposts before us. Among them, one is especially important: Lenczewska herself—the path along which God led her. Let us begin with that thread.

THERE IS A DESIRE TO KNOW GOD

Let us listen to the visionary. In 1987, Alicja wrote a testimony about her conversion: "I grew up in a Catholic family, but my Catholicism was for many years very superficial. And there were even periods of several years when I lived outside the Church, almost completely in clear contradiction to God's commandments." She adds that this was not the way to find happiness and that "there finally came a period when I felt, more and more clearly, the emptiness of such a life."

What becomes the turning point for her? Reading.

The Monastery of Philip Neri in Gostyń.

In a sense, Jesus will later refer to this, saying: "Strive to know the Truth about Me; desire it. Along with this knowledge, gratitude will grow in you. Ingratitude, too, is the fruit of ignorance." A confluence of circumstances prompts her to read religious literature—books that, moreover, touch her heart. "At the same time," writes Alicja, "seemingly by accident, religious books began to come into my hands. Among them are the ones talking about the Charismatic Renewal in the United States."

The living Church, the Church filled with the Spirit, drew her irresistibly. She notes: "I didn't dare to dream that I would ever be able to come into contact with such a group, although I really wanted to. After all, I did not have the opportunity to go to the US. Then someone randomly told me that there was a group like this in Szczecin, a few stops from my house." She comes to the meeting—and stays.

Soon, an unexpected coincidence occurs that changes everything. Alicja recalls: "Then there was a seminar preparing for the renewal, and during it, a trip to Gostyń for an animators' retreat (I went in place of the animator of the home group, who could not go)." It was as if Jesus had planned for Lenczewska to go.

FIRST ENCOUNTER WITH JESUS

"And there something happened that completely changed my life," writes the visionary. "There, Jesus appeared standing before me. More real, more true than anything that was in the chapel: than the people who stood next to me."

Alicja describes an experience familiar to many mystics, yet she explains it perhaps the best and most simply. Spiritual reality is stronger. The temporal proves less real—secondary and fleeting, like a mist. When Jesus comes, the temporal dimension becomes only a meaningless shadow. The moment when the supernatural becomes overwhelmingly real is the Eucharist.

➤ *The visionary records: "First, I got rid of the color TV and donated the money I received for it to charity."*

Many of us who know what Jesus said to St. Teresa of Ávila are not surprised by this. We read in Lenczewska's testimony: "It happened after I received Holy Communion.... Everything ceased to exist; there was only Him. His might, power, vastness were getting bigger and bigger, and I was getting smaller and smaller next to Him. The magnitude of a love was so great,

and unprecedented, before which one can only weep over one's ingratitude. And then the joy that He loves me. A joy that bursts the heart."

This encounter had to transform her. She confesses:

> *From that moment everything changed: the hierarchy of values, the structure of needs, the purpose of life. The only value, desire, and purpose became Him—Jesus Christ. And the most beautiful moments became my meetings with Him.... He gave me everything I longed for and for which I chased around the world for so many years. And He gave much more than I could have imagined and desired.*

Everything changed. Her experience must be real if her conversion and her new life are real.

GO, SELL EVERYTHING...

We read in her testimony:

> *Many of the things I had accumulated became unnecessary, and some even became a burden. First, I got rid of the color TV and donated the money I received for it to charity. Then I began removing other items that needlessly took up space in my house. I dedicated my time, my strength, and all that I had to serving God and my neighbors. My ailments and the hardships of daily life, which are never lacking, became an offering of atonement for my sins and for the sins of others.*

POLAND

Main altar of the basilica on Święta Góra near Gostyń.

After the first apparitions in Gostyń, Alicja Lenczewska's spiritual guide became Fr. Walter Rachwalik, who instructed her to systematically record her visions. The visionary recorded them in ordinary school notebooks from 1985 to 2010.

The Monastery of Philip Neri in Gostyń.

In Lenczewska's notebooks, we find the words of Jesus explaining the reason for making these notes: "What you are writing down is so that people will understand that I want to speak to everyone, to guide them, to warn them from evil, and to lead them on the path of salvation. I am with every person at every moment of his life. One must desire to hear Me, to listen to Me, and to carry out what I point out."

Through her confessor, Jesus instructed her to "reduce her life in the material world to the bare essentials, keeping only what is truly necessary." He said to her: "Holiness is found in everyday life, in bearing what is small and hidden, in giving thanks for what is tedious and exhausting."

> *Look at everything in light of the needs of My Kingdom, not according to your own preferences. Examine your every thought, word, and action through My eyes—consider whether they serve to build My Kingdom in the hearts of others and in your own heart.*

Once again, the same theme appears, as it did in the earlier apparitions: Jesus is still waiting for the generation in which "His Kingdom will come."

NOTES

Who is our visionary? Let us supplement her testimony with a few facts. Born in 1934 in Warsaw, she has lived in Szczecin since 1946. There she completed her education and began working as a teacher. She loved traveling, as well as mountain climbing, skiing, and walking by the sea. Together with her brother, she visited Bulgaria, Romania, France, Spain, Greece, Italy, and Morocco.

In the late 1950s, she fell in love and came close to the Sacrament of Marriage, but broke off the engagement due to her fiancé's struggle with alcohol. Later, she met an Italian man named Michele. They visited each other often, and Alicja planned to spend her life with him. However, it turned out that Michele was already married. She had no luck with fiancés. It was as if Jesus were saying to her: "This path is not for you."

BEGINNING

In 1982, her ailing mother came to live with her. It was a difficult but blessed time for Alicja. Daily contact with her mother, who was deeply faithful and prayed constantly, led Alicja onto the path of conversion. It was then that she began to seek out religious books. Her mother died in 1984. Not long afterward, the future visionary joined a Catholic Renewal community. Her encounters with Jesus began.

At fifty-three, she retired from teaching—though in truth, she had already taken on a new vocation two years earlier: she had been hired by the Savior. He did not speak to her only directly; His voice also came to her through her confessor.

When asked who He is, Jesus explains: "I am with you—with My mouth, with My hands, and with My heart beating among you."

It was her spiritual guide who instructed her to begin systematically recording her visions. She noted them in ordinary school notebooks from 1985 to 2010. In them, we find Jesus' explanation for why she was to keep these records: "What you are writing down is so that people will understand that I want to speak to everyone, to guide them, to warn them from evil, and to lead them on the path of salvation. I am with every person at every moment of his life. One must desire to hear Me, to listen to Me, and to carry out what I point out."

What else should we know about Lenczewska? Perhaps this: she was fifty-five years old when she received the gift of the invisible stigmata.

STRATEGY OF SATAN'S SERVANTS

In His apparitions, Jesus devotes a great deal of attention to the state of the world. He speaks of an unprecedented attack by Satan. Notably, He emphasizes that Satan does not act alone; he works through "his servants," and that today a "satanic generation" has appeared (Sister Lucia also wrote about this at the end of her life).

The Lord warns: "The purpose of the actions of Satan's servants in the world is to deceive as many souls as possible and to cast them into the depths of evil. Their actions aim to destroy and distort everything that God has created and to throw it all under the feet of Lucifer, who is eager for power and revenge against God and His creation."

He adds: "My enemy uses hatred and lies, which are the essence of his being and which lead to division."

What is the purpose of all this? Jesus explains: "The goal is the so-called new world—a new era—founded on principles

"I didn't dare to dream that I would ever be able to come into contact with such a group, although I really wanted to. After all, I did not have the opportunity to go to the US. Then someone randomly told me that there was a group like this in Szczecin, a few stops from my house."

Alicja joins the Renewal in the Holy Spirit Movement. Seventeenth National Vigil of the Renewal in the Holy Spirit, Jasna Góra, 2011.

Eucharist stained glass in the cathedral in Fribourg (Switzerland).

Christianity is either radical, or it nourishes anti-Christianity.

that are the opposite of natural and divine law. It is the so-called new order being created by the church of Satan."

"Now Satan, through his servants, is openly fighting against Me, in My people and in My apostles," Jesus continues. "And he is preparing a modern-day Golgotha for My Church."

Lenczewska records a warning from the Savior: "Tell My children that the attacks of evil are increasing more and more, and no one on this earth is so sheltered that he does not need to engage all his strength to be saved from the destructive power of evil."

The Church is not a place of earthly comfort, security, satisfaction, or temporal guarantees. The Church stands on a battlefield, and every member must take up arms. The stakes are life or death. Consequently, "one cannot, while consciously standing by Me and pledging allegiance to Me, at the same time make any concession to sin, which always has its roots in Satan—or to the weaknesses of human nature and the temptations of the world."

Christianity now is either radical or it feeds anti-Christianity. Alicja Lenczewska seeks to convey this truth to others. She assures them that the struggle has meaning, because it will end in the triumph of God.

ANTICHRIST AND HIS SERVANTS

Jesus assures her that Satan's march will be interrupted:

> *You, My faithful children, are called to overcome, to participate in the renewal of the face of the earth, and in My triumph in the souls of men.*

It is significant that Christ often uses the words *though* and *although* to frame what appears, from a human perspective, to be a certainty of defeat. For example, He says:

> *And the dawn and spring of the Holy Church are coming, though*

ANTI-CHURCH

> *there is an anti-church and its founder, Antichrist. Though there are Lucifer's prophets and priests. Though there is a world Sanhedrin directing the church of Satan on earth. Though they have subjugated governments and riches, and they seem to have poisoned everything and are leading the world to its destruction.*

Even though Satan seems to hold all the cards, he will still lose. Jesus offers a beautiful theological point:

POLAND

Satan cannot win, because there is no love in him. Jesus proclaims: "My kingdom is coming.... Believe! I have overcome the world.... Before this happens, the escalation of evil must be fulfilled. Then there will be the Miracle of the Resurrection of faith and love when I step in with power to put an end to the reign of Satan and his servants."

> *Antichrist is not God. He cannot create anything; he only seeks to destroy what God has created.*

Ultimately, his only ability—the ability to destroy—will lead him to destroy what he himself has built. Satan cannot win, because there is no love in him. God will win, because He is love. Hence Jesus

1985

Although martyrdom of Christians continues all over the world, the media consistently remain silent on this subject. Thousands of believers in Christ have lost their lives at the hands of the Islamic fanatics Boko Haram in Sudan.

"It is the time of the Church's sacrifice—the time of Christians' sacrifice. The time of the crucifixion sacrifice of My body, which is the Church.... The Church must die to be reborn anew through the resurrection in the fullness of God's power and shine with the radiance of the Holy Spirit."

Flag of the Christians of Sudan.

proclaims: "My Kingdom is coming... Believe! I have overcome the world."

CHURCH SACRIFICED

Before this can happen, "the escalation of evil must be fulfilled," Jesus explains, "just as it was fulfilled against Me two thousand years ago, it is now coming to its fullness against My Church." Jesus' Passion and death had a continuation; they ended in His Resurrection. It will be the same with the Church: "Then there will be the Miracle of the Resurrection of faith and love when I step in with power to put an end to the reign of Satan and his servants."

The theme of the crucifixion and death of the Church appears again and again in the Szczecin apparitions. It is as though the Church as we know it will cease to exist. Jesus further explains what will happen: "Christians and the Church must be crucified so that ... the resurrection of mankind in the Holy Spirit will take place. I will die again in My people so that the Holy Spirit will regenerate mankind. There is a time of sacrifice of the Church—a time of sacrifice of Christians. The time of the cross sacrifice of My body, which is the Church.... The Church must die (cf. John 12:24) in order to be renewed by Resurrection in the fullness of God's power and to shine with the radiance of the Holy Spirit."

The Lord goes on to explain: "On Golgotha died that which came from the world. In pain, My earthly body died.... So will My Church in pain give up what it took from the world. And it will seem to be dead. And Satan and his servants will rejoice, as they rejoiced then in Jerusalem. But the time of their apparent victory will be short, for the morning of the Resurrection of the Holy Church will come—an immortal Church, giving birth to new life on earth: the holiness of My children."

Jesus explains why "God is absent"—remember that formula: "I am hiding so as not to ensnare you with the magnificence of My gift. I desire happiness for you that no human being can imagine or foresee." In another place, He explains: "My child, how much I must hide Myself so as not to burn your soul with the fire of My love and not to kill your body with the power of My fatherly tenderness."

TESTAMENT

On June 24, 2009, in one of her last notes, Alicja Lenczewska shares her understanding of Christianity: "We must love Christ in people, because there He is thirsting for love. Not in abstract notions, but in actual people we know and meet, especially in those in whom there is a lack of love. We must look at people not from the perspective of our own egoism and claims, but from the perspective of Jesus, who is in them, identifies with them, and suffers without being loved or even noticed."

This is how Alicja strived to live. One of the most important lessons shown

to us by Jesus through the sign that is Alicja Lenczewska is that she chose other people's happiness over her own, giving up herself, her comfort, and her precautions.

It is about choosing to love Christ living in Heaven, living in the Church, and living in the people. This is Jesus' prescription for the renewal of the Church.

Is that all? No, because Alicja also records a brief statement from the Savior, who explains the Christian ideal this way: "I have given you everything and expect you to do the same." The Savior adds that this is what Holy Communion is all about, for it is "a meeting to give ourselves to each other: Me to you and you to Me."

The victory of the Church will be the victory of the Eucharist. This is another prophetic theological theme of the Szczecin apparitions, a truth known to the saints since the first generation of Christians.

Her quiet death in 2010 is her final sacrifice. It is the surrender of herself to Jesus, who died for every man so that no one would perish, but that all might have eternal life (John 3:16). Alicja Lenczewska dies, asking that her death—accepted by Christ—might serve His cause of saving the world.

Someday, it will be seen that this act was more important than all the pages she wrote, all her thoughts and words, and even her greatest deeds, which she carried out in union with Christ "for us men and for our salvation" (Credo).

For the Church must die, and Alicja is a member of the Church. Thus, Jesus' words apply to her as well: "My devoted servants ... in the sacrifice of martyrdom are the foundation and wall and vault of My temple. In it, I am alive and true, and in it, through My servants, I feed My children, restore life, and lead them to My Father's House."

It is amazing how true these words have proven to be after Lenczewska's death.

The victory of the Church will be the victory of the Eucharist. This is another prophetic theological theme in the Szczecin apparitions of Lenczewska—a thought known to the saints from the first generation of Christians.

Our Lady of La Salette Weeping.

19
JESUS IN DREAMS

Place of Apparition: Lebanon, Syria, Iraq, Jordan, Egypt, Sudan, Tunisia, Afghanistan, Greece, Turkey
Time of the Apparitions: The present day

In 2007, interviews conducted with hundreds of Muslims who had converted to faith in Christ were summarized. When asked why they had made this decision, one of the reasons stood out: numerous converts reported having had dreams that they understood as signs from God. They dreamed of Jesus.

19

JESUS IN DREAMS

MANY PEOPLE WHO CONVERTED FROM ISLAM

Do Muslims ask for Baptism? Yes. They come to priests, pastors, and Christian families, seeking an explanation of the faith of the Church. They begin reading the Gospel and declare that "Jesus is Lord." Why do they come? Many of them have had a dream—a dream about Jesus.

"We do not seek them out. They come to us of their own accord," says Archbishop Paul Desfarges, president of the North African Episcopal Conference. "One by one. They come because they are searching, because they are growing spiritually. Many of them—truly, many of them—have had a dream, a vision that shook them and changed their lives. And it is after this event that they come and knock on the door of the Church."

DREAM?

In 2007, interviews conducted with hundreds of Muslims who had converted to faith in Christ were summarized. When asked why they had made this decision, many gave the answers one might expect: they were drawn by the love of God revealed in Christianity, the beauty of the Gospel, and the brotherly love within the Christian community. Yet one reason, found across many testimonies, stood out: numerous converts reported having had dreams that they understood as signs from God. They dreamed of Jesus.

They heard His words about forgiveness. They felt His presence fill them with an unfamiliar peace and joy. They heard a voice speaking to them with the words of the Gospel—words that were entirely unknown to them. They saw Jesus appear to them in a way that was almost physical. And it was not always a dream: sometimes it seemed that an element of the supernatural had entered into their temporal reality, something akin to "resting in the Holy Spirit." In that moment, the light flooded them and changed their lives.

In the Muslim world today, Christian visions and dreams are widespread. People dream of Jesus in Lebanon, Syria, Iraq, Jordan, Egypt, Sudan, Tunisia, Afghanistan, and even in Greece and Turkey.

Jesus appeared to Muslims in a very realistic way; they even felt His physical presence. And it wasn't necessarily a dream. Sometimes, one could say that an element not of this world entered their temporal reality.

DREAMS IN ISLAM

Some might wonder whether these visions are truly genuine. It is claimed that in recent years dreams have become a popular topic in certain Muslim circles. Yet could such things really be discussed openly in Islamic societies, where conversion to Christianity is punishable by death? Perhaps it is different in refugee camps or in the West, where Baptism might help secure a coveted residence visa. There, it could happen that people awaiting an earthly paradise might claim to have had a supernatural dream. But that is not the case in the regions we are speaking of.

"I was surprised when I listened to these stories and realized the magnitude of the phenomenon," recounts Pastor Tom Doyle. "I know of no other group that experiences God in this way. About one-fifth of the world's population is Muslim—and so many of them dream about Jesus!"

Is this a gift from Heaven? "Yes," Doyle answers. "More Muslims have converted to Christianity in the past ten years than in all the previous centuries combined. It is a real revolution."

Some may ask why—alongside the testimony of the Catholic Bishop Desfarges—we also cite the words of a Protestant pastor. As it happens, most of the testimonies cited here come from Protestant sources. Why? In these difficult regions, Christians of all denominations work together to proclaim the Good News and to protect converts.

Could Muslims who become Protestants one day become Catholics? Members of the Catholic Church pray constantly for Christian unity. Every day, some pray for this intention, and every year all Christians are reminded of Jesus' prayer that "they may be one so that the world may believe" (John 17:21). The Week of Prayer for Christian Unity is traditionally celebrated from January 18–25, between the feasts of St. Peter and St. Paul.

One lesson we should take from these apparitions is that nothing is impossible for God. If He wishes to unite us, He will—perhaps even through these converts.

➤ *Christian visions are present throughout the Muslim world. People dream of Jesus in Lebanon, Syria, Iraq, Jordan, Egypt, Sudan, Tunisia, Afghanistan, as well as in Greece and Turkey.*

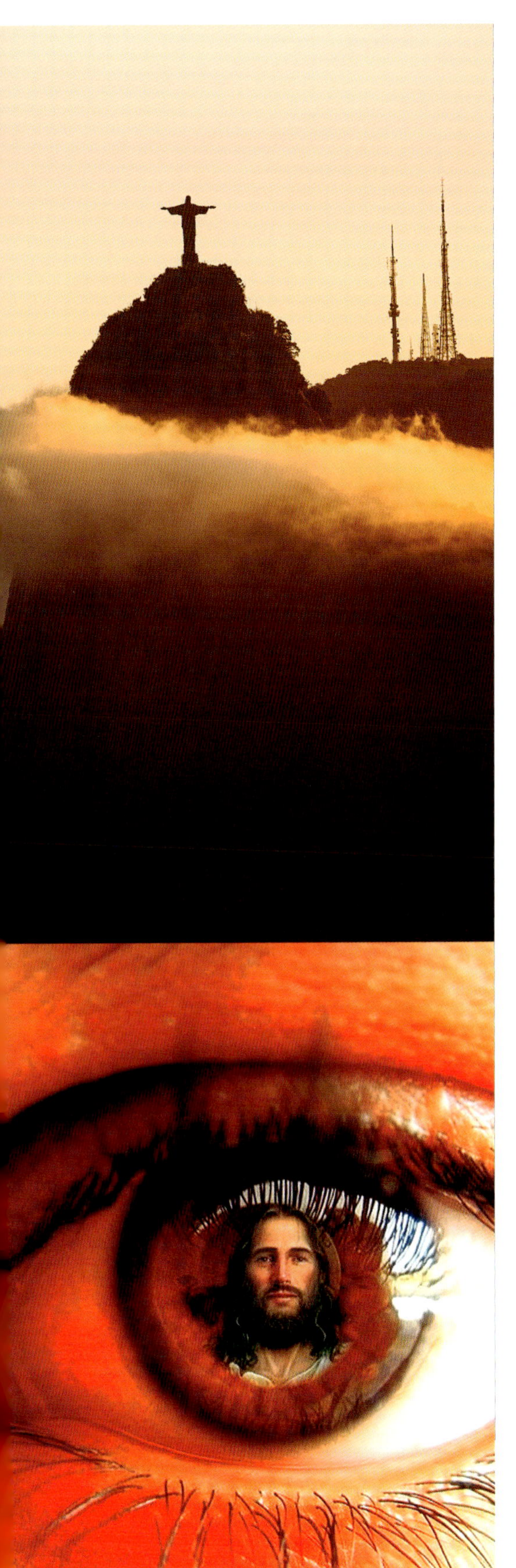

It is important to pray for unity, to believe in it, and to hope that through the power of Jesus Christ, we may once again become one Church.

WHY DREAMS?

For followers of Allah, dreams are one of the most important ways the supernatural world communicates with human beings. Islam itself began with a vision that the Prophet Muhammad experienced, and so it is not surprising that Muslims believe dreams can convey divine messages.

Why, then, does Jesus choose this particular means of communication?

There are three reasons.

First, Jesus is God. He acts as He wills. He may choose Our Lady to be the intercessor between Heaven and earth. He may choose to speak to Muslims through dreams. No one can forbid Him.

Second, Christianity has never shunned revelatory dreams. As much as forty-nine percent of the Bible consists of descriptions of visions and other mystical experiences. Dreams are one of the means through which God speaks—whether to the patriarch Jacob, to the prophets, or through the dreams of St. Joseph, the Magi, and even Pilate's wife.

Third, perhaps Jesus knows that within the Islamic cultural world, dreams are the best medium for conveying a message from Heaven. If so, He is using a cultural "filter"—meeting people where they are and speaking to them in ways that they will understand.

Perhaps that is why God so often speaks to Muslims through dreams.

"I was surprised when I listened to the stories," says Pastor Tom Doyle.

"I realized the magnitude of the phenomenon. I know of no other group that experiences God in this way," he says.

What is the result? Looking back over the past two decades, it is estimated that

"I was surprised when I listened to these stories and realized the magnitude of the phenomenon," recounts Pastor Tom Doyle. "I know of no other group that experiences God in this way."

One Islamic State militant ... once said that he "liked to kill Christians." One night, he had a strange dream. In it, he saw a man dressed in white who said to him, "You are killing My people."

between two and seven million Muslims have converted to Christianity. Why such a broad range? It is believed that perhaps only one in three converts is publicly known; the others belong to the underground Church. Let us not forget: in many Muslim societies, converting to Christianity is punishable by death.

Enough of introductory remarks. Let us now turn to some stories of apparitions from within the Islamic world.

ISIS MILITANTS

Let us begin with former Islamic militants who have left Islam, accepted Baptism, and are now evangelizing on their own—a whole new category of apostles.

One Islamic State militant—let us call him Muhamed—once said that he "liked to kill Christians." One night, he had a strange dream. In it, he saw a man dressed in white who said to him, "You are killing My people."

The night vision did not immediately change the militant's heart. When Muhamed was about to take another Christian's life, the man looked at him directly and said, "I know you will kill me, but I want to give you my Bible." After murdering him, Muhamed took the Bible out of curiosity and began to read it. Soon after, he had another dream. Jesus appeared to him again, calling him to become a Christian.

Before we return to Muhamed's story, let us consider another case. Omar, who—like

Muhamed—had fought with the Islamic State and taken many lives, also had a dream of Jesus. The Savior said to him, "Your sins can be forgiven. I love you. I died on the cross for you." This dream changed Omar's life entirely. He resolved to seek out Christians and ask who this Jesus was. Both Muhamed and Omar knew that if their companions discovered their questions, they would be killed.

At first, the Christians were afraid to speak with them. Muhamed and Omar tried to persuade them: "We are having dreams about Him. Tell us something about Him. We will not harm you." After a long period of trial and observation, they were invited to a community meeting. Needless to say, they remain part of the community to this day.

MOTHER OF A SICK CHILD

This story took place in Jordan, in a hospital run by Americans. One day, a Muslim woman with her sick son arrived

When he was about to take another Christian's life, the man looked at him directly and said: "I know you will kill me, but I want to give you my Bible." After murdering him, he took the Bible out of curiosity and began to read it.

at the hospital. The child received the care he needed. It seemed like thousands of other cases—at first. But the next morning, the mother was waiting for the doctor who had admitted them. "I saw Him during the night!" she exclaimed. "Who did you see?" the astonished doctor asked.

"Jesus!" she cried. "He came to me in a dream. He said He loved me and that He died on the cross for my sins. I have never felt so safe around a man!"

The dream repeated throughout the week. The woman received Baptism.

"He came to me in a dream. He said He loved me and that He died on the cross for my sins. I have never felt so safe around a man!"

DAILY DREAMS

Another remarkable story should be recalled. A Muslim convert—we will call him Jamal—was sharing his joy by telling others about Jesus. He knew he might pay for it with his life, but he could not hold back his happiness.

One night, Jamal was awakened by noises deep within his home. Someone had broken in. In a moment, a masked man stood over him, a gun in hand. Covering Jamal's mouth, the man said, "You're coming with me."

They left the house and moved down a dark street. At one point, the kidnapper pointed to a building and said, "We must go to the very top of that old house. It has five floors."

When they reached the roof, he said, "Now we jump to the roof next door. It's a little more than a meter. I've done it before. Hurry, and you will make it."

Jamal thought, "I'm about to die. Either he will shoot me or I will fall."

But he jumped—and made it.

The masked man then pointed to a barely visible door. "Do you see that door? Go inside." Jamal braced himself for torture, certain that no one would hear his cries.

But when Jamal entered, he saw ten men seated around a candle.

The kidnapper removed his mask and said, "We are imams. We have all begun having dreams about Jesus. We have started reading the Bible in secret, for if anyone finds out, we will die. We want to know Jesus. Can you help us?"

The safest way to bring Jamal to them had been to kidnap him.

They gathered secretly three times a week. Jamal, overjoyed, began to laugh uncontrollably—the great tension gave way to unstoppable laughter. He became their teacher.

SMILES AND TEARS

Hawa, a young Muslim girl from Somalia, had a dream. She dreamed of a man smiling at her with love, while tears streamed down His face. "Somehow, I knew He was crying because He missed me," she later recounted.

She began reading the Bible and, step by step, discovered Jesus' love for all people.

But her life had already been planned. She was engaged to a Muslim man. When her family learned of her conversion, they reacted harshly. Hawa was thrown out of her home and disinherited.

She was not alone. Her sister Zulfa also converted and suffered the same fate.

The two sisters became homeless and penniless. Worse still, while fleeing from an enraged uncle, Hawa fell into a ditch and broke a disc in her spine.

To survive, Zulfa baked bread over a smoky campfire and sold it. Over time, the smoke damaged her eyesight.

How did their story end? The Christian organization Open Doors, which supports persecuted Christians, found them. Medical care was arranged for them, and they received financial help to open a small business.

Perhaps by the world's standards it was not much. But the peace that filled these two young women was a treasure they considered worth any price—even the price of their lives.

ONE WORD FROM JESUS

Aisha lived in Jordan with her Muslim family. Her home life was marked by fear and anxiety. Her father was abusive, and religion in the household was a source of condemnation rather than consolation. Aisha felt certain that Allah disliked her and condemned her for everything.

Desperately longing to be loved, Aisha became pregnant at the age of seventeen. She knew that according to Islamic teaching, her father would be obligated to kill her to defend the family's honor. In despair, she chose to have an abortion. In Islam, she had been taught, such sins were unforgivable. She believed she was hated by Allah. Depression overwhelmed her, and suicidal thoughts haunted her.

One day, as she cried out in anguish to Allah for mercy, she heard a clear voice utter a single word: "Jesus."

Aisha lived in Jordan with her Muslim family.

They left the house and moved down a dark street. At one point, the kidnapper pointed to a building and said: "We must go to the very top of that old house. It has five floors."

Upon hearing the voice from Heaven, Aisha turned her prayers to Jesus and asked Him to reveal Himself to her.

"That was the first time I felt peace," she explains. "Peace washed over me when I prayed to Jesus."

She began reading the Bible. When she opened to the Epistle to the Romans and read, "While we were still sinners, Christ died for us" (Romans 5:8), she knew she had found the true God.

JESUS SPEAKS IN THE WORDS OF THE BIBLE

At dawn, an Iranian man living in a refugee camp nervously knocked on a pastor's door.

He told the pastor that during the night he had seen a man dressed in white who raised His hand and said, "Get up and follow Me."

The Iranian asked, "Who are you?"

The man replied, "I am the Alpha and the Omega. I am the Way to Heaven. No one comes to the Father except through Me."

"Who is He? What am I supposed to do? Why did He ask me to follow Him? How should I go? Tell me!" he pleaded with the pastor.

In response, the pastor pulled out a Bible and asked, "Have you ever seen this before?"

"No," he replied.

"Do you know what it is?"

Again, the answer was no.

The pastor opened to the book of Revelation and read aloud: "I am the Alpha and the Omega, the Beginning and the End."

The Iranian began to weep. "How can I find Him? How can I follow Him?" he cried.

They talked and prayed. Before parting, the pastor gave him a Bible and warned, "Hide it, because the Muslims in the camp may harm you."

But the man answered, "The Jesus I met today is more powerful than the Muslims in the camp."

An hour later, he returned—with ten more Iranians who said, "We also want the Bible."

THE MAN IN WHITE

Layla, a Muslim woman living in Athens, had heard of Jesus and was attracted to what she had learned about God. But she could not bring herself to follow

Amman, the capital of Jordan.

Him. Her entire world—her family, her heritage—was Muslim.

One day, she prayed:

"You know what, God? I have no excuse, absolutely none. I have run out of excuses. I do not know what to do, but following You would mean rejecting everything I have believed and everything my family has believed for generations. I cannot stand in between. I must either follow You or not. I cannot take this step alone. It is too hard. I need Your help."

After praying, she was not sure whether she was awake or dreaming when a man dressed in white entered the room.

She cried out, "Do not come near me! You are holy, and I am sinful. Do not come near me!"

The man replied, "Layla, I told you, and I am telling you again: I am the way and the truth and the life. No one comes to the Father except through Me."

That day, she chose Jesus.

OPEN DOORS

An elderly Afghan woman arrived in Europe, separated from her children who remained in her native country. She was deeply unhappy. An Iranian pastor prayed with her many times and explained that Jesus was the answer to her suffering. But like many Afghans, she was utterly uninterested in the Gospel.

One day, the pastor asked her, "If God reveals Himself to you and shows you the truth, will you follow Him?" She laughed aloud.

That same day, she passed by an aid center. Finding no one there, she sat down to rest, leaning against the door.

Suddenly, a bright light shone from behind her. It was so radiant that she covered her eyes. Then she heard a voice speaking in her own language:

"My daughter, My daughter, the door is open for you. Come!" She protested, "The door is closed!" Again the voice called: "I am the Son of God, Jesus. The door is open to you, My daughter. I am the door!"

Shaking as she later recounted the story, she said, "God spoke to me! I thought it was blasphemy—but now I know that Jesus is alive."

TAHER

Taher was a Muslim man from Iran. When his wife and children accepted faith in Jesus, he beat them and threatened to kill them. His family fled abroad. Time passed, and Taher, left alone, devoted himself even more fiercely to Allah, memorizing verses of the Quran and seeking Allah's favor.

"Please show me Your face," he pleaded. But the only answer was silence. For the first time, doubt crept in. "What if the god I serve does not exist at all—and my family was right?" he wondered. Desperate, he cried out: "I will believe in the God who appears to me."

◀ *Sisters Hawa and Zulfa were found by the Christian organization Open Doors, which supports persecuted Christians. Medical aid was organized for them. They also received financial support so they could open a small business that would provide them with a livelihood.*

"God spoke to me! I thought it was blasphemy—but now I know that Jesus is alive."

Jesus answered his prayer.

That night, Taher dreamed of a man riding a donkey who came up to him, embraced him, and said, "I will cleanse you of all your sins. You are free. I will give you rest. Believe in Me."

Taher asked, "But what if I sin again?"

The man answered, "I will wash away all your sins." Then He rode away.

Taher stood stunned. A second man approached him and asked, "Do you know who that man on the donkey is?"

"No," Taher replied.

"It is Jesus Christ. He cleanses you of your sins."

Taher awoke and pondered the dream. Falling asleep again, he dreamed the same dream. When he awoke the second time, fear gripped him. He had served Allah faithfully for forty-five years, had even made a pilgrimage to Mecca. How could he leave Islam?

A third time he slept—and a third time the dream came.

When he awoke, he had no more doubts: Jesus Christ is the true God.

We could recount hundreds of similar stories, but let us conclude with just one more.

It is not a story of dreams, but of miraculous deliverance.

Jordan Hilger, a reporter for Worthy News, wrote on March 22, 2019, about an extraordinary event in Africa:

> *Seventy-two Nigerian Christians who had converted from Islam were rescued after being kidnapped by Boko Haram. Their deliverance involved miraculous circumstances—angels, snakes, and even an apparition of Jesus.*
>
> *The group originally included seventy-six men, women, and children. Four men, who had been leading the group, became the first martyrs after refusing to renounce their faith. The others waited, terrified, for the same fate.*

But during the night, several mothers reported that their children had seen Jesus, who assured them that "everyone would be saved."

The next morning, the militants lined up the captives to kill them. Yet before a shot was fired, the attackers began shouting about snakes, dropping their weapons and fleeing. Some fell dead, defeated by an invisible force.

One child said to an adult who tried to pick up a weapon dropped by a fleeing militant, "You do not have to do this. Can't you see the men in white fighting for us?"

The child saw angels all around. All seventy-two believers were saved

During the night he had seen a man dressed in white who raised His hand and said, "Get up and follow Me." The Iranian asked: "Who are You?" The man replied: "I am the Alpha and the Omega. I am the Way to Heaven."

without a single human hand being raised in their defense.

WE LIVE AMONG SIGNS

God gives many signs to Muslims. He speaks through elements of their own deep tradition—for instance, in 1917, sending the Blessed Mother to Fatima.

The place where the greatest Marian apparitions of the twentieth century occurred is named for Muhammad's beloved daughter, Fatima—the second most honored woman in Islam, after Mary herself.

After Fatima's death, Muhammad wrote, "You will be the most blessed of all women in paradise, after Mary."

If God chose the parish of Fatima for the greatest modern apparitions, and made Mary the Messenger from Heaven, there can be no talk of coincidence.

In these supernatural events, Muhammad's daughter and the Mother of the Savior seem to meet. The former is but a shadow before the splendor of the latter, who comes not to condemn, but to call for conversion and repentance.

Mary comes to Fatima to proclaim: "Enough of offending God!"

Will all Muslims convert to Christianity through Our Lady of Fatima? Humanly speaking, it seems impossible. But Fatima is a miracle, not a natural event. With God, nothing is impossible.

It is important to pray for unity, to believe in it, and to hope that through the power of Jesus Christ, we may again become one Church.

Will Muslims convert to the Christian faith, and will Our Lady of Fatima be the bridge that enables them to transition from the old faith to the new? From a human perspective, it seems impossible. But the apparitions in Fatima are not of human origin—they are divine. What happens there is not a natural course of events, but a miracle. And within a miracle, everything is possible with God.

An old Portuguese legend tells how the village of Fatima received its name: in the twelfth century, a Muslim princess named Fatima fell in love with Gonzal Hermiguez, a Christian knight. She converted in order to marry him. After her death, the grieving knight named her favorite place after her—Fatima.

Does God have special plans for Islam today?

Although we have not recounted every thread woven into the modern apparitions and prophecies, the pattern the Lord is using seems increasingly clear.

God gives many signs that are understandable to Muslims. He refers to the deep tradition of Islam, for example, in 1917, by sending the Most Holy Mother to Fatima.

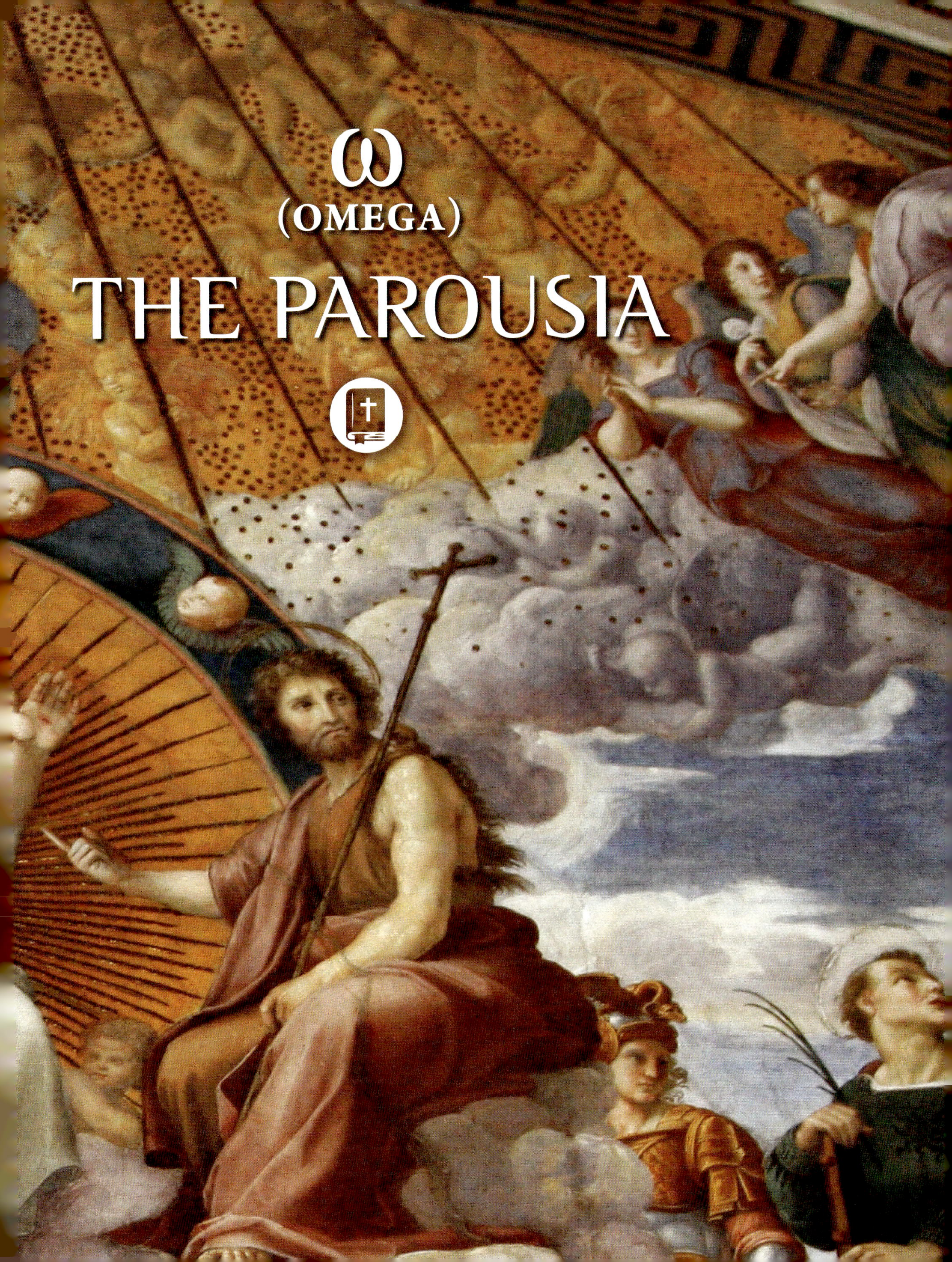

ω
(OMEGA)
THE PAROUSIA

On the previous page: Raphael, Disputation of the Blessed Sacrament *(detail), Vatican Museums (Vatican City).*

Place of Revelation: All temporality

(OMEGA)

THE PAROUSIA

ALL HUMANITY, THE FINAL MOMENT OF HISTORY

"And we await Your coming in glory," we repeat during the liturgy, as we rise from our knees after the eucharistic miracle has taken place on the altar, hidden from our earthly senses. We speak these words to Jesus, who is now physically present among us under the signs of bread and wine. We speak with Him. We assure Him that by our lives and by our words we proclaim His death and profess before the world the truth of His Resurrection. And in the same breath, we affirm our expectation of His return.

John Martin I, The Plains of Heaven, *fragment of the triptych* The Last Judgment, *Tate Gallery (London, United Kingdom).*

He will come, whether or not we are prepared. His return is a future historical fact, existing "in the perfect future tense." It is certain: the Lord will return in the greatest revelation the universe has ever known.

PLACE OF REVELATION: ALL OF TEMPORAL REALITY

We look forward to His coming in glory, to the moment when everything "will be made new" (cf. Revelation 21:5, "Behold, I make all things new"), when evil and its power will pass away, Satan will be cast into darkness, and all the prophecies of happiness will be fulfilled. We await the moment when Jesus will stand among us in Majesty, in Light, in Might—coming as the only Lord, the only Ruler, the only Owner of all things, visible and invisible.

THE FINAL REVELATION

We await His coming—true, visible, and glorious. The Parousia will be the new, final, and visible presence of Jesus: a definitive revelation (cf. 1 Thessalonians 4:13–18).

No longer will He come "in the great mystery of faith." We long for the day when Jesus will stand among us in Majesty, in Light, in Might—coming as the only Lord, the only Ruler, the only Owner of the cosmos—and take us to Himself in Heaven.

The Apostle to the Nations teaches "that He will bring about at the proper time, the blessed and only ruler, the King of kings and Lord of lords" (1 Timothy 6:15).

Once again, Jesus will enter history in a visible way. He will come again in the flesh—no longer hidden under the veil of faith as the eucharistic Servant, but revealed in great glory as the Lord of all existence.

When will He come? No one knows; God has not revealed the hour or the place of this most awaited event (cf. Mark 13:32). We

Peter Paul Rubens, Christ Triumphant Over Death, *Museu Nacional de Arte Antiga (Lisbon, Portugal).*

William Holman Hunt, The Light of the World, *Manchester Art Gallery (United Kingdom).*

▲ *Fresco* The Almighty on His Throne, *main monastery of the Serbian Orthodox Church (Visoki Dečani, Kosovo).*

➤ *Top: Piero di Cosimo,* The Crucifixion of Christ, *Museum of Fine Arts (Budapest, Hungary).*

➤ *Bottom: Andrea Previtali,* Salvator Mundi, *National Gallery (London, United Kingdom).*

know only that it will occur at the final time, when all is "ready" (cf. 1 Peter 1:5).

The date and place do not matter—especially since most of us will meet Jesus before the Parousia, at the hour of our bodily death. Thus, Benedict XVI reminds us that Jesus "wishes to shield His disciples of every generation from curiosity about dates and predictions, and instead wants above all to show the right path, which must be trod, today and tomorrow, to enter eternal life."

That "entry" into eternity will coincide with the Parousia only for one generation—the last one. Is it ours? We have no signs that would assure us the Lord will return in glory during our lifetime.

Thus, "our waiting for His coming in glory" is not tied merely to our personal situation but springs from Christian concern for all humanity. Every generation of Christians yearns for God's reign and the end of evil. Disciples of Jesus, moved by compassion for those who suffer and who may be lost, cry out to the Lord to close the book of history by His glorious return.

Someone may ask why God delays, since evil continues to bear fruit and—as the Blessed Mother lamented at Fatima—"many people go to hell." The answer is not unexpected: humanity has not yet prepared the world for the hour of Jesus' return. Thus, the liturgical acclamation in which we profess that "we

await" also means "we contribute to Your coming in glory."

FROM HEAVEN, THAT IS, FROM ABOVE?

The second coming of Jesus will be the greatest revelation in the history of the world. Naturally, we wonder: what will it look like? Do we know anything about it?

The angels announced it on the day of the Ascension: "This Jesus who has been taken up from you into heaven will return in the same way as you have seen Him going into heaven" (Acts 1:11).

"In the same way"? Does this mean we will see the cloud of God's presence and Jesus descending from it? Are we to interpret literally Paul's statement that we "wait for His Son from heaven" (cf. 1 Thessalonians 1:10)? Or that we "will be caught up together ... in the clouds to meet the Lord in the air" (cf. 1 Thessalonians 4:16–17)?

Such a literal reading is mistaken. "In the same way" means a real coming in a glorified body—but not necessarily

Moretto da Brescia, Jesus in Glory Hands the Keys to Peter and the Book of Teaching to Paul, *Abbey Church of San Nicola in Rodengo-Saiano (Lombardy, Italy).*

Icon of the Second Coming. Christ is enthroned surrounded by angels and saints (in the center), paradise is depicted below, with the bosom of Abraham (on the left), and the good thief (on the right) holding his cross. Greece, circa 1700. Sotheby's Auction House (London, United Kingdom).

John Martin I, The Great Day of His Wrath, *panel from the triptych* The Last Judgment, *Tate Gallery (London, United Kingdom).*

according to the cosmology of that time. The "heavens" where God dwells are not merely the skies above, and the "cloud" is not just a cloud drifting through the atmosphere. It is a visible sign of the Invisible, Infinite One.

We will be "caught up in the clouds"—drawn into the mystery of God's presence, beyond human comprehension or sensory grasp.

"Our future is 'to be with the Lord,'" Benedict XVI explains simply.

The New Testament's descriptions of the Lord's return, while realistic in form, are figurative in nature. When we read that the Parousia will be the Lord's "descent" (cf. 1 Thessalonians 1:10), it signifies not so much Jesus' coming down through the sky, but His entering into the fullness of the earthly realm.

Thus, St. Paul assures us: "For the Lord Himself ... will come down from heaven" (cf. 1 Thessalonians 4:16).

He has already "come down" once, in the Incarnation—and that was no mere descent from sky to earth.

It is also senseless to ask where the Parousia will take place. The angels, saying He would return "in the same way," never intended to suggest the Mount of Olives or any other specific location. "In the same way" refers to the reality of His coming, not to a physical site.

Jesus Himself warned: "They will say to you, 'Look, there He is!' or 'Look, here He is!' Do not go off, do not run in pursuit" (Luke 17:23). His coming, He said, will be like lightning that flashes from one end of the sky to the other (cf. Luke 17:24).

The Parousia will be sudden and unexpected (cf. Luke 17:30). It will be

THE PAROUSIA

a universal revelation: all humanity encountering Christ as He comes in glory (cf. 1 Thessalonians 4:16ff).

When the Lord returns, only God's Glory will remain, and all things will exist within it: the saved will dwell amid the "new heavens and new earth" (cf. Revelation 21:1).

All that is not "in the image and likeness of God" will vanish like the morning mist. The Evil One and all evil will be "driven out" (cf. John 12:31).

FIRST, THE PAROUSIA OF THE LAWLESS ONE

Before the Son of God returns, we are to face another Parousia. That knowledge comes to us from St. Paul. He assures us that before Jesus' glorious return, there will be another "momentous appearance": the coming of the Lawless One.

Peter Paul Rubens, Christ Triumphant Over Death and Sin, *Musée des Beaux-Arts (Strasbourg, France).*

Florentine Master, mosaic Christ Pantocrator and the Last Judgment, *ca. 1300, baptistery of St. John's Cathedral in Florence (Italy).*

A time will come, the apostle warns, when "the one who restrains" will be removed, granting the Lawless One license to act. That figure is the Lawless One, waiting for his opportune hour. When it arrives, "then the lawless one will be revealed" (cf. 2 Thessalonians 2:8).

Who is this emissary of Satan? Is it the Antichrist? We know that he will parody the Parousia we await, even posing as Christ Himself. "The coming of the lawless one," says Paul, "will be accompanied by the power of Satan ... with all power and signs and lying wonders" (cf. 2 Thessalonians 2:9)—a display of false wonders. Outwardly, it will appear divine.

That is why Paul fears that many Christians may be deceived by this satanic display of glory. The Parousia of the Lawless One, marked by a semblance of great power, will bring grave danger. His coming will reveal something that mimics God's might, accompanied by multiple phenomena Paul describes with near-synonymous phrases: mighty works, signs, and wonders—all of them great.

We may surmise something of the doctrine this Lawless One will preach to attract crowds. In *Jesus of Nazareth*, Benedict XVI suggests that we often

▲ Christ in Glory, *Metropolitan Museum of Art (New York, USA)*.

➤ *William Blake,* Vision of the Last Judgment, *1808, National Trust (Sussex, United Kingdom)*.

➤ *Francesco Bassano,* Christ in Glory.

imagine that if Jesus truly wished to be the Messiah, He would have inaugurated a golden age. Meanwhile, "the kingdom of man remains man's realm, and whoever claims to save the world perpetuates Satan's deception and hands the world over to him."

The Lawless One will promise an "earthly paradise"—a world without hunger or suffering, a place of satisfaction and merriment—heralding a "New Order."

Will many choose to follow this pseudo-God, who will cunningly forestall the true Lord's arrival? Yes, and that choice will be a rejection of the salvation brought by Jesus. Paul writes that the Lord will reveal which salvation is genuine: He appears soon after, and the false Parousia of the Lawless One collapses immediately before Christ's Parousia (cf. 2 Thessalonians 2:8). This satanic imitation of the Divine Ruler proves to be a figure made of mist; Jesus need not even fight him. With a single act and in a single moment, He destroys and annihilates him by the splendor of His coming—like light scattering darkness, like lightning flashing from horizon to horizon.

Nor is it only the Lawless One who meets defeat. Those who knowingly and willingly allow themselves to be seduced—choosing to use evil to build a "New Order," permitting Satan to blind them—will share in his downfall.

Thus they lose their share in the light meant for every human being. An apocryphal text, the *Gospel of Philip*, offers an image

Paul Gustave Doré, The Triumph of Christianity Over Paganism.

Annibale Carracci, Christ in Glory, *Pitti Palace (Florence, Italy).*

Peter Paul Rubens, The Risen Christ, *Pitti Palace (Florence, Italy).*

Stained-glass window of the Second Coming of Christ, St. Matthew's Lutheran Church (Charleston, SC).

that helps explain what becomes of Satan's servants on the day of the Parousia:

> *When they are in darkness, the blind and those who see do not differ from one another; but when the light comes, the one who sees beholds the light, and the blind remains in darkness.*

And that, for all eternity...

JOY, THE GREAT DAY

For God's servants, the final revelation of Jesus will be a day of rejoicing. This is suggested by the very word *Parousia*, which in the time of the New Testament referred to the emperor's ceremonial arrival—an event celebrated publicly and with great joy. A Parousia was a triumphal entry by the ruler, a festive occasion involving countless crowds. Sometimes new dating even began from an emperor's Parousia.

Such—only on an infinitely greater, cosmic scale—will be the Parousia of Jesus.

PREPARATION ON EARTH

The great feast of the Parousia calls for preparation. According to Scripture, it will be accompanied by purifying suffering (cf. 1 Thessalonians 5:3). It will also be linked, among other things, to persecutions (cf. 1 Peter 4:13ff).

Might that suffering refer to the period under the Lawless One, who uses evil to build an earthly paradise?

The world's eschatological future is full of questions we cannot fully answer. So, if we ask whether the sufferings that precede the Parousia are inevitable, we cannot say much. Perhaps we should echo St. John Paul II, who said that these sufferings are unavoidable, yet we can obtain from Jesus their "mitigation and transformation."

Humanity cannot evade them entirely, but it can lessen them.

What does that mean?

It is not true that humanity has no influence on the timing or circumstances of the Parousia, that all we can do is "watch" (cf. Mark 13:37). Once we understand that

Giovanni Battista Gaulli, The Triumph of the Name of Jesus, *Church of the Gesù (Rome, Italy).*

this evangelical watchfulness is action rather than passive observation, we realize that Christ's coming also involves human participation—specifically, the Church's involvement.

Although, in the end, even evil will be shown to serve God. Everything can hasten the hour of the final revelation.

CONFRONTATION

Let us pause our reflections and transport ourselves briefly to the 1976 Eucharistic Congress in Philadelphia, where Cardinal Karol Wojtyła spoke. In his homily on the threats to human freedom, he cried out in apocalyptic language, speaking of a double Parousia:

> *We are now facing the greatest historical confrontation humanity has ever gone through. I do not think that wide circles of American society, or the entire wide circle of the Christian community, realize this fully. We are now facing the final confrontation between the Church and the anti-Church, between the Gospel and the anti-Gospel, between Christ and the Antichrist. This confrontation is within the plans of Divine Providence. It is, therefore, in God's plan, and it must be a trial which the Church must take up and face courageously.*

The perceptive Archbishop Fulton J. Sheen adds that this anti-Church will likewise be a "mystical body," resembling in its outward forms the Mystical Body of Christ. This anti-Church will speak of a "golden age"—a promise of earthly salvation. People will flock to it.

The perceptive Archbishop Fulton J. Sheen adds that this anti-Church will likewise be a "mystical body," resembling in its outward forms the Mystical Body of Christ. This anti-Church will speak of a "golden age"—a promise of earthly salvation. People will flock to it.

"The devil is portrayed as a serpent," writes St. Cyprian, "because he moves in silence, appears peaceful, suggests easy paths, yet he is so cunning and treacherous ... that he tries to persuade people that night is day and poison is medicine. It is precisely through such trickery that he tries to undermine truth by deception. And he comes as an angel of light."

After that, the Antichrist will reveal himself in his own Parousia.

It will be a time of great deception for many—the greatest false revelation in history.

Yet we know that it will vanish, yielding to the revelation of God's glory, which will sweep away everything that is not the image of Christ. The anti-Church will disappear.

IS THE TIME NEAR?

Modern prophecies often repeat that we are nearing the "final revelation," the second coming of Christ into the world. Even St. Faustina Kowalska seems to confirm this joyful news. She writes that from Poland—faithful and obedient to God's Will—will come forth a spark to prepare the world for His final coming: "I have loved Poland in a special way, and if it is obedient to My will, from it will come forth the spark that will prepare the world for My final coming."

➤ *The Antichrist seated on Leviathan from the manuscript* Liber Floridus, *1120 (University of Ghent, Belgium).*

Perhaps that moment is indeed near, just around the corner of history. We cannot see it, but do the sensitive ears of

prophets already hear the rustle of angelic wings accompanying Christ's descent from Heaven? We do not know.

We do know that the day of the Parousia may arrive sooner or later. We, too, move the hands of the apocalyptic clock—perhaps even swiftly—through our time of purification. And that should be our primary concern.

INVOKING THE "PRE-COMING"

Benedict XVI reminds us of the prayer *Marana tha!*—"Come, our Lord!" (cf. 1 Corinthians 16:22). This was the prayer of the first generation of Christians. The last book of the New Testament, Revelation, also ends with this prayer: "Come, Lord Jesus!" (cf. Revelation 22:20).

Do we likewise pray in this way?

It seems that in our modern era, in our personal lives and in the world at large, it can be difficult to sincerely pray for the end of this world, for the coming of the new Jerusalem, for the last judgment, for the coming Judge—Christ Himself.

Yet even if for various reasons we hesitate to pray it wholeheartedly, we can still rightly and honestly echo the prayer of the first Christians: "Come, Lord Jesus!"

Why?

> *We want an end to this unjust world. We likewise want to see the world fundamentally transformed, to witness the birth of a civilization of love—a world without violence, without hunger. We want all this, but how could it ever happen apart from Christ's presence? Without Christ's presence, the world will never truly be just or renewed. And so, in a different yet more profound manner, we also can—and must—urge, today, in the circumstances of our times: Come, Lord! Come in Your own way, known to You alone. Come where injustice reigns, where*

Giovanni Battista Gaulli, The Triumph of the Name of Jesus, *Church of the Gesù (Rome, Italy).*

Domenico Ghirlandaio, Christ in Heaven with Four Saints and a Donor, *Municipal Art Gallery (Volterra, Italy).*

violence prevails. Come to refugee camps..., to so many hidden corners of the earth. Come where drugs hold sway. Come also to the wealthy who have forgotten You and live only for themselves. Come where You remain unknown. Come in Your own manner and renew today's world. Come also into our hearts. Come and renew our lives. Enter our hearts, so that we ourselves might become God's light, Your presence. In this sense we pray with St. Paul: Marana tha!, "Come, Lord Jesus!" And let us pray that Christ will truly be present in our world today and renew it.

That is the mission of the Church, which—yes—shall become the "Mother of the Parousial Christ."

WOJTYŁA'S IDEA

Lastly, let us recall the vision of the Parousia that Cardinal Karol Wojtyła (later John Paul II) presented to Pope Paul VI during the Lenten retreat in the Vatican in 1978.

The Cardinal—who would that very year become Bishop of Rome—explained to Paul VI that Mary "is to be the Mother of the Parousial Christ." Indeed, it is obvious: Jesus, who died, rose, and will return, has the body He received from the Virgin Mary.

However, Wojtyła adds that this "second coming ... must be prepared by the Holy Spirit, no longer in the Virgin's womb, but in the entire Mystical Body." In his vision of the final times, the Church will be "like Mary": holy, immaculate, pure, filled with grace, filled with God, and alien to the world.

A Marian Church: devoid of worldly securities and influence, lacking palaces or wealth. A poor and persecuted Church, considered unimportant in the eyes of the world.

That will be the place of the Son of God's new coming to earth.

Thus, when we call upon the day of Christ's revelation in glory, we also pray for a Church so united with God that there is room in her for the Parousia.

➤ *Paul Gustave Doré,* The Valley of Tears, *Musée des Beaux-Arts de la Ville (Paris, France).*

THE PAROUSIA

What will this Church look like? That is not our theme here. Suffice it to say that it may well consist of small, fervent communities — a Church "as little as yeast," as Benedict XVI once taught.

Might it become such through its purification?

One thing is certain: God will not let His plans remain unfulfilled, nor will He allow the Creation of humankind to be pointless, with Hell as our destiny. He will not accept such an outcome.

This divine refusal is upheld by a Church without blemish.

That small seed will transform the world into "another world," transfigured by the Parousia.

It will be the greatest revelation yet to take place within the Church.

We remember that all true revelations have taken place in the Church; we know some of them. The Parousia will be their final culmination.

Christ Pantocrator — image in a wall niche of the Holy Trinity Monastery, (Meteora, Greece).

Giovanni Battista Gaulli, Christ in Glory, *Sotheby's Auction House (London, United Kingdom).*

Illustration Credits

List of Illustration Sources Photographs are described in the following order: from top to bottom—left page, right page.

α THE REVELATION OF THE INCARNATION TO THE ANGELS

Sailko/ CC BY 3.0/ Wikimedia commons. https://blogs.futura-sciences.com, MET Museum/CC0. Wikimedia Commons/public domain. Wikimedia Commons/public domain, Wikimedia Commons/public domain, Wikimedia Commons/public domain. Antiquary/ CC BY 4.0/Wikipedia. Wikimedia Commons/public domain, Wikimedia Commons/public domain. Wikimedia Commons/public domain, Wikipedia/public domain. Storye book/ CC BY-SA 4.0/Wikimedia commons/, Reddit.com. Wikimedia Commons/public domain, Michael Kranewitte/ CC BY-SA 3.0/ Wikimedia commons/. Wikimedia Commons/public domain, Faber/ Wikimedia Commons/public domain, Wikimedia Commons/public domain. Wikimedia Commons/public domain, Wikimedia Commons/public domain, tuxpi.com. Wikimedia Commons/ public domain, Wikimedia Commons/public domain. Wikimedia Commons/ public domain, Wikimedia Commons/public domain, Wikimedia Commons/ public domain. Wikimedia Commons/public domain, Wikipedia/public domain, Francesca Ferrito/ CC BY-SA 4.0/ Wikimedia commons.

β AROUND THE NATIVITY OF THE LORD

Wikimedia Commons/public domain. Wikipedia/public domain, Jos. Luiz Bernardes Ribeiro/ CC BY-SA 4.0/Wikipedia, Sailko/ CC BY 3.0/ Wikimedia commons, Wikimedia Commons/public domain. Ian and Wendy Sewell/ CC BY 3.0/ Wikimedia commons, Neil Ward/ CC BY 2.0/ Wikimedia commons, Wikimedia Commons/public domain. Zerooooo/Wikipedia/public domain, Freedom's Falcon/Wikimedia Commons/public domain. DE.MOLAI/Wikipedia/public domain, https://www.flickr.com/photos/iz4aks/ CC BY 2.0/ Wikimedia commons. Wikipedia/public domain, Bukvoe/ CC BY-SA 4.0/ Wikimedia commons. National Library of Wales/ CC0/Wikimedia commons/, Jesse / Flickr.com, Paweł Teperski /Flickr.com, Seethe Holy Land/Flickr.com, Wikimedia Commons/public domain. Antoine Taveneaux/ CC BY 3.0/ Wikimedia commons, Wikimedia Commons/public domain, Ralf Roletschek/ GFDL 1.2/ Wikimedia commons. Wikimedia Commons/public domain, Fallaner/ CC BY--SA 4.0/Wikimedia commons. Fczarnowski/CC BY 3.0/ Wikimedia commons. Wikimedia Commons/public domain, Wikimedia Commons/public domain, Wikimedia Commons/public domain.

γ THE BETHLEHEM EPIPHANY

Wikimedia Commons/public domain. Brooklyn Museum/CC0. Wikimedia commons/ public domain. Wikimedia Commons/public domain, Wikimedia Commons/public domain, Wikimedia Commons/public domain, Wikimedia Commons/public domain, Raimond Spekking / CC BY-SA 4.0 /Wikimedia Commons. Wikimedia Commons/public domain, Wikimedia Commons/ public domain. Wikimedia Commons/public domain, Jastrow/ Wikimedia Commons/public domain, Wikimedia Commons/public domain. Jochen Jahnke/CC BY 3.0/ Wikimedia commons, Wikimedia Commons/public domain. Wikimedia Commons/public domain. Jastrow/ Wikimedia Commons/public domain, Wikimedia Commons/public domain, Wikimedia Commons/public domain. Wikimedia Commons/public domain, Sailko/ CC BY 3.0/ Wikimedia commons. Wikimedia commons/ public domain. Wikimedia Commons/ public domain, Wikimedia Commons/public domain, Marie-Lan Nguyen/ Wikimedia Commons/public domain. Luc-Olivier Merson/ Wikimedia Commons/public domain. Petar Milošević//Wikimedia Commons/public domain, Wikimedia Commons/public domain. renee hawk /Flickr. com. Yuropoulos/ CC BY-SA 4.0 /Wikimedia Commons.

Δ MORE THAN A MAN

Welleschik/ CC BY 3.0/ Wikimedia commons. Wikimedia Commons/public domain. Wikimedia Commons/public domain. Wikimedia commons/ public domain, Wikimedia Commons/public domain, Wikimedia Commons/public domain. Wikimedia Commons/public domain, Wikimedia Commons/public domain, Wikimedia Commons/public domain. Wikimedia Commons/public domain. Wikimedia commons/ public domain. Berthold Werner/ Wikimedia Commons/public domain, Wikimedia Commons/public domain. The Yorck Project/Wikimedia Commons/public domain. Wikimedia Commons/public domain. Wikimedia Commons/public domain, Wikimedia Commons/public domain, Metropolitan Museum of Art/ CC0/ Wikimedia commons. Wikimedia Commons/public domain, Sibeaster /Wikimedia Commons/public domain. Wikimedia Commons/public domain, Wikimedia Commons/public domain. Gloumouth1/CC BY-SA 4.0/.

ε VERAIKONY

Wikimedia commons, Wikimedia Commons/public domain. C messier// CC BY-SA 4.0/ Wikimedia commons. Wikimedia Commons/public domain, Koppchen/ CC BY 3.0/ Wikimedia commons. Wikimedia Commons/public domain. Wikimedia Commons/public domain. Wikimedia Commons/public domain, Wikimedia Commons/public domain, Fahrenheit 451, Wikimedia Commons/public domain. Wikimedia Commons/public domain, Wikimedia Commons/public domain, Wikimedia Commons/public domain. Alamy/ Secondo Pia, Prawdziwe oblicze Boga/Fronda, courtesy of prof. Manuela Rodrigueza Almenara. Wikimedia Commons/public domain, Wikimedia Commons/public domain. Wikimedia Commons/public domain, Wolfgang M./ CC BY 3.0/ Wikimedia commons, Wikimedia Commons/public domain, Wikimedia Commons/public domain. han santing/ Flickr.com. Wikimedia Commons/public domain, randlfrost/Flickr.com, Wikimedia Commons/ public domain. randlfrost/Flickr.com. Wikimedia Commons/public domain, randlfrost/Flickr. com. Sitomon/ Wikimedia Commons/public domain, Reinhard Dietrich/ CC BY-SA 4.0 /Wikimedia Commons, Piotr Karczewski.

ζ "TABORIZATION"

Wikimedia Commons/public domain, Fahrenheit 451. carol zwilling/Flickr.com. shalev-cohen-/ unsplash, F.lix Bonfils/Wikimedia Commons/public domain. Wikimedia Commons/public domain, Wikimedia Commons/public domain. J.rg Bittner Unna/CC BY 3.0/ Wikimedia commons, Wikimedia Commons/public domain. Wikimedia Commons/public domain, Wikimedia Commons/public domain, Wikimedia Commons/public domain. Wikimedia Commons/public domain, Wikimedia Commons/public domain, Wikimedia Commons/public domain. Dr.hhorn/ CC BY-SA 4.0 /Wikimedia Commons. Wikimedia Commons/public domain, shalev-cohen-/unsplash, https://www.flickr.com/photos/pldrtbrennan/ pldrtbrennan/ CC BY 2.0/ Wikimedia. Annesov/CC BY 3.0/ Wikimedia commons, shalev-cohen-/unsplash, shalev-cohen-/unsplash. Wikimedia Commons/public domain, Wikimedia commons/ public domain, Wikimedia Commons/public domain, Wikimedia Commons/public domain, Wikimedia Commons/public domain. Wikimedia Commons/public domain, Wikimedia Commons/public domain. Wikimedia Commons/public domain. Rvin88/CC BY 3.0/ Wikimedia commons, Wikimedia commons/ public domain, British Library Add. MS 59874/ Wikimedia commons. Brooklyn Museum/ CC0.

η THE SIGN OF THE EUCHARIST

National Library of Wales/ CC0/ Wikimedia commons. Wikimedia Commons/public domain. Wikimedia Commons/public domain. Wikimedia Commons/public domain, Wikimedia Commons/public domain, Wikimedia Commons/public domain, Wikimedia Commons/public domain. Бернгардт/ CC BY-SA 4.0/ Wikimedia commons. Wikimedia Commons/public domain, Wikimedia Commons/public domain, Wikimedia Commons/public domain. Wikimedia Commons/public domain. simon/Flickr. com, Wikimedia Commons/public domain. Wikimedia Commons/public domain. Wikimedia commons/ public domain, benjamin/Flickr.com, Onceinawhile/CC BY-SA 4.0/ Wikimedia commons, See The Holy Land - Flickr: Mount Zion/ CC BY-SA 2.0/Wikimedia commons, GadgetSteve/ CC BY-SA 4.0/Wikimedia commons. Wikimedia Commons/public domain. P.R. Binter - private trip by P.R. Binter/ Wikimedia Commons/public domain, Wikimedia Commons/public domain, Wikimedia Commons/public domain. Olivier Jules/ CC BY 3.0/ Wikimedia commons, www.blogtalkradio.com, theresa sismilich/Flickr. com. Krzysztof Żyła/Flickr. com, Junior/Wikimedia Commons/public domain. liem bui/Flickr. com, carlo raso /Flickr.com, hen megonza/Flickr.com. Abxbay/ CC0/Wikimedia commons, Mathiasrex/Maciej Szczepańczyk/CC BY-SA 4.0/Wikimedia commons, richard boudreau /Flickr. com. Artur Nowacki/Flickr. com.

θ A CHRISTOPHANY IN SHEOL

Artur Nowacki/Flickr. com, Tarkan18/CC BY-SA 4.0/Wikimedia commons, Wikimedia Commons/public domain, Wikimedia Commons/public domain, Wikiart/public domain, Edal Anton Lefterov/ CC BY 3.0/ Wikimedia commons. Wikimedia Commons/public domain, Wikimedia commons/ public domain. Jos. Luiz Bernardes Ribeiro/CC BY 3.0/ Wikimedia commons. Wikimedia Commons/public domain, Wikimedia Commons/public domain. Wikimedia Commons/public domain, TED/Flickr. com. Wikimedia Commons/public domain. Wikimedia Commons/public domain, Wikimedia Commons/public domain, Wikimedia Commons/public domain. Wikimedia Commons/public domain. Wikimedia commons/ public domain, Lawrence Lew/Flickr. Wikimedia Commons/public domain. Sailko/CC BY 3.0/ Wikimedia commons, Wikimedia Commons/public domain, Wikimedia Commons/ public domain.

ι THE RESURRECTION

Paata Vardanashvili (www.paata.ge)/ CC BY 2.0/ commons/public domain, Wikimedia Commons/public domain, tanyasid/123RF. www.freebibleimages.org. Wikimedia Commons/public domain, Wikimedia commons/ public domain, Wikimedia Commons/public domain. Tetraktys/CC BY 3.0/ Wikimedia commons, Jastrow/Wikimedia Commons/public domain, Wikimedia Commons/public domain. Wikimedia Commons/public domain, Wikimedia Commons/public domain. Wikimedia Commons/public domain, Wikimedia Commons/public domain. Wikimedia commons/ public domain, https://www.flickr.com/photos/jlascar/10350972756/in/set-72157636698118263/ CC BY 2.0/ Wikimedia commons, Wikimedia Commons/public domain. Kyle Taylo/ CC BY 2.0/ Wikimedia commons, Wikimedia Commons/public domain, Berthold Werner/ CC BY 3.0/ Wikimedia commons, Fallaner/CC BY-SA 4.0/Wikimedia commons. Ondřej Žváček/ CC BY 2.5/ Wikimedia commons, adriatikus/ CC BY 3.0/ Wikimedia commons. photos4health /Flickr.com, Jlascar// CC BY 2.0/ Wikimedia commons.

1. THE MOST IMPORTANT HEART

Wikimedia Commons/public domain, Fr. Lawrence Lew/Flickr. com. Jl FilpoC/CC BY 4.0/ Wikimedia commons. Wikimedia Commons/public domain, granpik suffolk/Flickr. com, Bremond/ CC BY-SA 3.0/ Wikimedia commons, Andreas Praefcke/ CC BY-SA 3.0/ Wikimedia commons. Fr. Lawrence Lew/ Flickr. com. Adam Cardinal Maida/Flickr. com, Dominican foundation/Flickr. com, Nicholas Breidgam/Flickr. com. Majella1851r/CC BY-SA 4.0/ Wikimedia commons. Andrew Guidroz II/Flickr. com, Fr. Lawrence Lew/Flickr. com, Wikimedia Commons/public domain, Wikimedia Commons/public domain. Fr. Lawrence Lew/Flickr. com. Didier Descouens/ CC BY-SA 4.0/ Wikimedia commons, Jan Sokol/ CC BY-SA 3.0/ Wikimedia commons, Mmahr/ CC BY-SA 3.0/ Wikimedia commons. Iglesia Valladolid/Flickr. com, Fr. Lawrence Lew/Flickr. com. Fr. Lawrence Lew/Flickr. com. Wikimedia Commons/public domain, Rian Barrion/Flickr. com. Wikimedia Commons/public domain.

2. "IT SEEMS TO ME ..."

Wikimedia Commons/public domain. Randy Greve/Flickr. com. Mongolo1984/ CC BY-SA 4.0/ Wikimedia commons. vitaesanctorum.wordpress.com. Toni Pecoraro/Wikimedia commons/ public domain. Wikimedia Commons/public domain, Matalyn/ CC BY 2.0/ Wikimedia commons, Sailko/ CC BY-SA 3.0/ Wikimedia commons. RAA Castro/ Flickr, Wikimedia Commons/public domain. Randy Greve/Flickr, Wikimedia Commons/public domain. Sailko/ CC BY-SA 3.0/ Wikimedia commons. Wikimedia Commons/ public domain, Wikimedia Commons/public domain. Wikimedia Commons/ public domain. Marche Tourism/Flickr, Fr. Lawrence Lew/Flickr. com. Marche Tourism/Flickr. com. Wikimedia Commons/public domain, Achille Ballerini/ Flickr. com. bart-ms/pixabay. com.

3. A MAN OF NOBLE APPEARANCE

Fr. Lawrence Lew/Flickr. com, Dave Overcash/Flickr. com. Wikimedia Commons/public domain. Stebunik/ CC BY-SA 3.0/ Wikimedia commons, Wikimedia Commons/public domain, Wikimedia Commons/public domain. Wikimedia Commons/public domain, Wikimedia Commons/public domain, Kertraon/Wikimedia Commons/public domain, fotolia.com. Carnage 2000/ CC BY-SA 3.0/ Wikimedia commons, fotolia.com. Georgius LXXXIX/ CC BY-SA 3.0/ Wikimedia commons, Wikimedia Commons/public domain, Thaler Tamas/ CC BY-SA 3.0/ Wikimedia commons. Georgius LXXXIX/ CC BY-SA 3.0/ Wikimedia commons, Stebunik/ CC BY-SA 3.0/ Wikimedia commons. Wikimedia commons/ public domain, Wikimedia Commons/ public domain. Dave Overcash/ Flickr. com. Fr. Lawrence Lew/Flickr. com. Fr. Lawrence Lew/Flickr.com.

4. LIVING WITHOUT PUBLICITY

FMA Thailand/Flickr. com. Kubek89/Flickr. Wikimedia commons/ public domain, courtesy of Zofii Chmielewskiej. courtesy of Mirosława Wąsika, Wikimedia Commons/public domain. Wikimedia Commons/public domain, courtesy of Zofii Chmielewskiej. Wikimedia Commons/public domain, courtesy of Zofii Chmielewskiej, Wikimedia Commons/public domain, Rafał T/ CC BY-SA 3.0/ Wikimedia commons, Wikimedia Commons/public domain. Wikimedia Commons/public domain. courtesy of Zofii Chmielewskiej, courtesy of Andrzeja Olejnika. courtesy of Andrzeja Olejnika, LuzynaS / CC BY-SA 3.0/ Wikimedia commons. robert walsh/Flickr. com, courtesy of Andrzeja Olejnika. courtesy of Andrzeja Olejnika, Wikimedia Commons/ public domain.

5. GOLDEN ARROW

Krzych.w/ CC BY-SA 3.0/ Wikimedia commons, courtesy of Zofii Chmielewskiej. Jastrow/Wikimedia Commons/public domain. Jmhullot/ CC BY-SA 3.0/ Wikimedia commons. Wikimedia commons/ public domain, Fahrenheit 451, Wikimedia Commons/public domain, Wikimedia Commons/public domain. Fr. Lawrence Lew/Flickr. com. Wikimedia Commons/public domain, Ozeye/ CC BY-SA 3.0/ Wikimedia commons. Guillaume Piolle/ CC BY-SA 3.0/ Wikimedia commons, Wikimedia commons/ public domain.douard Hue/ CC BY-SA 3.0/ Wikimedia commons. Wikimedia Commons/public domain, Wikimedia Commons/public domain, Wikimedia Commons/public domain. Reinhardhauke/ CC BY-SA 3.0/ Wikimedia commons. courtesy of ks. Krzysztofa Jędrzejewskiego, Jean-Pol GRANDMONT/CC BY 4.0/ Wikimedia commons. Goldmund100/ CC BY-SA 3.0/ Wikimedia commons.

6. GIVE ME CHILDREN SO THEY LOVE YOU BETTER

Pline/ CC BY-SA 3.0/ Wikimedia commons. Sam Beebe/Ecotrust/ CC BY-SA 3.0/ Wikimedia commons. Wikimedia Commons/public domain, Wikimedia Commons/public domain. Wikimedia Commons/public domain, Wikimedia Commons/public domain. Percy s a carballo/ CC BY-SA 4.0/ Wikimedia commons, Wikimedia Commons/public domain. SAHER/ CC BY-SA 3.0/ Wikimedia commons, Wikimedia Commons/public domain. www.corazones.org, www.corazones.org. www.corazones.org, www.corazones.org. www.corazones.org. www.corazones.org. www.corazones.org, www.corazones.org.

7. "I WOULD LIKE TO CEASE LOVING THEM"

VoxDomini.pl, VoxDomini.pl. Jürgen Gl.sener/Creative Commons ShareAlike 1.0/ Wikimedia commons. Vincenzo De Maria/Flickr.com. Wikimedia/public domain, Wikimedia/public domain, pasquale vitale/ Flickr.com, packy 1976/ Flickr.com, roberto acuna /Flickr.com. Stanisław Marciniak, Wikimedia, Lino M - Flickr.com/ CC BY-SA 2.0, Wikimedia/public domain. Wikimedia/public domain, Wikimedia/public domain, LianeM/Fotolia.com, franciscan universiti pilgrimage /Flickr.com. Giovanni Cingolani/Fotolia.com, defendero6/Fotolia.com, angelospeed/ Fotolia.com, Wikimedia/public domain, Christa Eder/ Fotolia.com, Wikimedia/ Mazaki/ CC BY-SA 4.0. valeria2valeria/ Flickr. com, saginaw/ Flickr. com, saginaw/ Flickr. com, Itto Ogami// CC BY-SA 3.0/ Wikimedia commons. indiadiaz/ Flickr. com, saginaw/ Flickr. com. fotolia.com, Wikimedia/public domain.

8. IF TO LOVE, THEN WITHOUT LIMITS

Fotolia. com. Marco Saracco- fotolia.com. Wikimedia/public domain, Wikimedia/public domain. eleakorn/fotolia.com, Wikimedia/public domain. Opusdei28/ CC BY-SA 4.0, Wikimedia commons, toshiki/ Flickr. blue moon art cathy/ Flickr. com, blue moon art cathy/ Flickr. com. Jos. Luiz Bernardes Ribeiro/ CC BY-SA 3.0/ Wikimedia commons, Erwin/ Flickr. com. Wikimedia/ public domain, Wikimedia/public domain, Wikimedia/public domain, " Mikils/CC BY-SA 3.0/ Wikimedia commons. fistra/fotolia.com, Lalupa/CC BY-SA 3.0/ Wikimedia commons, ErdonZello/ Flickr. com. Wikimedia/public domain, cath/ Flickr. com. sean murray/ Flickr. com, tina Johnsson /Flickr. com. ErdonZello/ Flickr. com, black murphy/ Flickr. com, ErdonZello/ Flickr. com. Lucia altenhofen/ Flickr. com. Wikimedia Commons/public domain, CarlosIRT/ CC BY-SA 3.0/ Wikimedia commons. www.stgemmagalgani.com.

9. MISSION IN THE EAST

Wikimedia Commons/public domain. obogoslovi zagreb/ Flickr. com. obogoslovi zagreb/ Flickr. com, Wikimedia Commons/public domain. Pudelek (Marcin Szala)/ CC BY-SA 3.0/ Wikimedia commons, Marcin Konsek/CC BY-SA 4.0, Wikimedia commons. gnuckx/ CC BY 2.0/ Wikimedia commons. Judgefloro /Wikimedia Commons/public domain, Roberta F/ CC BY-SA 3.0/ Wikimedia commons, obogoslovi zagreb/ Flickr. com. obogoslovi zagreb/ Flickr. com. Roberta F./ CC BY-SA 3.0/ Wikimedia commons, Želimir Gogić @ bosnasrebrena.ba/ CC BY-SA 3.0/ Wikimedia commons.

10. TO ERASE THE KISS OF JUDAS

Fraxinus/CC BY-SA 3.0/ Wikimedia commons. Fahrenheit 451. Wikimedia Commons/public domain. Wikimedia Commons/public domain, Fahrenheit 451. Wikimedia Commons/public domain, Wikimedia Commons/public domain. Wikimedia Commons/public domain. www.cicbue.edu.ar/capilla/ oratorio-madre-pierina, www.fic.org.ar, Tstude/Wikimedia Commons/public domain, +iirhys82192ii+/ Flickr. com. +iirhys82192ii+/ Flickr. com.

11. INFANT OF GOD

diego esquivel/cathopic. Wikimedia Commons/public domain. Monika Dydek /CC BY-SA 4.0, Wikimedia commons, Miranda Lotte/ Flickr. courtesy of Zgromadzenia Si.str Służebniczek Najświętszej Maryi Panny Niepokalanie Poczętej. Jacquemart/ Flickr. com, courtesy of Zgromadzenia Si.str Służebniczek Najświętszej Maryi Panny Niepokalanie Poczętej. Lowdown/ CC BY-SA 3.0/Wikimedia commons, Wikimedia Commons/public domain. courtesy of Zgromadzenia Si.str Służebniczek Najświętszej Maryi Panny Niepokalanie Poczętej, Gorofil/CC BY-SA 4.0, Wikimedia commons. Karol Pilch (Karol91)/ CC BY-SA 3.0/Wikimedia commons, courtesy of Zgromadzenia Si.str Służebniczek Najświętszej Maryi Panny Niepokalanie Poczętej, courtesy of Zgromadzenia Si.str Służebniczek Najświętszej Maryi Panny Niepokalanie Poczętej, Wikimedia Commons/public domain, Wikimedia Commons/public domain. courtesy of Zgromadzenia Si.str Służebniczek Najświętszej Maryi Panny Niepokalanie Poczętej.

12. THE KING

Courtesy of Zgromadzenia Si.str Służebniczek Najświętszej Maryi Panny Niepokalanie Poczętej. Wald-Burger8/ CC BY-SA 3.0/ Wikimedia commons, Wikimedia commons. Toby Hudson//CC BY-SA 3.0/ Wikimedia commons, Rama/CC BY-SA 2.0 fr 781. Wikimedia commons, courtesy of Fundacji Serca Jezusa, Wikimedia commons, courtesy of Fundacji Serca Jezusa. courtesy of Fundacji Serca Jezusa, dzieki uprzejmości Fundacji Serca Jezusa. Aneta Lazurek// CC BY-SA 3.0/ Wikimedia commons, Fr. Lawrence Lew/ Flickr. com, WorldKnowledge0815/ CC BY-SA 3.0 de/ Wikimedia commons. Andreas F. Borchert/CC BY-SA 4.0/ Wikimedia commons, courtesy of Fundacji Serca Jezusa. Tennessee123/CC BY-SA 4.0/ Wikimedia commons, Kiejstut9/ CC0/ Wikimedia commons. Wikimedia Commons/public domain, Leszek Stojanowski-Han/ CC BY-SA 4.0/ Wikimedia commons, Wikimedia Commons/public domain. Zygmunt Put Zetpe0202/CC BY-SA 4.0/ Wikimedia commons. Zygmunt Put Zetpe0202/CC BY-SA 4.0/ Wikimedia commons, Zygmunt Put Zetpe0202/CC BY-SA 4.0/ Wikimedia commons.

13. THE MERCY OF GOD

Oskierro/ CC BY-SA 4.0/ Wikimedia commons. Zygmunt Borowski /Flickr. com. Wikimedia Commons/public domain. courtesy of władz gminy Głogowiec, courtesy of władz gminy Głogowiec, Fahrenheit. Wikimedia Commons/public domain, Fahrenheit 451, Andrzej Olejnik/TekstProjekt, Wikimedia/public domain, Piotr Gaborek/Flickr.com. Andrzej Otrębski/CC BY-SA 4.0/ Wikimedia commons, Wikimedia/public domain. courtesy of Zgromadzenia Si.str Jezusa Miłosiernego, Hospicjum w Wilnie, courtesy of Zgromadzenia Si.str Jezusa Miłosiernego, Hospicjum w Wilnie. Harner Blake/ GPL/ Wikimedia, Wikimedia Commons/public domain. Pimke/ CC BY-SA 3.0/ Wikimedia commons. Higroskopijny/ CC BY-SA 3.0/ Wikimedia commons, Krystyna Pruchniewska/ CC BY-SA 3.0/ Wikimedia commons, Piotr Drabik/Flickr.com. Anna Michalska/Fotolia.com. rpzambrano /Flickr. com. catholic church england and wales /Flickr.com. X ziomal X/ CC BY-SA 3.0/ Wikimedia commons.

14. REPAIRING THE WORLD

courtesy of ks. Krzysztofa Jędrzejewskiego/Licheń. Archiwum wydawnictwa, Archiwum Autora, Archiwum Autora, Archiwum Autora. PedroMonteiro/ Fotolia.com, PedroMonteiro/Fotolia.com, Christian Mueller/ Fotolia.com, Mario Rodriguez/ Fotolia.com. Archiwum Autora. Archiwum wydawnictwa. Archiwum wydawnictwa, antiball/fotolia. com. Archiwum wydawnictwa. Archiwum wydawnictwa, Archiwum Autora, Archiwum wydawnictwa, Archiwum wydawnictwa.

15. "YOUR LOVE BURNED ME"

Archiwum Autora, Archiwum wydawnictwa. Alessandro Guzzi/CC BY-SA 4.0, Wikimedia commons. Gachepi/ CC BY-SA 3.0/ Wikimedia commons. Patrick Robles/ Flickr, Peter Potrowl/ CC BY-SA 3.0/ Wikimedia commons, Peter Potrowl/ CC BY-SA 3.0/ Wikimedia commons. Gachepi/ CC BY-SA 3.0/ Wikimedia commons. www.aascj.org.br. Clary Paco/ /CC BY-SA 4.0, Wikimedia commons, www.martherobin. com, www.visionsofjesuschrist.com. P. Houy/ CC BY-SA 4.0/ Wikimedia commons. myrim horngren/ Flickr. com. Eva Maria/ Flickr. com. Woehrling/ CC BY-SA 3.0/ Wikimedia commons, somebody675/ CC BY-SA 3.0/ Wikimedia commons. Foyer de Charit. de Baye// CC BY-SA 3.0/ Wikimedia commons.

16. BURNED OFFERING

Peter Potrowl/ CC BY-SA 3.0/ Wikimedia commons. V.tor Reis - Pr.prio/ CC0/ Wikimedia commons. http://alexandrinabalasar.free.fr, http://alexandrinabalasar.free.fr, Wikimedia Commons/public domain. Manuel Anast.cio/ CC BY-SA 2.5/ Wikimedia commons, toshkiakyma/ Flickr.com, www.pilgrim-info.com. alexandrinabalasar.free.fr, Vitorreis2// CC BY-SA 3.0/ Wikimedia commons, alexandrinabalasar. free.fr. alexandrinabalasar.free.fr. alexandrinabalasar.free. fr, alexandrinabalasar.free.fr, alexandrinabalasar.free.fr. alexandrinabalasar. free.fr, alexandrinabalasar.free.fr, alexandrinabalasar. free.fr. alexandrinabalasar.free.fr, alexandrinabalasar.free.fr. alexandrinabalasar.free.fr, alexandrinabalasar.free.fr, alexandrinabalasar.free.fr, alexandrinabalasar.free. fr. alexandrinabalasar. free.fr. anjo-sozinho/ CC0/Wikimedia commons, V.tor Reis// CC0/Wikimedia commons.

17. SIXTEEN-HOUR CONFESSION

Manuel Anast.cio/ CC0/Wikimedia commons. tongeron91 - https://www.flickr.com/ photos/tongeron91/6149674521/ CC BY-SA 2.0/Wikimedia commons. Ulrichulrich// CC BY-SA 3.0/ Wikimedia commons. mariateresacarloni. org. mariateresacarloni.org, Toni Pecoraro/ Wikimedia Commons/public domain. cepatri55// CC BY-SA 2.0/Wikimedia commons, Diego Baglieri// CC BY-SA 4.0, Wikimedia commons, Belmetauro - https://www.flickr.com/ photos/ belmetauro/4465245532/ CC BY-SA 2.0/Wikimedia commons. mariateresacarloni.org. Wikimedia Commons/public domain, Suradnik13/ CC BY-SA 3.0/ Wikimedia commons. Pkravchenko/CC BY-SA 3.0/ Wikimedia commons, https://deutsch.radio.cz/symbol-deswiderstands- kardinal-josef- -beran-8163160/ Fair use/ Wikimedia commons, Mieremet, Rob / Anefo/ CC BY-SA 3.0 nl/Wikimedia commons. mariateresacarloni.org.

18. ANTI-CHURCH

mariateresacarloni. org. cathopic. Mateusz War/CC BY-SA 3.0/ Wikimedia commons, Fahrenheit 451. Jan Jerszyński/ CC BY-SA 2.5/Wikimedia commons, Jakub Zasina / CC BY-SA 2.5/Wikimedia commons. Wikimedia Commons/public domain. adrian/Flickr, Maciejw/ CC BY-SA 3.0 pl/ Wikimedia commons, Fallaner/CC BY-SA 4.0/Wikimedia commons. carlosphotos /123RF.com. Przemysław Jahr/Wikimedia Commons/public domain. Martin Thurnherr/Wikimedia Commons/public domain, whiskey/ Flickr. com, Wikimedia Commons/public domain. compare fibre/unsplash. com, Farel Anna/Flickr. com, tiffany Lange/Flickr. com, The Compass News - 20190529_Spain and Portugal El Camino Pilgrimage_1063/ PDM-owner/Wikimedia commons. https://lausanne.org, nikolastan - https://www.flickr.com/ photos/81433534@N00/2191031467/ CC BY 2.0/ Wikimedia commons.

19. JESUS IN DREAMS

John Kultan/Flickr. Com. geralt/pixabay. com. alex wood/unsplash. com. Alessandro/Flickr. com, maxpixel.net. David Stanley/ CC BY 2.0/ Wikimedia commons. Andrea Leopardi/unsplash. com, ashraf fekry/Flickr. com. KELLEPICS

/pixabay. com. Mo Eid/Pexels. com, Mati-foto/pixabay. com. jeffjacobs1990/ pixabay. com. AMISOM Public Information - https://www.flickr.com/photos/ au_unistphotostream/27469932863/ CC0/ Wikimedia commons. Berthold Werner/ CC BY 3.0/Wikimedia commons. Nessma Elaassar/ CC BY-SA 4.0/ Wikimedia commons. Wikimedia Commons/public domain. domiciado murillo quesada/Flickr. com. lauranna/Flickr. com. yueshuya/pixabay.com. jeffjacobs1990/pixabay.com.

ω THE PAROUSIA

Fr. Lawrence Lew/Flickr. com, Andrey Mironov/ CC BY-SA 4.0. ELEN/123RF. com. Wikimedia Commons/public domain. Wikimedia Commons/public domain, Wikimedia Commons/public domain. Unknown author/ CC BY-SA 4.0/ Wikimedia commons. Wikimedia Commons/public domain, Wikimedia commons/ public domain, Wikimedia Commons/public domain, Wikimedia Commons/public domain. Wikimedia Commons/public domain. Rama/ CC BY-SA 2.0 fr/ Wikimedia commons, Wikimedia Commons/public domain. Metropolitan Museum of Art/C00/ Wikimedia commons, Wikimedia Commons/public domain, Wikimedia Commons/public domain. Wikimedia Commons/public domain, Wikimedia Commons/public domain. Hen Megonza/ Flickr. com, Cadetgray/ CC BY-SA 3.0/ Wikimedia commons. Jean-Christophe BENOIST/ CC BY 2.5/Wikimedia common. Wikimedia Commons/ public domain. Philippos/ CC BY-SA 3.0/ Wikimedia commons, Wikimedia Commons/public domain. Wikimedia commons/ public domain.

The Polish publisher states that it has exercised due diligence to locate the current holders of the economic copyright to the photographs. In the event of any inadvertent error in the spelling of a nickname, first name, surname of an author, or in the license designation, we undertake to correct such inaccuracies in subsequent editions of the book.

About Sophia Institute

Sophia Institute is a nonprofit institution that seeks to nurture the spiritual, moral, and cultural life of souls and to spread the gospel of Christ in conformity with the authentic teachings of the Roman Catholic Church.

Sophia Institute Press fulfills this mission by offering translations, reprints, and new publications that afford readers a rich source of the enduring wisdom of mankind.

Sophia Institute also operates the popular online resource CatholicExchange.com. Catholic Exchange provides world news from a Catholic perspective as well as daily devotionals and articles that will help readers to grow in holiness and live a life consistent with the teachings of the Church.

In 2013, Sophia Institute launched Sophia Institute for Teachers to renew and rebuild Catholic culture through service to Catholic education. With the goal of nurturing the spiritual, moral, and cultural life of souls, and an abiding respect for the role and work of teachers, we strive to provide materials and programs that are at once enlightening to the mind and ennobling to the heart; faithful and complete, as well as useful and practical.

Sophia Institute gratefully recognizes the Solidarity Association for preserving and encouraging the growth of our apostolate over the course of many years. Without their generous and timely support, this book would not be in your hands.

www.SophiaInstitute.com
www.CatholicExchange.com
www.SophiaTeachers.org